There is a famous interview between Napoleon and Balasov on the eve of the Russian campaign which is more correctly described by Tolstoy, an avowed romancer working on a few fragments of knowledge, than by historians working on the amplest records.

Harold Temperley : *Research and Modern History*

PENGUIN BOOKS

WHO WAS THE MAN IN THE IRON MASK?

Hugh Ross Williamson (1901–78) was a prolific author of history, novels and plays. He was Assistant Editor of the *Yorkshire Post* from 1925 to 1930, Editor of the *Bookman* from 1930 to 1934 and Acting Editor of the *Strand Magazine* from 1934 to 1935. He was Director of the London General Press from 1936 to 1942, and again from 1968 until his death. He became an Anglican Priest in 1943, until he was reconciled to the Catholic Church in 1955. His books include *The Poetry of T. S. Eliot* (1932); *John Hampden* (1933); *Charles and Cromwell* (1946); *The Gunpowder Plot* (1951); *Guy Fawkes* (1964); *Kind Kit* (1972), an informal biography of Christopher Marlowe; and *Historical Enigmas* (1974; published in Penguin as *Who Was the Man in the Iron Mask?*, 2002). He also published an autobiography, *The Walled Garden* (1956).

Who Was the Man in
the Iron Mask?
and Other Historical Enigmas

HUGH ROSS WILLIAMSON

PENGUIN BOOKS

PENGUIN BOOKS

Published by the Penguin Group
Penguin Books Ltd, 80 Strand, London WC2R ORL, England
Penguin Putnam Inc., 375 Hudson Street, New York, New York 10014, USA
Penguin Books Canada Ltd, 10 Alcorn Avenue, Toronto, Ontario, Canada M4V 3B2
Penguin Books India (P) Ltd, 11 Community Centre, Panchsheel Park, New Delhi – 110 017, India
Penguin Books (NZ) Ltd, Cnr Rosedale and Airborne Roads, Albany, Auckland, New Zealand
Penguin Books (South Africa) (Pty) Ltd, 24 Sturdee Avenue, Rosebank 2196, South Africa

Penguin Books Ltd, Registered Offices: 80 Strand, London WC2R ORL, England

www.penguin.com

Historical Whodunits first published by Phoenix House Ltd 1955
Enigmas of History first published by Michael Joseph Ltd 1957

First published as *Historical Enigmas* by Michael Joseph 1974
Published as a Classic Penguin under the title *Who Was the Man in the Iron Mask?* 2002

1

Copyright © Hugh Ross Williamson, 1955, 1957, 1969, 1974

Contents

Epistle Dedicatory

to
Ken Hughes

My dear Ken,

There are many good reasons why this book should be dedicated to you apart from friendship and my gratitude to you for admitting me to the 'inside' so to speak, of your two great historical films, *The Trials of Oscar Wilde* and *Cromwell*. The fact that you actually wrote the scripts as well as directing gives you a special place among those of us whose work and pleasure it is to try to bring the past to life for the edification of the present. And of the many varieties of historian you are, I think, the most to be envied in that you use the most vivid and popular of the media as your means of communication. The more you have to simplify, the more – in order to avoid distortion – you have to know. So to your films I offer my radio-broadcasts, which had something of the same problem. The majority of pieces in this book (which include *Historical Whodunits* and *Enigmas of History,* both now long out of print) were originally broadcast on a popular wavelength, commissioned by Kenneth Adam and directed by Paul Stephenson, and thus demanding certain restrictions of time and style.

In the first chapter I have tried to discriminate between the various methods of writing history – that is to say, of communicating the past to the present – so I will not repeat myself here but, in this matter of simplicity be content to epitomize it by quoting G. K. Chesterton's : 'If you say "the social utility of the indeterminate sentence is recognized by all criminologists as part of the sociological evolution to a more humane and scientific view of punishment", you can go on talking like that for hours with hardly a movement of the grey matter inside your skull. But if you begin to say "I wish Jones to go to gaol and Brown to say when Jones shall come out", you will discover with a thrill of horror that you are obliged to think.'

Yet, as the duty of an historian is, in the words of a good one, A. J. P. Taylor, 'to understand what happened and why it happened', the communication of it at all, except to one's friends in conversation, savours of self-indulgence. To which I shamelessly plead guilty – as you do. I shall never forget the thrill of discovering while working in the Manuscript Room of the British Museum that the letters which King James I addressed to 'My only sweet and dear child' were written to his favourite, the Duke of Buckingham, and not to his son, Prince Charles, who had been wrongly catalogued as the addressee since the eighteenth century. The result was that the history of the reign of James I needed reassessment and that the question of his possible poisoning by Buckingham (which had never been doubted until in Victorian days S. R. Gardiner questioned it) needed re-examination.

My discovery could be communicated to the academic in the ordinary way in my biography of Buckingham but its implications seemed to me sufficiently important to the ordinary man 'interested in history' to be worth a broadcast on the poisoning of King James I. Otherwise Gardiner's outmoded account of the end of the reign was likely to command popular acceptance.

At whatever level one chooses to communicate history – by academic treatise, by popular studies of a period, by novel, play or film – there is for all of us the crucial problem of selection, which is the art of simplifying without falsifying. Thirty packed volumes would be little for a full life of Cromwell. Your film, which as I remember ran for over four hours before the cuts necessitated by commercialism, could touch only the fringe of the life. And to the problem of selection are added, when the form chosen is novel, play or film, the harder problems of transposition and invention. The events of a year may have to be compressed into snatches of dialogue. Here there is only one rule. Any invention must conform scrupulously to what might have happened and not violate strict historical possibility.

One of the impermissible inventions, for example, even though Schiller used it for dramatic purposes, is that which allows Queen Elizabeth I to meet Mary Queen of Scots. From first to last Mary pleaded with Elizabeth for such a meeting. Adamantly from first to last Elizabeth refused. Both queens believed that such a meeting would result in Elizabeth succumbing to Mary's charm. Thus to represent such a meeting is to falsify history at the deepest level not only of events but of character and to plunge into the world of what may be pejoratively called 'costume fiction'.

I'm quoting this example not only because it is so well-known but because it has affected criticism of your *Cromwell*. Some pseudo-highbrow critic had, in his mind, confused it with Charles and Cromwell and you were accused of serious distortion in allowing them to meet. But quite obviously this was an invention quite different in kind from an Elizabeth-Mary meeting, since it violated no probability and distorted no character. Also, for what it is worth, there are firm historical records of their meetings – one, for example, if any reader wants chapter and verse, on 4 July 1547. Nevertheless, in an article on *Cromwell* in a prominent Sunday newspaper, the meeting of the two was cited as an example of your flouting of history. My correcting letter was refused publication and the lie that Charles and Cromwell never met has gained increasing credence among the pseuds.

To have an opportunity of righting this publicly is, I think, an additional reason for dedicating this book to you. Another is the hope that you may find in it a subject for another film in which you may establish for the many the truth of a matter which is still distorted by the Oxford propaganda-historians – the Gunpowder Plot, for example, or the murder of the princes in the Tower. There is only one that you must not touch – the divorce of Queen Caroline, (which was not, of course, allowed to be broadcast). The consequences of too much curiosity might be dangerous and I myself have given my word that I will do no further work on it. But, apart from that one, another film please, to bring the past, as you can, magnificently back to us.

Yours affectionately,

Hugh

Foreword

THE immemorial instinct of mankind 'to tell sad stories of the death of kings' is no longer enough for the historian. Nowadays he has to know the texture of the shroud and its cost per foot in terms of a fluctuating pound linked to the export price of wool. The President of the Historical Association, in his Jubilee Address, in 1956, recalled the remark of the Cambridge College porter: 'The men going in and out of this gate used to be gentlemen; now they are only scholars.' One sees what the porter meant. And anything can happen when history ceases to be a gentle hobby.

What in fact has happened Dr Butterfield hinted in that same address, when he said, 'The early part of the twentieth century saw historians building up their institutional organization. Together with the development of more serious teaching in schools and universities, this established history as a profession and a vested interest.'

Thus he defined accurately (though not perhaps intentionally) the nature of the catastrophe which today has overtaken historical writing. It has become a vested interest. Text-books and examinations, prestige and preferments, degrees and doctorates, royalties and emoluments are now involved in its orthodoxies. It must be a 'science'; it must have a 'method'; it must flourish 'facts'; it must announce 'conclusions'.

But, as I have been perhaps over-pertinacious in pointing out, it can unfortunately do none of these things. 'History' can record only a millionth part of the 'facts', is unable, in consequence, to draw any 'conclusions' which can rightly be termed 'scientific' and has no 'method' other than that which applies equally to any form of investigation, from designing an aeroplane to solving a murder – that is to say, finding out as much as possible, expressing and using that knowledge honestly, testing the conclusions and admitt-

13

ing that, at any moment, something new may be discovered which will invalidate the tentative solution.

I shall not be so tedious as to repeat here the theory of history which I have already elaborated on more than one occasion; but I feel bound, in charity, to warn any of the young into whose hands this book may fall that they should on no account incorporate my conclusions in their examination answers. To do so would be to ensure very low marks, if not actual failure. It is not that what I have written is not, to the best of my knowledge, research and belief, as near the truth as it is possible to get. It is that, *if* it is true, it reduces most of the vested interest textbooks to absurdity; and this, as it would have considerable economic repercussions, could never be allowed.

If for example it is impossible to be certain of a simple fact like the identity of the executioner of Charles I, why should anyone suppose it possible to write an authoritative assessment of an extremely complicated subject like the origin of the Civil War? If Queen Victoria ought not to have succeeded to the throne until 1849, what happens to learned treatises on the constitutional development of the Cabinet under Melbourne? If Mary Tudor, who was the undoubted daughter of Henry VIII, was right in believing that her 'half-sister' Elizabeth was not – and she was presumably in a better position to assess it than was Mr Froude or even Professor Pollard – what reliance can be based on those who attribute Elizabeth's outlook to her inheritance from her Royal father? And so on.

For myself, it does not 'matter' one way or the other, any more than it 'matters' whether Henry VII murdered the princess in the Tower, whether Cecil organized the Gunpowder Plot, whether William Rufus was a pagan sacrificial victim or whether Queen Elizabeth was an accessory before the fact in the murder of Amy Robsart. I think that all these things are so, because all the evidence I have been able to discover points relentlessly to those conclusions. But obviously, on my own theory of history, I may be wrong. If I am, no great harm is done. I have tried my best to find out what happened to certain people and to discover what kind of people they were and failed. And even if I am right, it is no more than a story which, perhaps, later writers will be able to fill in in a little more detail.

But, the effect on the vested interest of my being right would be shattering. It would mean that the books and the examination papers would all have to be rewritten and reset. It would mean more importantly the collapse of all those pretensions to 'scientific scholarship'; for there really would be little more point in having Chairs of History than Chairs of Memoir-Writing or Chairs of Detection or, more pertinently, Chairs of Propaganda.

It is always difficult to find a simple example to illustrate a theory, but it so happens that, in a review in the *Times Literary Supplement* of a book on the Dead Sea Scrolls, there appeared a passage which explains my point with exactitude. The reviewer wrote that the author of the book 'claims that, because the first cave showed no signs of occupation after A.D. 70, all the documents found in it must have been written and deposited there before that date. This, however, clashes with the only *firm historical allusion* in this group of texts . . . the statement in the commentary on Habakkuk that the enemy sacrificed to their standards. . . . The only occasion on which the Romans are *known* to have sacrificed to (as distinct from venerated) their standards was in the autumn of A.D. 70 when the Roman soldiers forced their way into the precincts of the Temples at Jerusalem. To say that this must refer to some other unknown occasion is to *adopt a method* by which anything may be proved of anything.' (My italics.)

The reviewer thus reveals the assumptions underlying academic history. The first is that everything that happened is recorded – rather as a full list of all coming-out dances appears in *The Times* newspaper. The second is that, if a thing is not recorded, it cannot, by 'historical method' be presumed to have happened. The third is that, if a thing is recorded, it is both accurate and unique and must be the factor given precedence in any investigation.

The absurdity of these axioms is, I should have thought, self-evident; yet on their acceptance all the propositions of academic history rest. In this particular case there is no reason whatever to suppose that the recorded instance in A.D. 70 of the Romans sacrificing to their standards is the only occasion on which it happened; nor is there any reason to suppose that 'veneration', as a ritual, necessarily excluded 'sacrifice' merely because it was not reported. For all anyone knows, such sacrifices may have been a conventional annual or even monthly occurrence. The incident in Jerusalem has thus no bearing on the dating of the cave. That must be considered in the light of other evidence; and if such evidence is sufficient to give a reasonable certainty that the cave was deserted at the time of the Jerusalem episode and that, therefore, the already written Scrolls cannot refer to it, the only correct proceeding is that which the author has followed – postulate an 'unknown' (i.e. formally unrecorded or so far undiscovered) occasion.

But this, cries the reviewer in alarm, voicing the panic of all academic historians, is 'to adopt a method by which anything may be proved of anything'. If the overstatement be put in the terms that 'nothing can be *proved* from documentary evidence' he is perfectly right. Nothing can. That is my point. 'Documentary evidence' alone is worthless, simply because what on any point has survived cannot be presumed to be the total documentary evidence and therefore cannot be properly evaluated, even supposing it be genuine and accurate, (which, in cases of critical and disputed events, it often is not). 'History' cannot be more, when it is honest, than an enquiry into possibilities; and 'documentary evidence' is only one, and not the most important, of its components.

I will not pursue the matter further except in self-defence to acquaint the non-academic reader with one line of attack which has been directed against my innocent enquiries. Academics, defending their vested interest, occasionally find that they have to admit that their official version of history has been shaken. The evidence is too strong to ignore, but, they say, people of my kind go too far in the opposite direction. The favourite phrase is 'the swing of the pendulum'. The Gunpowder Plot, for instance, may not be all that S. R. Gardiner thought it was, but it is ridiculous to suppose that it is all I think it is. The pendulum has swung too far.

Seldom has an analogy been more misleading. If a detective enquiry exonerated from murder one suspect, would anyone claim that Scotland Yard should be on its guard lest the swing of the pendulum might lead them to suspect someone else? If the alleged motives of A have been successfully disproved, must we guard against the swing of the pendulum leading us to enquire into the possible motives of B?

The story of the Emperor's New Clothes is pertinent. The

child's perception that the Emperor was in fact unclothed must have been very galling to the tailors, who had published accounts of the clothes which they had made and which they said he was wearing. Did they explain, in self-defence : 'Well, we agree that the Emperor's clothes are not altogether like those we originally described to you; but you will notice that the coat he has on, although not perhaps a long coat, in the proper meaning of the word long, cannot correctly be described as a short coat either. There have been far shorter coats. And if the breeches are not scarlet silk, they seem to have an appearance of red in the strong sunlight and the sheen is not unlike that of silk?'

Such a reaction on the part of a vested interest, whether of tailors or of dons, is not only comprehensible but even disarming; and the child would have to be very childish indeed if he expected anything else from them, especially as, in the words of a writer in *The Times* newspaper in the November of 1956, 'in the best-informed Senior Common and Combination Rooms . . . what was taught to little Arthur still in essentials holds water'.

On the other hand, he might hope that some of the disinterested spectators in the crowd would see, if not the king's nakedness, at least the tailors' point in denying it. But that I must leave to my readers . . .

HUGH ROSS WILLIAMSON

CHAPTER 1

History and the Writer

HENRY FORD'S remark that 'history is bunk' is famous enough to be included in *The Oxford Dictionary of Quotations,* and has been quoted with scorn for fifty years or so. It is time that someone pointed out that, in one sense, Henry Ford was right.

This can be verified by anyone who merely enumerates the events of a single day. Of all the hundreds of things that have happened to each individual, how many are remembered and what is their significance? A diary entry may memorialize one or two events of importance to the recorder which, at some later date, may be recalled as facts connected with that day and year – like 'Battle of Hastings, 1066', 'Passing of Reform Bill, 1832', and so forth on a larger stage of life. But the significance of the facts – their relationship to the life of the recorder and *his* history and their place in the chain of causation, *their* history – is impossible to determine.

Further, there is no way of knowing whether the recorded events were the really important happenings of that particular day. Only the future can decide whether, for instance, a casual word to a stranger, or a routine decision taken without a second thought, were, because of their eventual consequences, what made that day crucial.

And even if by some miracle one of the important facts is recorded and its significance partially understood, it would still be impossible for the diarist to escape from the prison of his own individuality and see himself, and what had happened to him, objectively in relation to the general scheme of things.

Thus, on the tiny stage of one person's life for one day, a negative answer must be given to the three questions : Do you know the significance of the facts you have selected for recording? Are they, in any case, the 'significant' facts? Can you evaluate the chosen facts in relation to other people? And if the possibility of so small a 'history' must be denied, how much more when, magnified a million million times, the stage is the world itself and the duration is recorded time? To those who have the temerity to say 'History teaches . . . ' or to discuss the 'verdict of history' or to postulate a 'science of history,' the only possible answer is Henry Ford's 'Bunk!' And it is bunk because of the inescapable impossibilities. It is impossible to draw a moral or to give a verdict when only a billionth part of the facts is known, and the significance of the few facts which happen to have been recorded is incomprehensible. Nor is any 'science' possible when the observer is part of the process he is observing. What takes their place is a combination of myth, propaganda, and guess-work. Academic history can never be more than that, despite the fact that an Oxford history don spoke recently of deducing 'useful lessons by rational methods from the facts of history'.

The propaganda element is the easiest to see, since our generation fortunately takes for granted the selection and manipulation of facts for the production of a totalitarian 'history'. And what is normally necessary to a dictatorship, because of its nature, is equally necessary to every state, whatever its political complexion, in the abnormal conditions of war as well as to every party engaged in civil war or revolution. Even the mild combat of a general election demands the distorting-glass of propaganda. All parties tend so to pass over certain facts in silence, and so to stress others out of all proportion, that if the various election manifestoes were accepted at their face value, there would be a series of mutually contradictory 'histories' of the pre-election years. The fact that no one takes them seriously, and that, in any case, each can be checked against the others, is a legitimate matter for patriotic self-congratulation that we are not as those countries where the official propaganda is enforced as 'history' and the rival versions and their authors destroyed. But it has the disadvantage that the unscholarly may assume that it was always so and forget that most of what he is taught in history books is merely the enforced propaganda lines of a succession of victorious parties which have eliminated their rivals.

This is particularly true of the whole of the period from 1485 to 1688, within which limits most of the 'mysteries' treated in this book fall. The Tudor propaganda against the Plantagenets, the Protestant propaganda against the Catholics, the Parliamentary propaganda against the Stuart dynasty, are successive waves of calculated falsehood for which allowance must perpetually be made. And mental readjustment is the harder because it is precisely that propaganda which, with modifications, has become the text-book history taught generation after generation to school-children.

The modifications are accomplished by the two remaining stages of propaganda history. Of these the first is the misrepresentation of past events to support or excuse some later revolutionary action. A simple example is Magna Carta. Most medievalists are today agreed that, as far as facts can be ascertained, the struggle for the Great Charter was the conservative action of a number of powerful and selfish nobles against a king who was politically wiser than they were. For three centuries at least no one bothered much – as far as 'history' went – about Magna Carta. Shakespeare could write a play about King John without even mentioning it. But when in the seventeenth century the wealthy landowners wanted some legal precedent for curtailing the Royal power, they disinterred Magna Carta and publicized it as an enlightened and 'progressive' action taken by unselfish lovers of their country against a reactionary and misguided tyrant.

The third stage of propaganda history is the incorporation of various successful party views into a connected version of events which groups other equally carefully selected events round them, and if Henry Ford described the result as 'bunk' he was anticipated in his perception by nearly two centuries by one who had perhaps more authority to say it. Sir Robert Walpole, our first Prime Minister, ruled England for twenty-one years, and for forty-five took a leading part in the difficult and dangerous politics of the early eighteenth century. He, if anyone, knew the difference between what really happened and the version of the happenings given to the public. When he was dying he asked to be read to. What would he like? they asked. 'Anything,' he said, 'anything but history, for that is bound to be false.'

The falsity, however, goes deeper. Behind the particular of

propaganda lies the general of myth. Certain historians, that is to say, assume that 'history' as a whole can have a 'meaning' – or, at least, a 'plot' like a novel – and that they know what it is. The usual myth, underlying most school and university text-books, is the myth of progress. Events are selected and narrated in such a way as to make a kind of pageant with the apotheosis of the present day as a grand finale. We stand near the crest of a hill, looking back upon the main road which leads clearly up to us and will take us on to the summit not far ahead. That, broadly speaking, is what has become known as the 'Whig interpretation of history' or 'the Liberal view'. Though it is less popular than it was – since recent events have engendered a healthy scepticism and reference to history books of the late nineteenth century provoke rueful hilarity – man's addition to optimism will probably prevent its total disappearance.

Another myth, which has much in common with it, is what may be called 'the myth of the Missing Acorn'. Devotees of this myth, when they see an oak tree, having only one preoccupation – to find the acorn from which it grew. Instead of looking at the tree, they elevate the missing acorn into an object of veneration. They talk about the Saxon folk-moot and the grandeur of free institutions and fail to notice that Parliament is now in fact a collection of careerists, backed by rival financial interests, who have surrendered their personal judgments to the demands of party whips and who are without real power – since, as G. K. Chesterton noted as long ago as 1917, 'a vote is now about as valuable as a railway ticket when there is a permanent block on the line'.

Or, to take a rather different application of the same myth, they do not look at the One Holy Catholic and Apostolic Church as it is today in every country in the world; they try to reconstruct what it may have been like in a small community in Palestine in the year A.D. 40 and then express indignant surprise that the two do not look the same.

The Acorn myth can be combined with the Progress myth to give almost any desired result, for by varying the stresses practically any pattern can be made. Some of the variations are the Ebb-and-Flow and the Demand-and-Response and the Hegelian Dialectic – thesis, antithesis, synthesis : the ever lasting pendulum.

There are, however, two 'myths' which stand apart from the rest in that they postulate an objective and unchanging principle by reference to which the meaning of history can be seen. One is the Christian; the other is the Marxist. The Marxist myth sees history as a struggle for power; the Christian as the dealings of God with the world.

The principle of objectivity which governs both can be illustrated by reference to the most easily accessible of all history books – the Old Testament. This is 'history' interpreted as the dealings of Jehovah with the Chosen People, with whom he made a unique Covenant. The objective principle is this Covenant relationship. Foreign policies, armed invasions, sociological trends, national calamities, the careers of great men, are all treated as illustrative, in one way or another, of that principle and are entirely subsidiary to it. It, on the one hand, dictates the selection of events recorded and, on the other, gives meaning to any event, great or small, which may be selected.

In a similar way, Marxism sees laws and constitutions, wars and revolutions, political groupings and economic policies, as by-products or weapons of the unchanging class-struggle for power, irrespective of the details of nationality or period. And Christians see them as the working out of the New Covenant – the relationship of Christ-in-the-Church with the world outside the Church – as the Jews saw (and see) them in relation to the Old.

These 'objective myths', it will be noticed, differ in kind from the various forms of the subjective Progress-Acorn myth. By postulating an independent criterion, they escape the fatuousness of trying to find a pattern from billions of events. They do not pretend to arrive at 'a philosophy of history'; on the contrary, they make history part of their philosophy. A Christian believes one thing, a Marxist materialist another. But both have already their criterion of 'significance' and this they apply to history. They say not 'history teaches' but 'history illustrates'.

The process of writing academic history is, then, something like this. Unless the writer is a Catholic or a Marxist, he selects whichever conventional myth his temperament dictates (or, if he wishes to make a name for himself, he invents a new one); then he puts a small selected period under a microscope, collecting and tabulating what details he can find. If he makes them conform to a popular myth on the one hand and the current propaganda-fashion on the other, he will be said to have written 'a first-class work of scholarship of permanent value to all future historians', which means that his work will be repeated by other historians for generations to come. If he fails to relate his detailed field work to the mythological pattern, he will have produced only 'a work which may have a certain value to those interested in a rather narrow period but which shows a disappointing lack of historical method'. If he is so unfortunate as to discover that the conclusions forced on him by his field work show the accepted myth to be nonsense and the popular propaganda to be falsehood, he will be guilty of 'a paradoxical and misguided work which no reputable historian is likely to take seriously'.

It is pleasant to be able to record that nearly all the academic history now being written in England falls into the first category, for, as a writer in *The Times Literary Supplement* recently pointed out, since 'it has become bad taste to expose the errors or inadequacies of a professional historian for fear of endangering his promotion', we have become 'stifled in this soft lotus-land of English history, compounded of complacency, timidity, and incompetence in equal parts'. Or, as the epigram has it, 'history never repeats itself, but historians always repeat each other'.

Some of us see a way of escape by reorientating 'history' to the oldest and most discredited of the myths, which is radically different from all I have so far mentioned – the Great Man myth. This, which is compatible with Christian but incompatible with Marxist 'objectivity', insists that 'history' is nothing but the relationship and interaction of characters and that, under God, events are determined, destinies of people shaped, and forms of government altered by men and women who, by birth or genius or beauty, are in a position to impose their will upon their fellows. This truth has been best summed up in the *mot*, 'It was not the Carthaginian army which crossed the Alps : it was Hannibal'. And still less was that epic crossing an inevitable manifestation of the decreased purchasing power of the Roman *denarius* or a by-product of a constitutional crisis in Carthage.

Thus, the changes and revolutions of the sixteenth and seventeenth centuries in England were not caused by economic evolution, religious beliefs, or the necessity for constitutional reform. They were caused – in the precise way in which they happened – by the characters and passions of a few men and women who could control or influence nations. The meaning of history – in so far as it is discoverable at all – is to be found in what people do. It is the people who matter and the religious, constitutional, and economic circumstances are valuable only in so far as they further an understanding of the people.

Not 'the people' in the mass; but the leaders, the great men and those with effective power behind the scenes. History is about them, just as classic tragedy is about them. The tragic hero must, by definition, be a great man because it is part of the tragedy that his weakness or failure affects, because of his position, the lives of many innocent, uninvolved people. History is made in the same way. The decision of, say, Henry V to renew the war with France involved the two countries of England and France in ruin. The Spanish Armada can be better understood by really *knowing* Philip of Spain and Elizabeth I of England, Medina Sidonia and Francis Drake, than by analysing the life of a seaport community in the year 1588.

The Great Man myth, different in kind from the other myths, has become discredited mainly because it discredits them. It draws no conclusions; it insists that every person and every circumstance is unique; it does not affect philosophic preferences or religious beliefs, since what concerns it are the beliefs of the people involved whatever they may be; it makes no pretensions to finality or conclusiveness, since all that is claimed is that, *on the evidence available,* sifted and examined and weighed with care, So-and-so seems to have been such-and-such a kind of person; it has no ulterior motive except to tell as 'truly' as possible a 'real-life' story. Lastly, it involves the maximum of scientific research and discipline from the historian. He must know the general circumstances and the particular circumstances; he must know a wide circle of people about the person he is writing about – their family circumstances, their economic position, their temperament, character, religious beliefs, and political leanings; their appearance, their clothes, their health. He must know, in fact, the whole period in as much detail as he knows the contemporary scene merely as a background for his portrait; and he must get to know the people as well as he knows his own family.

When he comes to the portrait itself, he must go to primary sources – manuscript letters and diaries and memoranda. The hand-writing of a letter may tell him much – if it is written carefully or if it is dashed off in a hurry. He cannot rely on printed ver-sions; and the abstracts made by previous historians, like the short summaries in Calendars, are often misleading. As the groundwork of everything there is this patient accumulation of data, the constant checking of hypothesis with known fact, the conscientious accuracy which will ruthlessly scrap an accepted theory when awkward and incompatible facts make their appearance, which make the training of the historian analogous to that of the scientist and provides the only sense in which history can rightly be called a 'science'. But, though the historian has to submit to the scientist's training, he has to forgo the scientist's reward. He can never say 'This is a complete and successful experiment.' For, however much information he may accumulate on any given point, his ignorance is still more profound than his knowledge. He can only say 'This is the outline, as far as it can be ascertained, and it may be shown tomorrow, by the discovery of a document, to be quite wrong.'

The Great Man myth, avoiding the falsity and tendentiousness of the other subjective myths, admits that all history is a form of fiction; and this is not the least of its drawbacks in the eyes of the professors, who dislike being reminded that they are merely a species of story-teller. Yet this third element, which I referred to at the beginning as 'guess-work', is inescapable in all history and essential if any connected story is to be told. In the context of the Great Man myth it is seen at its least harmful and can make academic history approximate towards those higher forms of history – the historical novel and the historical play.

Academic history is, in general, imaginative fiction of a low order because there is no room in it for the use of a genuinely creative imagination. Even when the writer has grasped the fact that history is the interaction of character and not the invention and propagation of myths, he is still circumscribed by the demands of his 'scientific' conscience and the extent of his discoveries. He cannot invent speeches and thoughts for his people; he can only record what he can prove, by the citation of documents they actually did say or write or appeared to think.

An example may clarify this distinction. In 1688, James II had a stormy interview with seven Anglican bishops who refused to acknowledge the Royal Prerogative and to read the Declaration of Indulgence. At the end of it he is recorded as having said, 'I tell you there are seven thousand men, and of the Church of England too, that have not bowed the knees to Baal.' The latest biographer of the king comments on this that he is 'borrowing the phraseology of the Puritans but conveying little meaning' – which, if the remark is taken as recorded, is quite true. And, in text-book history, this is all that can be said because this is all that is recorded. But an historical novelist, recreating the scene – that is to say, using a genuinely creative imagination – cannot leave the matter there. He must solve the meaning, for James, especially on such vital occasions, was not in the habit of talking nonsense. And he might notice that in that room, standing before the king, were the seven leaders of the Church of England, refusing to acknowledge lawful authority but encouraging revolution – a 'false god'. They might be presumed to know that the Scriptures usually referred to such apostasy as 'bowing the knee to Baal'. Thus he might write the sentence, 'There are seven of you, my Lords. But I tell you there are seven thousand men – and of the Church of England too – who have *not* bowed the knee to Baal.' That not only makes sense but is surely what – in some form or other – the king said. The historical novelist's reconstruction is better history than the academic historian's recording.

It is hardly necessary to say that by 'historical novel' I do not mean 'costume romance', which has no connection with history and little with literature but, where it is not thinly disguised pornography (on the principle that you can get away with things if they are set in the reign of Charles II or the Regency which would be impossible in modern dress), is the work of writers who lack the power of invention and find in what they would call 'history' ready-made plots, situations, and characters. With the help of a few popular history books to give their story a kind of verisimilitude, they decorate their chosen plot and people with their own fancies and produce a world which has little connection with anything but their own and their readers' day-dreams.

The historical novelist, on the other hand, has to do all the scientific groundwork of the academic historian before he can add to it his own imaginative vision. One instance will suffice – Miss Prescott's *The Man on a Donkey,* which makes the Pilgrimage of Grace live again with a vivid accuracy without parallel in English historical writing.

Not long ago one of our Professors of History criticized a book on Wolsey in which 'Wolsey communed at night with his soul in a remarkable monologue, unknown to the *Letters and Papers of Henry VIII* or any other historical source'. He was quite right. In academic history this was an unpardonable lapse because, by its nature, it cannot invent in this way. But the test of an historical novelist is that he could, in fact, write that monologue so that the professor, conversant with all the historical sources, would immediately applaud the 'truth' – and even the inevitability – of it.

The problem of the great Greek dramatists is not, perhaps, irrelevant. They and their audiences were both familiar with the stories they were interpreting. They could not invent a new ending for Oedipus. Agamemnon had to die at the hand of his wife. Hippolytus was, from the beginning, doomed. The dramatists' task was, given the stubborn facts, so to interpret them that an aspect of truth emerged which should compel the audience's belief. In other words, the artist there – as everywhere – was required not to invent, but to interpret.

In the modern world 'history' takes the place of the classical stories. Wolsey, whatever you may do to him, must fall. He is as much a victim of *hubris* as Oedipus. Charles I, like Agamemnon, must perish by an axe. Bonnie Prince Charlie, from the beginning, is doomed to defeat. And the historical writer, in so far as he is an artist, has to communicate to the reader the inevitability of the end; for that is the only 'truth' within his grasp.

In the solution of most historical mysteries, the initial approach is that of the historical novelist or dramatist. One begins, so to speak, with a climax of character and circumstance and works

backward. A king is murdered or a queen's rival mysteriously dies;
innocent people are hanged for a crime they did not commit; an
impostor's deception affects the policies of entire kingdoms. The
first question, as in any detective inquiry, must be about the persons and their motives. As a rule, it is in the disentangling of the
motive that the myth-propaganda background of history as a
whole emerges as a subject for scrutiny. For many of these mysteries
are mysteries only because the myth has been accepted and the
propaganda mistaken for 'truth'.

This can be seen most clearly, perhaps, in the case of the
murder of Sir Edmund Berry Godfrey. At this distance of time,
we can assess the worth of any contemporary judgment in the
light of the mob-hysteria inflamed to a point of insanity (probably without parallel in English history) by the deliberate propaganda of unscrupulous politicians. We understand why this was
done. And we know that the men hanged for the murder were
entirely innocent. Thus, while to contemporaries the mystery was :
Which particular Catholics murdered him? to us it is : Which
particular Protestants?

But in other cases the clues are less clear because the propaganda is still too strong in its hold on popular imagination, and has
not been officially discredited by historians. Anyone today who
believes in the *bona fides* of Titus Oates could do so only out of
ignorance so profound that it would put him outside the circle
of serious consideration; no historian, of whatever school, could
consider him worthy of an argument. But if he should choose to
believe in the Tudor caricature of Richard III, he would find
serious historians to support him, since that particular matter has
not, for various reasons, ever sufficiently engaged attention. And
for ten people who would immediately agree with my suggestion
that the murder of Godfrey was *ipso facto* a Protestant achievement, only one would be likely to support the thesis that the
mystery of the princes in the Tower is not whether Richard III
or Henry VII had them murdered, but the date of Henry VII's
order.

Another factor is the interrelation of some of the mysteries.
Godfrey and James de la Cloche both belong to the same politico-
religious situation. There is some connection, even though it may
be fortuitous and irrelevant, between the murder of Overbury

and the Campden Wonder. And, above all, there is an essential link between the death of Amy Robsart and the murder of Darnley. Many years ago, Andrew Lang called attention to the superficial resemblances: 'As regards Amy Robsart and her death, Elizabeth was in a position almost as equivocal as was Mary Stuart in regard to the murder of Darnley. Before the murder of Darnley we do not hear one word to suggest that Mary was in love with Bothwell. For many months before the death of Amy (Lady Robert Dudley) we hear constant reports that Elizabeth has a love affair with Lord Robert and that Amy is to be divorced or murdered. When Darnley is killed, a mock investigation acquits Bothwell, and Mary loads him with honours and rewards. When Amy dies mysteriously, a coroner's inquest, deep in the country, is held, and no records of its proceedings can be found. Its verdict is unknown. After a brief tiff, Elizabeth restores Lord Robert to favour. After Darnley's murder, Mary's ambassador in France implores her to investigate the matter with all diligence. After Amy's death, Elizabeth's ambassador in France implores her to investigate the matter with all diligence. Neither lady listens to her loyal servant; indeed Mary could not have pursued the inquiry, however innocent she might have been. Elizabeth could! In three months after Darnley's murder, Mary married Bothwell. In two months after Amy's death Cecil told (apparently) the Spanish ambassador that Elizabeth had married Lord Robert Dudley.'

But the more important point – to which Lang would not agree – is that Elizabeth was guilty and Mary was innocent and that the attempts to make Mary appear guilty were surely not unconnected with Elizabeth's experience. And throughout the cases of Amy Robsart, Kirk o' Field, the Gowrie Conspiracy, and the Gunpowder Plot there is one constant which is a pointer to the solution of them all – the policy and character of the Cecils, father and son.

Finally, because in writing shortly of historical mysteries it is necessary on the one hand to have an extensive knowledge of the background and on the other to reduce the actual problem, without distorting it, to its simplest possible terms, I have – with four exceptions, the first three and the last – dealt only with those which fall within the period which I have studied for fifty years and written about for thirty-five, the sixteenth and seventeenth centuries. One has managed to acquire a little understanding of the people and events of those two great centuries; though one must emphasize once more that, in the nature of things, there can be no claim to have *solved* anything. I can only hope that the asking of the questions and the suggestion of the possible clues will prompt the readers to answer the simpler question, 'What do *you* think?'

CHAPTER 2

The Death of William Rufus

2 August 1100

WILLIAM, surnamed 'the Red', the third and favourite son of William the Conqueror, ascended the throne of England at the age of thirty on his father's death in 1087. During the thirteen years of his reign, he showed himself a brilliant soldier and an efficient administrator. He was not an orthodox Christian, and to the Church he maintained the attitude of a persecutor, consistently plundering Church lands, openly declaring that neither St Peter nor any of the saints had influence with God and that he would ask none of them for help. He was angry if anyone added the usual reservation 'if it be God's will' to anything he ordered to be undertaken, and he regarded himself in a way which can only be construed as 'divine'. He also compared himself with Alexander the Great – and the comparison was generally admitted, with the additional speculation as to whether he was not also the reincarnation of Caesar.

He thus earned the unanimous disapproval of the ecclesiastical chroniclers who were the historians of the time and who set the mould for his reputation as the 'bad king', *par excellence,* in the child's history book sense. The story of his accidental death while hunting in the New Forest – the result, so it is usually averred, of an arrow aimed by his favourite, Walter Tirel, at a stag – is one of the historical tales known to most readers from childhood. There are many conflicting accounts of the episode, elaborations of the stark words of the *Chronicle,* 'On the morrow after Lammas Day was the King William in hunting from his own men with an arrow offshot.' But who shot the arrow, whether it was accident or treason or revenge, whether the motive led back to Henry, the king's brother, who succeeded him, or to one wishing to right the wrongs of an overtaxed country or a pillaged Church, may be argued for ever. There is not only insufficient evidence now. There was insufficient evidence then. The truth remains impenetrably

33

hidden and no historical research can ever reveal it. And to arrive at a possible solution, the first step is to try to see Rufus and his background as they were, freed from the bias of ecclesiastical propaganda.

'From the beginning to the end there is a kind of glamour about the Red King and all that he does.' So wrote E. A. Freeman, the great historian of the Norman Conquest, who is, on the whole, bitterly hostile to Rufus. 'It might be going too far to say that William Rufus was the first gentleman . . . but he was certainly the first man in any prominent place to whom the whole set of words, thoughts, and feelings which belong to the titles of knight and gentleman were habitually and ostentatiously thrust forward. When William plighted his word as *probus miles,* no man kept it more strictly.'

Rufus's friend, ally, and companion-in-arms for the last two years of his life was William IX of Aquitaine, better known as the 'Count of Poitou', the first of the Troubadours whose famous *Song of Nothing,* with its belief in overruling Destiny, is a well-known example of the so-called 'enigmatic' verse in which are enshrined the doctrines of that Catharist dualism which the Church had finally to root out with fire and sword in the Albigensian Crusade and to crush intellectually through the teaching of St Dominic and his Order of Preachers.

Another of Rufus's friends was that Welsh prince, Bledri or Bleheris, who (scholars think) was the original author of *Perceval and Gawain,* the first of the great 'Grail' romances, written before the story was 'Christianized' and the Grail in the later Arthurian cycle disguised as the Chalice of the Last Supper. Bleheris, as Dr J. L. Weston points out, enshrined in this 'earliest form of the Grail story' the record of an actual anti-Christian ritual 'having for its ultimate object the initiation into the secret of the sources of life, physical and spiritual. . . . The *mise en scène* of the story, the nomenclature, the march of incident, the character of the tests, correspond to what we know from independent sources of this Nature Ritual.'

The nearest parallel to Rufus among the Kings of England is

Richard Cœur-de-Lion, who also was a paladin of chivalry, who also was a Troubadour – the great-grandson, in fact, of Rufus's friend, the Count of Poitou – who also died mysteriously from an arrow wound at the close of the century, 1199, as Rufus did at its opening, 1100. Like Rufus, Richard plundered the Church and taxed the country almost beyond the limits of endurance. Like Rufus, Richard was an open homosexual (for, in the Catharist cult, of which the Troubadours were the poets and missionaries, procreation was the gravest of sins). But, unlike Rufus, Richard led a crusade, which, in the eyes of the ecclesiastical chroniclers, atoned for all faults – with the result that, in popular imagination, Richard the Lion Heart has come to stand at the opposite pole to William Rufus. Richard has been idealized, his virtues exaggerated, his faults glossed over; William has had every shadow darkened. What – to take one instance – in Richard's case is represented by the immortal story of Blondel has, in William's, become, in Freeman's words, 'The vices of Rufus were literally the works of darkness, works which even his own more outspoken age shrank from dwelling on in detail.'

Yet, of the two, William seems the 'better' man and could well have been the pattern on which Richard modelled himself. He had a greater magnanimity than the Lion Heart, and if in courage and chivalry they were equals, William was a finer soldier, both as leader and as strategist. Dr Margaret Murray's estimate of Rufus is not exaggerated, 'A dutiful son, an able and competent ruler, a faithful friend, a generous enemy, recklessly courageous, lavishly open-handed, and never known to break his plighted word.' And it is as well that in any consideration of his death, this portrait be kept in mind.

But of much greater importance are the beliefs of the great dualist heresy, which almost defeated Christianity during the eleventh, twelfth, and early thirteenth centuries. In *The Arrow and the Sword* I dealt with them, in relation to the death of Rufus, and only the barest epitome of the conclusions can be given here. In Rufus's day there were three main strands of dualism. Inside the Church there was Catharism (not yet excommunicated), with the Troubadours as its poets. Outside the Church there were the philosophic pagans, inheritors of the Neo-Platonism of the Druids and the modified Zoro astrianism which the Romans had introduced in the worship of Mithra, the literature of which was in the not-yet-Christianized romances of the Grail. Thirdly, there was 'witchcraft' proper, the Old Religion of the people, which was in fact fertility worship – the Dianic cult, whose rites took place in a forest at full moon – and against which ecclesiastical legislation had been directed, with varying lack of success, from the seventh century onward.

None of these movements, which interpenetrated each other at various levels, was 'wicked' in the sense that is said, 'Evil, be thou my good'. On the contrary, they all worshipped 'good' in an exalted sense. Dualism interprets the cosmic process as a struggle between the Good and Evil principles, just as Christianity does. Its quarrel with Christianity is not essentially in the realm of ethics or even mysticism, but in that of faith and history. The dualist contends that evil may finally triumph. The Christian insists that, on Calvary, evil was finally defeated through the one perfect and sufficient Sacrifice made there in the blood and death of God. But where the Christian sees the Sacrifice as unrepeatable (though in every Mass its effects are daily conveyed to the faithful who thus become incorporated in it), the dualist – at least, on the popular level – postulates its constant repetition. The King-God must generation after generation, century after century, give his life for his people. To avoid confusion with Christian terminology, the victim is known as the 'Devil'.

That, in the year 1100, the Ango-Norman 'devil' was William Rufus is the one hypothesis which seems to fit all the facts of the mysterious death in the depths of a forest at sunset on the morrow of 'the Gule of August', the great 'witch' festival. And, incidentally, it explains the conflicting accounts of the event – those of the rhymers and romancers who conveyed the true significance of it to posterity, and those of the monks who, understanding it no less clearly, made every effort to represent it merely as the vengeance of Heaven on a wicked and blasphemous ruler.

Once this background is seen, many perplexities vanish, for a wealth of clues all point to the same conclusion. That 1100 was a crucial year in which the 'Devil' had to die for his people

– that is, voluntarily to give his life that Good might triumph over Evil in the community for which he was responsible – is, I think, unquestionable. Freeman, who, writing long before *The Golden Bough,* is quite unaware of these esoteric matters, admits, 'At least within the range of the Red King's influence, that year seems to have been marked by that vague kind of feeling of a coming something . . . coming events do cast their shadows before them in a fashion which, whether philosophy can explain it or not, history must accept as a fact. And coming events did pre-eminently cast their shadows before them in the first half of the year 1100. In that age the feeling that weighed on men's minds naturally took the form of portent and prophecy, of strange sights seen and strange sounds listened to. There is not the slightest ground for thinking that all these tales were mere inventions after the fact.'

Not only the year but the day – the morrow of Lammas – is what one would have expected. The chief festivals of the Old Religion were pivoted on a May–November cycle – May Day, the Gule of August, 1–2 November, and 2 February – a division of time which follows neither the solstices nor the agricultural seasons, but which there is some reason to believe was connected with the breeding seasons of flocks and herds. On the November Sabbat of 1099, a great tide came up the Thames, obliterated houses and villages and swept away men, oxen, and sheep. This must have heightened the superstitious dread which already hung about the closing of the century, more particularly since the force of Evil was traditionally personified by the Great Dragon of the Sea. At the beginning of May a substitute victim was offered. William's nephew, Richard, was killed in the New Forest. The version given out was that one of his attendants, loosing his bow at a stag, accidentally shot him – the precise terms 'officially' used of Rufus's own death when, his substitute having proved unacceptable, he faced his own demanded death at the next, the August, Sabbat.

His nephew's death at the beginning of May seems reasonably to explain why Rufus's death was so generally expected on 1 August – for it was known in Italy, in Belgium, and in Devonshire on the day it happened. (In one part of Devonshire, indeed, it was known before it happened, for it was on the Sabbat itself that Peter de Melvis met a countryman bearing a dart and saying, 'With this dart your king was killed today.' Allowance has not been made for Rufus's procrastination till 'the morrow of Lammas'.)

The various accounts of the death of Rufus abound in touches which convey its true significance. It is consummated in the depths of a forest at sunset on the site of a pre-Christian holy place. He stands under (or the arrow glances from) an oak, the Royal tree. His slayer stands under an elder tree, the tree of doom, which traditionally is both the tree of the Cross and the tree on which Judas hanged himself. The king partakes of a kind of last sacrament of herbs and flowers. In most of the accounts he is slain by an arrow loosed by his intimate, Tirel, after Tirel's hesitation and the king's command, 'Shoot, in the Devil's name, or it will be the worse for you.' On the night before his death, he has had strange dreams. In one, he was being bled when his blood suddenly gushed up towards heaven so as to obliterate the daylight; in another, he was alone in a chapel in a forest whose walls were hung with purple tapestries of Greek workmanship, embroidered with ancient legends. These suddenly disappeared, leaving the walls and altar bare and on the altar a naked man, whom the king tried to eat. But the man said, 'Henceforth you shall eat of me no more' and vanished. In another version it is, even more significantly, the body of a stag.

It should by now be clear enough why William, the grandson of Robert 'the Devil', was surnamed the Red King – an appellation used by contemporary writers also as a proper name. For red, the colour of blood, has always and everywhere been the 'witch' colour. To take one example, Frazer points out that 'we have it on the authority of Maneto that they used to burn redhaired men and scatter their ashes with winnowing-fans, and it is highly significant that this barbarous sacrifice was offered by the kings at the grave of Osiris. We may conjecture that the victims represented Osiris himself who was annually slain, dismembered, and buried in their persons that he might quicken the seed in the earth.' The oxen that were sacrificed were also red and were, indeed, disqualified by the discovery of asingle white or black hair.

The point is too obvious to be laboured, but it is worth mentioning that when, after Rufus's death, his body was taken from the

New Forest to Winchester, the contemporary chronicles insist that the blood dripped on the earth throughout the entire journey. Though this is an actual impossibility, it is consistent with the belief that the blood of the Divine Victim must fall on the ground to fertilize it. Memory of the track of blood is kept to this day in the local name of a footpath across a field at Romsey, 'Kingsway', and the tradition of 'King's Lane' at Hursley and at Compton; while for many centuries in the forest itself the legend persisted that the oak against which Rufus was slain budded every Christmas Day.

One final point may be mentioned to complete the picture. William's favourite oath – the one which he never broke and the only one which bound him – was *per vultum de Luca* (in French *Li vo de Luche*), 'by St Luke's face'. This is usually interpreted as referring to the famous crucifix, 'the Holy Face of Lucca', which is itself an equivocal effigy capable of a Cathar interpretation. But as Freeman points out, some of the earlier writers assumed that the oath was quite simply what it seemed to be – 'by the face of Luke'. And surely those earlier writers are right. For the face of Luke, is, in ecclesiastical heraldry and symbolism, the bull which is his emblem. Rufus's oath, if equivocal, was quite simple. He was swearing on the Great Bull, which can be interpreted simply as the Mithraic Oath or as the more homely cult-oath on the horned animal. The famous oath in fact is comprehensible at all three levels of dualism – the Cathar heresy within the Church, the philosophic paganism outside it, and the simple folk-magic which knew the 'Devil' as the horned god, the bull – or the stag in whose guise Rufus died.

With these clues in mind, we can now turn to the account of the king's last day as preserved by William of Malmesbury and Orderic. At his hunting lodge in the New Forest – probably at Brockenhurst – William had spent a restless night. After his dream – if it was a dream – of his blood rising to the heavens and darkening the skies, he called for a light, forbade his chamberlains to leave him, and remained awake till dawn.

During the morning, he tried to calm himself by doing some

routine work, and when the early dinner was ready, he ate and drank more than usual, in an attempt at least to appear undisturbed.* After dinner, as he was putting on his boots for the hunt, a smith craved audience and offered him six new 'catapults' – 'arrows it would seem designed not for the long bow but for the more deadly arbalest or crossbow' as Freeman puts it. Whatever they were, they were special arrows. The king accepted them, complimented the craftsman on his work, kept four for himself and gave two to Walter Tirel with the remark, 'It is proper that the sharpest arrows should be given to him who knows how to inflict the death-dealing strokes.'

As they were continuing in talk which is not recorded, a monk arrived from Abbot Serlo at Gloucester, whose new cathedral had been consecrated a fortnight previously. It told of the dream of a monk in which Holy Church had been seen calling on God for vengeance on the king. William laughingly turned to Tirel and said, 'Walter, deal justly (*fac rectum*) with what you have heard.'

'So I will, my Lord,' answered Walter.

On this exchange, Freeman comments, 'I do not quite see what these words mean.' Their significance, however, is obvious enough in their context; and the whole scene becomes charged with dramatic irony at its most intense. Rufus gives his intimate the weapons of death and then the authority to use them. His laughter at the monk's message, with its strange appropriateness, is surely an authentic and remembered touch; nor does there seem any justification for Freeman's translation of *rex in cachinnum resolutus est* as William 'burst into bitter laughter'. If one had to invent a word to describe what the chronicler leaves unadorned, 'bitter' is not a choice that meets the situation.

There follows immediately a somewhat lame explanation by the king of that laughter which is obviously meant to answer the unspoken questions of those courtiers who were not in the secret, and who could make as little sense as Freeman did later of the

---

*William of Malmesbury uses phrases which Freeman notes as 'odd', and which are certainly emphatic, to convey the disturbance of his mind and his attempt at indifference: *Seriis negotiis cruditatem indomitae mentis eructuans* and *Ferunt; ea die largiter epulatum, crebioibus quam consuererat poculis frontem serenasse.*

quick exchange with Tirel, 'I am surprised at Serlo's fancy in writing like this : I always thought him a good old abbot. It is very simple of him, when I am so weighed down by affairs, to trouble to put the dreams of his snoring monks into writing and to send them all this way to me. Does he think I am like the English, who throw up their journey or their business because of the snoring or dreams of old women?'

Those are his last recorded words, though in a later version of the story, the king is said still to hesitate and tell those around who are puzzled by his reluctance to start the chase immediately, that he is sick and sad a hundredfold more than they can understand. But he overcomes his fear at last, mounts his horse, and rides into the depths of the forest accompanied only – according to William of Malmesbury – by Walter Tirel.

Of the death there are many accounts. Tirel shooting at a stag misses it and hits William, who, breaking off the shaft, dies without a word. Tirel shoots; the arrow glances off a tree and kills the king, who, with his last breath, urges Walter to fly for safety. The king stumbles and falls upon one of his own arrows. The king, shooting at a stag, finds the string of his bow breaks; the stag stands still with amazement; the king calls, 'Shoot, in the Devil's name, or it will be worse for you'; Tirel shoots and his arrow pierces the king to the heart. A herd of deer comes by; the king dismounts to take better aim; Tirel places himself near an elder tree; a great stag passes near by; Tirel's shot, badly aimed, kills the king; Tirel at once flees, but a passing hunter, in response to the dying king's request, picks some herbs and flowers, which he makes the king eat as a kind of last communion.

Long after, Walter Tirel, beyond the reach of English justice and 'with nothing to hope or fear', is said by the Abbot Suger to have denied that he had any part in the death of the king. But it is difficult to see how any account of the death could have come except, in the first place, from him. Only one version – that of Gerald the Welshman – mentions another name than Tirel's; and this, which substitutes for it that of Ralph of Aix, is obviously ill-informed since it speaks of the priory of Dunstable and events there at a time when that priory was not founded.

What is probable is that none of the accounts is the truth, and, paradoxically, that the later romances of the early Troubadours are more certain guides to the truth than the earlier versions. From them, we can see, at least the *nature* of the death, even if the details remain an impenetrable mystery and the only 'historical' verdict must for ever remain, 'On the morrow after Lammas Day was the King William in hunting from his own men with an arrow offshot.'

CHAPTER 3

The Princes in the Tower
? 1485

THE STORY OF the princes in the Tower of London, murdered there by order of their wicked uncle, Richard 'Crookback',
is too famous to need retelling, for the perennial popularity of
Shakespeare's *Richard III* ensures that it is known to each succeeding generation of Englishmen. That melodrama is a direct and
almost literal dramatization of a 'Life' of the king which the play-
wright found included in his source-book for the 'Histories', Holin-
shed's *Chronicles*. The authorship of this 'Life' was attributed to
Sir Thomas More, and it was first published separately in 1557,
over seventy years after King Richard's death and over twenty
after More's own martyrdom. The publisher, one of More's
relations by marriage, William Rastell, noted that it had been found
in More's own hand-writing and had been composed about 1513.
A version had appeared in 1543, incorporated with Hardyng's
Chronicle, and a Latin version was printed with additional matter
at Louvain in 1566. The English version in More's 'own hand', from
which Rastell said he was printing, has disappeared. The only
known Latin manuscript version (in Arundel MS. 43) is not in
More's hand, and there is no known manuscript original of the
Louvain edition.

It is possible that More was the author, but the 'Life' may
equally well have been the work of Cardinal Morton, in whose
household the young More was educated. Morton is known to
have been 'much delighting' in the young More's 'wit and forward-
ness', and there is no intrinsic improbability in the suggestion made
by some scholars that the manuscript was in More's handwriting
because Morton dictated it to him or because he translated it
from Morton's Latin original. In any case, Morton is the contemporary authority behind it, since More himself was a child of
five at the time of the events it purports to narrate.

Whatever the truth of the authorship – whether Morton

dictated it or whether More 'worked up' Morton's memoirs as a literary exercise – the work bears little relation to any kind of historical truth. A third of it consists of conversations and speeches which have no source but the author's imagination. Its relationship to ascertainable facts may be gauged from its first statement that 'Edward IV lived fifty and three years, seven months and six days' when in point of fact he lived forty years, eleven months, and twelve days. Its tone is so blatantly tendentious that even Professor Pollard refers to it as 'that flaming piece of Tudor propaganda' and Sir James Ramsey dismisses it as 'a mere historical romance'. As long ago as 1878 Stubbs rejected its evidence with regard to the deaths of the Princes, 'Edward V ended his reign on 25 June 1483 and, with his brother Richard, then disappears from authentic history. How long the boys lived in captivity and how they died is a matter on which legend and conjecture have been rife, with no approach to certainty. Most men believed, and still believe, that they died a violent death by their uncle's order.'

This 'belief' is based on one effective source and one only – More's 'Life'; and this continued credence is itself something of an historical phenomenon. But the non-historian is not really to blame for his credulity when, despite the fact that 'More's' accuracy has been completely disproved for at least half a century, the *Dictionary of National Biography* still solemnly affirms that Edward V and his brother were murdered by order of Richard III 'according to an irrefragable account first given in detail by Sir Thomas More'.

The Richard III of More, at least in its dramatized version as the *Richard III* of Shakespeare, is never likely to be displaced from the national consciousness; nor is there any reason why it should be, as a piece of psychological fiction. But Morton's propaganda-romance has little relation to any facts, and the interesting question for the historian is not, Did Richard III murder the Princes? but, When did Henry VII order their death?

To understand the situation at the accession of Richard III, it is necessary to go back to the early years of the reign of his elder brother, Edward IV. On May Day, 1464, Edward IV, who was then twenty-two, secretly married Elizabeth Woodville, five years his senior, a widow with two children. When, in the autumn, the marriage was publicly proclaimed, there was an immediate outcry. In the eyes of the whole country, the medieval idea of kingship was tarnished. Even if commoners did not share the nobles' indignation that their sovereign had broken with all tradition and married an obscure commoner, they were as scandalized as anyone that the bride was a widow; for the pre-nuptial virginity of a queen was considered essential, and (as, in Denmark, Caspar Weinreich noted in his Chronicle) according to English custom 'no widow is considered fit to be Queen'. On the Continent generally, Edward's solecism was attributed to the fact that Elizabeth Woodville had been his mistress. Others attributed it to sorcery. This feeling in the country, at all levels, never died and an acute Italian visitor, Dominic Mancini, observed at the end of Edward's reign, that Elizabeth Woodville was always conscious that 'according to popular usage she was not the legitimate wife of the King'.

Edward's mother, the Duchess of York, was the most outspoken. Since her eldest son's action in marrying Elizabeth showed him base-born, she is said to have been willing to substantiate that he had, in fact, been born out of wedlock. Certainly she told him publicly that it was 'a high disparagement to the sacred majesty of a prince, that ought as nigh to approach priesthood in cleanness as he doth in dignity, to be defiled with bigamy in his marriage'.*

Nevertheless, throughout the nineteen years of their married life, Elizabeth Woodville never lost her hold over Edward. She held him by apparent submission, by an almost timid demeanour, by soft and caressing words. When in the later years of their marriage, his infidelities were the talk of England, she held him more subtly by providing as the boon companions of his exploits her younger brother and the two sons of her first marriage. According to a foreign observer, who was sent to make an objective report on England for a French diplomat, Edward IV 'was licentious in the extreme; he pursued with no discrimination the married and the unmarried, the noble and the lowly. Although he had many promoters and companions of his vices, the most important and especial three were the Queen's two sons and one of her brothers.'

*Though, as we shall see, this may have had more than one meaning.

His most notorious mistress, Jane Shore, he shared with his elder stepson and with Lord Hastings, who had privately contracted with Elizabeth that his daughter should marry that stepson.

Elizabeth Woodville's one passion was power – power in her own right. She spared no effort to aggrandize her family, and her success may be estimated from a mere recital of the marriages and positions she secured for them. Of her five brothers, the eldest, who was created Earl Rivers, married the richest heiress in England, and the youngest, at the age of twenty, married the Dowager Duchess of Norfolk, who was eighty – a match which, universally known as 'the diabolical marriage' and taking place in the year of her own coronation, increased the general hatred felt for her. Of her remaining brothers, one was entrusted with effective command of the army and navy; one was made Bishop of Salisbury; and one was, by the king's influence, made Prior of the Order of St John of Jerusalem against the wishes and protests of the brethren.

The marriages of her six sisters gave the family great territorial power – one marrying the Duke of Buckingham, one the Earl of Arundel, one the Earl of Kent, one the Earl of Essex, one Lord Strange, and one the heir of Lord Herbert.

Her elder son, Thomas, was, while still in his teens, created Marquess of Dorset – the sixth marquessate ever to be bestowed in England 'where the title was exotic and unpopular to a degree' – and her first husband's brother was made Viscount Lisle.

As she advanced her own, she never ceased to plot for the destruction of the king's family. Her main and increasing attack was against his second brother, George, Duke of Clarence. She had reason. Clarence was not only heir-presumptive to the throne for the first six years of her marriage, until the birth of her son Edward; he was still, in the popular estimation which would not admit the marriage's validity, heir-presumptive even after that event. In this capacity, he was a perpetual menace to her security. 'Witty and well visaged', as a contemporary Englishman described him, he was popular with the people. According to Mancini, 'the Queen's alarm was intensified by the comeliness of the Duke of Clarence, which would make him appear worthy of the crown; besides, he possessed such a mastery of popular eloquence that nothing upon which he set his heart seemed difficult for him to achieve'. Moreover, Clarence was not tactful. He never forgave her marriage to his brother. He said she was a sorceress, and 'by bitter and public denunciations of Elizabeth's obscure family and by proclaiming that the king, who ought to have married a virgin wife, had married a widow in violation of established custom' he added fuel to her flames.

Also, and more pertinently, he probably knew a more dangerous secret.

This secret was that, for quite other reasons than her widowhood, Elizabeth Woodville was not Edward's legitimate wife and that, in consequence, his children could not inherit the throne. Two or three years before the marriage, Edward had solemnly plighted his troth to Lady Eleanor Butler, daughter of the Earl of Shrewsbury. Such a contract was, in the fifteenth century, as binding as marriage itself. Indeed, the French chronicler, Philippe de Commines, says that Robert Stillington, Dean of St. Martin's and Keeper of Edward's Privy Seal, who drew up the contract and witnessed the troth-plight, told him that he afterwards actually married Edward and the Lady Eleanor. Whether or not this was true, it did not affect the legal situation, since the betrothal alone was sufficient to invalidate the subsequent Woodville marriage. Nor did the fact that the Lady Eleanor eventually entered a convent at Norwich, where she died in 1466, alter the situation with regard to the legitimacy of the children who were to become known to history as 'the princes in the Tower'.

The Duchess of York knew of the Butler contract (which was presumably made for political reasons among the uncertain chances and changes of the Wars of the Roses) and it may have been this, quite as much as Elizabeth Woodville's widowhood, which prompted her angry outburst about 'bigamy' to her son, knowing that he would understand the hidden meaning of it. And it is at least possible that, at some point, she confided the secret to her second son, George, Duke of Clarence, who in her eyes would remain the legitimate heir to the throne. As for Dr Stillington, he was rewarded for his work and for his secrecy. In

1466, the year of Lady Eleanor's death, he was made Bishop of Bath and Wells and the following year Lord Chancellor.

The duel of words and wits between Elizabeth Woodville and the Duke of Clarence culminated in Clarence's judicial murder in 1478. The final act was that of the king himself who personally introduced a Bill of Attainder against his brother. Clarence characteristically offered wager of battle. Edward refused it. And in the wordy strife where 'not a single person uttered a word against the Duke except the king; not one individual made answer to the king except the Duke', the king was the inevitable victor. The Duchess of York tried frantically, but unavailingly, to reconcile her sons. Their youngest brother, Richard, Duke of Gloucester, rushed back from the North where he kept the Marches against the Scots, to remonstrate with Edward against this act of fratricide. But Edward was adamant.

At this distance of time, it is easy enough to discern in the strange proceedings and accusations a dominant note which is false, equivocal. The apparent charges are so obviously not the real charges. On them alone even his uxorious thraldom to Elizabeth Woodville would not have made Edward actually kill his brother. And those writers are surely correct who see in the action the king's fear that Clarence, in his hatred of the queen and in the headiness of his increasing popularity, would play as his trump card the Butler pre-contract. No sooner was Clarence secretly done to death in the Tower of London – tradition has it by being drowned in a butt of malmsey as his own gay choice of death when his brother, as a last mercy, offered him a choice – than Stillington was arrested and sent to the Tower on the vague charge of 'uttering words prejudicial to the King and his state'. The coincidence is, at least, remarkable. But the Bishop of Bath and Wells had no desire to share Clarence's fate. He gave the necessary assurances and was released after three months' imprisonment. For the rest of Edward's reign, the dangerous matter remained a secret. Only Richard, Duke of Gloucester – who knew nothing of it – swore vengeance on the Woodvilles. 'Richard was so overcome with grief for his brother,' reported Mancini, 'that he could not dissimulate so well but that he was overheard to say that he would one day revenge his bother's death.' The future Richard III was at that time twenty-five.

Edward IV died on 9 April 1483. By his will he appointed Richard sole guardian of his children and Protector of the Realm during young Edward's minority. Neither Elizabeth Woodville nor her family was to have any part in the governance of the kingdom. It was as if, freed at last from her influence, he had made what amends he could from beyond the grave. Richard was in York when the news of his brother's death reached him. He called together the nobility of the district, made them swear allegiance to the twelve-year-old Edward V and, with six hundred followers, all attired in mourning, set out for London, intending on the way to meet his nephew at Northampton and conduct him in state to the capital.

The Woodvilles, not unnaturally, saw things differently. Their richest harvest was in store for them – a long period of unchallenged power during which they could rule in the boy-king's name. And they had a considerable initial advantage – the actual custody of the child. Edward was in Ludlow in charge of Elizabeth Woodville's eldest brother, Lord Rivers, her younger son, Sir Richard Grey, and her nephew, Sir Robert Haute. In London, the Tower was commanded by her other son, the Marquess of Dorset. On 24 April, Rivers and Grey set out for London with 2,000 men-at-arms taking the king with them, while in London Dorset seized the arms and treasure of the Tower to fit up a naval force to command the Channel. Though as early as 21 April Richard was named Protector in an official document, Rivers and Dorset issued Orders in Council in their own names, excluding that of the Protector; nor is there any doubt – on this point both contemporary chroniclers, Rous and the Croyland Monk agree – that they were conspiring for Richard's death.

Richard, as soon as he learnt what was happening, acted with his accustomed swiftness. Rivers and Grey, who, unaware of his knowledge, had ridden into Northampton with a few gentlemen merely to delay him by an exchange of courtesies while Edward was sent by another route to London, were arrested, and the king intercepted and brought back to Northampton. The conspirators were arrested and eventually executed and England saved from another civil war. Elizabeth Woodville fled to sanctuary in Westminster.

On 4 May Richard entered London in state with Edward V,

whom he sent to stay at the Bishop of London's palace near St Paul's, while he himself went to his mother, the Duchess of York, at Baynard's Castle (which stood at the foot of St Andrew's Hill, to the west of the cathedral). The coronation was fixed for 22 June and Parliament summoned for 25 June. But during the interval the course of events was radically changed by Richard's becoming for the first time aware of the irregularity of his brother's marriage. As he was staying with his mother, it would seem probable that she, in the first place, told him of it; but the first public intimation was when Stillington revealed it at a Council meeting on 8 June. From that moment it was clear to everyone that Edward V could not succeed to the throne, since his illegitimacy debarred both him and his brother. Clarence's son, the eight-year-old Earl of Warwick, was of attainted blood and thus equally ineligible. The only possible king was Richard. He commenced his reign on 25 June 1483, to the general satisfaction of all but the Woodville faction. Edward V and his brother were given apartments in the Tower, where they were kept as much for their own safety as the country's.

The Woodvilles, however, were not disposed to accept the situation. During Richard's absence in the North a new plot was hatched. Negotiations were opened with the twenty-six-year-old Henry Tudor, a Lancastrian in exile in Brittany, whose claim to the English succession was tenuous in the extreme. He was the great-grandson of an illegitimate son of a younger son of Edward III. The Woodvilles held out to him the bait of marriage with Elizabeth Woodville's eighteen-year-old daughter – her eldest child by Edward IV and the sister of the princes in the Tower. Henry was to invade from Brittany at the same time as the Woodville faction, led by one of Elizabeth Woodville's brothers-in-law, raised a rebellion at home.

Again Richard triumphed. But it was his last victory. The combination of treachery eventually succeeded; in the August of 1485 he was killed at the battle of Bosworth, and 'the last and most doubtful of all the usurpers, a wanderer from the Welsh marches, a knight from nowhere, found the crown of England under a bush of thorn'.

Henry Tudor was king by right of conquest, but to establish himself with any hope of permanency the marriage with Elizabeth was a necessity. And herein lay the dilemma. By marrying her, he legally reversed her illegitimacy; but, in so doing, he also reversed that of her brothers and Edward V was beyond cavil king. By the very act of securing his title by marriage, Henry Tudor destroyed his title. And to this problem there was only one answer – the princes in the Tower must die.

'But', the legend objects, 'they were already dead.' The worth of the legend, however, may now be better estimated. The evidence of Polydore Vergil, Henry's official historian, who did not come to England till 1502, is obviously worthless, since he was merely transcribing the royal propaganda line on an event of which he could have no knowledge. The one effective source was Morton, whose credentials must now be examined.

A lawyer who took priest's orders for financial reasons, John Morton became one of the greatest pluralists known to ecclesiastical records under Henry VI. After the defeat of the Lancastrians, he quickly changed sides and offered his services to Edward IV, who made him Master of the Rolls and Bishop of Ely, and employed him on a diplomatic mission in the course of which he accepted a bribe of 2,000 crowns a year from the King of France. On his return he attached himself to the Woodville faction, whose 'brains' he became. At Ludlow on Edward's death, he was the architect of their plan to seize power. It was he, again, who inspired the second rebellion and the overture to Henry Tudor. Though he was one of Richard's deadliest enemies, Richard forgave him the first time – after a short imprisonment – and on the second occasion Morton managed to escape to the Continent where he attached himself to Henry Tudor and intrigued on his behalf for the rest of Richard's reign. After Bosworth his services were rewarded. He was made in rapid succession Lord Chancellor, Archbishop of Canterbury, and (through Henry's petition to the Pope, Alexander Borgia) Cardinal. In his lifetime he was hated and feared by all classes, both because of his 'avaricious and grasping' conduct and because he so disgraced the priesthood that he did not scruple to reveal to Henry 'the confessions of as many lords as His Grace listed'; and, for posterity, he is enshrined in history as the inventor of 'Morton's fork' – the argument that those who spend little must have saved much and those who spend much must have much. On his word rests the effective charge that Richard had murdered his nephews.

Apart from the intrinsic improbability of such an act – for Richard had nothing, while Henry had everything, to fear from the boys' existence – there is one piece of evidence against it which is as conclusive as anything can be in such a matter. In the Act of Attainder which Henry drew up after his victory, King Richard is reviled for every kind of cruelty and tyranny. No slander is omitted which might help to justify Henry's usurpation. But there is no mention in it of the murder of the princes. As the Tower was in the new king's possession in less than a week after Bosworth, it is surely a legitimate deduction that this startling omission was due to Henry's knowledge that they were still there, alive and unharmed.

The probable date of their murder was about the beginning of July 1486. One of Henry's first acts was to order that the original act proclaiming the illegitimacy of Edward IV's children should be removed from the Rolls and burnt and that, on pain of imprisonment during his pleasure, every copy of it was to be surrendered. Stillington was imprisoned and, though he was pardoned, he was rearrested later, and never emerged from his captivity. Richard's illegitimate son, John of Gloucester, was similarly imprisoned and – if not actually murdered – left to die. Clarence's son, Warwick (whose attainder Richard had reversed and who was therefore, after the princes in the Tower, indisputably Edward IV's heir), was arrested, imprisoned in the Tower, and eventually executed. The marriage to Elizabeth was delayed until the January of 1486, and in the February of 1487 Elizabeth Woodville had all her lands and possessions confiscated and was immured in a nunnery for the rest of her life. Even Bacon, the great apologist of the Tudors, comments on this action of Henry's that it was 'probable there was some greater matter against her which the King, upon reason of policy, would not publish'. The reason for this treatment of her which, even at the time, was 'taxed as rigorous and undue' may have been that she realized that Henry had killed her sons.

On 16 July 1486 – that is, almost a year after Bosworth – Fabyan, an alderman of London, clothier by profession, who kept a diary, noted that 'common fame' was ordered to spread the report that Richard III had put the princes in the Tower 'to secrete death'.

On the same day, a certain Sir James Tyrrel, received (for the second time) a pardon and was appointed Constable of Guisnes to which he was bidden to repair and where he remained for the next six years. At the end of that time, in 1502, Tyrrel helped the Earl of Suffolk – another nephew of Edward IV and a claimant to the throne – to escape into Germany and safety. Henry at once ordered Tyrrel's arrest, sent the entire garrison of Calais to besiege him in Guisnes, promised him his safety if he would come aboard a ship to discuss terms and, having got him there, immediately had him brought to England where he threw him in the Tower and beheaded him without trial. That same year, 1502, the first written story of the murder of the princes appeared, by Henry's official journalist, Polydore Vergil. His version is that Richard 'lived in continual fear, for the expelling of whereof by any kind of means he determined by death to dispatch his nephews, because so long as they lived he could never be out of hazard; wherefore he sent warrant to Robert Brackenbury, lieutenant of the Tower of London, to procure their death with all diligence, by some means convenient. From thence he departed to York, where he was joyfully received of the citizens. . . . But the lieutenant of the Tower at London after he had received the king's horrible commission was astonished with the cruelty of the fact, and fearing lest if he should obey the same might at one time or other turn to his own harm, did therefore defer the doing thereof in hope that the king would spare his own blood, or their tender age, or alter that heavy determination. But any one of these points was so far from taking place, seeing that the mind therein remained immovable, as that when King Richard understood the lieutenant to make delay of that which he had commanded, he anon committed the charge of hastening the slaughter unto another, that is to say, James Tyrrel, who, being forced to do the king's commandment, rode sorrowfully to London, and, to the worst example that hath been almost ever heard of, murdered those babes of the issue royal. This end had Prince Edward and Richard his brother; but with what kind of death these silly (harmless) children were executed it is not certainly known.'

When it is added that Tyrrel, of whom nothing is recorded since Bosworth, reappears in history when he is given a general pardon on 16 June 1486 and becomes knight of the king's body, accompanying Henry to his visit to York; that he is, for some reason, given another pardon on 16 July, when he is made Constable of Guisnes and virtually banished to France; that, as we have seen, he is arrested by treachery and killed without trial in 1502 because he shows himself still sympathetic to Richard III's nephew; and that, as soon as he is dead, his name appears by Henry's orders in the first written 'official' account as the murderer of the princes, we may conclude that this account is in fact true, except in one particular : the name of Richard has been substituted for that of Henry.

CHAPTER 4

The Identity of Perkin Warbeck
1491 to 1499

'PERHAPS THERE is no individual in the whole course of English History', said Sir Frederic Madden in 1837, 'whose character and pretensions have been enveloped in greater mystery or occasioned more discussion than those of the person who in the reign of King Henry VII assumed the title of Richard, Duke of York, and who is better known under the name of Perkin Warbeck.'

During the nineteenth century, the debate tended to be whether he was, in fact, what he claimed to be – the younger of the two princes in the Tower – and it was decided in the negative. But this decision (which there seems no reason to challenge) did not imply that therefore he was what he made himself out to be in the confession he signed when he was in Henry VII's power; though this false alternative is now usually accepted. Gairdner, the historian who finally disposed of Perkin's claim to be Richard of York, is also careful to point out that his 'confession' is worthless as evidence since 'it only represents what the king said of Warbeck and not what Warbeck said of himself. . . . We know from Bernard André that Henry ordered it to be printed, so we cannot doubt it served his purpose to make it known.' The mystery of his true identity, in fact, remains unsolved, but it is to the highest degree improbable that the young man who managed to persuade 'the Pope, the King of France, the Archduke, the King of the Romans, the King of Scotland, and almost all the Princes of Christendom' that he was the last Plantagenet King, Richard IV, was really the son of a Tournai boatman who with some difficulty learnt English at the age of seventeen. His kingly bearing, his admitted facial resemblance to Richard, Duke of York, his recognition and enthusiastic support by Margaret of Burgundy (the sister of Edward IV and Richard III and thus his pretended aunt), the devotion to him of James IV of Scotland, who gave him his own cousin in marriage – all suggest that, even allowing for Warbeck's utility as a pawn in the political and diplomatic struggle, he had some connection with the man he claimed to be.

This, indeed, is reflected in the rumours of the time. The citizens of Cork – who, like the rest of Ireland, remained faithful to the house of York and particularly to the memory of George, Duke of Clarence, who had been Lord Lieutenant of Ireland – believed him to be either a son of Clarence or a bastard of Richard III. Another current story was that Edward IV had been openly his godfather and secretly his father. And even some of the later arguments against his actually being Richard IV rest only on the assumption that Richard III murdered the princes in 1483 instead of Henry VII in 1486,* and thus beg the whole question.

The probable identity of Warbeck is revealed in a letter from the Milanese ambassador in Flanders to the Duke of Milan on 17 February 1495, in which he says, on the authority of the Emperor Maximilian I, that 'this Duke of York (Perkin) is not the son of King Edward but is the son of the Duchess of Burgundy and the Bishop of Cambrai'. On this Pollard comments, 'The story would not be inconsistent with Perkin's upbringing by foster-parents in Tournai; it would explain some of the mystery about his career; and yet it would not be one which Henry could publish, for princes observed, even then, the *convenances* in their relations with one another.'

---

*For example, Ferdinand and Isabella of Spain offered to send to Henry VII in 1496 the names of several people who knew Perkin, among them a Portuguese knight named Ruy de Sosa. He is *au courant* with the whole affair, well informed and in good faith. Having been on an embassy from Portugal to England, he is quite well acquainted with the Duke of York, whom he has seen. Two years later he saw the other man (Perkin) in Portugal.' On this, Warbeck's latest biographer – Jean-Didier Chastelain in *L'Imposture de Perkin Warbeck* (1952) – comments, 'Ruy de Sosa may have been "well informed and in good faith" but he indubitably had a bad memory. The last time he could have seen the Duke of York was at the beginning of April 1483, and Perkin Warbeck, whom he alleges to have met in Portugal "two years later", did not arrive in that country till after Easter 1486.' But, assuming that the arguments in the previous chapter are valid, there is no reason why the Portuguese should not have seen Richard of York in 1484, and had he been in fact Richard York escaped from the Tower, he might have been expected to have arrived in Portugal some time before the June of 1486. In none of his proclamations does Perkin Warbeck suggest that the murderer was Richard III; he merely says he escaped murder.

If this be true – and it is the one explanation which would fit the known facts – then Warbeck was actually the cousin of the man he claimed to be; the affection of his 'aunt' and her un-wavering loyalty to him was maternal; and his answer to Henry VII, in the presence of the Bishop of Cambrai (who, on an embassy to England, had particularly asked to see him), that 'he solemnly swore to God that the Duchess Madame Margaret knew as well as himself that he was not the son of King Edward', is one of the supreme moments of dramatic irony in English history.

The theory both makes Warbeck's success intelligible and obviates the difficulty of assuming that all the princes and nobles who supported him in various countries did so in bad faith.

Perkin is first heard of in Portugal, in the late spring or early summer of 1486, as a twelve-year-old page in the service of Lady Brampton, the widow of a Yorkist refugee, one of Richard III's supporters. That several people connected with the Spanish Court met him there, we know from the letter of Ferdinand and Isabella. In particular it would seem probable that, at that time, he first met Sir Bernard de la Force, one of the friends and councillors of Richard III whom that king on his accession in 1483 had specially selected as envoy to Spain to conclude the peace-treaty between England and Castile. At any rate, ten years later – in 1496 – Perkin, then in Scotland, wrote a private letter to Sir Bernard at Fuenterrabia, asking him to find out the King of Spain's attitude to his claim to the English throne and referring to Sir Bernard's son, Antony, 'which hath full lovingly given his long attendance upon us in sundry countries'.

The importance of this early Spanish period in Warbeck's life, which has been too much neglected by historians, is that it shows that from the very beginning he was surrounded by friends of his uncles, Edward IV and Richard III, and was living not only in a courtly atmosphere but in the place and at the time which might have been expected had he in fact been Richard, Duke of York, escaped from Henry VII's assassins. His training for his impos-ture was begun early and was carefully superintended by those who were aware of and in touch with the actualities of events. It was not – as it is always presented as being – a later idea, born of the accidental circumstance that, in 1491, the citizens of Cork, by rea-son of his unmistakable features, acclaimed him as a Plantagenet.

Nor is there any evidence (apart from his 'confession') that, as an obscure youth ambitiously determined to make his way in the world, he left Lady Brampton at the end of twelve months and took service with 'a Breton trader, Pregent Meno', who eventually happened to take him to Ireland on business. There is no reason to suppose that Perkin left his Yorkist surroundings on the Continent until in 1491, at the age of seventeen, his training was completed and he was entrusted to Meno to take to the one remaining part of Henry VII's realm still fanatically Yorkist – the Ireland which had recently shown its devotion by crowning in Dublin a pretender, Lambert Simnel, as Edward VI.

Pregent (Pierre Jean) Meno – whose personality also has been strangely neglected by historians – was far from being merely an unknown 'Breton trader'. He was of such importance that he was allowed the privileges of Irish citizenship; he was given (in exchange for thirty sacks of wool and a payment of 300 livres) the right to the customs dues at the two ports of Dublin and Drogheda; and he was eventually appointed, in spite of his 'foreign-ness', Governor of Carrickfergus. Such a man would be the obvious choice of the Yorkists for introducing Perkin to Ireland and for arranging and observing the young man's reception there. He was notably successful. Warbeck's claim to be the rightful Richard IV was supported not only by the people as a whole but by the Earls of Desmond and Kildare. Having thus established himself, the 'Merchant of the Ruby' – to give Perkin the name by which he was referred to at the time – accepted an invitation from the King of France, brought to him by Etienne Frion, who had once been Henry VII's French secretary but was now his bitter enemy. On receiving it, he crossed to France where he spent several months as the honoured guest of Charles VIII. He was lodged in the Château d'Amboise and given a guard of honour. Here he received the homage of many English Yorkists, including Sir George Nevill and Sir John Taylor. But in the October of that year, 1492, Henry VII decided to invade France, and in the Treaty of Etaples, which concluded that bloodless war, one of the conditions of peace was the expulsion of Warbeck from French soil.

So Perkin came at last to the court of his mother, Margaret of Burgundy, who immediately recognized him in his pretended rôle as her nephew, named him 'the White Rose of England', gave him a guard of thirty halberdiers dressed in the livery of the House of York, and attached to him as his special counsellor, Hugh of Melun, Knight of the Golden Fleece and Governor of Termonde. By her efforts on his behalf, she gained recognition for him from the King of Denmark, the Duke of Saxony, and the Emperor himself.

At last seriously alarmed, Henry VII sent an army of spies into the Low Countries. When they had managed to discover Perkin's foster-parents, John and Catharine Warbeck, he had the imposture officially proclaimed and broke off trade relations with Flanders.

Chief among Henry's spies was Sir Robert Clifford who, posing as a violent Yorkist, managed to get himself not only trusted by the exiles in Flanders but actually used by them as their liaison with those still faithful to the Plantagenets in England. At the appropriate moment – at the end of 1494 when Perkin, supplied with money by the Emperor Maximilian whom he had visited in Vienna, was preparing for an invasion of England – the necessary arrests were made. Stanley, Fitz-Walter, Montfort, Thwaites, Lacy, Daubeney, Astwood, as well as many ecclesiastics, including the Dean of St Paul's and the Provincial of the Dominicans, were thrown into prison on the charge of high treason in corresponding with Perkin's *entourage*. Stanley (who had saved Henry VII's life at Bosworth) and six others were executed, the rest kept in captivity.

Of all men Henry as a usurper was most conscious of a king's weakness in the days of rebellion or invasion. After Bosworth he had executed for high treason, attainted and confiscated the land of men whose only crime was loyalty to the rightful and acknowledged king, Richard III. His introduction of this entirely novel principle had provoked an outcry, expressed by a lament in the *Croyland Chronicle*, 'O God, what security are our kings to have henceforth that in the day of battle they may not be deserted by their subjects who, acting on the awful summons of a king, may, on the decline of that king's party, as is frequently the case, be bereft of life and fortune and all their inheritance.' Now that he found himself in the reverse position he thought it advisable to make Parliament enact that no one supporting a king in actual possession of the crown could be subjected to the penalties of high treason.

The menace of invasion, however, was not serious. In the summer of 1495, Perkin with a small fleet carrying about 5,000 mercenaries appeared off the coast of Kent. An exploratory party which landed near Deal was repulsed by the local levies and six of its leaders – two Spaniards and four Englishmen, including the younger Montfort – taken prisoner. Henry had them hanged at various places along the coast as an encouragment to the natives; and Perkin, realizing that a frontal attack on England was useless, sailed on to Ireland and the hospitality of the Earl of Desmond. Thence, in due time, he crossed to Scotland where he was welcomed by James IV, who gave him one of his kinswomen in marriage.

The attitude of James IV to the pretender is of some importance in any estimate of the personality of Warbeck. The accusation that the Emperor and the King of France were content to use him as a pawn against Henry VII, though it may be true, does not necessarily imply disbelief in his claims; and their abandonment of him for economic reasons would probably have taken place even if he had been able to furnish positive proof that he was the rightful King of England. Whoever was the *de jure* ruler, they had to deal with the *de facto* monarch. Yet it may be conceded that, on the whole, their support of him is no real evidence of their belief in him. Margaret of Burgundy, who remained faithful to his cause even when others withdrew, was sufficiently actuated by her desire to revenge her house in general and her brother, Richard III, in particular, to use unscrupulously any instrument she found to her hand – and one of the darker tones of the whole story is that she may quite coldly have sent her son to death in order to avenge her brother. But the attitude of James IV is a different matter. He was, when Perkin arrived at Stirling, twenty-three – a year older than the adventurer. Of all who met him, James was the closest to him in understanding. He not only immediately made him his own cousin by marriage : he incurred the bitter hostility of Henry VII by refusing to marry Henry's eldest daughter when that honour was offered him as the price of abandoning Warbeck.* He maintained his help even when Warbeck, speaking as Richard IV of England, refused to promise him some of the English border-country as the price of his support. He rode with Warbeck on an expedition into England; and when his guest finally left Scotland, he made a diversionary raid to draw Henry's attention to the north while Warbeck was effecting his landing in the south.

*Though he did, in fact, marry her later after Warbeck's death.

The conventional interpretation of Warbeck's leaving Scotland is that James IV, succumbing to the King of England's diplomacy, gave him his *congé* and disembarrassed himself of both Perkin and Lady Catherine Gordon. This view, which is ultimately based on the false assumption that because he did not in fact return he was not intended to return, has now been demolished by M. Jean-Didier Chastelain in his chapter on 'The Attitude of James IV'. Without entering into all the arguments, it should be enough to say that Henry's envoy to James – who is assumed to have caused the change of policy and have expedited Warbeck's departure – did not arrive in Edinburgh till 10 July 1497, four days after Perkin had left Scotland on the last stage of his adventure. What is more to the point, James IV never retracted his belief that the adventurer was indeed Richard of York, even after his confession of imposture and his death at Tyburn.

Thus it would seem that the one man most competent to judge – one who was Warbeck's own age, who was the nearest to the heart of events, who had opportunity of knowing him intimately and observing him minutely for nearly two years at court, in council, and in war – was convinced of his royal Plantagenet blood. Such a circumstance strengthens the presumption that he was a nephew of Richard III, even though he was not the nephew he pretended to be.

Warbeck landed at Whitesand Bay, near Land's End, on 7 September 1497 and was immediately joined by a host of Cornish men. He captured St Michael's Mount where, for safety, he left his wife when he proceeded to Bodmin where he was proclaimed Richard IV, King of England. His welcome was overwhelming; 4,000 men took service under him and accompanied him in a triumphal march to Exeter, which, however, he failed to take by siege. It is significant that one condition of the six-hour truce which Devonshire granted him was that no inhabitant of Exeter should be allowed to join him. Had they been free to do so, there is little doubt that his army would have exceeded the 7,000 who were with him, swearing to fight to the death, by the time he arrived at Taunton. There the Royal troops barred the way, with Henry

himself, safely at the head of the reserves, offering a pardon to all
the rebels who should submit. The result was a foregone conclusion.
There was not even a battle. Perkin's army melted away and he
himself, with three companions, fled to sanctuary at Beaulieu Abbey
at the edge of the New Forest.

He was eventually persuaded to surrender himself to Henry
on the promise of pardon. Though his life was spared – for the
moment – he was forced to write a confession and was imprisoned
in the Tower, after being held up to the ridicule of the London
mobs. The confession which is, on the positive side, worthless has
a certain negative value. The one person Perkin refused to incriminate or even mention was Margaret of Burgundy. Nor, for some
reason, did Henry insist on it. Might not that reason be that the
Bishop of Cambrai was on a visit to Henry VII and that the
unpublishable truth was known? Perkin's two confessions were made
publicly, first at Westminster and then at Cheapside, in the June of
1498. A few weeks later, the Spanish ambassador reported to
Ferdinand and Isabella, 'Of Perkin there is nothing to be said,
except that he is kept with the greatest care in a tower where
he sees neither sun nor moon. The Bishop of Cambrai wished to
see him, because he had formerly transacted business with him. The
king, therefore, sent a few days ago for Perkin and asked him in my
presence why he had deceived the Archduke and the whole
country. Perkin answered, as he had done before, that the
Duchess, Madame Margaret, knew as well as himself that he was
not the son of King Edward. The king then said to the Bishop of
Cambrai and to me that Perkin had deceived the Pope, the King
of France, the Archduke, the King of the Romans, the King of
Scotland, and almost all the princes of Christendom except Your
Highnesses. I saw how much altered Perkin was. He is so much
changed that I, and all other persons here, believe his life will be
very short.'

He lived, however, another year. Henry's objective now was
not so much to get rid of Perkin, who was harmless, as to find
some reason for publicly executing the Earl of Warwick, Clarence's
son – the undoubted heir to the throne – who was also in the
Tower. He was able to use the one to destroy the other. By a
characteristically Tudor ruse, he allowed the two youths to be
together, encouraged through *agents provocateurs* their attempts

to escape from their captivity, and then executed them both for trying to escape.

Warwick, because of his rank, was beheaded. His base-born cousin, Warbeck, was sentenced to hanging, drawing, and quartering at Tyburn, where he died 'with much humility' in the presence of a dense throng of Londoners.

It is unfortunate that no evidence exists of Warbeck's demeanour during these last days; but it is at least possible that a tradition lingered on to find its expression in John Ford's magnificent play *Perkin Warbeck,* where at the end Warbeck turns on the low-born and accommodating Lambert Simnel, his precursor in impostorship, with :

> *But, sirrah, ran there in thy veins one drop*
> *Of such a royal blood as flows in mine,*
> *Thou wouldst not change condition to be second*
> *In England's state, without the crown itself.*
> *Coarse creatures are incapable of excellence:*
> *But let the world, as all to whom I am*
> *This day a spectacle, to time deliver,*
> *And by tradition fix posterity*
> *Without another chronicle than truth,*
> *How constantly my resolution suffered*
> *A martyrdom of majesty.*

CHAPTER 5

The Parentage of Queen Elizabeth I
1532 to 1536

JANE DORMER, friend, companion and lady-in-waiting of Queen Mary Tudor, left it on record that Mary would never call Elizabeth sister 'not be persuaded she was her father's daughter. She would say she had the face and countenance of Mark Smeaton.'

As no portrait exists of Mark Smeaton, who was tried and executed for adultery with Elizabeth's mother, Anne Boleyn, we have no means of forming our own judgement on the likeness; but at least we can see that there is little resemblance between Elizabeth and her presumed father, Henry VIII. Elizabeth seems to have been, in appearance, very much her mother's daughter. She had Anne's nose with startling exactitude, Anne's mouth and forehead, Anne's high cheek-bones and pointed chin. As Anne's eyes were said by observers to be 'black and beautiful', so were Elizabeth's. But Elizabeth's exquisite hands, of which she was very proud and which all who saw her mentioned as of outstanding beauty, were not her mother's nor had they anything in common with the pudgy coarseness of Henry VIII's. Her hair is supposed to have been like the king's – reddish, as Mary's was – but it must be remembered that Elizabeth was totally bald before she was thirty and that the reddish wigs that she wore for forty-two of her forty-five years as queen were intended to create precisely that impression.

As in appearance, so in character. Elizabeth's could hardly be better described than in that passage in which Paul Friedman, in his standard biography of Anne Boleyn, sums up her mother: 'She was incredibly vain, ambitious, unscrupulous, coarse, fierce and relentless. . . . Her virtues, such as they were, were her own. So we may pass no harsher judgment on her than was passed by Cromwell when, speaking confidentially to Chapuis of the woman whose destruction he had wrought, he could not refrain from extolling her courage and intelligence. Among her good qualities he might also have included her warm and constant attachment to her friends.'

Elizabeth's chief accomplishments were music and dancing. Even when she was fifty-six, six or seven galliards a morning, besides music and singing, were her custom. And in earlier days – she was thirty-one – one of her questions to Melville, Mary Queen of Scots' envoy, was whether Mary played well on the lute and virginals. When Melville answered : 'Reasonably for a Queen', he was allowed to hear her playing 'exceedingly well' on the virginals and was detained an extra day to watch her dance, at which he was bound to admit that the Queen of Scots 'danced not so high and disposedly as she did'.

Mark Smeaton was a dancer and Court musician.

It seems, therefore, not altogether pointless to consider the implications of Dr Ortiz's information to the emperor on 23 May 1536 about what he had heard in Rome – that 'in order to have a son who might be attributed to the King, she [Anne] committed adultery with a singer who taught her to play on instruments.'

As Smeaton's unwavering admission of guilt before, during and after his trial is of little evidential value because he was tortured, it is best to start the enquiry by examining the strength of Mary Tudor's belief that Elizabeth was not her sister. How tenaciously did she hold it?

Mary and Elizabeth

The dominating factor of European politics during the reign of Mary Tudor was the rivalry between France and Spain. Compared with these two powers, England and Scotland were little more than pawns which must be preserved from falling into the rival's hands, or moved so as not to obstruct the greater pieces' advance. And as Scotland 'belonged' (in this sense) to France, so England 'belonged' to Spain. Mary Stuart, queen, from her infancy, of Scotland, had been sent to France when she was six to be brought up at the French court until the time came when, at sixteen, she was to marry the dauphin. She was twelve when Philip of Spain married Mary Tudor, Queen of England, and so brought England into the rival orbit.

But Mary Queen of Scots was also Mary Tudor's heir, since Elizabeth, born while Henry VIII's true wife, Catherine of Aragon, was still alive had been declared illegitimate both by the Pope and (temporarily) by Henry VIII and the obedient English Parliament.

Thus the one object of Philip of Spain, while he was King-Consort of England (from 1554 to 1558) was to prevent at all costs the succession of Mary Queen of Scots to the English throne, should he and Mary Tudor have no issue. He wished to ensure this by marrying Elizabeth to his first cousin, Emmanuel of Savoy, while at the same time persuading Mary to recognize her as her heir.

This, in the circumstances, should have been the easiest of things to accomplish. Mary was an infatuated wife who would do anything, it seemed, that he asked. For Philip's sake, she brought England into war on the Spanish side, which lost Calais, the last English possession in France. She gave him freely of her money. She endured his interminable-seeming absences. But this one thing she would not do. She would neither allow Elizabeth's marriage nor proclaim her her heir, because these actions violated her conscience. Believing her not to be her sister, she would do nothing which could imply that she was.

In doing this she was acting against her own interest, for as long as Elizabeth remained in England and unmarried, she was the centre of all pro-French intrigue, and a perpetual danger to the queen. As the Spanish ambassador noted in the last year of the reign : 'Elizabeth was brought up in the doctrines of the new religion, she was formerly of the French faction, she hates the Queen . . . . All the plots and disorders that have troubled England during the last four years have been aimed at placing its government in Elizabeth's hands sooner than the course of nature would permit, as witness the actions of Peter Carew, the Duke of Suffolk, Courtenay, Dudley, the Frenchman Bertheville, Stafford and others, in which affairs the French and Elizabeth were involved.'

Thus it would have been to Mary's own advantage and safety to have arranged Elizabeth's marriage, quite apart from the consideration of pleasing Philip. But she could not do it. Her simplicity and honesty – even Pollard admits that 'she was the

most honest of the Tudors' – and the deep religious faith which
made her, if anything, over-scrupulous in matters of conscience forbade that concession.

The Duke of Savoy first visited England in the December of the
year in which Philip and Mary were married, 1554. Mary received
him with every courtesy, gave him the Garter, put Somerset House
at his disposal – but refused to let him see Elizabeth. Events on the
Continent recalled him after a very short stay so that it was not
until 1556 that the matter of the marriage became practical
politics.

At the beginning of 1557, rumours were abroad that Mary
had given her consent and that the marriage had been arranged.
'The King of France has heard with great regret that negotiations are going on for a match between the Duke of Savoy and the
Lady Elizabeth', wrote Simon Renard to Philip. 'They say that the
Queen has given her consent. . . . They intend to move to declare
that the Lady Elizabeth is a bastard, hoping thus to upset Your
Majesty's plans.' But the news of Mary's consent was false and it
was she who was considering having Elizabeth declared a bastard
by Act of Parliament and debarred from the succession.

Philip, from Brussels, wrote an angry letter to his wife charging
her, on her conscience, to consent to the marriage which would be
for the good of the Catholic cause in Europe. She had already
been taken to task by one of his religious advisers who, Mary
said, 'propounded questions so obscure that, to my simple understanding, there was no comprehending them : as for instance :
"Who was King in Adam's days?" and said, withal, "that I was
bound to conclude this marriage by an article in my creed."' 'I
beg in all humility', she wrote, 'that Your Highness will defer this
matter till your return and then it will be manifest whether I am
culpable or not. Otherwise I shall live in apprehension of Your
Highness's displeasure, which would be worse to me than death;
for I have already begun to taste it too much to my regret.'

The crucial passage in this long letter runs : 'I will say nothing
now except, seeing you hold that I should examine my conscience
to know if it is in conformity with the truth or no, to supplicate
Your Highness most humbly to name and appoint what persons
you judge fit to speak with me about this affair, *for that which my
conscience holds, it has held these four and twenty years.*' It was

twenty-four years since Elizabeth's birth. The passage in italics is omitted in the Protestant historian, John Etrype's *Ecclesiastical Memorials* and subsequent historians who have copied him.

Philip sent his confessor, de Fresneda, to persuade Mary 'for the safety and quiet of the Kingdom and religion, lest Elizabeth, feeling herself spurned should . . . take an anti-Spanish husband, to give her the hope of the succession.' But Mary remained adamant and, according to the Venetian ambassador – whose secret service was excellent – she obstinately maintained that 'Elizabeth was neither her sister nor the daughter of King Henry, nor would she hear of favouring her.'

Philip himself came to England in March and was followed shortly by the Duchess of Lorraine who was to take Elizabeth back with her for the marriage. But, despite everything, Mary would not give way and at the beginning of May the duchess returned to the Continent without Elizabeth.

During this last visit of Philip to his wife, from March till July, 1557, the matter must have been settled privately between them, for thereafter the project was quietly dropped. But in the spring of the following year, another suitor appeared. Philip's special envoy to Mary, Count Feria, reported it. 'An ambassador of the King of Sweden came here recently. Several days passed without his having audience of the Queen or even demanding it. His mission appears to consist of two parts : one about commercial affairs between England and Sweden and the other to negotiate a match between the Lady Elizabeth and the King of Sweden's son, for which purpose he brought a letter from the young man accrediting him to the Lady. Before he had been received by the Queen, he went to present his letter to the Lady Elizabeth. . . . When this ambassador first arrived, the Queen was greatly distressed, thinking that Your Majesty would blame her because the proposed match a year ago [with Savoy] had not come off. Now that the Lady Elizabeth has answered that she does not wish to marry, the Queen has calmed down; but she takes a most passionate interest in the affair. She now realizes that her pregnancy has come to nothing and seems afraid Your Majesty will urge her to take a decision [about marrying off Elizabeth]. Figueroa and I think Your Majesty ought to do this, grasping the occasion supplied by this ambassador and the pregnancy matter. . . . I do not think the Queen will wish to prevent Elizabeth from succeeding, in case God grants no issue to Your Majesties.'

Mary dealt with the matter in her own way. She summoned the Swedish ambassador, told him that, after having committed such a breach of etiquette as to deliver a letter to her sister before presenting his credentials, he had better go home and never return with such a message, and curtly dismissed him. Yet, in spite of her realization that, if Elizabeth had to marry, Savoy would have been the match dictated by interests or religion, as Philip had insisted, Mary still would not recognize Elizabeth as her sister. She knew now that all hope of her own child-bearing was gone; she was desperately sick (she had in fact only five more months to live); yet, not until nine days before her death, when eaten with cancer and exhausted with a fever, she was unable even to read a letter, did she yield to the importunities of her councillors, badgering her round her bed, and name Elizabeth her successor.

She had kept her conscience in the matter, against all odds, clear to the end.

In face of these facts, it seems to me impossible to deny that, whoever Elizabeth's father may have been, Mary believed that he was Mark Smeaton, as she told Jane Dormer; and for this belief she had reasons which, in her own mind, could not be shaken. Against her inclination, against her self-interest, against her love for her husband and against the cause of the religion that was so dear to her, she took the only course she considered compatible with 'that which held her conscience for four and twenty years'. What proof she had, we cannot know; but, judging by events, it seems to have convinced Philip when at last she told him of it.

According to Girolamo Pollini, whose *L'Historia Ecclesiastica della Rivoluzion d'Inghilterra* was published in 1594, Mary 'was present assisting with the relatives and friends of Anne Boleyn in the lying-in chamber when Elizabeth was born; and there she heard, among the ladies and persons of court, such scandals relative to the conduct of the mother as made her declare that "she was sure the infant was not her sister." ' This would provide some basis for her belief, but it is unlikely in view of her later conduct that she had no surer grounds than what one historian has characterized as the 'evil reports' of 'malignant busybodies'. Mary at the time of Elizabeth's birth was seventeen and must have known Smeaton, who had been at Court as a favourite dancer and musician for some years.

St Thomas More

That Mary believed Elizabeth to be Smeaton's child is, obviously, taken by itself, no proof that she was so in fact; and the next evidence worth examining is a curious remark made by St Thomas More.

St Thomas More died a martyr for the Catholic faith on 6 July 1535, because he refused to acknowledge Henry VIII 'the supreme head on earth of the Church of England.' There was no doubt or equivocation about this on anyone's part and More himself put it beyond a peradventure when he described the Act of Supremacy which gave Henry and his successors this status, as 'an Act of Parliament directly repugnant to the laws of God and His Holy Church, the supreme government of which, or of any part thereof, may no temporal Prince presume by any law to take upon him, as rightfully belonging to the See of Rome, a spiritual pre-eminence by the mouth of our Saviour Himself, personally present upon earth, only to St Peter and his successors, bishops of the same See, by special prerogative granted.' He pointed out that 'this realm, being but one member and small part of the Church might not make a particular law disagreeable with the general law of Christ's universal Catholic Church, no more than the City of London, being but one poor member in respect of the whole realm, might make a law against an Act of Parliament to bind the whole realm' and that 'no more might this realm of England refuse obedience to the See of Rome than might the child refuse obedience to his own natural father.'

And on the scaffold he called the crowd 'to bear witness with him that he should now there suffer death in and for the faith of the Holy Catholic Church'.

Originally, in 1531, the king's claim to the Supremacy had been couched in the terms . . . 'of the Church and Clergy of England, whose especial Protector, single and supreme Lord and, as far as the law of Christ allows, even Supreme Head, we acknowledge His Majesty to be'. The saving clause 'as far as the law of Christ allows' meant that the oath could be taken by anyone without a violation of conscience. But in the November of 1534, after More had been in prison for six months, it was tightened and 'as far as the law of Christ allows' was omitted. Thus More was not arrested specifically on the grounds for which he was, in the end, martyred and canonized.

What led to More's imprisonment was his refusal to take the Oath of Succession, which he was asked to swear in the April of 1534 – that is to say, seven months after Elizabeth's birth. A Succession Act was a constitutional innovation. This was the first ever passed to regulate the succession to the throne of England and it insisted among other things, that Henry's lawful heirs were his issue by Anne Boleyn. Protestant no less than Catholic writers have assumed that More's refusal to take the oath was based on the obvious ground that this would be to declare invalid Henry's marriage to Catherine of Aragon which the Pope had declared valid and thus to become implicated in the whole question of Papal jurisdiction. When Cranmer and Cromwell asked that More might be allowed to take the oath in a modified form, Henry, influenced by Anne Boleyn's 'importunate clamour', refused on the ground that 'it might be taken not only as a confirmation of the Bishop of Rome's authority, but also as a reprobation of the King's second marriage.' Thus Henry, as well as later commentators, assumed that the implied theological issue could have constituted More's reason and that he resisted the oath (the penalty for which was imprisonment, not death) on the same – or at least similar – grounds of Faith, for which he ultimately and unequivocally died.

But did he?

It seems to me that not sufficient attention has been paid to a passage in a letter he wrote while in prison to Dr Nicholas Wilson who was also in prison for refusing the oath and, unsettled in mind, was asking More's advice. In the course of his answer, More wrote : 'As touching the oath, the causes for which I refused it, no man wotteth what they be, for they be secret in mine own conscience; some other, peradventure, than those that other men would ween and such as I never disclosed to any man yet, nor never intend to do while I live.'

This description hardly fits any of the reasons adduced which were precisely what 'other men would ween', since the validity of Henry's first marriage and the relevance of the Papal condemnation were obstacles apparent to everyone. Nor can More's 'such as I never disclosed to any man yet nor never intend to do while I live' by any stretch of language or imagination be applied to the Royal Supremacy, which had already been a matter of three years' public argument and which, as we have seen, still contained, at that point, a 'conscience clause'.

More, as a statesman, a friend of King Henry's and Wolsey's successor as Lord Chancellor, was prepared to bow to authority as far as it was in conscience possible. Lord Acton, indeed, has blamed him for the lengths to which he carried his submission. He was even prepared to accept the Act of Succession as being within the competence of Parliament, provided he was not asked at the same time to recognize the Boleyn marriage. In the question of the divorce of Catherine, he had so scrupulously refused to 'meddle' that he asked one of Catherine's partisans not to call on him and told him that any letters he might receive he would feel bound in honour to show to the king. Yet against Anne Boleyn, he was immovable.

Months before there was any question of an Oath of Succession, he made a gesture which can only be construed as reflecting on her personally. Although he was a former Lord Chancellor and still a member of the Council, and as such, had a strictly official position, he refused to attend Anne's coronation, when requested to do so by the Bishops of Durham, Bath and Winchester.

The notice which may have determined this refusal is thus defined by his latest biographer: 'The coronation was a religious act. . . . After the anointing Mass was said and the new Queen "kneeled before the altar where she received of the Archbishop the Holy Sacrament." This was something more than an act of state; it was the sanctification of a union made in defiance of the Pope who had not yet pronounced his decision on the validity of the marriage between Henry and Catherine. It may have been some such view of the matter that kept Thomas More away from the coronation.'*

It may indeed have been so, but such a theory seems to me reading history backwards by using knowledge of what More eventually died for and applying it to an earlier and different situation. Also it credits More, the lay statesman, accommodating

*E. E. Reynolds: *Saint Thomas More,* p. 279.

to the utmost and anxious to obey the king, his benefactor and friend, with an outlook more in keeping with that of a bishop such as St John Fisher. Had the Pope already pronounced on the invalidity of the marriage of Henry and Anne Boleyn – which in fact he did not until five weeks after Anne's coronation – the situation would have been radically different. As it was, it would surely have been more in keeping with all that we know of More for him to conform where nonconformity was not yet demanded and when he could plead, without stretching his conscience, the excuse of official duty.

His refusal seems to me to have been what Anne considered it at the time – an action which reflected on her personally. And it would be explicable if More's secret 'such as I never disclosed unto any man yet nor never intend to do while I live' was that the child she was within three months of bearing was not Henry's. It would also have been consonant with his refusal ten months later to take the oath to Henry acknowledging the Royal succession was first to the sons of Anne 'and for fault of such sons of your body begotten . . . to the eldest issue female, which is the Lady Elizabeth.'

In any case, it is not too much to claim that More, by his own testimony, knew a secret which must never be spoken and which, in some way, concerned Elizabeth I's mother.

Anne Boleyn and Mark Smeaton

Anne Boleyn was tried, found guilty and executed in the May of 1536 on the charge 'that the Lady Anne Queen of England having been the wife of the king for the space of three years or more . . . did falsely and traitorously procure . . . divers of the king's daily and familiar servants to become her adulterers and concubines.'

Three of the men tried and executed as her lovers were Henry Noreys,* Gentleman of the King's Bedchamber, Keeper of his

*There was a general rumour that Noreys was Elizabeth's father. Elizabeth when she was queen showed excessive favour to Noreys's son; but it seems more likely that the implication of Noreys and Bryerton, as leading members of the Boleyn faction, was as much political as personal; and that Elizabeth's later close friendship with the younger Noreys was not because he was her brother, but because his father had been so chivalrous a champion of her mother.

Privy Purse and one of his favourites; Sir Francis Weston, the son of the under-treasurer of the exchequer, who from being a royal page had risen to the rank of Gentleman of the Privy Chamber, had married a rich heiress and, at the coronation of Anne, had been created a Knight of the Bath; and William Bryerton, nephew of Sir William Bryerton (one of Henry's ablest captains) who, like Weston, had risen from page to Gentleman of the Privy Chamber.

All pleaded not guilty and there is every possibility that they were telling the truth. The jury had been carefully chosen, and, as Wolsey had once remarked : 'If the Crown were prosecutor and asserted it, juries would be found to bring in a verdict that Abel was the murderer of Cain.'

An attempt was made to save Sir Francis Weston, whose rich and powerful family had occasionally opposed the Boleyns; but this, even with the support of the French ambassador, was unsuccessful. Henry's minister, Thomas Cromwell, to keep in the good graces of the king (who was already courting Jane Seymour) had at all costs to get rid of Anne, and he had no intention of leaving a 'Boleyn faction' to trouble him after her execution.

That Anne was a loose woman and that she had had several lovers, is denied by no one; but that the actual charges against Noreys, Bryerton and Weston, as framed in the indictment, are true seems improbable. To quote Friedmann, 'even if it be admitted that Anne was one of the most depraved women of an extremely base court it is most unlikely that she behaved in the manner described in the indictments.'

Even more unlikely – indeed the charge may be dismissed as preposterous – is the accusation of incest with her brother, George Viscount Rochford. The only evidence brought forward is that she was occasionally alone with him! In his case, the reason for his death is comprehensible enough. He was sufficiently intelligent and self-assertive to be a natural leader – was, in fact, already 'in opposition' to Cromwell and would never have rested till he had avenged his sister's death. He was also fatally indiscreet and had announced both that Henry was impotent and that Elizabeth was not the king's child.

At his trial, Rochford defended himself against the charge of incest with such cogency, passion and eloquence that the betting among the people was ten to one that he would be acquitted. But to the charge that he had used expressions showing that he doubted whether Elizabeth was Henry's child he made no reply and when he was handed a paper with a question written on it which he was forbidden to read aloud, he, knowing that nothing would prevent his judicial murder, proclaimed the contents in a loud voice – 'that the King was not able to have relations with his wife : that he had no virtue or potency in him.' This, as Chapuis, the Spanish ambassador, reported to Charles V, infuriated Cromwell who was anxious not to have suspicion cast on Elizabeth's paternity, since Henry though now determined to have her technically bastardized in law was, comprehensibly, equally determined to insist that he was her father.

The fifth man who was charged with adultery with Anne was Mark Smeaton, who stands in a different category from the others. He was of no political significance, being not a 'gentleman' but 'of low degree'; from first to last – from whatever motive – he admitted the amour and died the terrible death of disembowelling, castration, hanging and quartering (the others were simply beheaded) without retracting it. When Anne heard that his last words on the scaffold were : 'Master, I pray you all pray for me, for I have deserved death', she is reported to have said : 'Has he not then cleared me from the public shame he hath done me? I fear his soul will suffer for the false witness he hath borne.'

To reconstruct the story of Mark Smeaton and Anne at this distance of time, with all the key documents destroyed, is almost impossible. The sources that remain are, among official records, his indictment and the mention in the Privy Purse expenses of some forty grants to him of shirts, hose, shoes, buskins, boots and money in the three years before Elizabeth's birth*. There are ambassadorial dispatches; a Spanish *Chronicle of King Henry VIII,* which gives a detailed account of matters as they were known to Spanish merchants living at the time in London; a contemporary French life of Anne Boleyn which gives a strange and highly-coloured account,

---

*The Privy Purse accounts (Add. Mss. 20,030) are from 17 November 1529 to the end of December 1532. They thus stop about nine months before the birth of Elizabeth. The accounts for these three years were preserved by coming into the hands of Sir Orlando Bridgeman in 1634. Although at present other accounts are missing, they may yet of course be discovered.

of which some portions can be checked against other narratives; a memorial to Cromwell from George Constantine (who was an eye-witness of the executions); letters of Cromwell and others; gossip and popular ballads, such as Cavendish's metrical account of Smeaton's parentage :

My father a carpenter and laboured with his hand,
  With the sweat of his face he purchased his living,
For small was his rent and much less was his land :
  My mother in cottage used daily spinning.

and other occasional references.*

To some extent, the sources may be used to check each other to arrive at as much 'certainty' as can be found for most events of the time. One can say, for example, that undoubtedly Smeaton was the first to be arrested, since Constantine, Chapuis, Cromwell, Bulkeley, the Spanish chronicle and two French accounts all agree on the point. And, where they can be compared, the statements of Cromwell, Constantine and the Chronicler (between whom there can have been no collusion) support each other so well that the *Chronicle* substantially may be relied on.

As far as it can be pieced together from the sources that have survived the destruction of the main documents, the story runs thus.

*Bishop Burnet, in his *History of the Reformation* (published in 1679, the year the 'Popish Plot' scare was at its height, as a piece of Protestant propaganda), says that he took great pains in searching for documents which might throw some light on the proceedings and managed to find an entry in the private note-book of Sir John Spelman, one of Smeaton's judges, which ran: 'As for the evidence of the matter, it was discovered by Lady Wingfield, who had been a servant to the Queen and becoming suddenly infirm before her death, did swear this matter to one of her...' Here the page containing the vital information is torn off and with it the other notes of the judge have disappeared.

There is nothing in Burnet's character or methods which makes it improbable that he himself destroyed both this and any other document which he found embarrassing to his cause. The Lady Wingfield story is uncorroborated, as Cromwell, in his letter to Gardiner, names no one in particular, saying merely that Anne's servants could not hide 'the Queen's abomination' any longer. Burnet's avowed purpose is to exonerate, as far as possible, Anne as the patroness of Protestantism and his alleged 'Wing-field fragment' enables him to contend that the main evidence against her and her lovers was hearsay evidence of an oath of a dead woman.

Mark Smeaton, who was in Anne's service while she was still only Henry's mistress, was sent for one morning when she lay in bed 'in her lodging above the King's' when they were staying at Winchester. She wished him to play that her ladies might dance.

He was young and very handsome and as she watched him she set her heart on having him for her lover. Since he himself would not take advantage of her obvious interest, she took into her confidence an old waiting-woman named Margaret, who lay at night in the ante-chamber of her room, between it and the gallery where, within hearing, the rest of Anne's ladies slept.

In his antechamber there was a cupboard where sweetmeats, candied fruits and preserves were kept. Here, one night, Margaret concealed Smeaton. When all was quiet Anne called out : 'Margaret, bring me a little marmalade' and the waiting-woman, leading Smeaton by the hand, said : 'Here is the marmalade, my lady.' Then Anne, so that the ladies in the gallery could hear – as they had heard but not understood the rest of the exchange – called out : 'Go along; go to bed.'

Smeaton continued so much in the queen's favour that she gave him considerable gifts, which he spent on dress, jewels and horses. In time he became overbearing and insolent, after the manner of favourites, and quarrelled with some of the courtiers, in particular Sir Thomas Percy, the brother of the Earl of Northumberland.

Anne, on hearing of this, sent for Percy and ordered him to make up his quarrel with Mark. Percy, though forced to obey, continued to bear such a grudge that he went to Cromwell, told him of the favour Anne was showing to Smeaton and pointed out that the musician could not have acquired by fair means all the money he was in the habit of spending.

This was exactly what Cromwell needed. He asked Percy secretly to watch his enemy, with the result that, on 29 April, 1536, Percy was able to report that he had seen Smeaton, early in the morning, coming out of Anne's apartments.

That particular meeting between Anne and Smeaton in the palace at Greenwich was too well-authenticated for it to be denied and Anne's account of it ran : 'Upon Saturday before May Day I found him standing in the round window in my Chamber of Presence and I asked why he was so sad and he answered and said it was no matter and then I said : "You may not look to have me speak to you as I should to a nobleman, because you be an inferior person." "No, no, madam, a look sufficeth me and thus fare you well." '

She also said that this was the only time she had spoken to him since the occasion when she sent for him to play the virginals in her bedroom at Winchester.

It will be noticed that Anne's explanation of Smeaton's sadness was that he was hopelessly in love with her. Smeaton's later explanation, probably under torture, was that Noreys and Bryerton were his rivals. These statements give the particular complexion to the affair that each speaker wanted – Anne of being innocent but accused of adultery by a love-crazed menial, Smeaton of deserving mercy by giving the names of two people whom Cromwell wished to remove. But, if the words were actually spoken – and the scene seems to me vividly true – there is surely a third possible interpretation. Smeaton must have been aware of the climate of the court, where it was quite well known that Henry had tired of Anne and was paying his attentions to Jane Seymour. The whole atmosphere was one of impending disaster and in less than three weeks, as it happened, both Smeaton and Anne would be dead. What was more natural than that he should make a desperate attempt to leave while there was still time and, in coming to say farewell, give Anne a warning to which, because he was a mere musician outside politics, she would pay no heed? Not only will the words bear this construction, but the situation seems to demand it.

In any case, Smeaton later that morning left the Court and, on his way back to London, he was arrested and taken to a house in Stepney where next day he was interrogated by Cromwell himself. Constantine wrote : 'I cannot tell how he was examined, but upon May Day in the morning he was in the Tower. The truth is he confessed it, but yet the saying was that he was first grievously racked, which I could never know of a truth.' The chronicler says that the torture was by a knotted cord being tightened round his head. Another account is that he was induced to sign the deposition which incriminated himself and Anne as well as Noreys and Bryerton, not by torture but by the implied promise of Sir William Fitzwilliam, Lord High Admiral, who, seeing his hesitation and terror, said : 'Subscribe, Mark, and you will see what will come of it.'

The only thing certain is that, for whatever reason, Smeaton never denied his relations with Anne and the other four never admitted them. 'No one', said Sir Edward Baynton, who was given the task of searching for evidence, 'will accuse her, but alonely Mark, of any actual thing.' And, as we have seen, when all hope of his life being spared (if he ever had such hope) was gone, Smeaton persisted, at the edge of death, in his plea of guilty. And as he had pleaded guilty at his trial, no examination was necessary there. The indictment referred to a single act of adultery, on 26 April, 1534, to which Anne had 'procured and incited' him a fortnight earlier. That April, seven months after Elizabeth's birth, Anne had told Henry she was pregnant, which, as she had to admit in September, was untrue.

Anne and Henry

Anne's acquaintance with the king had begun soon after 1521, when she returned from France (where she had been brought up at Court), to find that her younger sister, Mary, was Henry's mistress. The king soon transferred his affections to the vital, sophisticated newcomer into the Boleyn household, who, however, knowing the rumours that he intended to divorce his wife, Catherine of Aragon and marry someone who could give him an heir, is said to have kept him at arm's length as the surest way to inflame his passion and ultimately gain the Crown. Whatever their relationship may have been Anne was a power to be reckoned with in the late 'twenties though she did not become Henry's officially recognized mistress till the autumn of 1532, when the death of the old Archbishop of Canterbury, William Warham, who had stubbornly resisted all the king's attempts to divorce Catherine, meant the disappearance of the last obstacle to eventual marriage. The new archbishop, Cranmer, could be counted on to do whatever Henry ordered and was, indeed, appointed only for that purpose.

Anne accompanied Henry to France as his *maîtresse-en-titre* in the October of 1533, returning to England in mid-November. In December, Cranmer arrived from Italy to be made Archbishop of

Canterbury and, according to accepted belief, Henry and Anne were secretly married on 25 January 1533.*

When Elizabeth was born, Henry made no attempt to hide his disappointment and irritation at the sex of the child; and within six months, he had tired of Anne and was beginning to show interest in Jane Seymour.

It was at this point – the April of 1534 – that Smeaton was said to have committed adultery with Anne and that Anne told Henry she was pregnant. The news, false though it was, had the effect of making the king show her once more some consideration and courtesy – which abruptly stopped when she had to confess that she was mistaken. In the February of 1535, Henry was considering divorcing her and only refrained because it was pointed out to him that, if he did, he would have to return to Catherine of Aragon. He would not be able to make a third marriage with Jane Seymour while two discarded wives were still alive.

During 1535 Anne realized that her only hope of holding Henry was by bearing him a son. She was pregnant again in the September of that year, but miscarried in January 1536, on the very day of Catherine of Aragon's funeral. Henry had no pity. He went to her bedside and told her that he now saw God would not give him a son and that when she recovered, he would speak to her. She knew then, since Catherine's death had removed the obstacle to Henry's marriage with Jane Seymour, that her divorce was merely a matter of time, though it is improbable that she foresaw her death.

After Anne's arrest and trial, three months later, as Rochford's proclamation of Henry's impotence and Smeaton's admission of his own adultery, made it impossible for the king to bastardize Elizabeth by adducing proof that Elizabeth was not his child, another excuse had to be found. Though this simple solution was apparently

---

*Jane Dormer, however, said that the marriage was only four months before Elizabeth's birth on 7 September and that, for that reason, Camden had concealed the date – as, indeed, he has. The 25 January date, which is now assumed by all historians, rests on Cranmer's statement in a letter which he wrote on 17 June, that it took place 'about St Paul's day' (one may be permitted to suppose that had Cranmer known the true state of Anne's pregnancy, he would have ante-dated it), combined with the Duke of Norfolk's information to Catherine of Aragon on 9 April, that the king had been married to Anne Boleyn for over two months.

originally under consideration and the Spanish ambassador actually heard a rumour that it was being used. Henry for mere pride's sake, would not hear of it. He insisted that Elizabeth should be recognized as his daughter, yet be proclaimed a bastard. The only method of doing this was to find that his marriage to Anne had been invalid from the beginning. Cranmer, who had originally declared it valid, immediately obeyed Henry and two days before Anne's execution solemnly declared it null on the grounds that a man could not properly marry the sister of his mistress. And as Mary Boleyn had admittedly been the king's mistress before his marriage to Anne, Anne could never have been truly Henry's wife.

In all this tangle of lying, chicanery and lust, anything like certainty is even more impossible than usual in history. And there is, to complicate the matter still further, the implication in Friedmann's verdict, with which few who have studied the matter will disagree : 'While I am strongly of the opinion that the indictments were drawn up at random and that there was no trustworthy evidence to sustain the specific charges, I am by no means convinced that Anne did not commit offences quite as grave as most of those of which she was accused. She may have been guilty of crimes which it did not suit the convenience of the government to divulge. At the trial some hints to this effect were thrown out and, though proof was not adduced, they were likely enough to have been true.'

It must also be added that, as a statute had been passed in the autumn of 1534 making treasonable any statement capable of being interpreted as a slander upon the king's issue, it had become, in fact, impossible to accuse Anne officially of misconduct before Elizabeth's birth, however much evidence there might have been.

We may, therefore, sum up the matter by saying that, though 'proof' is lacking, Mary Tudor's tenaciously-held belief and open assertion that Elizabeth was the daughter of Anne Boleyn and Mark Smeaton equally cannot be 'disproved' and that what facts are known support rather than rebut the claim.

CHAPTER 6

The Murder of Amy Robsart

8 September 1560

CUMNOR HALL in the year 1560 was a one-storey building built round a quadrangle. It had once been the sanatorium of the monks of Abingdon Abbey, five miles away. When the abbey had been suppressed by Henry VIII, twenty-two years before, the abbot had been allowed to retain it as his private residence. It had then passed into the hands of Dr George Owen, physician to Henry VIII, Edward VI, and Mary, who had died in 1558. The present tenant, who leased it from the Owen family, was Antony Forster, the Treasurer of the Household of Lord Robert Dudley (better known to history by his later title, Earl of Leicester). And in Cumnor Hall, on the evening of 8 September 1560, Lord Robert's wife, Amy Robsart, was found dead at the foot of a staircase.

Her death was convenient to her husband. The queen, Elizabeth I, whose twenty-seventh birthday was the day before the murder, was infatuated with him; and it is possible that he was in love with her. The diplomatic question of the day in all the courts of Europe was whether, if he should become a widower, he would marry her and become king-consort. No one showed any surprise when his liberation was accomplished – though divorce had been discussed as an alternative to poison – and a pamphleteer summed it up, 'When he was in full hope to marry the Queen, he did but send his wife aside to the house of his servant, Forster of Cumnor, where shortly after she had the chance to fall from a pair of stairs and break her neck, but yet without hurting of the hood that stood upon her head.' The cynicism of this description, reflecting the universal disbelief, becomes the more obvious when it is realized that 'a pair of stairs' means a staircase with a landing in the middle of it. As Cumnor Hall had only one storey, Amy, had she tripped and fallen down the whole flight (which, in any case, would have been almost physically impossible), could have done little more than bruise herself.

There was an inquest; but the coroner's verdict has been destroyed. There was, so it was said, an immediate burial at Cumnor; but the parish register has been destroyed. There was, later, a splendid funeral at Oxford; but when, a few years ago, the coffin was examined, there was nothing in it but a little dust. The queen, for appearance sake, took immediate measures in Council against Lord Robert; but the Privy Council register for that year has been destroyed. The trail has been further obscured for posterity by the fact that, to guard Queen Elizabeth's reputation, Sir Walter Scott in immortalizing the event in *Kenilworth* altered the date by fifteen years and represented the queen as unaware of Amy's existence; and that certain academic historians, acting on the same chivalrous principle of 'No scandal about Queen Elizabeth', have shown, if not so much disparity, a vagueness about crucial dates quite as effectively misleading. Professor Neale, for example, in his *Queen Elizabeth* puts as 'probably 8 September' a conversation which was certainly 6 September (as Professor Black, in his *The Reign of Queen Elizabeth* correctly states). To the question of the date we shall return later, but it may be pointed out at once that there is a vital difference between discussing the death of a person on a Friday, when she is perfectly well, and talking about it on the Sunday, after she is known to be dead.

No one who has seriously studied the matter is likely to doubt that the queen had guilty foreknowledge of the murder of her lover's wife, though the Tudor-Protestant propaganda line, obscuring this, is still potent in 'popular' history. And no one, either then or now, has doubted that Amy Robsart was murdered at her husband's instigation – though the actual murderer and the method employed must for ever remain a mystery. What is of major interest in the case is the part the death of Amy Robsart plays in the political struggle, at home and abroad, and in particular its relationship to the duel between Dudley and Cecil for control of the queen – that duel which was to be carried on throughout their lives. High politics hinged on the personal tragedy at Cumnor.

On the fatal Sunday, 8 September 1560, there were known to be two people in Cumnor Hall besides Amy Robsart. There was a

Mrs Odingsell, known as 'the widow that liveth with Antony Forster' and so, presumably, the housekeeper. She was the aunt of the Richard Verney who was probably the actual murderer. He had been Dudley's page, was devoted to his interests, and in the previous April – when reports were rife that Dudley intended to poison Amy – had been sent for by his master. Though he had written apologizing that, at the moment, it was impossible for him to come, he had added cryptically, 'I and mine shall always be to my best power advanced in any your affair or commandment where opportunity offereth.' There are no means of tracing Verney's movements on 8 September. The 'libel', known as *Leicester's Commonwealth,* states that 'Sir Richard Verney who, by command-ment, remained with her [Amy] that day alone, with one man only, and had sent away perforce all her servants from her, to a market two miles off, he, I say, with this man, can tell how she died'. The writer of the pamphlet says that the other man was killed in prison, where he lay for another offence, because he 'offered to publish' the facts; and that Verney about the same time died in London after raving about devils 'to a gentleman of worship of my acquaintance'. All that one can say with certainty is that there would have been nothing obviously suspicious for Verney, accom-panied by a friend, to pay a Sunday call on his aunt, Mrs Odingsell, at Cumnor Hall.

Mrs Odingsell, we know, wished to remain in the house. It was a fair day at Abingdon – 'Our Lady's Fair', it was called, because the date was the Feast of the Nativity of the Blessed Virgin Mary – and Amy either let her servants go or deliberately sent them there. The theory that she ordered them to go was advanced by those who wished to establish she had planned to commit suicide; but their absence did not leave her alone, for when Mrs Odingsell protested that she would stay, since otherwise Amy would be alone for her midday meal, Amy replied that 'Mrs Owen could bear her company at dinner'.

Mrs Owen, either the widow or the daughter-in-law of old Dr Owen, was occupying some of the rooms at Cumnor Hall, which was still, in spite of being let to the Forsters, the family house. It is possible that Amy, a lonely, deserted, frightened woman of twenty-seven, wished to have a meal privately with the one person in whom she might be able to confide and who stood outside the circle of her husband's relations and retainers. In any case, according to Blount, a relative of Dudley's whom he sent down to Cumnor to report to him on the matter, Amy 'came to Mrs Odingsell, who refused that day to go to the fair, and was very angry with her'.

Mrs Odingsell's action, since it could not be for the purpose of safeguarding Amy, would be quite comprehensible on the theory that she was, in fact, privy to the murder. Not only would she be expecting a visit from her nephew, but it would be essential for someone to be at Cumnor Hall to prevent Mrs Owen making a peregrination of the house and discovering Amy's body at the foot of the stairs. This was not, in fact, found till the late evening, when the servants returned from the fair; but there is no doubt that the death occurred much earlier in the day and the body was arranged in the position in which the servants – independent witnesses – discovered it. All that Mrs Odingsell would have to do would be to explain to Mrs Owen that Amy had gone to Abingdon with her servants; to admit Verney and his companion to do the murder and place the body in position (after which they could leave and establish for themselves a cast-iron alibi for the day) and then to guard against any discovery of it till the servants returned at nightfall. No one can say that this is the way it happened; but anyone can see, on the tiny shreds of evidence that have survived, that this is the way it could have happened.

Contemporary gossip gives a clue, for what it is worth, to the method employed. When, earlier in the century, Cumnor Hall had been converted from the monks' sanatorium into a private house, certain structural alterations had been inevitable. Among these was the blocking up of several doors. Amy, so the accepted story went, was on some excuse or other persuaded to change her ordinary room for one which had a secret doorway, of which she was unaware, at the head of the bed. Through this her murderer entered and either strangled or smothered her and then dropped the body from a height to break the neck before placing it at the foot of the stairs.

It is worth noting, in this connection, that after Amy's death, Forster (who was rewarded for his services to Dudley by large grants of land in fifteen different counties) bought Cumnor Hall from the Owens and almost entirely rebuilt it. Even with this precaution, its secrets were kept doubly sure by Forster's will, which gave Dudley on his death the option of buying it from his heirs. Dudley bought it.

At the time of the murder, the three principal characters involved – Amy, Dudley, and Elizabeth – were all twenty-seven, though Amy was older than Dudley and Dudley older than Elizabeth within the year. Dudley and Elizabeth had known each other from childhood. Dudley and Amy did not meet until they were seventeen. Amy was the only daughter and heir of a Norfolk knight, of better family than the parvenu though powerful Dudleys. A Robsart had been standard-bearer to Henry V at Agincourt. As Robert Dudley was a younger son and Amy was a considerable heiress, the match was considered suitable by Dudley's father – who, as Earl of Warwick and later Duke of Northumberland, was the virtual dictator of England, ruling in the name of the puppet boy-king, Edward VI.

Edward noted the marriage (at which Elizabeth was present) in his diary, 'Lord Robert Dudley, third son of the Earl of Warwick, married Sir John Robsart's daughter, after whose marriage there were certain gentlemen that did strive who should take away a goose's head which was hanged alive on two cross-posts.' As he was thirteen, his greater interest in the goose was natural enough.

When Edward died, Northumberland, unwilling to relinquish his power, attempted, with the aid of other Protestant noblemen who were equally unwilling to relinquish their plundered ecclesiastical wealth, to subvert the succession and enthrone Lady Jane Grey, the wife of his son, Lord Guildford Dudley – Robert's elder brother. Robert actually made at King's Lynn the official proclamation of his sister-in-law, Jane, as queen; with the result that when the rightful queen, Mary I, had crushed the rebellion and was safely on the throne, he found himself in the Tower. His brother, his father, and Lady Jane Grey were all executed; and he himself owed probably his life and certainly his release to the intervention on his behalf of Philip of Spain, husband of Mary I. Dudley showed his gratitude to Philip by, immediately on his release, serving with the Spanish forces on the Continent against the

French – a point of considerable importance in understanding the political balance of the years following the Robsart murder.

While Robert Dudley was in the Tower, and afterwards during his service abroad, his wife Amy continued to administer his estates for him. She also had permission to visit him in prison, though there is no evidence as to how often she exercised this privilege. What is more to the point is that, at the same time, Elizabeth was also a prisoner in the Tower, suspected of connivance in the Dudley and other conspiracies. (There is no reason to doubt her guilt, either in that or in later plots, but Mary was unwilling to have her sister's blood on her hands and eventually released her.)

Tradition suggests that it was during their confinement in the Tower that Elizabeth and Dudley first fell in love, and there is no doubt that, on Dudley's return from campaigning abroad – in the year of Mary's death and Elizabeth's accession to the throne – Elizabeth showed openly her infatuation for him. He was made Master of the Horse (which meant that he had to be in continual attendance on her); money and honours were showered on him, the two became inseparable to the point that Elizabeth's confidante, Kate Ashley, begged her on her knees to consider her reputation; and, throughout Europe, it became common knowledge that 'she is in love with Lord Robert Dudley and never lets him leave her'.

Amy, as might be expected, was neglected entirely. She was sent by her husband to live with some friends in Berkshire and finally to Cumnor Hall and death – a mere twenty-two months after Elizabeth's accession.

One of the traps for the unwary in the study of history is the ease with which events may be, almost unconsciously, 'read backwards'. During the most famous part of Elizabeth I's reign, Philip of Spain was the national enemy and the Earl of Leicester was the leader of the ultra-Protestant War Party urging attack even when it was dangerous. Moreover, Philip of Spain, as the leader of Catholic Europe, was the champion of the rights of Mary Queen of Scots. Because the events of 1587 and 1588 – the execution of the Queen of Scots and the repulse of the Spanish Armada

– have acquired the status of a national legend, this grouping has become fixed in popular imagination like a label for a waxwork tableau.

It is thus necessary to emphasize that the conventional values bear no relation whatever to the position in the September of 1560. Then Lord Robert Dudley, the young man who was to become Earl of Leicester, was not only the personal friend of Philip of Spain (who, until two years before had been King of England), but Philip was, for dynastic reasons, 'backing' his marriage with Elizabeth. Philip was also bitterly hostile to the claim of Mary Queen of Scots to the English succession since Mary was, at that time, Queen of France, and the cementing of an alliance between England and France would have been a serious blow to Spanish plans for hegemony in Europe.

The reports of the Spanish ambassador in England to Philip on the subject of Dudley's relations with Elizabeth, and the possibility of their marriage once Amy Robsart is dead, must therefore be considered as of cardinal importance, written with the extreme of care and objectivity. They are not 'hostile' reports or the mere retailing of gossip, but an attempt to give Philip the material for an informed judgment on a matter of the highest policy.

In the April of 1559, the Spanish ambassador reports, 'Lord Robert has come so much into favour that he does whatever he likes with affairs, and it is even said that Her Majesty visits him in his chamber night and day. People talk of this so freely that they go so far as to say that his wife has a malady in one of her breasts and the Queen is only waiting for her to die to marry Lord Robert.'

That summer, a new ambassador, Alvaro de Quadra, Bishop of Aquila, was sent over specifically to watch the situation. 'I have heard from a certain person who is accustomed to give veracious news', he writes in the autumn, 'that Lord Robert has sent to poison his wife. Certainly all the Queen has done in the matter of her marriage is only keeping Lord Robert's enemies and the country engaged with words until this wicked deed is consummated.'

The talk of poison continued. In January 1560, the ambassador discussed the matter with a German diplomat who was to report verbally about 'the poison for the wife of Milord Robert' – 'an important story and necessary to be known'.

There is, incidentally, another sidelight on this poison. In

Leicester's Commonwealth it is asserted that Forster and his companions, seeing that Amy was 'sad and heavy' (which, in the circumstance, is hardly surprising), sent over to Dr Bayly, the queen's Professor of Physics at Oxford, for a prescription, 'meaning also to have added somewhat of their own for her comfort', and that Dr Bayly refused to prescribe anything, 'misdoubting [as he after reported] lest if they poisoned her under the name of his potion, he might have after been hanged for a cover of their sin'. As, when the pamphlet appeared, Dr Bayly was alive, famous and secure, he could easily have contradicted it. As he did not, the presumption is that it is true and that he, seeing (as the writer puts it) 'the small need which the good lady had of physic', refused to be involved since he guessed – or knew – what was intended.

In this January of 1560, when the method of poison was favoured, de Quadra reported that the country was getting restive, 'Either I am deceived and know nothing of the English people or they will do something to set this crooked business straight. There is not a man who does not cry out on him and her with indignation. . . . She will marry none but the favoured Robert.' In March he repeated it, 'There is not a man in England who does not cry out on him as the Queen's ruin. . . . Every day he presumes more and more and it is now said that he means to divorce his wife.' It was at this point that Dudley sent for Verney.

Among the people the scandal grew to such proportions that in August, three weeks before the murder, Anne Dowe of Brentford was sent to prison for openly asserting that the queen had had a child by Lord Robert, which possibly connects with the French ambassador's report that 'he had been assured by a person who was in a position to know that Lord Robert had slept with the Queen on New Year's night'.

With this background we are able the better to estimate the position a day or two before the murder.

On Friday, 6 September, the Court was at Windsor and de Quadra went down to have an audience with the queen. Though he, naturally, was concerned with foreign affairs, the overriding topic of the moment was the struggle between Dudley and Cecil, the queen's secretary.

William Cecil, twelve years older than Robert Dudley, had been in the service of Dudley's father, Northumberland, but had, with his unerring political instinct, deserted him at the right moment, just as he had deserted his former master, who had 'made' him, just before his fall. There was thus no love lost, merely on family grounds, between Dudley and Cecil; and the dislike was inflamed, if possible, but the fact that Dudley had been in prison under Mary, whereas Cecil, whose enormous wealth was founded on grants of plundered monasteries and who had been one of the architects of the Protestant revolution, had made terms with Mary and even wormed his way into the confidence of Cardinal Pole. But as soon as Mary was dead, he had thrown off the mask and was now Elizabeth's most trusted adviser, busily engaged on forcing her further in the Protestant direction than she herself wished to go. William Cecil, as one biographer has put it, 'was a cat always lighting on his feet on the winning side, a master in the art he so vividly described as "throwing the stone without that the hand be seen".' The one moment that his position was in deadly danger was at the beginning of September 1560, when Elizabeth's infatuation for Dudley had disturbed every balanced calculation.

After de Quadra's audience with Elizabeth on 6 September, Cecil talked somewhat freely to the ambassador. 'After my conversation with the Queen,' wrote de Quadra, 'I met the Secretary Cecil, whom I knew to be in disgrace. Lord Robert, I was aware, was endeavouring to deprive him of his place. He said that the Queen was conducting herself in such a way that he thought of retiring. He said it was a bad sailor who did not enter a port if he saw a storm coming on, and he clearly foresaw the ruin of the realm through Robert's intimacy with the Queen, who surrendered all affairs to him and meant to marry him. He said he should ask leave to go home, though he thought they would cast him into the Tower first. He ended by begging me in God's name to point out to the Queen the effect of her misconduct and to persuade her not to abandon business entirely, but to look to her realm; and then he repeated to me twice over that Lord Robert would be better in Paradise than here.

'Last of all he said they were thinking of destroying Lord Robert's wife. They had given out she was ill; but she was not ill at all; she was very well and taking care not to be poisoned.'

On the following day, Saturday, the queen's birthday, the ambassador managed to have a word with her, 'The Queen told me on her return from hunting that Lord Robert's wife was dead, or nearly so, and begged me to say nothing about it.'

Rather more than twenty-four hours later, on the Sunday evening, Amy was found dead at the bottom of the staircase, though the official news of it did not reach Windsor and the queen till Monday. Either on the Monday evening or the Tuesday morning de Quadra added a postscript to his letter : 'Since this was written the Queen has published the death of Lord Robert's wife and has said in Italian, *Si ba rotto il collo*. She must have fallen down a staircase.'

It is an interesting psychological point that Elizabeth should have chosen Italian for the announcement she knew to be untrue, even though speculation about its possible connection in her mind with an 'Italianate' situation is profitless. But there can surely be no doubt of her foreknowledge of the event. Twenty-four hours before the murder, when Amy is quite well and taking care not to be poisoned (which may explain why she wished to dine alone with Mrs Owen), Elizabeth tells de Quadra she is dead or 'nearly so'. And the whole setting – the end of Elizabeth's twenty-seventh birthday hunting party; her plea for de Quadra not to mention the fact in his ambassadorial capacity; and indeed her reference to the matter at all – suggests that the proposed murder was occupying her mind to the point of depriving her of her customary caution.

The reactions to the murder were immediate. Less than ten days later, Dr Leaver, one of the famous preachers of the day, wrote from Coventry that 'the country was full of mutterings and dangerous suspicions, and there must be an earnest searching and trying of the truth'. No one believed that Amy Robsart had met her death by accident, and in the pulpits 'preachers harped on it in a manner prejudicial to the honour and service of the Queen'. When it was realized that, as soon as the decencies of official mourning were over, Dudley intended to marry the queen, the English ambassadors in Scotland and France sent frenzied messages that, for the sake of English prestige in those countries, such a match must at all costs be stopped. Randolph, from Edinburgh, said that the news 'so passioneth my heart that no grief I ever felt was like unto it'. Throckmorton in Paris wished only to crawl away somewhere and die, and emphasized to Cecil 'how much it imports the Queen's honour to have the reports of Amy's death ceased'. He reported the Parisian attitude in a letter on 28 October, 'One laugheth at us, another revileth us, another threateneth the Queen. Some let not to say : What religion is this, that a subject shall kill his wife and the Prince not only bear withal but marry him?'

Throckmorton was given no satisfaction, because there was none to give. His position became intolerable. 'I am withal', he wrote, 'brought to be weary of my life.' Four months later he was told plainly to stop his inquiries. That letter he endorsed, before filing it, 'A warning not to be too busy about matters between the Queen and Lord Robert.'

De Quadra's position was more delicate. His official policy was to support the match; but he could not in honesty refrain from warning Philip of the dangers of continuing the policy. 'She is in fair way', he wrote, 'to lie down one evening the Queen and wake next morning plain Madame Elizabeth, she and her paramour with her.' For several weeks he took the line that the proposed marriage had become a matter for such scandal that it could hardly enter into the exchanges of diplomacy. No one could tell whether or not the guilty pair would be swept away, but if they should hold on precariously to power they would hardly be in a position to maintain the oppression of Catholics; for their marriage would hopelessly split the ruling Protestant set. And it was this split that, above all, Cecil feared and consequently he used every weapon at his disposal to prevent a marriage which would mean his own irretrievable ruin.

In the January of 1561, it appeared that the marriage would be accomplished. Dudley's brother-in-law, Sir Henry Sidney, came to de Quadra with an extraordinary proposal. He said that Elizabeth longed to shake herself free of 'the tyranny of Cecil' and to 'put religion right'. The way to do this, he suggested, was by her marriage with Lord Dudley. If Philip of Spain would openly support the marriage, Dudley, as soon as he was king-consort, would lead in person a delegation to the Council of Trent and thus bring England back into the Catholic fold. Two days later Elizabeth herself broached the subject and thus made it clear that Sidney's approach had her knowledge and approval.

De Quadra, of course, could do nothing without instructions from

Spain; and by the time that he got Philip's authority to proceed once Elizabeth, 'whose words are little to be depended on', had committed herself in writing, the situation had changed. Cecil had countered by proposing a meeting of the Council to consider the proposed marriage. Meanwhile, a papal nuncio was on his way to England. It had been decided that the queen should meet him on the river out of London, which would avoid any religious or diplomatic difficulties, and that on St George's Day a great celebration should be held, at which both the marriage decision and the concessions to the Catholics, blessed by the nuncio, were to be announced.

But before that 23 April, Cecil had struck. He had been busy preparing the weapon which he and his son after him were to use with consummate skill for the next half-century – the fabrication of bogus 'Catholic plots'. On 14 April, a priest named either Devon or Cox, was seized at Gravesend. His courage gave way under torture and he confessed that he was the chaplain of Sir Edward Waldegrave, at whose house he had said Mass daily. He was on his way to Flanders to distribute money in alms among the more poverty-stricken of the English Catholic exiles there. About the same time, Cecil intercepted a letter from one of the imprisoned bishops hoping that, through the good offices of the nuncio, he and his fellow-sufferers might at last regain their liberty.

Even Cecil found it difficult to combine these into a plausible scare of a widespread plot to re-establish Catholicism by force of arms and foreign help; but by arresting about two hundred Catholics in various parts of the country, he contrived to disseminate alarm, while in the Council he could always rely on the Protestant 'new men' like himself to give legal form to whatever he wished to do. 'This way is full of crooks,' he wrote. 'I found my Lord Marquis (Winchester) my Lord Keeper (Sir Nicholas Bacon) and my Lord of Pembroke in this matter my best pillars. Yet I was forced to seek byways, so much was the contrary labour by prevention. . . . When I saw the Romish influence toward, I thought it necessary to dull the Papists' expectation by discovering of certain Mass-mongers and punishing them. . . . I find it hath done much good.'

Thus when the Council met to discuss the reception of the nuncio, the climate was such that the whole scheme came to nothing.

Cecil, seconded by Sir Nicholas Bacon, declared that anyone who voted for the nuncio's reception would be guilty of treason. 'By this one word "treason" he brought it about that, though many wished the Nuncio should be heard, he was in fact refused by the common vote of all.'

The plan of the Dudley marriage was wrecked for ever; for by cutting off Elizabeth and Dudley's one ally, Spain, Cecil had ensured that henceforward they were at his mercy.

There is one other significant fact. In all the subsequent attempts of Cecil to harass de Quadra – corrupting his secretary, seizing his mails, spying on his visitors, charging him with sending hostile reports – one matter is not touched on : the death of Amy and its consequences. Cecil was quite willing that the black charges should stand as a shackle to the guilty pair to present them escaping his control when he had effectually cut them off from access to Catholic support. Nor is there anywhere reflected in the negotiations of the time any disposition on the part of Elizabeth, Dudley, Cecil, or Sir Henry Sidney to doubt or deny that Amy Robsart was murdered. The callous manner in which the murder was spoken of, both in anticipation and in retrospect, joined by the bold determination to ignore the public opinion of Europe, is incompatible with a belief in the innocence of the queen.

In those early days it may not have mattered to her; but as she grew older and found the one man she loved (for of her love for Robert Dudley there is no doubt) always forbidden by Cecil to be her husband, it may be that she learnt the meaning of servitude to a blackmailer; and that the real clue to the Cecilian influence throughout the reign is to be found on that Friday and Saturday morning before Amy Robsart died.

CHAPTER 7

Holyrood and Kirk o' Field

9 March 1566 and 10 February 1567

ON THE NIGHT of Saturday, 9 March 1566, in the Palace of Holyrood in Edinburgh, Mary Queen of Scots was locked tightly in her husband's arms. The position was not of her choosing. She had been pushed there by the armour-clad Lord Ruthven to prevent her interfering while he and his confederates murdered her Italian secretary, David Riccio. 'Take your good wife, my lord', he said, 'and cherish her while we do what must be done.'

The occasion had been planned with forethought by her husband, Henry, Lord Darnley, a drunken sensualist of twenty-one. As she was six months with child, it was hoped that the shock, if it did not kill her, would at least dispose of the child who, were he a boy, would end Darnley's hopes of the Crown Matrimonial of Scotland.

That no chance should be neglected, Darnley had insisted that Riccio should be killed before Mary's eyes. The utmost violence was desirable. Fawdonsyde, one of Ruthven's band, actually cocked his pistol at her, but she beat it down with the flat of her hand before she was overpowered. She saw Riccio dragged through the open door and there butchered, stabbed by fifty-six dagger thrusts.

The queen, at the time of the murder, was twenty-three. She had been born when her father, King James V of Scotland, was dying, so she had been queen from her cradle. At the age of five and a half, she had been sent to France to be betrothed to the dauphin (heir to the French throne), whom she married ten years later. During his short eighteen months' reign as Francis II of France, he was also technically King of Scotland, for Mary had granted him the Crown Matrimonial which conferred equal power and status on him, so his signature was necessary – and even took precedence over Mary's – on all State documents. Francis died a few days after Mary's eighteenth birthday, and eight months later she left the French Court, the centre of European culture, to face the comparative barbarism of her native land, a land of which she was now the sole sovereign.

Her arrival there had been unpropitious. 'There was never seen', a chronicler recorded, 'a more dolorous face of heaven than was at her arrival, which two days after did so continue; for beside the surface wet and the corruption of the air, the mist was so thick and dark that scarce might any man espy another the length of two pair of butts [wine casks]; the sun was not seen to shine two days before or two days after.'

But there was more than climatic inconvenience. The previous year the Scottish Parliament, controlled by the Protestant lords, had officially outlawed the Catholic religion of which Mary was so devout an adherent; and one preacher saw in the weather a reflection of the 'sorrow, dolour, darkness and all impiety' which she brought with her.

Nevertheless, official gaiety, as far as it could, continued, and among the foreign deputations which arrived in Edinburgh to bring their congratulations was that from the Duke of Savoy. And so, a month or two after Mary's own landing, there entered Scotland, in the train of the Savoy ambassador, a small, ugly Piedmontese of about twenty-eight years of age named David Riccio. His family had served in the lower ranges of Italian diplomacy and David was travelled, cultivated if not cultured – and musical. He had a magnificent bass voice, as well as being a skilled lutanist and an adequate composer, and as Mary's domestic quartet of singers lacked a bass, it was not surprising that when the Savoy Embassy left Scotland, Riccio stayed behind, at a salary of £40 a year, to complete the quartet. For three years the Italian remained a comparatively obscure person at Court, but at the end of 1564, Mary's French secretary, who was not altogether trustworthy, was dismissed and Riccio appointed in his place. So when, in the February of 1565 Henry Stewart, Lord Darnley, arrived as a potential bridegroom for his cousin the queen, Riccio was already a person of some influence.

Mary became utterly infatuated with Darnley, and Riccio encouraged the romance, taking it upon himself to act as Darnley's adviser. They became inseparable. Indeed, their friendship was such that they would sometimes 'lie in one bed together'. And when, in July, the royal marriage took place – to the fury of Queen Elizabeth of England and the Protestant Scottish lords – the new king and the influential private secretary of the queen remained on excellent terms.

The rift came quickly enough. Mary refused to grant Darnley the Crown Matrimonial and Riccio refused to counsel her to do so. To gain this, which had become an obsession, Darnley was prepared to do anything, not excluding murder.

There was at Court another man who considered the Crown, or at least the power appertaining to the Crown, should belong to him, the queen's bastard brother, James Stewart, Earl of Moray. From first to last he was his sister's deadliest enemy. He had never forgiven the illegitimacy which had robbed him of the throne. His eyes were for ever fixed on it, and, if he could not be king, he could be regent. Skilfully, hypocritically, always 'looking through his fingers', he was behind every plot against Mary, but he had a genius for never being actually on the spot when his seditious plots were carried out, and he was very careful about what he signed. At thirty-five, he was the richest, the ablest and, in some ways, the most powerful man in Scotland and had no difficulty in persuading, buying, or blackmailing men of all ranks to carry out his plans. Abroad he had the support of Elizabeth of England and her Minister, William Cecil.

Moray objected to the Darnley marriage so violently that he raised a revolt, with the express purpose of capturing the queen and her consort. Known ironically as 'the Chaseabout Raid', it was spectacularly unsuccessful and that October (1565) Moray and his accomplices fled to England.

By winter, after six months of marriage, Mary's passion for her husband had cooled. She had discovered that the young man, tall, handsome, and athletic was also drunken, overbearing, jealous, and indiscreet. The circumstance which had fanned the original flame – that he, at six-foot-two, was actually taller than her six-foot and so made an admirable dancing-partner – was negligible in comparison with his scandalous conduct and general unreliability. Early in the New Year, the English ambassador reported :

'I cannot tell what mislikings of late there hath been between her Grace and her husband; he presses earnestly for the Crown Matrimonial, which she is loth to grant until she know how well he is worthy to enjoy such a sovereignty. In the court are divers contentions, quarrels, and debates; nothing so much sought as to maintain mischief and disorder. David Riccio yet retaineth his place, not without heart-grief to many that see their sovereign guided chiefly by such a fellow.'

That Riccio's flamboyant conduct and tactless exhibition of his privileged status with the queen gave genuine offence to many of the Scottish nobles is beyond dispute. But Darnley's belief that it was the Italian who was the real cause of the queen's refusal to grant him the Crown Matrimonial was as foolish as his pretence that Ricco was Mary's lover. The notion was useful as propaganda but preposterous as fact. Riccio's real offence was that, unlike his predecessor in the queen's service, he was totally loyal to her and could not be suborned. Darnley and the Protestant lords, though in opposite camps, could heartily agree on the need to destroy Riccio. But the murder of the wretched little man was almost incidental to the real plot. Darnley and his erstwhile enemies now saw that they stood to gain a great deal by joining forces. Moray, in England, was in desperate straits. He had not '200 crowns in the world' so that 'necessity forces him to somewhat, how full of peril soever it be'. Moreover, the Scottish Parliament was to meet early in March, and it would declare all Moray's goods forfeit, so that from his point of view the 'somewhat' was urgent.

The removal of Riccio was to be merely the pretext for a *coup d'état,* the purpose of which was the reinstatement of Moray and his party on the one hand and the achievement of the Crown Matrimonial by Darnley on the other. The brutal and gory method of Riccio's removal, threatening as it did the life of the queen and of her unborn child, was particularly agreeable to both her husband and her brother. The matter was too dangerous for either of the parties to trust each other without a signed undertaking. Two 'bonds' were drawn up. In the one, the Protestant lords undertook 'to give the Crown Matrimonial to the noble and mighty Prince Henry by the Grace of God, King of Scotland and husband to our Sovereign Lady, for all the days of his life'. In the other, Darnley undertook to remit 'all faults and crimes by-past, of whatsoever quality of the said earls, lords, and their complices and to permit them to use and enjoy all their lands that they had before their passage to England'.

Thus safeguarded from one another, the syndicate proceeded to the murder. About eight o'clock on that Saturday evening, 9 March 1566, an armed party led by James Douglas, Earl of Morton – Moray's friend and ally – seized the Palace of Holyrood, overpowered the porter at the main gate, and took his keys. They were met by Darnley, who led eighteen of them with swords, daggers, and pistols ready, through his own apartments and up the private stairway to the queen's small cabinet where she was having supper with the Countess of Argyll and Lord Robert Stewart (her illegitimate brother and sister), and Riccio.

Darnley entered alone and, as he and Riccio had been playing tennis amicably during the afternoon, the Italian saw nothing to be alarmed about. But panic seized him when, a moment later, the sinister, corpse-like figure of Lord Ruthven entered the room and said to the queen : 'May it please Your Grace that yonder man, Davy, come out of your privy chamber, where he has been too long.'

Mary said : 'What offence has he committed?'

'He has offended against your honour,' Ruthven replied.

The queen ordered Ruthven to leave. The rest of the armed men then poured into the room and dragged Riccio, who was clinging pathetically to the queen's skirts, to the door. There, while Mary looked on with horror, they killed him, leaving Darnley's dagger in his heart.

The success of the conspiracy seemed complete. Mary was a prisoner in Holyrood, and the effective government of Scotland had passed to Darnley, as the puppet of the lords. Moray had planned to arrive shortly in Edinburgh to be pardoned and, by emphasizing his absence, to make clear that he was in no way involved in the unfortunate event. But the conspirators had left one thing out of their calculations – the strength of character of the queen. Within a few days, she had persuaded Darnley to betray the names of all his accomplices and to escape with her from Holyrood to Dunbar.

As she put it in her letter to her brother-in-law, the King of France :

'We made the King comprehend our position and how he himself might be reduced to greater straits if the conspirators prevailed against us. We had already resolved to liberate ourselves from this captivity and secretly communicated with the Earls of Bothwell and Huntly [Bothwell's brother-in-law] to devise some method of doing so. Then these noblemen, being without fear and willing to sacrifice their lives, to this end arranged to let us down at night from the walls of our palace in a chair by ropes and other devices they had prepared.'

James Hepburn, Earl of Bothwell, was thirty, a Protestant, hereditary Lord High Admiral of Scotland, and one of the great Border nobles. Though he had known Mary at the French Court and though, during her rule in Scotland, she had realized that he was one on whose loyalty she could rely, this courageous action – by which he undoubtedly saved her life – seems to have been the beginnning of her favour to him. 'His dexterity in escaping,' she wrote later, 'and how suddenly by his prudence not only were we delivered out of prison, but also that whole company of conspirators dissolved, we shall never forget.'

Once at liberty, Mary outlawed the major conspirators who, headed by Morton, had fled to England. She pardoned Moray on condition that he 'broke relations with the conspirators and retired from court'. And Darnley made a proclamation that upon 'his honour, fidelity, and the word of a prince', he never took 'any part of the said treasonable conspiracy, whereof he is slanderously and falsely accused' nor ever 'counselled, commanded, consented, assisted, or approved the same'.

The reply of the infuriated conspirators was to send Mary a copy of the bond Darnley had signed. Moray's reaction was to send a secret messenger to England asking Queen Elizabeth to show her favour to Morton and the rest of the conspirators as 'his dear friends'. Cecil's move was to send into Scotland an *agent provocateur* posing as a Catholic, to try to manoeuvre Mary into another compromising position.

For the rest of that year, 1566, Darnley, shallow and treacherous, remained the most constant source of Mary's anxieties. After the birth in June of their son, the future James VI of Scotland and I of England, she decided that the only solution lay in the annulment of her marriage to him.

Darnley, on his side, was terrified that Mary would accede to Moray's entreaties for the pardon of Morton and the other murderers of Riccio. His fellow conspirators would then be free to return to Scotland and settle their account with him. He even contemplated escaping from Scotland in an English ship.

Such, in the barest outline, was the situation just before Christmas 1566, six weeks before Darnley was murdered at Kirk o' Field.

During the week before Christmas, three things happened. On 17th December, the prince was baptised and Darnley, though he had threatened to absent himself, was present at the ceremony. On 23rd December, the jurisdiction of the ecclesiastical courts (which had been abolished in 1560) was restored, and the Archbishop of St Andrews, as Papal Legate, was empowered to hear cases of nullity. And on Christmas Eve Mary signed a pardon for Morton and the other murderers of Riccio. Darnley, realising that he was now in mortal danger, fled that same day from Stirling to take refuge in his father's castle at Glasgow. Here, surrounded by family retainers, he felt safe.

When he arrived, he was ill with syphilis though Mary believed him when he called it smallpox. He sent for her, but she had fallen from her horse and was recovering at Seton. Nevertheless, she sent her own physician to him and followed as soon as she was able to. Her great fear was that the child would catch the infection and on 14th January, 1567 she took James from Stirling to Edinburgh. But disease was not her only dread. Her greater fear was that Darnley and his father, Lennox, were plotting to kidnap the child. With both Darnley and the baby prince safely on board the 'English ship' on the way to Elizabeth, the diplomatic situation would be even more tense. Mary's fear was well justified, as proved by a letter from her ambassador in Paris saying that he had heard the rumour and adding : 'I would right humbly beseech your Majesty to cause the captains of your guard to be diligent in their office.'

In leaving the prince in Edinburgh, Mary was leaving him in the care of the one man she could trust, Bothwell, who was Sheriff of Edinburgh and Captain of the Queen's Guard. The fact that Bothwell attended her on her ride from Edinburgh to Glasgow when eventually she went to visit Darnley, was, in the circumstances, the most natural thing that could happen. The suggestion that Bothwell was her lover (romantic enough now, but cold, deliberate propaganda at the time) and that together they set out to lure Darnley to Edinburgh, and to death has long been exploded, though unfortunately it is still believed by sentimentalists. It was equally natural that Bothwell, in his official position, should superintend the lodgings which Darnley was to occupy on his return to the capital. What is important, in the light of what followed, is that Mary did not want Darnley to go to Edinburgh at all, but to Craigmillar where he could take special baths. It was Darnley, terrified of an attempt on his life by the murderers of Riccio, who insisted on being with Mary as his one guarantee of safety. He may also have had other reasons.

Mary and Darnley arrived in Edinburgh on Monday, 27th January, 1567, and Darnley was installed in what was known as Kirk o' Field, a piece of ground which had at one time been the garden of the Collegiate Church of St Mary-in-the-Fields and the site of the houses of the adjoining Dominican friary. Of the old conventual quadrangle of lodgings, the principal was a small house abutting on the town wall, through which a door led into a narrow by-lane. Overlooking it was Hamilton House, the new palace of the Hamiltons – hereditary enemies of the Lennoxes, Darnley's family – in which was living the old Archbishop of St Andrews.

The little house, built over an arched crypt, had once been a deanery and contained two principal rooms, both small, one over the other. It had been made as splendid as possible for Darnley's reception. A magnificent French bed with a silk mattress, one of Mary's gifts to him, was put in the upper room. Cloth of gold adorned the walls, the table had a rich green velvet covering, and the double-seated Chair of State was draped with watered silk of red and yellow, the colours of Scotland. Darnley's page, Taylor, shared this room with him; next to him, in a smaller room, his three other servants slept.

Despite the cramped space, Darnley seems to have been happy enough. On 7th February, when he had been there just over a week, he wrote to his father saying that his health was greatly improved by reason of 'the loving care of my love, the Queen, who doth use herself like a natural and loving wife'. He still indeed wore his taffeta mask to hide the ravages of his 'smallpox' but he was so much better that he proposed to ride with Mary to Seton three days later for the last stage of his convalescence. They intended to start as early as five o'clock in the morning of Monday, 10th February. But by two o'clock that morning he was dead.

On that last day of Darnley's life, Sunday, 9th February, Mary spent most of the day with him at Kirk o' Field – she had slept there in the room below his on both the Wednesday and the Friday

– and left him in the evening only because she had promised to grace the marriage-festivities of four of her servants. Even then, so that Darnley should not feel neglected among the gaiety, she left the supper-table at Holyrood and, with Bothwell and several companions, visited Kirk o' Field once more. She left finally at midnight, five hours before she and Darnley planned to start for Seton.

As she was leaving with Bothwell and the rest, she noticed one of Bothwell's former French servants, whose nickname was Paris, standing by the door. Paris had recently entered her own service and in the hearing of them all, she said, just as she was mounting her horse : 'Jesu, Paris, how begrimed you are !' The dirt on his face is supposed to have been the gunpowder which he and the other servants of Bothwell were busy planting in the crypt of the house upstairs while Mary was talking to Darnley. According to the propaganda-romantic story, she knew what was happening.

Quite apart from the fact that such an action would have been entirely alien to everything that is known of her character, and dismissing even her confessor's later assurance to the world that she knew nothing of the murder of her husband, this remark alone surely testifies to her innocence. Had she really been an accomplice in the plot, the last thing she would have done would be to call everyone's attention to the fact that Paris's face was black with gunpowder.

About two hours after the queen left Kirk o' Field an explosion rocked Edinburgh, and an official party, commanded by Bothwell (who, as sheriff, was responsible for law and order) set out to discover what had happened. The bodies of Darnley and his page, Taylor, were found lying in the garden some distance from the house, with no traces of gunpowder on them.

Some women who lived in the alms-houses swore that, some time before the explosion, they heard Darnley scream : 'Pity me, kinsmen, for the love of Him Who pitied all the world.' And in the muddy field near the bodies was found the court slipper of one of Darnley's kinsmen, Archie Douglas, a professional 'bravo' who was one of the Riccio murderers recently returned from banishment.

It seems, therefore, reasonable to suppose that the actual murder of Darnley took place in the garden of Kirk o' Field before the explosion. What may have happened is that Archie Douglas with other Douglases of the Morton 'band' whom Darnley had betrayed the year before were the actual murderers and that the method was strangling or suffocation. It was suggested at the time that a handkerchief dipped in vinegar had been used. But we shall never know the precise details of the crime. Possibly Darnley heard men below bringing in the gunpowder, was alarmed, went to investigate, and died trying to escape. Or did he leave the house for quite another reason?

There is another theory (which in my opinion is the only one which takes into account all the known facts of the situation) that the plot was in fact Darnley's, who intended to kill Mary and rule as regent for the prince with the aid of Moray. According to this view, Darnley intended to escape from the house before the explosion, explaining that he had not had time to warn the queen. His clothes, including his cloak, were taken by Taylor into the garden before the 'escape'. Up to that point all went according to plan. But Paris had, during Mary's last visit to Kirk o' Field, discovered the gunpowder in the crypt (which accounted for his begrimed face) and had told Bothwell. Bothwell had therefore prevented Mary from returning to Kirk o' Field for the night, which Darnley, as is known, had almost hysterically urged her to do and as some maintain she had promised to do. Bothwell then came himself to Kirk o' Field to watch events and may have been responsible for the firing of the gunpowder, unaware of the other plot afoot to kill Darnley.

In support of the theory that Darnley had laid a plot to kill Mary, it is argued that no one could have put quantities of gunpowder into the crypt without the knowledge of Darnley's three servants and that Darnley dismissed them all that evening, so that they were not injured by the explosion. It is certainly odd that they escaped if they had not known what was about to happen. Above all, it must be remembered that Darnley was not a helpless invalid, as the propaganda-romantic version represents him, but that he had ordered his three 'great horses' to be saddled ready for the ten-mile ride to Seton in a few hours time.

Nor is there any doubt that Mary herself believed that she was the intended victim of the plot. The following day she wrote to her ambassador in Paris: 'The matter is horrible and so strange as we believe the like was never heard of in any country. . . . Always, whoever have taken this wicked enterprise in hand, we assure ourselves that it was dressed for us as well as for the King; for we lay for the most part of all the last week in that same lodging, and were then accompanied with the most part of the Lords that are in this town that same night at midnight, and of very chance tarried not all night, by reason of some masque in the Abbey.' I endorse the comment of George Scott-Moncrieff (himself a profound Mary-scholar) that the theory of the double-plot cannot be 'totally dismissed, even if it can never be proved.'

The one certain thing about the gunpowder explosion at Kirk o' Field is that Darnley was not killed by it. On the bodies of Darnley and his page, found at some distance from the house, was 'no fracture, wound or bruise'. They had been strangled or suffocated *before* the explosion. The second point is that the Riccio murderers, who had determined to avenge themselves on Darnley, were known to be in the neighbourhood. The third is that Bothwell was now aware that there was gunpowder in the cellars and, after he had escorted Mary back to Holyrood, he returned to Kirk o' Field.

It is, therefore, at least possible that once Darnley accepted that the queen would not return to Kirk o' Field for the night, he settled down to wait there until five o'clock but, hearing noises outside, and suddenly realising that he was alone in the midst of his mortal enemies, he made a desperate attempt to escape, only to be caught and suffocated by the Douglases. As the Savoy ambassador put it :

'The prince, hearing the rumour of the people round about the house and that they were trying false keys to open it, rushed out of it by a door that led to the garden in his shirt with his pelisse and there was strangled and then taken out of the garden into a little orchard without the walls of the grounds.'

Meanwhile, Bothwell, as soon as the queen and the courtiers had retired for the night in Holyrood, determined to pay Darnley out in his own coin and returned to Kirk o' Field to fire the gunpowder, unaware, of course, that Darnley was already dead.

Whoever the actual murderers were and however the crime was accomplished – and the mystery is never likely to be solved – there is no reasonable doubt that the man behind it all was Moray. After he was pardoned and recalled from England, he was never absent – except when it was dangerous to be present – from his sister's side. He pretended to befriend both Darnley and Bothwell, playing on Darnley's jealousy and on Bothwell's growing affection for the queen. And, as in the Riccio murder, the meeting of Parliament constituted a deadline for him, so now he had to accomplish an even more sensational *coup* before the end of that year 1567. In December Mary would be twenty-five, and on her twenty-fifth birthday she would, by Scottish custom, have the right to annul or confirm all grants made during her minority. Moray knew well that at that moment his power and his wealth would be taken from him. But in the event, Mary, on her twenty-fifth birthday was his prisoner in Lochleven Castle and he was Regent of Scotland, ruling in the name of the baby prince.

The murder of Riccio and the murder of Darnley cannot be considered in isolation from each other. The real object of both was to kill the queen. In the first, Darnley was Moray's tool. It is just possible that he was Moray's tool at Kirk o' Field as well and was hoist with his own petard.

As Mary escaped the explosion, means had to be found to discredit her. Almost immediately Moray, with his associates made a new 'bond', this time urging Bothwell to marry the queen :

'Weighing and considering how our Sovereign the Queen's Majesty is now destitute of a husband, in which solitary state the Commonwealth of this Realm may not permit Her Highness to continue and endure . . . and in case the former and affectionate service of the said Earl [Bothwell] may move Her Majesty so far to humble herself to take to husband the same Earl, we [Moray] and every one of the undersubscribing, upon our honour and fidelity . . . promises to further, advance and set forward the said marriage.'

So ran the bond which succeeded where gunpowder had failed. It was a trick, but a very successful one. Bothwell, blind to Moray's intrigue, kidnapped the queen and forced her to marry him. This event took place little more than two months after Darnley's murder. As it was recorded in the *Diurnal of Occurrents in Scotland* :

'Upon the twenty-fourth day of April, our Sovereign Lady being riding from Stirling to visit her son in Edinburgh, James, Earl of Bothwell, accompanied with seven or eight hundred men and friends, whom he caused to believe that he wished to ride against thieves in Liddesdale, met our Sovereign Lady betwixt Kirkliston and Edinburgh, at a place called the Bridges, and there took her person to the castle of Dunbar.'

From that moment, Moray had won everything. As Claude Nau, Mary's secretary, wrote :

'They designed to make Bothwell their instrument to ruin the Queen, their true and lawful sovereign. Their plan was this, to persuade her to marry the Earl of Bothwell, so that they might charge her with being in the plot against her late husband and a consenting party to his death. This they did shortly after, appealing to the fact that she had married the murderer.'

How successful they were, history bears witness. The legend of passion, adultery, and murder, false in every particular though it is, is liable still to obscure the truth. For the real meaning of Kirk o' Field is a trifle prosaic compared with the romance. It has nothing to do with the love of Mary Queen of Scots; it has to do with the hate of her bastard brother and the political requirements of Cecil and Elizabeth I of England.

CHAPTER 8

The Gowrie Conspiracy
5 August 1600

'IT IS A GREAT COMFORT,' an old Scottish lady is reported to have said, 'to think that at the Day of Judgment we shall know the whole truth about the Gowrie Conspiracy at last.' Until then, unfortunately, we must be content with conjecture as to how the Earl of Gowrie and his brother, the Master of Ruthven, were brought to their deaths on the afternoon of 5th August, 1600. For the evidence has been destroyed. The only contemporary account is – since he ruthlessly suppressed any others – the narrative of King James VI of Scotland (not yet become James I of England), and this is palpably false. Many books have been written since, endeavouring to elucidate the matter; but the truth remains elusive.

The Ruthvens had never been notably friendly to the Stuart house. It was Patrick, Lord Ruthven, who had roughly handled Mary Queen of Scots on the occasion of the Rizzio murder; it was his son, William, who had kidnapped James when he was sixteen in the so-called Raid of Ruthven and had imprisoned him in the Ruthven mansion, Gowrie House, in Perth, until he consented to sign an announcement that he was remaining there of his own free will. James, however, had managed to escape, turn the tables on the kidnapper, and eventually execute him on the evidence of a private confession which he had been induced to write on the Royal promise of pardon.

His sons, the present Ruthvens – John, Earl of Gowrie, now twenty-two, and Alexander, Master of Ruthven, aged nineteen – thus regarded the thirty-four-year-old king, not without some justification, as their father's murderer, even though he had pleaded that at the time he was not his own master and had subsequently restored their confiscated estates as evidence of his good faith.

Apart from this deep-seated and hereditary hostility, however, James had other reasons to fear and dislike the young Ruthvens. He was in debt to them to the extent of £80,000, and as recently as 26th June, 1600, the elder brother had successfully opposed in the Convention his demand for 100,000 crowns to prosecute his negotiations for the English succession, to which Gowrie was also popularly supposed to have a claim. (The young earl, while a student in Padua, had in fact adopted, as an additional device on his crest, an armed man pointing to a crown and uttering the words, 'For thee alone'.) Also the Gowries were suspected of association with the witch-cult – their grandfather had certainly tried to get Mary Queen of Scots into his power by means of a 'necromantical jewel', which was also, in other circumstances, used by their sister, who married the great Montrose – and they were idolised by the Presbyterian Kirk. There was thus no lack of reasons for the royal animosity.

At the end of July 1600, James had written secretly to each of the brothers. The two letters were destroyed, and there is now no means of knowing whether or not the Ruthvens' sudden return on 2nd August from their castle in Atholl to Gowrie House in Perth was in response to the king's orders. Nor can it ever be known why the Master of Ruthven rose at four in the morning of 5th August and rode from Perth to Falkland, where the king was, for a private interview with him at the stables before His Majesty began his day's hunting.

James's version of the matter was that the Master had come to inform him that in a secret room in Gowrie House he had imprisoned a stranger with 'a great wide pot all full of coined gold in great pieces' whom he had discovered the previous evening wandering in the fields near Perth. Even his brother, the Master said, knew nothing of it, and he had come now so that James might have the first knowledge of it and accompany him to Perth to see it. The king objected that, as it was not treasure trove, the Crown had no right to it.

The Master countered that, if the king did not take it, someone else would. The gold was foreign coin.

Obviously, said James, it had been brought into Scotland for a seditious purpose, probably by the Jesuits, and the chances were that the man was a priest in disguise. He would send a servant with a warrant back to Perth with the Master, so that Gowrie and the magistrates could examine the prisoner and his hoard.

If others touched the money, said the Master, James 'would get a very bad account made to him of that treasure'.

Eventually the king promised to consider the matter when the hunt was over. It lasted, as a matter of fact, until eleven, and at every check – so the king said – the Master had urged him to leave it and ride with him to Perth. Immediately after the kill they set out to find the pot of gold.

The story was obviously pure invention : if it could be known who invented it – James or the Master – the responsibility for the subsequent happenings would be easier to assess. On the face of it, it seems incredible that, if it was the Master's message, James could have for one moment believed it. Nevertheless, he solemnly informed his suite of it, to be told bluntly by Lennox, 'I like not that, sir, for it is not likely.'

Possibly, suggested James, the Master was mad?

'I know nothing of him,' replied Lennox, 'but as an honest, discreet gentleman.'

It seems that the importance of this conversation is that it sowed suspicion in the mind of Lennox, who would certainly never have countenanced a plot to destroy the Ruthvens but whose co-operation in the events of the afternoon was essential. James emphasised the strangeness of the story by saying openly that he suspected some 'treasonable device'. He then set off for Perth with a company of twenty-five, including Lennox, Mar, Erskine, and John Ramsay, the page who was his 'favourite' of the moment. It seemed a small company with which to dare possible treachery, but by a happy coincidence there happened that day to be in Perth three hundred armed King's men, Murrays under Tullibardine.

When the Royal party was within a mile of Gowrie House, the Master of Ruthven rode on ahead to inform his brother of their approach. The earl, who was dining with three neighbouring lairds, was both surprised and suspicious. He told his old tutor that he knew of no business that could bring the king to Perth, but, as Provost, he hurried out to give His Majesty an official welcome. He apologised that, as their arrival was unexpected, there was insufficient food in the house for the Royal dinner, and James had to wait an hour while the steward sent out for some grouse and ordered to be made ready 'a shoulder of mutton and a hen'.

The king, instead of hurrying in search of the gold, spent this interval drinking and talking with the earl, who was gloomy and uneasy. Meanwhile the Gowrie steward inquired of the Master the reason for the Royal visit. The Master replied, 'Robert Abercromby, that false knave, has brought the King here to cause His Majesty to take order for our debt.' This statement was subsequently suppressed by James, though Abercromby, the Court saddler, was never called in evidence to deny it, so it seems probable that it was, in fact, the reason given by the king to the Master, who remained in complete ignorance of the pot of gold concoction he was supposed to have told.

When James had at length dined, he went upstairs alone with the Master. As they left the Great Hall, the Master, addressing the company, apparently on behalf of the king and certainly in his presence, said, 'Gentlemen, stay, for so it is High Highness's will.'

Lennox, however, who was on edge with suspicion, rose to follow the king, but was checked by Gowrie's remark that 'His Majesty was gone up quietly on some quiet errand' – 'the obvious meaning of which,' as one of the historians of the time has pointed out, 'is preserved in local tradition.' The Master seemed destined to be the next favourite.

There is no doubt that the two went alone upstairs, along the Great Gallery where the earl's famous pictures hung, through a heavy door, which they locked behind them, into the gallery chamber, at the far corner of which was a turreted room. There they stayed undisturbed for about two and a half hours.

When they had left the Great Hall, the suite dined and then, accompanied by Gowrie, went into the garden, which sloped down to the river, to while away the time, pacing to and fro, talking and eating cherries.

Some time between five and six in the evening, the earl's equerry came to them with the unexpected report that James had mounted and was riding away from Perth. Gowrie at once cried, 'Horse! Horse!' and hurried with the others into the courtyard. But at the outer gate the porter informed them that the king had not left the house.

'You lie, knave!' said Gowrie. 'He is forth at the back gate and through the Inch.'

'That cannot be, my lord,' replied the porter, 'for I have the keys of all the gates.'

Gowrie, turning to Lenox, said that the king was always away first, adding, 'Stay, my lord, and I shall gang up and get the verity thereof.' With this he ran into the house and returned immediately with the news that James had indeed gone. But, as they were standing by the gate, deliberating what to do and where to find the king, they heard James's voice crying out, 'Help, my Lord Mar! Treason! Treason! I am betrayed! They are murdering me!' Looking up they saw at the window of the turret room the king's head 'wanting his hat, his face being red, and a hand gripping his cheek and mouth'.

Immediately Lennox and Mar, followed by most of the others, rushed into the house, up the broad staircase, through the long gallery, but found themselves stopped by the locked door. They tried to break it down, but the ladder they were using as a battering-ram broke in their hands. They sent for hammers and for as long as half an hour they beat at the door, managing at last to make a hole in the panel, but still unable to open it.

On the other side of the door, in the gallery chamber and the turreted study, murder was being done.

There were two people in particular who remained apart from the others and whose movements suggest a preconcerted plan. One was Ramsay, the page; the other was Erskine, a man of James's own age who had shared his education in boyhood. If the plot were of James's making, there was no need for any but these two to have been privy to it. Ramsay, who almost certainly originated the false report that James had ridden away, had separated himself from the rest of the company and, instead of going into the house, ran immediately up the small, dark, spiral staircase, known as the Black Turnpike, which led direct from the courtyard into the gallery chamber. He thus came to the room where the king and the Master were – inside the great doors separating it from the gallery which the others were trying to break down from the gallery side. How did Ramsay know this entrance? The most reasonable supposition is that the king (who, by reason of his earlier imprisonment in Gowrie House, knew the geography of it as well as anyone) had told him. Why was the door at the head of the spiral staircase unlocked? If it was not merely left open by the Master, who was unsuspicious of anything amiss, it must have been unlocked by the king during the few moments when, as we shall see, he left James alone. Whichever was the reason, the fact that, immediately the king gave the signal by shouting from the turret window, Ramsay had no difficulty in at once going up the winding staircase and into the room where the king was, suggests the innocence of the Master and the guilt of James.

As for Erskine, he and his brother, as soon as the alarm was raised, set on the astonished Gowrie and tried to kill him. Gowrie was rescued by one of his retainers but, by the Tullibardines who were conveniently outside the gate at that moment, was forced further down the street and had to fight his way back to his own house. Erskine did not wait for this but, as soon as he had picked himself up from the ground, rushed back to the Black Turnpike staircase and, collecting three companions, followed Ramsay.

When Ramsay arrived in the turret room he found James and the Master 'striving and wrestling together in each other's arms'. James had the Master's head under his arm and the Master, 'almost upon his knees', had his hand on the king's face and mouth in an effort to prevent him screaming. Behind the king and the Master, Ramsay said he saw a man standing; but this – as we shall see – was pure invention. There was no one but the two wrestlers in the turret and it was admitted that the Master had not drawn his sword.

As soon as James saw Ramsay enter he called out, 'Strike him low! Strike low! He is wearing a secret mail doublet.' Ramsay, however, struck high. He drew his dagger and slashed at the helpless Master's face and neck. Then he and James pushed him, dazed and bleeding profusely, down the little staircase.

It is of some importance to notice that the Master could easily have been taken prisoner. If James alone was capable of holding him, he could, with the additional assistance of the lusty seventeen-year-old Ramsay, have been secured for trial and questioning without difficulty. As it was, Erskine, coming with his companions up the stairs, found the dying Master, announced 'This is the traitor' and killed him. His last words were, 'Alas! I was not to blame for it.'

Meanwhile, hard on Erskine's heels, Gowrie came running to the

Black Turnpike. Stepping over the dead body of his brother, he too went into the gallery chamber, where Ramsay was, reinforced by Erskine and the other three murderers of the Master. The king himself was now hiding in the turret study, and Gowrie, looking round, immediately demanded, 'Where is the king?'

Ramsay said he had been killed. At this news Gowrie 'shrank from the pursuit', dropped his guard, and was promptly killed by the others.

A few minutes later, Lennox, Mar, and the rest at last succeeded in breaking down the locked door and joined Ramsay and Erskine in the gallery chamber. The king, seeing that all was safe, came out of the turret room and, kneeling down by the corpse of Gowrie, 'out of his own mouth thanked God of that miraculous deliverance and victory, assuring himself that God had preserved him from so despaired a peril for the perfecting of some greater work behind to His glory and by procuring by him the weal of His people that God had committed to his charge'.

Outside in the town all was pandemonium. The citizens of Perth, summoned by the clanging of the town bell, were assembling to inquire what had happened to their beloved Gowrie. 'Bloody butchers,' they shouted, 'give us back our Provost or the King's green coat shall pay for it.' And, 'Come down, you son of David, you have slain an honester man than yourself' – a tribute not so much to James's wisdom as the 'Scottish Solomon' as to the suggestion that Rizzio was his father. Had it not been for the presence of Tullibardine's force, the Ruthvens might have been avenged there and then. As it was, after two hours of rioting, during which James himself appeared at the window in a futile effort at pacification, the crowd dispersed; and at eight o'clock it was safe for the king to be hurried out secretly by the back gate, rowed down the river to the Inch and, strongly guarded, escorted back to Falkland.

Once there he immediately sent a force to arrest the Ruthvens' two young brothers. The children, however, with their mother escaped across the Border; one of them died in exile; the other was arrested three years later, on James's accession to the English throne, and, without a trial, imprisoned in the Tower for twenty years. The vast Gowrie estates were confiscated by the Crown and the name of Ruthven abolished for ever. Thus James by one stroke performed the economic feat of turning a considerable liability into a still more considerable asset. Also he had the satisfaction of discovering that Gowrie was indeed connected with the witch-cult, for in the dead earl's pocket was found 'a little close parchment bag, full of magical characters and words of enchantment'.

The king gave suitable rewards to his servants. Erskine got the Gowrie estate of Dirleton, was raised to the peerage with that title, and later became, by the king's favour, Viscount Fenton and Earl of Kellie; Ramsay was knighted, pensioned, and eventually created Viscount Haddington and Earl of Holderness; Tullibardine received the Sheriffship of Perth, and another of the Murrays the castle and barony of Ruthven, the name being changed to Huntingtower.

James's main task, however, was to convince the world that the Ruthvens had been justly punished as authors of a monstrous plot against his sacred person. He encountered scepticism early. On the following day, the ministers of Edinburgh refused to hold services of thanksgiving for His Majesty's 'miraculous delivery from that vile treason', on the grounds that the various reports of the affair 'fought so together that no man could have any certainty'. They consented, however, to celebrate the occasion in the more guarded terms of an escape from a great danger.

When the news reached England and France, those Courts were polite but incredulous of James's version, which was as follows :

When after dinner he and the Master reached the turret study they found not, as Ruthven had promised, a man with a pot of gold, but a man in armour whose dagger Ruthven immediately snatched and held at James's heart. He warned James not to cry out or to attempt to open the window, and suggested that the king's conscience must be heavy with the murder of the Gowries' father. The king, with dignity, justified himself on that matter, pointing out that he had been a minor and that he had since made what amends he could, and expatiated on the sin of regicide with such eloquence that not only did the armoured man 'tremble and quake like one condemned', but the Master promised James safety so long as he refrained from calling for help. He then, having made the king promise not to open the window, locked James and the mysterious stranger in the turret and went downstairs to consult his brother.

James, relieved of his presence, turned to his companion for information about these strange proceedings, but the man replied that he knew nothing at all, having himself been locked in without any instructions. James then pointed out that, though he could not break his royal word by opening the window, there was nothing to prevent his companion from doing so. The man obeyed, but at that moment the Master unfortunately returned, realized the situation, told James that 'His Majesty behoved to die', and tried to bind his hands with a garter; whereat the king closed with him and so far overcame him as to manage to reach the window to utter the call for help which the waiting courtiers heard.

The obvious defect of this version, besides its inherent improbability, was that it accounted for so comparatively little of the two and a half to three hours spent by James and the Master upstairs; its counterbalancing merit was that, since the Master was dead and the man in armour had unaccountably disappeared, it could not be disproved.

However, as doubts of the Royal veracity persisted, and as people understood quite well why James must insist that there was a third person in the room all the time, it became essential to find the mysterious stranger. Among the list of 'possibles' submitted to the king was the name of Andrew Henderson, the Gowries' chamberlain, a small, red-faced man with a sandy beard. James, who had specified a 'black, grim fellow' remarked that 'he knew that face well enough : it was not he'. But, as the quest became more urgent, he decided that it was he after all – a belated identification which was confirmed by Henderson's own confession, for which he was given his life and a reward.

Henderson's account of the matter was modelled on James's version, though he naturally modified it in certain particulars in order not to appear so quiescent in defence of majesty as the king suggested. Some of the discrepancies he retracted, in deference to his sovereign, in his second deposition, but there remained sufficient to render the mystery even deeper.

Henderson said he accompanied the Master on the early morning visit to Falkland : but no one saw him there. He said he was sent back to Perth to warn the earl of the king's arrival for dinner; but Gowrie obviously never got the message, nor were there any preparations made for the meal. Even in the turret no one saw him except James – and Ramsay, who averred that, on his first entry, 'he saw a man standing behind His Majesty's back whom he noways knew, nor remembers what apparelling he had on'.

There is, in fact, no reason to suppose that the king's story, from the pot of gold to the man in the turret, is anything but a tissue of lies invented to give some sort of explanation which should obscure the fact that he went to Perth with the nineteen-year-old Master for some reason which only they themselves knew, spent the greater part of the afternoon alone with him, and subsequently had both him and his brother murdered by the Royal *mignons*. There is not a shred of reliable evidence that the Gowrie brothers were, on that day, implicated in a plot to murder him. There is, on the other hand, a very strong presumption that the king, who had motives enough, arranged a situation which enabled him to get rid of the Gowries. Assuming James's guilt, the story makes sense in every particular; assuming the Gowries' guilt, improbability treads on the heels of improbability. James's responsibility is now hardly questioned by impartial investigators; though, at the time, the official version of the matter was so thoroughly enforced that no copy of the contemporary Ruthven apology is known to exist, and 5 August was appointed to be observed in all times to come as a day of thanksgiving for the king's escape from a vile treason.

Yet to arrive at a solution for the events of 5 August is not in fact to solve the Gowrie mystery. All writers tend to assume that the verdict rests on a clear alternative, and defenders of the king have tried to prove that, *on that day,* the Gowries were intending to kidnap James. What, it seems to me, is more likely is that the king, by his actions that day, anticipated a Gowrie plot which had not yet come to fruition. A full understanding of the position is only possible by reference to the question of the succession to the English Crown; what might seem at first sight a Scottish feud is in reality a reflection of European high politics.

Elizabeth I of England had not, in the nature of things, much longer to live and the burning topic of the hour was her successor. This successor she obstinately refused to nominate, and the dozen or so candidates inevitably became centres round which intrigue could gather. The two strongest were James of Scotland and the Infanta Isabella, daughter of Philip II of Spain (who had, of course, been King of England). The Catholics, on the whole, supported the latter; the Protestants, the former. In England, the Earl of Essex, Elizabeth's last and most famous favourite, was the leader of the Protestant party and had, at least from 1598, been in correspondence with James. This had driven his rival, Robert Cecil, the queen's Secretary of State, temporarily to support the claims of the Infanta and to intrigue (much against his will and for the only time in his life) with the Catholics.

Because, in the end, Cecil triumphed, and Essex, after raising his abortive rebellion, was executed, the historian has too often thought in terms of that triumph in 1601 when looking at the events of the previous year. And, the general reader, aware only that it was Cecil who corresponded with and eventually placed on the English throne James VI of Scotland as James I of England (who, to the end of his life in 1612, he could therefore manipulate like a puppet), thinks not unnaturally of Cecil and James as being on terms of friendship. He forgets that Cecil was only able to approach James at all after Essex was dead and that, in the year of the Gowrie mystery, 1600, Cecil was James's most deadly enemy.

A further complicating factor was that Gowrie himself had some kind of claim to the English throne. It was tenuous in the extreme. According to an anonymous and dateless manuscript referred to in a life of Gowrie published in 1818, Elizabeth I, in the April of 1600, granted to Gowrie – who was certainly then in London – the guard and honours appropriate to a Prince of Wales. The justification for this would seem to be that Gowrie, through his mother (said to be a direct descendant of Henry VII), was Elizabeth's cousin; and there is at least to be said in support of the theory that the father of the Burnet who wrote the *History of His Own Time* at the end of the century 'took great pains to inquire into the particulars of that matter' so that he could tell his son 'one thing which none of our historians have taken any notice of', namely, Gowrie's Tudor descent which made him, failing James and his issue, heir to the English throne.

More important than the actual claim (which even if it were valid was so weak as to be negligible) was the fact that Gowrie was intensely ambitious and, while a student at Padua, added to his ancestral device what was described as, 'On the dexter a chivaleer, garnish'd with the Earl's coat of arms, pointing with a sword upward to an imperial crown, with this device, *Tibi Soli*'. A version of this in the Workman manuscript differs from it in that the figure points at the crown with his open right hand while keeping the left on the sword-hilt; but in either case the meaning is sufficiently clear. In 1609 the English ambassador to Italy forwarded to James, now King of England, a copy of the arms which Gowrie had left at Padua, with the comment that 'hath your Majesty now a view, *in umbra*, of those detestable thoughts which afterwards appeared *in facto*, according to the said Earl's own *mot*. For what other sense or allusion can the reaching at a crown with a sword in a stretched posture . . . yield to any intelligent and honest beholder?'

Gowrie was also, it may be remembered, the idol of the Presbyterian Kirk; so that if Cecil, uneasy in his forced pro-Catholic position with regard to the succession, should be looking for a Protestant claimant to set against James in Scotland, who would fit his purpose better than Gowrie?

On his side, James was deep in plots with Essex. He had promised, when the time was ripe, to prepare an army and march at the head of it to the Border, whence he would demand from the English Government (which meant, in effect, Cecil) the open acknowledgment of his right to the succession. He would support the demand by sending as his ambassador the Earl of Mar, to prosecute it at the English Court. The move was to be timed to coincide with Essex's attempt to get control of the Government by his insurrection in London, and Mar was to arrive by 1 February 1601. Essex did make his attempt that February and paid for it with his life, and Mar did eventually arrive, though not in precise time; so it may be inferred that James's promise was an essential part of Essex's scheme. He kept James's answer always in a little black bag hung round his neck, which he managed to destroy before he was arrested; and James, for his part, always referred to Essex as 'my martyr'.

It is obvious, therefore, that at the time of the Gowrie Conspiracy, nothing would have suited Cecil better than the temporary disappearance of James in a Scotland where kidnapping the king had become a favourite political pastime. Nor could he have found a more suitable instrument than that wild and ambitious young man, the Earl of Gowrie, whose pretensions to the Crown the cunning politician could turn to his own uses. Seen in this light, the compliment paid to Gowrie at the English Court in the April of 1600 is not surprising. It was an obvious move in the game.

In Scotland itself Cecil had a sufficiency of spies, agents, and pensioners – Logan, the Mowbray brothers, Archie Douglas, and in particular Locke, his 'go-between in his darkest intrigues against James' and his agent with Gowrie. There was also the wild Bothwell (nephew of Mary Queen of Scots' husband) who had already, with the help of Gowrie's mother, kidnapped James once and who, in 1600, was secretly on the way back to Scotland.

Gowrie had a castle, manned and provisioned, at Dirleton near North Berwick. Opposite it, just off the coast and refusing communication with the shore, a large English ship was hovering. The Governor of Berwick was in close communication with Cecil.

Merely to recite these circumstances is to conclude that there was almost certainly a plot afoot, inspired by Cecil and implemented by Gowrie, to kidnap James and hold him prisoner until, in England, Cecil, in Queen Elizabeth's name, had dealt with Essex. But to say that this plot was to mature on 5 August, and that it explains the curious and fatal events of that day, is to try to prove too much. The happenings cannot be twisted to fit that thesis.

What can be argued – and what is, it seems to me, weighing all the evidence, true – is that James anticipated the plot by getting rid of the Gowries. For the slaughter of the Ruthvens he alone was to blame; yet he might well have pleaded, had the conventions of politics allowed, that they had brought that subtle and sudden doom on their own heads.

CHAPTER 9

The Gunpowder Plot
1604 to 1605

At seven o'clock on the evening of Saturday, 26 October 1605, the thirty-year-old William Parker, fourth Baron Monteagle, was about to sit down to supper in his mansion at Hoxton, a village five miles or so from London, when one of his footmen, whom he had sent out on errand over the street, approached him with the news that he had been 'met by an unknown man of a reasonable tall personage who delivered him a letter, charging him to put it in my Lord his master's hands'.

Monteagle broke the seal and started to read the letter. It was written in an unknown and somewhat illegible hand, without signature or date, and he called one of his household to help him decipher it. It had no punctuation, no capital letters, and several mis-spellings. Correcting these for the modern reader's convenience, the anonymous letter ran :

'My Lord, out of the love I bear to some of your friends I have a care for your preservation; therefore I would advise you, as you tender your life, to devise of some excuse to shift of your attendance at this Parliament; for God and man hath concurred to punish the wickedness of this time. And think not slightly of this advertisement but retire yourself into your own country where you may expect the event in safety; for, though there be no appearance of any stir, yet I say they shall receive a terrible blow, this Parliament, and yet they shall not see who hurts them. This counsel is not to be condemned because it may do you good and can do you no harm, for the danger is past as soon as you have burnt the letter and I hope God will give you the grace to make good use of it, to Whose holy protection I commend you.'

Though 'somewhat perplexed what construction to make of it' Monteagle, according to the official report, 'as a most dutiful and loyal subject did conclude not to conceal it. Whereupon not withstanding the lateness and darkness of the night in that season of the year, he presently [immediately] repaired to His Majesty's palace at Whitehall and there delivered the same to Robert Cecil, Earl of Salisbury, His Majesty's principal Secretary.' But the letter held no surprises for Cecil. Not only had he written it; he was also expecting it. For the Catholic Lord Monteagle was his tool in this, the most spectacular 'frameup' in British history.

This may seem an extraordinary contradiction to what most history books say about the Gunpowder Plot: they tell how Guy Fawkes and his conspirators, unknown to the Government, plotted to blow up the Houses of Parliament. The idea of the Government's involvement in the plot first came to me when discussing my book on James I with the late Lord Beaverbrook. He pointed out that I had not considered that the plot might have been fostered by the Government. Having examined the evidence in this light, it seems that his politician's intuition was almost certainly correct.

But to continue the story, the letter to Monteagle was read by two men. One was the little hunchback, Robert Cecil himself, and the other – 'the wisest fool in Christendom' – was the cowardly, drunken, slobbering, homosexual James I. These two then interpreted the letter officially as evidence of a 'gunpowder plot'. In consequence, the cellars under the House of Lords, where Parliament was to assemble on 5 November, were searched and, at the appropriate moment on 4 November, a Yorkshire soldier-of-fortune, Guy Fawkes, was 'discovered' in charge of barrels of gunpowder and was duly arrested.

As for Lord Monteagle, his reward for delivering an anonymous letter which he protested he did not understand was a pension of £700 a year for life (about £20,000 in the currency of today) with other privileges. 'There was a great deal more to be rewarded', wrote a lawyer who over a century ago realized that the Gunpowder Plot was not what it seemed, 'in Monteagle's conduct than the mere delivery of the anonymous letter. He became a party to a State intrigue.' And he added that 'when such expert artists as Cecil and Bacon framed and propagated a State fiction in order to cover a State intrigue, they took care to cut off or divert the channels of history so effectually as to make it hopeless at the distance of three centuries to trace the truth.'

And yet much of the truth has been traced. The whole affair was suspected at the time of being a Government 'frame-up'. On

10 December 1605, for instance, an English observer wrote to a correspondent abroad : 'Those that have practical experience of the way in which things are done hold it as certain that there has been foul play and that some of the Council secretly spun a web to entangle these poor gentlemen' (the so-called 'Gunpowder Plotters') and the theory that what 'plot' there was was of Cecil's making has now been accepted by most historians of the period. Above all, events have made it possible for us in the second half of the 20th century to understand and therefore to assess the 'climate' of the Gunpowder Plot where those in the sheltered 19th century could not.

The use of torture to extort signatures to convenient statements; the forgery of documents; the unscrupulous use of propaganda; the services of the *agent-provocateur;* the sudden deaths of vital witnesses; the art of the 'double-cross' (which was known at the time of the Plot as 'practising') and, more important, the 'double-doublecross' – all these concomitants of a revolutionary period are part of our day-to-day European experience, which make possible a better understanding of the past.

The construction of 'plots' by governments is a standard device of statesmanship. Though the device neither originated nor ended in 16th- and 17th-century England, that was a most propitious era for its use. Sir Henry Wotton (who died in 1639) went so far as to admit that 'plots' were necessary to maintain a politician's reputation. The best way, he said, for a Government to gain approval for unpopular or even impossible measures was to stir up public indignation against any party opposed to the Government. If Government spies could suggest an 'enterprise' to a few fanatics, goad them on, and then 'unmask' the affair, so much the better for the Government's purposes.

Few statesmen of any country have been more expert in manufacturing such 'plots' than the Cecils, father and son. William Cecil, Lord Burghley, was Secretary of State to Queen Elizabeth I from her accession in 1558 to 1572 when he became her chief Minister till his death in 1598, and his son Robert Cecil, Earl of Salisbury, whom he trained as his successor, continued his policy for the beginning of the reign of her successor, James VI of Scotland and I of England.

The problem with which the Cecils were faced was how to

destroy Catholicism in England. In order to justify the increasingly cruel anti-Catholic legislation of Elizabeth's reign, 'plots' to assassinate the queen had to be continually 'discovered'. For her life was the thread on which the new Church and State precariously depended. All the 'plots' were spurious – a fact which was suspected as long ago as 1901 by the Protestant historian Martin Hume who wrote :

'The accusations that have been repeated by nearly every historian from Elizabeth's time to our own of widespread and numerous plots to assassinate the Queen are to a large extent unsupported by serious evidence. Pamphlets and broadsides, professing to give the whole story of the various murder-plots, were numerous and have formed the basis of our historical relations for three centuries; but they were written in nearly every instance with political or party aspect and, from the nature of the case, were necessarily based upon an imperfect or partial statement of the facts.'

The Cecils even toyed with the idea of a gunpowder plot as early as 1587 and, in a modified form, they used it in what is known as the Des Trappes Plot. The object of Cecilian policy was in this case to immobilize the French ambassador and to counter his pleas to Elizabeth I on behalf of Mary Queen of Scots. Two scoundrels were produced and provided with forged documents showing that they had been bribed by the French ambassador to tie a bag of gunpowder under Queen Elizabeth's bed. The whole thing was not only a complete fabrication, but was admitted to be so when, after the execution of Mary Queen of Scots, the French ambassador received apologies from the Government and was invited to treat the matter as a joke.

To get rid of Mary Queen of Scots the much more elaborate 'Babington Plot' had been concocted, in which more careful forgery and more experienced *agents provocateurs* were necessary. She was executed after this plot to dispose of Queen Elizabeth and put Mary on the throne had been 'discovered'. But the idea of gunpowder was kept in reserve and was finally employed, with Cecil's brilliant psychological acumen, on Mary's son, James I. Since James's father, Darnley, had been killed as a result of the gunpowder plot of Kirk o' Field and since he himself was terrified by physical violence, an apparent attempt by Catholics to get rid of him in the same way as Darnley was calculated to drive him to the edge of unreasoning fury. No vengeance would seem excessive; no anti-Catholic legislation too severe. There is more than his temperamental sadism in his instructions to torture Guy Fawkes: 'The gentler tortours are to be first usid unto him, *et sic per gradus ad ima tenditur*; and so God speed your good work.'

Robert Cecil's technique in the Gunpowder Plot of 1605 was, through the agency of Lord Monteagle, to foster in the minds of a body of desperate men the idea of striking a blow for the Catholic cause which should so disorganize the Government that it would be possible for the Catholics to set up a new régime with James I's daughter Elizabeth on the throne.

Most of these men were connected by blood or marriage. Robert Catesby, their leader, Thomas Wintour, the brains of the Plot and his elder brother, Robert, a financial subscriber to it, Francis Tresham and Lord Monteagle, the head of the 'cousinage', were all first cousins. John Grant was the Wintours' brother-in-law; Robert Keyes and Ambrose Rookwood, who owned the best stable in England, were connected with the Wintours' maternal branch. John and Christopher Wright were, through their mother who had been imprisoned for her Catholicism for fourteen years, related to the Wintours by marriage; and Thomas Percy, the oldest and most eminent of the conspirators – a man of forty-five, cousin of the Earl of Northumberland, and one of a group of landed gentry in their twenties and early thirties – was married to the Wrights' sister. Only Guy Fawkes, who had been at school with the Wrights; Thomas Bates, who was Catesby's servant; and Sir Everard Digby, a wealthy young man devoted to Catesby, who was brought into the Plot at the last moment for financial reasons, were outside the 'family'. Yet, when the matter was 'discovered', they were interpreted as being 'the whole body of Catholics' and were said (in the teeth of every particle of evidence) to have been inspired by the Jesuits who, in fact, in obedience to Papal policy, had gone to every conceivable length to prevent the Plot as soon as they heard of it.

When the Plot was 'discovered', Robert Cecil announced: 'It has pleased Almighty God, out of His singular goodness, to bring to light the most cruel and detestable Conspiracy against the person of His Majesty and the whole State of the Realm that ever was conceived by the heart of man at any time or in any place wheresoever.' And he issued an official account of the matter which has been the basis of all school histories and popular accounts of the Gunpowder Plot ever since. This official account (as epitomized by its greatest defender, the Victorian historian S. R. Gardiner) runs as follows.

In February 1604, King James banished all Catholic priests. Immediately, a Catholic named Robert Catesby proposed to a few of his friends a plot to blow up King, Lords, and Commons with gunpowder at the opening of Parliament. The king had two sons, Henry and Charles, and a little daughter, Elizabeth. Catesby, expecting that the two princes would be destroyed with their father, intended to make Elizabeth queen and to take care that she was brought up a Roman Catholic. Guy Fawkes, a level-headed soldier, was summoned from Flanders to manage the scheme. The plotters took a house next to the House of Lords and began to dig through the wall to enable them to carry the powder into the basement. The wall, however, was nine feet thick, and not being used to mason's work, they made little progress. In the spring of 1605, James increased their anger by reimposing fines on the Catholic laity. Soon afterwards their task was made easier by the discovery that a coal-cellar reaching under the floor of the House of Lords was to be let. One of their number, Percy, hired the cellar and introduced into it barrels of powder, covering them with coals and billets of wood. Parliament was to be opened for its second session on 5 November, and during the preceding evening Fawkes went to the cellar with a lantern, ready to fire the train of powder in the morning. One of the plotters, however, had betrayed the secret. Fawkes was seized, and his companions were pursued. All the conspirators who were taken alive were executed and the persecution of the Catholics became even more vicious than ever.

In outline, this is probably a fair account of certain simple facts. The plotters did behave in this way and these things did happen. But it is the omissions which are the more important, since they point to the controlling brain behind the plot being Cecil, with Monteagle as his tool.

Why, for instance, was the assembly of Parliament prorogued from 7 February when the conspirators were not ready, till 3 October, and again on 28 July when they were still not ready, from 3 October till 5 November? How did they get the gunpowder, which was a Government monopoly? The records of the stores for it for the relevant period are missing and Cecil subsequently refused to allow an investigation into the leakage of gunpowder from the Tower to continue beyond the beginning of 1604. How did the conspirators manage to hire the 'cellar' which was owned by a Government official who conveniently died – apparently of a heart attack – on the morning of 5 November? Why, when some of the conspirators were being rounded up in the Midlands on 8 November, were Catesby and Percy shot? Percy had first-hand knowledge of the king's promise of toleration to Catholics and Catesby alone knew the full story of the Plot. Officially, Cecil protested that he wanted them taken alive. This could quite easily have been done, since there were only a dozen men without fire-arms against several hundreds armed. The man who shot them was given a liberal pension (two shillings a day for life) which lends colour to a contemporary's remark that 'some will not stick to report that the great statesman, sending to apprehend these traitors, gave special charge and direction for Percy and Catesby : "Let me never see them alive." '

Of the arrest of Guy Fawkes, Cecil gave three mutually con-tradictory official accounts, so that some people were told he was arrested in the street, some in the cellar, and some in his room. There are considerable discrepancies even between Fawkes's con-fession elicited under torture and the official edition. The true facts are unknown.

One circumstance alone is sufficient to destroy the case for the authenticity of the official story. It was the essence of the Govern-ment's case that it did not know the names of any of the con-spirators except Percy, who owned the 'cellar', and Fawkes, who was in charge of it, until after Fawkes's confessions under torture on Saturday, 8 November. Yet early on the morning of Tuesday, 5 November, the servant of a hatter named Hewett, the landlady of two of the minor conspirators, Rookwood and Keyes, the servant of Rookwood, and other obscure people who had no obvious con-nection at all with the plot were arrested and brought not even before an ordinary magistrate but before the Lord Chief Justice himself.

It would seem that the Government was far from being in the dark about the Gunpowder Plot until the famous anonymous letter

to Monteagle a week before the 'blow' was planned; they had probably been aware of it for eighteen months and 'the little comedy
at Hoxton', when the mysterious letter was delivered, was merely
a piece of stage management designed to lead to the public discovery.

Of course, we cannot produce absolute proof that Monteagle
was involved. But if we accept the hypothesis that the Plot was a
Government frame-up, then the Government would have needed a
stool-pigeon, and Monteagle was the obvious choice. When we
look more closely at Monteagle's circumstances and his relationship
with the Government before and after the Plot, his complicity
seems even more likely.

By birth and wealth, Monteagle held a special position among
the great Catholic families. Until the death of Queen Elizabeth I,
Monteagle was at one with his co-religionists, but on James's accession he decided on conformity and wrote to the king, announcing
the change.

'I protest to Your Majesty before Almighty God, I have simply
and only propounded to myself the true service of God and sal-
vation of my own soul; not gain, not honour, not that which I do
most highly value, Your Majesty's favour or better opinion of me,
holding it contentment enough to myself that God hath in mercy
enlightened my mind to see His sacred truth, with desire to
serve . . .'

What Monteagle desired to serve must remain a secret, for the
letter is here mutilated, but at least by the March of the following
year, 1604 (about the time the gunpowder idea was first discussed)
he had managed to have his title, which came to him from his
mother, confirmed and had secured the re-grant of certain lands.
By the beginning of 1605, Cecil was supporting him in a lawsuit
against the Earl of Hertford and by the September of that year
– a few weeks before the delivery of the letter – King James personally asked as a favour from the King of France the release of
Monteagle's brother who was imprisoned at Calais for a violent
outrage he had committed there – a request which the French
king granted only with extreme reluctance.

In the light of his favour with the king and intimacy with Cecil,
Monteagle's other known activities during the same period are of
some interest. During 1605, he was in close touch with his cousins
who were planning the conspiracy. Thomas Wintour accompanied

him on visits to Bath, Lancashire, and the country-houses of the Catholic gentry. With Tresham and Catesby, he visited the Jesuit Provincial, Father Garnet, whom he asked to procure for him a colonelcy in the troop of English Catholics serving in Flanders 'but would not have it known yet'. In the July of 1605, Father Garnet asked him and Catesby whether they thought the Catholics in England 'were able to make their part good by arms against the King' and Monteagle replied : 'If ever they were, they are able now. The King is so odious to all sorts.'

At the end of October, Monteagle went to Richmond to see the Prince of Wales, ostensibly to discover in conversation whether he intended to be present at the opening of Parliament on 5 November. He then told Wintour that 'the Prince was thought not to be there' – a piece of information which caused Catesby to change his plans. That was on the Friday. On Saturday, Monteagle received the anonymous letter.

Once the Plot was 'discovered', Monteagle was rewarded with silence as well as with money. His name was safeguarded, and where it appeared in the examinations of the prisoners, it was passed over or erased even when it referred to events in which Monteagle had taken part but which had no reference to the Plot. From the document which referred to Monteagle's visit to the Prince of Wales, an official copy was made which omitted that particular episode. The document which narrated the conversation with Father Garnet was suppressed altogether. Before the trial of the conspirators, Cecil wrote in his own hand a private note to the Lord Chief Justice : 'You must not omit, you must deliver, in commendation of my Lord Monteagle, words to show how sincerely he dealt and how fortunately it proved that he was the instrument of so great a blessing as this was.'

The Plot may have already existed in the minds of the conspirators and was encouraged by Monteagle with Cecil's connivance. Or it may have been put there by Monteagle on Cecil's instigation. But why did this dedicated band of Catholics lend themselves to the scheme of murder which was condemned by their religion and which their priests, when they heard of it under the seal of confession, did their utmost to stop? The answer is to be found in the condition to which Catholicism in England had been reduced at that time.

Some twenty years earlier, in 1581, William Cecil had made it high treason to endeavour to convert anyone to the old Faith. To be present at Mass meant a year's imprisonment as well as a fine; and every person above sixteen was fined £20 a month (in the currency of the time) for non-attendance at Anglican services (a penalty soon adjusted to the confiscation by the Crown of two-thirds of their property). To ensure that the Act worked properly, informers were rewarded.

Despite these new measures, which made every Catholic priest guilty of high treason merely because of his priesthood, a stream of priests continued to come to England from the Continent so that, secretly, Catholics might still receive the Sacraments. Cecil soon realized that, if England were shut off completely from the Continent, Catholicism would be effectively eradicated.

New measures were therefore enacted. All Jesuit and seminary priests were banished from the country on pain of death; it was a felony to maintain them; any person who did not inform against them incurred a fine and imprisonment 'at the Queen's pleasure'; any English subject being educated abroad was to return within six months and take the Oath of Supremacy (i.e. to deny his Catholicism) or incur the penalties of high treason; no children were to be sent 'beyond the sea' without special licence from the Government and spies were sent abroad to supply descriptions of English Catholics who might try to return. (In one of the manuscripts of the period, there is an account of 295 Englishmen, with careful descriptions of each of them, written by a spy of Cecil's, who had been given the hospitality of the English College in Rome.)

What the legislation meant to the ordinary Catholic gentleman may be gathered from the following – if anything, understated – account by a Protestant historian, written in 1878 (before the discovery of much new material which confirms it in every particular).

'The truth is, a detestable system had now begun to spring up under which no one with any conscience or religious scruples could hold himself safe for an hour. An army of spies and common informers were prowling about the length and breadth of the land, living by their wits, and feeding partly upon the terrors of others and partly upon the letter of the law as laid down by the recent Acts

– wretches who had everything to gain by straining the penalties to the utmost, for they claimed their share of the spoil. Armed with warrants from weak magistrates, who were themselves afraid of suspicion, or, failing these, armed with an order from the Privy Council, which was only too easily obtained, they were nothing better than bandits protected by the law, let loose upon that portion of the community which might be harried and robbed with impunity. In some cases the pursuivants, after arresting their victims and appropriating their money, were content to let them alone; in others, they kept them till a ransom might come from friends; in any case, there was always the fun of half-scuttling a big house and living at free quarters during the search, and the chance of securing a handsome bribe in consideration of being left unmolested for the future.'

It was against these intolerable conditions that Catesby and his cousins and friends were determined to protest – by blowing up Parliament House with gunpowder at the beginning of the session. When the idea was mooted – presumably by Monteagle – Catesby said : 'In that place they have done us all the mischief and per-chance God hath designed that place for their punishment !'

When Thomas Wintour pointed out that if the design failed – as it probably would – the attempt would bring such scandal on Catholicism that not only their enemies but their friends would justifiably condemn them, Catesby replied : 'The nature of the disease requires so sharp a remedy.'

The question as to who wrote the famous anonymous letter to Monteagle is one of those problems which, like the identity of the Man in the Iron Mask, has fascinated succeeding generations. A variety of suggestions have been put forward, but they all have one common weakness; they assume that the Plot was genuine and that therefore the letter came from one of the conspirators, anxious that Monteagle should not take his place in the House of Lords on the fatal morning of 5 November.

Even if this were true, it would have been a strange way to send the warning. Several other Catholic peers had, in fact, been warned. Digby had warned some of his friends and Catesby had persuaded three peers to absent themselves. Had a mere warning been intended, the melodramatic method at Hoxton (even sup-posing the writer had had the knowledge that Monteagle's house there had been opened just for the evening) would hardly have been suitable. But, as the point of the communication was not a private word to Monteagle but a public excuse for Cecil to move openly, the would-be detective must obviously start from the hypothesis that the writer was either one of the Government agents employed on such matters or a trusted servant of Monteagle himself.

In my book *The Gunpowder Plot,* which was published in 1951, I said that it was unlikely that we would ever find out who had written the letter. But, with the publication in 1969 of the latest book on the Plot, *Guy Fawkes* by Francis Edwards, S.J., the writer of the letter has been more or less discovered. It was, as might have been guessed, Robert Cecil himself.

Father Edwards suddenly noticed a superficial resemblance between the Secretary's handwriting and that of the anonymous letter. The deliberate disguising of the script made certainty difficult, so Father Edwards consulted a leading authority on handwriting, accustomed to giving expert evidence in forgery cases in the courts of law. The verdict, based on a microscopic examination, was that Robert Cecil could, without any doubt, have written it and that there is a 70 per cent probability that he did. What made it less than certain were the special factors of the ink and paper having aged, but there is in the expert's mind no reasonable doubt that Cecil is the writer.

At the time, however, the most important question was the letter itself. Cecil knew that the weak point of the Plot was that many people would doubt the existence of the letter, and was determined to convince the world that there really had been a letter – the one and only way he could know of the Plot. It was therefore exhibited to the world with relentless persistence. It was printed in the *King's Book* (the official Government account of the Plot) and every other account of the affair; while transcribed copies were sent to the Ambassadors at foreign Courts and other public personages.

After the letter had been returned from Monteagle, Cecil's actions became even more obscure. There are at least three official accounts written by Cecil which cannot by any possibility all be true; on every single point they are utterly and hopelessly at variance. As one historian of the Plot has put it :

'We are told that King James was the first to understand and interpret the letter which had baffled the sagacity of his Privy Council; that the Lords of the Council had fully interpreted it several days before the King saw it; that the said Lords would not credit the King's interpretation; that the King would not believe their interpretation; and that neither the one nor the other ever interpreted it at all, that His Majesty insisted on a search being made in spite of the reluctance of his Ministers; that they insisted on the search in spite of the reluctance of their royal master; and that no such search was ever proposed by either; that Knyvet [J.P. for Westminster] was dispatched expressly to look for gunpowder, with instructions to rummage the firewood to the bottom, leaving no cover in which a barrel might lie hid; and that, having no instructions to do anything of the kind, nor any reason to suspect the existence of any barrels, he discovered them only as a piece of luck, so clearly fortuitous as to be clearly providential. On this last point especially the contraditions are absolutely irreconcilable.'

Nothing, indeed, is known for certainty, except that somehow, somewhere, Guy Fawkes was arrested either late in the evening of 4 November or early in the morning of 5 November, and brought before Cecil; and that he was tortured into a confession which, together with a forged confession of Thomas Wintour – later captured – forms the sole basis of the Government's account of the famous Plot in which no one was harmed except the conspirators.

The trials of the eight surviving conspirators – the two Wintours and Grant; Fawkes, Keyes, and Bates; Rookwood and Digby – took place at the end of January 1606. There was no doubt about the result. On the last days of the month they were executed in two batches, all under the penalty of high treason. They were hanged for a short time, cut down and castrated while still alive, their hearts plucked out, their entrails burnt before their faces and, after death, their bodies quartered.

Francis Bacon, who was present at the executions said that Digby (who was cut down immediately so that he might suffer more because on the scaffold he had said that his only motive was religious 'in which regard he could not condemn himself of any offence to God') was still alive when his heart was plucked out and,

at the executioner's cry of 'Behold the heart of a traitor', he said
'Thou liest!'

Digby was the first to die, Fawkes the last. Though Fawkes was
so weak with torture that he could hardly climb the ladder, even
with the hangman's help, he insisted on climbing as high as he
could. It was the last instinct of his soldier's training and it cheated
the mob of their pleasure. His neck was broken in the fall.

CHAPTER 10

The Murder of Sir Thomas Overbury
14 September 1613

HENRY HOWARD, Earl of Northampton, Knight of the Garter, Lord Privy Seal, Lord Warden of the Cinque Ports, was one of the more curious and sinister characters of the reigns of Elizabeth I and James I. His father was the poet, Surrey, who had been executed by Henry VIII because he stood too near the throne. His elder brother was the Duke of Norfolk who had planned to marry the imprisoned Mary Queen of Scots and had in consequence been executed by Elizabeth I. Henry Howard too had fallen into disgrace and, when the queen confiscated the Howard estates, into such dire poverty that he had known actual hunger as he lounged on Paul's Walk among the booksellers and poor scholars. But at the end of the queen's reign, he attached himself to the all-powerful Cecil and was rewarded with titles and honours on the accession of James I. But as long as Cecil lived, he was without real power. The most learned Englishman of his day, he packed the great palace he built for himself, Northampton House (on the site of Northumberland Avenue), with treasures of every kind, of which the greatest was his unrivalled library. A Catholic by birth, he openly changed his religion five times and was known as a devotee of witchcraft. A bachelor, his ruling passion was power for his house; but he was too wary an intriguer not to realize that, as long as Cecil lived, it was impossible to displace him. When Cecil died – in 1612 – Northampton was already seventy-one and had only two years of life left to him. But in that time, as the directing mind behind the intrigue which brought the Howard family back to power, he at last achieved his object.

The Howards had already made several efforts to ensnare the king by his favourite bait of boys. They had schooled what poor relations with pretty faces they could muster, given them a wardrobe, washed their faces in buttermilk, perfumed their breaths and thrown them in James's way. As they had had no success they decided to change their tactics and ensnare the boy James himself had chosen, Robert Ker. Ker had been one of James's pages in Scotland, the son of a knight of one of the Border families. When James came to England, he had gone soldiering in France for a time and on his return to London had caught the king's eye in a tilting-match, in which he was unhorsed and broke a leg. The king visited him daily and the implications were clear to the Court. 'Lord!' wrote an observer, 'how the great men flocked to see him and to offer to his shrine in such abundance that the King was forced to lay a restraint, lest it might retard his recovery by spending his spirits.' The king, keeping Ker to himself, decided to mould him into the perfect companion. He taught him Latin every morning – though, as one ungenerous commentator remarked, someone ought to have taught him English, 'for he is a Scotch lad and hath much need of better language'. James knighted him, created him Viscount Rochester and, on Cecil's death in the May of 1612, made him virtually his successor by the simple means of refusing to appoint a new Principal Secretary of State but doing all important business through bed chamber men of whom Ker (made Keeper of the Signet) was inevitably the chief.

The Howard plan, masterly in its simplicity, was to entrap Ker into marriage with Frances Howard, Northampton's great-niece, whom he had virtually brought up. The girl, no more than a beautiful and dissolute child, had been married at the age of thirteen to the young Earl of Essex, aged fifteen, the year before Ker had come to the king's notice. At sixteen she was carefully thrown in Ker's way while her husband – whom she loathed – was as far as possible kept out of hers. Ker's disinclination was overcome by various means, including the use of love-philtres, witchcraft, aphrodisiacs; and her husband's inclination by drugs to produce impotence, if not by an actual slow poison. The treatment was successful! Certainly by the time of Cecil's death, Frances Howard was Ker's mistress and the only remaining enterprise was to bring about a divorce from Essex.

There was, however, one notable obstacle, Sir Thomas Overbury. He was thirty-one, Ker twenty-five. The two had first met in

Scotland, eleven years before, and for nine years they had been inseparable – the David and Jonathan of the Court. The queen, who hated both of them for sufficiently comprehensible reasons, dubbed Overbury 'the keeper of the king's keeper'. Not that Overbury was without a reputation of his own. Ben Jonson had praised his poetry; and his prose 'Characters', which had an engaging wit, gave him a literary standing. He had travelled in France and the Low Countries and written about each a book which showed him a skilled political observer. Cecil himself had been his patron and he could have had what career he chose. Unfortunately for himself he chose Ker; but as that choice was made when Ker was nothing but a poor page in disgrace and the magnificent future could certainly not have been foreseen, Overbury was not open to the charge that could be levelled against Northampton. In the beginning Overbury had encouraged the *affaire* between Ker and Frances Howard, but immediately he realized that the king, too infatuated to refuse his minion anything, was prepared to get the Bench of Bishops (who, of course, were his nominees) to grant Frances a decree of nullity on the grounds of her husband's impotence – grounds which, as everyone knew, were demonstrably false – Overbury did all in his power to break the relationship. He wrote a bitter new poem called *The Wife* which Frances, as well as others, saw was intended for her. He quarrelled with Ker in a gallery at Whitehall, shouting at him, 'If you marry that filthy, base woman you will utterly ruin your honour and yourself. You shall never do it by my advice or consent; and if you do, you had best look to stand fast.'

'I can stand well enough on my own legs,' retorted Ker, 'but i' faith I will be even with you for this.'

But, of course, the one thing which Ker, with his new responsibilities, was completely incapable of doing was to stand on his own legs. As soon as Cecil was dead, the king and Ker had, from sheer necessity, to recall Overbury from France where he had been living in unadmitted exile. He came at once, and within a fortnight he was handling an ever-increasing amount of the king's business – advising on foreign affairs, opening and dealing with ambassadors' dispatches, and disposing of offices – which, without him, Ker was completely incapable of doing. Overbury's advice seems to have been sound, for, although the whole of the period of Ker's

dominance of the king was one of confusion, venality, and extra-
vagance, things certainly became far worse after Overbury was
dismissed and sent to the Tower.

His dismissal was inevitable. For one thing, he knew too much.
For another, he had the stupidity not to perceive the Howard
intrigues to get rid of him in a more conventional fashion – or, if
he saw them, the equal stupidity of over-estimating his own
strength. The final trap was baited by Northampton who persuaded
the king to appoint Overbury as ambassador to Russia. When the
news was conveyed to him, he said that he was not prepared to
leave the country and that he did not believe the king could make
him. However much it might be pretended, he said, that the
proposal was for his own good and his advancement in the king's
service 'he would not leave this country for any preferment in the
world'.

This was contempt. The same evening Overbury was lodged in
the Tower. That was 21 April 1613. On 16 May the king
announced the appointment of the Divorce Commission. In spite
of the king's commands, a few of the bishops proved unexpectedly
recalcitrant, for the evidence was over-whelmingly against the
desired verdict and not all the bishops shared the obliging venality
of Lancelot Andrewes. By September the matter was still undecided,
and Overbury, though in fast confinement where he was slowly
being poisoned, was still a menace. On 14 September he was finally
disposed of; on 25 September the divorce was granted by a
majority of two only – seven to five; on 26 December Frances
Howard went on the arm of her 'brideman', her great-uncle
Northampton, to her second marriage (the bishop who officiated
was, as if to give the crowning touch of cynicism, the same who
had married her to Essex). Ker had been created Earl of Somerset
and his bride given £10,000 worth of jewels as the king's wedding
present. She chose to dress in white, with her hair down, as a sym-
bol of her virginity and innocence. So Ker's marriage to this young
adulteress and murderess was at last compassed and the triumph
of Northampton and his house was complete.

The means of Overbury's murder might for ever have remained

as secret as those of most 'deaths' in the Tower during Tudor and Stuart days had not two circumstances combined in the summer of 1615 to bring it to light. The first was the confession of the apothecary's boy who had, on 14 September 1613, delivered at the Tower the fatal poison which had killed Overbury. The second was James's infatuation with a new young man, George Villiers, and his consequent wish to rid himself of the jealous and possessive Ker. Without this the confession itself would undoubtedly have been stifled. As it was, Trumbull, the envoy at Brussels, when the dying boy in exile cleared his conscience, thought it too dangerous to commit to paper. On a visit to England, he told Winwood, one of the king's secretaries. Winwood proceeded carefully to collect more evidence before he allowed it to come to the king's ears three months later.

In the consequent trials of all those involved (except Northampton, who was dead), the story of the murder was made unequivocally clear. We know the story in as much detail as any plot in history. The minor actors, as well as the major, omitted to destroy incriminating letters (though at the last moment Ker, by using the Privy Seal, managed to get hold of and burn one damaging collection of them), and Frances Howard, the principal, made a confession and pleaded guilty when it became obvious that everything was known.

The first step, taken as soon as Overbury was imprisoned, was to change the Lieutenant of the Tower. Northampton persuaded the king to dismiss the existing holder of the office and appoint a creature of his own, Elwes, who could be relied on to connive at the murder. Secondly – again on Northampton's recommendation – Overbury was given as his keeper a man named Weston, an apothecary's assistant who was one of a gang of dispensers of poisons and love-philtres collected round a procuress, Mrs Turner, the confidante of Frances Howard. As Ker still pretended friendship towards Overbury and ostensibly was endeavouring to prevail upon the king to release him, it was quite easy for Frances to send to the prisoner 'tarts and potts of jelly' and wine on behalf of herself and her husband.

Overbury's constitution was strong enough to withstand them for some time. 'This scab is like a fox; the more he is curst, the better he fareth,' Elwes wrote apologetically to Frances. But against the continual stream of poison, he had no eventual hope. Mrs Turner sent him partridges dressed in a sauce in which cantharides was used instead of pepper; Frances Howard, tarts sprinkled with white arsenic in place of sugar; Weston administered rose algar and sublimate of mercury. Overbury began to be mortally ill, having sometimes 'as many as three score stools and vomits, some mixed with blood'.

The game, however, was played carefully. The king's own physician, Dr Mayerne, was sent to see Overbury, and, when he was out of London, Dr Craig, the Physician in Ordinary to Prince Charles. Overbury's brother-in-law, Lidcote, was allowed to visit him. But when, in spite of the poisons, in spite of Dr Mayerne's diagnosis of 'consumption and flatus hypocondriacus' and Mayerne's brother-in-law de Loubell's twenty-eight pointless prescriptions, Overbury still lived, his murderers threw discretion to the winds. When, on 14 September 1613, de Loubell prescribed an enema, they had one prepared which contained sublimate of mercury. They paid an apothecary's boy twenty pounds to deliver it and so at last death was secured. It would have been the 'perfect murder' had not, two years later, the apothecary's boy feared the Last Judgment.

Northampton wrote immediately to Elwes, 'Noble Lieutenant, if the knave's body be foul, bury it presently; I'll stand between you and harm; but if it will abide the view send for Lidcote and let him see it to satisfy the damned crew.' In Northampton's calculations, the only danger now lay in the 'damned crew' of Overbury's relations, for both his father and his mother had been petitioning for his release on grounds of illness which they may have suspected to have been not altogether natural. Almost immediately after writing the letter he sent another, 'If they have viewed then bury it by and by; for it is time, considering the humours of that damned crew that only desire means to move pity and raise scandals.' Northampton also wrote to Ker, who was on Progress with the king, 'Sweet Lord, Overbury being viewed, there was found on his arm an issue and on his stomach twelve kernels, each as big as three-pence; one issue on his back with a tawny plaster on it. This was strange and ugly. He stunk intolerably, as he was cast in a coffin with a loose sheet over it. God is gracious in cutting off ill instruments.' Of the guilt of Northampton and

Frances Howard, of Elwes and Weston and Mrs. Turner, there is no shred of doubt. Nor, on the other hand, is it seriously suggested that the doctors were guilty of more than a wrong diagnosis and a modicum of incompetence. In neither of these matters is there any mystery. The guilt of Ker has occasionally been urged – he was, of course, found guilty at his trial, since James wanted to get him out of the way – but his innocence is even clearer than that of the physicians. Not only did Frances Howard, in her confession, exonerate him completely, but his own admissions – that he had indeed connived at the imprisonment of Overbury to teach him a lesson and to render him harmless while the divorce went through, but that he was entirely ignorant of the poison-plot – have about them the ring of unmistakable truth. The one mystery that remains unsolved is the secret he threatened to reveal which implicated the king.

It was not till the end of August 1615 that Winwood took to James the story of the murder so far as he had managed to collect it. James thereupon demanded from the Lieutenant of the Tower a full written report, which reached him on 10 September. As he was on Progress and would not return to London till 16 October, he wrote careful instructions to the Lord Chief Justice to begin some preliminary inquiries based on Elwes's written account. The lesser actors were arrested and questioned, and by the end of the first week in October it was clear that the principals were Ker and Frances Howard, now Earl and Countess of Somerset. On 14 October Somerset was with the king at Royston, when he was told that he was required as a witness. At first he refused to obey the summons, calling on James to support him in his attitude.

'Nay, man,' retorted James, 'for if Coke sends for *me,* I must go.'

Of the king's parting with Somerset, we have an eyewitness account, 'The Earl of Somerset never parted from him with more seeming affection than at this time when he knew Somerset should never see him more; and had you seen that seeming affection (as the author himself did) you would rather have believed he was in his rising than in his setting. The Earl when he kissed his hand, the

King hung about his neck, slobbering his cheeks saying, "For God's sake, when shall I see thee again?" The Earl told him "On Monday" (this being on the Friday). "For God's sake let me," said the King, "shall I? shall I?" Then lolled about his neck. Then, "For God's sake, give thy lady this kiss for me." In the same manner at the stairs' head, at the middle of the stairs, and at the stairs' foot.' But no sooner was Somerset safely in his coach than the king was heard to exclaim, 'Now, the De'il go with thee, for I shall never see thy face again.'

Between that occasion and the actual trial of Somerset on 26 May 1616, James made every effort to persuade him to plead guilty, assuring him that, if he did so, he would pardon him. But Somerset was firm in his protestations of innocence. He also let it be known that James dared not allow the trial for fear of revelations which might be made. As the country in general was getting more and more suspicious that the whole thing was a 'put-up job', there was enough substance in this threat to make James redouble his efforts. To the new Lieutenant of the Tower, he wrote a letter which was one of the most dishonest that came even from his pen.

Referring to Somerset's cursory dismissal of his former overtures, he wrote : 'Although I fear that the last message I sent to your unfortunate prisoner shall not take the effect that I should wish it should, yet I cannot leave off to use all means possible to move him to do that which is most honourable for me, and his own best. You shall therefore give him assurance in my name that, if he will yet before his trial confess clearly unto the Commissioners his guiltiness of this fact, I will not only perform what I promised by my last messenger, but I will enlarge it according to the phrase of the civil law *quod gratiae sunt ampliandae*. I mean not that he shall confess if he be innocent, but you know how evil likely that is, and you yourself may dispute with him, what should mean his confinement now to endure a trial when he remembers that this last winter to the Chief Justice that his cause was so evil likely as he knew no jury could acquit him.

'Assure him that I protest upon my honour, my end in this is for his and his wife's good : you will do well, likewise, of yourself to cast out unto him that you fear his wife shall plead weakly for his innocency and that you find the Commissioners have, you know not how, some secret assurance that in the end she will confess of him; but this must only be as from yourself, and therefore you must not let him know that I have written unto you, but only that I sent you private word to deliver him this message.

'Let none living know of this, and, if it take good effect, move him to send in haste for the Commissioners to give them satisfaction; but if he remain obstinate, I desire not that you should trouble me with an answer, for it is to no end, and no news is better than evil news.'

Whether or not the Lieutenant went to the lying lengths suggested by the king, he had no success. Somerset merely retorted that the king himself had a hand in the poisoning – which, in view of James's jealousy and dislike of Overbury and the fact that the Royal physician had attended him and diagnosed merely flatulence, would be a dangerous remark to be made publicly in Westminster Hall at the trial. The immediate result was that it was now impossible for James to communicate with him without running the risk of being thought an accessory; yet so urgent was the king's need of his confession that he wrote a further letter to the Lieutenant in which he said : 'If he would write or send me any message concerning this poisoning, it needs not be private; if it be of any other business, that which I cannot now with honour receive privately, I may do it after his trial, and serve the turn as well; for except either his trial or his confession precede, I cannot hear a private message from him without laying aspersion upon myself of being accessory to his crime; and I pray you urge him, by reason, that I refuse him no favour which I can grant him, without taking upon me the suspicion of being guilty of that crime whereof he is accused.'

Somerset remained adamant. He, who knew the king better than anyone living, had no trust in his word.

The evening before Somerset's trial, the Lieutenant of the Tower found himself in such a dilemma that he had again to have recourse to the king. Somerset had flown into a rage, told him that, if he wanted to get him to Westminster Hall the next day, he would have to carry him by main force and added that the king would not, even at this eleventh hour, dare to have him tried.

James thereupon made the necessary arrangements. The Lieutenant was instructed to have a man standing each side of Somerset during the whole of the trial, each with a cloak over his arm ready to muffle him and drag him from the court if he mentioned the king; and the Lord Chancellor was instructed that, in the case of such a scene, he was to disregard the law, have the prisoner withdrawn, and continue the case against him in his absence.

Nevertheless, in spite of these precautions, the next day was one of the worst in James's life. 'Who had seen the King's restless motion all that day,' wrote an observer at Court, 'sending to every boat landing at the bridge, cursing all that came without tidings, would easily have judged that all was not right and that there had been some grounds for his fears of Somerset's boldness; but at last, one bringing him word that he was condemned, all was quiet.'

Somerset, though he still refused to plead guilty and defended himself with notable ability, was not indiscreet. He betrayed none of the king's secrets. The danger over, James was merciful in his fashion. He quashed the death sentence and sent the undoubtedly innocent earl, with the undoubtedly guilty countess, to the Tower for six years.

But the mystery remains. What was the secret which Somerset threatened to reveal and to preserve which James took such panic-stricken pains?

There have been many theories. Some have thought that it had something to do with the death of Henry, Prince of Wales, whom the king, his father, disliked, whose sudden death was popularly ascribed to poison, and who had once been Ker's rival for Frances Howard's affections. Others believe the secret to have been political, and that Somerset, aware of James's secret promise to Spain to negotiate a marriage between Prince Charles and the Infanta and to have the children of the marriage brought up as Catholics, was prepared to divulge it. The effect on a country which had been raised to fever heat against the Catholics by the Gunpowder Plot of ten years before would have been incalculable. Somerset could also have given a list of those in the English government in Spanish pay and thus precipitated a crisis dangerous in the extreme. Others again have supposed that the suggestion that the king was in fact implicated in the murder is true and that it is confirmed by the fact that during the trial Dr Mayerne retired to Bath and did not give evidence. And lastly there is the theory that Somerset intended to expose the immoralities of the Court.

Though in an earlier book, *George Villiers, First Duke of Buckingham,* I inclined to the belief that the clue was to be found in the political situation as regards Spain, a closer study of the trial and the circumstances have convinced me that the last theory is nearest to the truth. The Overbury affair is intensely personal, and love and hate and jealousy and revenge are the essence of it. That it happened at Court is almost incidental. It could have happened anywhere. And it is ultimately out of character with the people concerned that the climax of the personal struggle should be concerned with high politics.

A return to the events of the late summer of 1615, when James decided to allow the allegations of poison to be officially investigated, may clarify the issue. Observers of the situation at the time were quite clear on the point. Winwood was said to have acquainted the king with the confession of the dying apothecary's boy, 'knowing how willingly he would have been rid of Somerset; yet the King durst not bring it in question, nor any question ever would have been, had not Somerset sought to cross him in his passion of love to his new Favourite, in which the King was more impatient than any woman to enjoy her love'.

It so happens that we know, from a later letter of Villiers's, the date of the start of his intimacy with the king. It was on 31 August 1615, at Farnham, on the summer Progress – which had been a running duel between Somerset and Villiers. A little earlier, at Lulworth in Dorset, James had sent Sir Humphrey May, a courtier with a reputation for tact, to try to reconcile them. But Somerset (who had thrown discretion to the winds after the king had pointedly broken the planned itinerary by suddenly visiting Villiers's mother on the anniversary of his first meeting with Villiers in the August of 1614) showed himself irreconcilable.

'My Lord,' said May, 'Sir George Villiers will come to you to offer his services and desire to be your creature; and therefore refuse him not. Embrace him – and your Lordship shall still stand a great man, though not the sole Favourite.'

When Somerset retorted that he would do nothing of the kind, May told him plainly that this was actually the command of the king who wished Villiers to 'take his rise under the shadow of his wings'.

Half an hour later, Villiers came to Somerset and said, 'My Lord, I desire to be your servant and your creature, and shall desire to take my Court preferment under your favour; and your Lordship shall find me as faithful a servant unto you as ever did serve you.'

Somerset gave him a 'quick and short answer': 'I will none of your service and you shall none of my favour. I will, if I can, break your neck and of that be confident.'

And since then, records the courtier, 'breaking each other's necks was their aims'.

Villiers found several ways in which to annoy Somerset, whose temper made him only too vulnerable, and at the end of August played his trump card of surrendering to the avid king. It was precisely at this moment that Winwood gave the king the information about the Overbury murder; and within ten days James had decided to have the matter investigated, knowing that such a decision must finally ruin Somerset.

In the nine months between that time and the trial, Villiers consolidated his position to an extent that surprised even those accustomed to the Jacobean court. James could not bear him out of his sight, writing frantic letters to him to return post haste 'so that the whiteness of his teeth might shine upon him again'. And on 23 April 1616 – a bare month before Somerset's trial – Villiers was rewarded for his complaisance by being given the highest order of chivalry – the Garter.

All this Somerset knew and could have told.

CHAPTER 11

The Poisoning of King James I
5 March 1625

On 5 March, 1625, King James I, who was at his favourite country residence at Theobalds, was taken ill of a tertian ague. It was not considered serious and on 11 March, he was well enough to sign and dispatch a safe-conduct for the Conde de Gondomar, the former Spanish ambassador who was then in Spain, to return to England. Among other things, Gondomar was bound to bring an adverse report on the Duke of Buckingham's recent conduct in Spain, and the gossip at court was that he was returning at the king's invitation 'to put a flea in the Duke's ear'. Nobody, least of all Buckingham, doubted that the Spaniard's coming would 'mean the Duke's discredit'. The day after the safe-conduct was signed, James was sufficiently strong to contemplate being moved to Hampton Court and Buckingham, who had been going to and fro between Theobalds and his own residence, Wallingford House, in London, arranged with his mother to send to Dunmow for a special plaster made by a doctor there.

The Countess of Buckingham applied the plaster to the king's wrists, in defiance of protests from his doctors; and James grew rapidly worse. As soon as the plasters were taken off and normal medical treatment restored, the king once more improved. On 21 March the plasters were again applied and the king grew so very much worse that one of the doctors, Craig, used such strong language that he was ordered to leave Court, while another, Hayes, was called out of bed to take the plasters off.

Buckingham then had prepared by his own servant, Baker, a special julep which he took to James with his own hand. James drank twice but refused the third time. This was on 22 March.

On 23 March, all hope of the king's life was abandoned. The bishop in attendance on him told him that his end was near and the next day he received Holy Communion in company with all his attendants except Buckingham, who excused himself on the grounds that he had stomach-ache.

On 27 March, James died. Immediately afterwards a paper was brought to the doctors to sign 'that the ingredients of the julep and the plasters were safe', but, even knowing what the displeasure of the now all-powerful Buckingham meant, they refused. (Their conduct in this matter was sworn on oath by the physicians themselves before a select committee in 1627.)

When, in 1626, Buckingham was impeached by the House of Commons, the thirteenth article of the charge referred to these events, though the specific accusation of poison was avoided. To save the duke, Charles I dissolved Parliament.

For over two hudred years after James's death, the theory that Buckingham poisoned him was never seriously called in question. The only problem which engaged the attention of historians was whether or not King Charles I was privy to it; or at least implicated in the sense in which the accusation was put by Milton : 'To omit other evidences, he that would not suffer a Duke that was accused of it to come to his trial must needs have been guilty of it himself.'

When, in 1653, Bulstrode Whitelock was the English ambassador to Sweden, he found Queen Christina interested in the subject. She asked him the details of the matter. He had been in the 1626 Parliament, and a lawyer and the son of a judge, had weighed the evidence carefully. After his recital of the facts of the case, Queen Christina replied : 'Certainly he was poisoned' and thus endorsed the general contemporary verdict.

The reversal of this verdict to such an extent that the mere asking of the question nowadays is held 'unworthy of a serious historian' is due entirely to S. R. Gardiner, who is accepted, without any attempt at verification, by academic historians. In the fifth volume of his *History of England,* published in 1883, Gardiner assumes that the medical evidence for poisoning is worthless. This conclusion, he bases on a pamphlet written in 1862 and published in Calcutta by Dr Norman Chevers, Principal of the Calcutta Medical College : *Did James the First of England die from the Effects of Poison?* Gardiner dismisses the weighty circumstantial evidence as worthless because, he says : 'the only ground for supposing it to have any value is cut away once it is understood that Buckingham had no object in poisoning the King.' As Gardiner's own reconstruction of that background is one of his own more obvious inaccuracies and his treatment of the event is marked by his usual technique of suppressing awkward facts, his opinion is of little value. It has not even the merit of making a real case; for Dr Chevers admits that the administration of the julep, even if it were quite harmless, would aggravate the illness and pronounces that 'nothing could have been less appropriate', citing as an example 'a Superintendent's Surgeon in the Bengal Medical Service who died in 1856, whose fatal attack was excited by a draught of beer shortly followed by one of milk'. Thus, if the question is put in the form: 'Did Buckingham kill the King?' ignoring the question of poison, Dr Chevers's pamphlet is not on S. R. Gardiner's side.

One may therefore pose the question as an unsolved historical mystery.

The Evidence of Poison

It is most convenient to start with the strongest argument against actual poison, which is that James's health was so ruined by his long debaucheries that his end was only to be expected. This is substantially the argument of Dr Chevers in his pamphlet.

The Venetian envoy, reporting to the doge two years before the king's death wrote 'Good principles and feelings are extinguished in him. He loves nothing but himself, his own convenience and his pleasures. He distrusts everyone, suffers from extreme weakness of mind and is tyrannized over by constant fear of death.'

The French ambassador, the Comte de Tillières, who left England after a five year's stay in the June of 1624, noticed that Buckingham, whose early ascendancy over James was due to simple and overpowering sexual infatuation, was now keeping that control by additionally encouraging all James's vices. In the October of 1623, he wrote: 'The weightiest and most urgent affairs cannot drive this King to devote to them even a day, nay, an hour, or to interrupt his gratifications. These consist of his betaking himself to a remote spot where, out of the sight of men, he leads a filthy and scandalous life and gives himself up to drinking and other vices. . . . It appears as if the more his strength wastes away, the more these infamous passions increase and, passing from the body over to the mind, assume a double power.' And in the February of 1624, he noted : 'Buckingham confirms him in everything and hopes that, the more he abandons himself to all pleasures and to drunkenness, the weaker will be his understanding and spirit and so much the easier will he be able to rule when the other ties of connection are dissolved.'

These are objective reports of foreigners, intent only on getting the exact truth to report to their masters; and their evidence, as far as Buckingham is concerned is confirmed by the duke's own letters to James. In the July of 1624 for instance, when he feared the rivalry of one of his younger relatives in James's affections, he writes that he wonders 'whether you love me now better than at the time I shall never forget at Farnham, where the bed's head could not be found between the master and his dog.' And in the October of 1624, he wrote (adding, comprehensibly, at the end : 'I pray you burn this letter') of a man who had come to him with a remedy for James's indispositions : 'I confess so long as he concealed the means he wrought by, I despised all he said; but when he told me that which he hath given Your Sovereignship to preserve you from all sickness ever hereafter was extracted out of a turd, I admired the fellow and for these reasons : that, being a stranger to you yet he had found out the kind you are come of and your natural affections and appetite and so, like a skilful man, hath given you natural physic.'

The picture emerges of an ageing debauchee wrecking – and encouraged to wreck – his health with excesses, under the superintendence of the favourite. Of the king's chronic drunkenness, there can be no doubt. It was reported and commented on from all quarters and, as early as 1621, de Tillières had mentioned that he was 'lost in pleasures and buried for the greater part of his time in wine'. When, after death, James's body was opened by his physicians they found 'his heart of an extraordinary bigness, all his vitals sound, as also his head, which was very full of brains; but his blood was wonderfully tainted with melancholy; and the corruption thereof supposed the cause of his death.'

The tertian ague, attacking such a constitution, was obviously serious though it need not have been mortal; and the most significant fact seems to be that James was recovering until the application of the plasters to his wrists and stomach.

Such plasters were the commonplace of contemporary treatment for the disease. 'The pulses of the wrists' and the pit of the stomach, were the spots chosen for the application of these external remedies. One such prescription was a compound of 'frankincense, cinnabar, camphire, wood-soot, turpentine and the like'; another 'used by the vulgar' was a hard-boiled egg split and applied hot to the wrists. Bruised spiders and tobacco were one recipe and another a combination of yarrow and rue with the buds of honey-suckle, bramble and elder. A favourite concoction was mouse-ear with vinegar and salt, wall-pepper, shepherd's purse, sundew and vervain.

The composition of the plaster applied to James is not ascertainable, but one of the Royal physicians, Dr George Eglisham, about a week after the king's death, was on a visit with Sir Matthew Lister to the Earl of Warwick's house in Essex, near Dr Remington, the Dunmow doctor (who was Warwick's physician) who had supplied the plaster. They sent for Remington to ascertain from him the ingredients. After Remington had told them that it was 'mithridate spread upon leather', Sir Matthew Lister produced a piece of the actual plaster which had been applied to the king. On examining it, Dr Remington was much surprised and offered to take an oath that it was not the same that he had sent to the duke.

Dr Eglisham, a Scot, had been James's physician since 1616. His hobby was writing poetry and he seems to have been both eccentric and extreme in his views. Shortly after his appointment as Royal physician he had undertaken to prove in his *Duellum Poeticum* that the king's boyhood tutor, George Buchanan, had been guilty of 'impiety towards God, perfidy to his Prince and tyranny to the Muses'. His famous pamphlet accusing Buckingham of murder, *Prodromus Vindictae;* was published in 1626, the year after James's death, and must be treated with considerable reserve, if only because immediately after its publication, Eglisham fled to the Continent to escape punishment by the infuriated duke.

To treat the pamphlet with reserve, however, is not entirely to dismiss it as evidence. For one thing, all the doctors agreed with Eglisham at least to the extent that, knowing the danger of offending Buckingham, they all refused to certify that the plaster was harmless. For another, it was published at a time when its reference to living persons could be verified and – had not Charles dissolved the 1626 Paliament to save Buckingham from having to answer for his conduct – would have been either verified or disproved at the Bar of the House of Lords. And, finally, much of the material in it is corroborated by other writers.

Eglisham's account runs : 'The King being sick of a tertian ague, which in the spring was of itself never found deadly, the Duke took this opportunity, when all the doctors of physic were at dinner, upon the Monday before the King died, to offer to him a white powder to take, the which he a long time refused; but, overcome with his flattering importunity, at length took it in wine and immediately became worse and worse, falling into many swoonings and pains and violent fluxes of the belly, so tormented that His Majesty cried out aloud of this white powder : "Would to God I had never taken it ! It will cost me my life."

'In like manner also the Countess of Buckingham, my Lord of Buckingham's mother, upon the Friday, the physicians being also absent and at dinner and not made acquainted with her doings, applied a plaister to the King's heart and breast; whereupon he grew faint and short-breathed and in a great agony. Some of the physicians, after dinner returning to see the King, by the offensive smell of the plaister perceived something to be about him hurtful to him and searched what it should be and found it out and exclaimed that the King was poisoned. The Duke of Buckingham entering commanded the physicians out of the room, caused one of them to be committed prisoner to his own chamber and another to be removed from Court; quarrelled with others of the King's servants in his sick Majesty's own presence so far that he offered to draw his sword against them in His Majesty's sight. And Buckingham's mother, kneeling down before His Majesty, cried out with a brazen face : "Justice, justice, sir, I demand justice of Your Majesty !" His Majesty asked her for what? "For that which their lives are no ways sufficient to satisfy; for saying that my son and I have poisoned your Majesty." "Poisoned me?" said he : with that, turning himself, swooned; and she was removed.'

That some such scene took place, there can hardly be any doubt. Meade, in one of his letters to Sir Martin Stuteville informed him that the Countess of Buckingham 'would needs make trial of some receipt she had approved but, being without the privity of the physicians, occasioned so much discontent in Dr Craig that he uttered some plain speeches, for which he was commanded out of Court, the Duke himself (as some say) complaining to the sick King of the word he spake'.

Dr Craig, who was as definite as Dr Eglisham in his belief that Buckingham had poisoned the king, was one of a family of physicians and lawyers. His father, Dr John Craig, an M.D. of both Basle and Oxford, had been James's physician before he became King of England and, in that capacity, had accompanied him south. His uncle, Sir Lewis Craig, had been an advocate, trained in France and, as Lord Wrightslands, had become a Scottish judge. His grandfather, Sir Thomas Craig, had been famous as an advocate, a justice and an authority on feudal law. With this background and training, Dr Craig was likely to be more accustomed to weighing evidence and less predisposed to emotionalism than Dr Eglisham. His nephew by marriage, the father of Bishop Burnet, who was in London at the time of the king's death 'did very much suspect an ill-practice in the matter', having heard his uncle's evidence.

James Howell, the writer, traveller and diplomatist who was later to become historiographer-royal to Charles II, was at Theobalds at the time of James's death and, in a letter to his father, mentioned the complaints of the doctors that a plaister had been applied to the 'outside of the King's stomach' by the Countess of Buckingham, though he committed no other comments to paper. Bishop Goodman, who was also there, though he entirely exculpates Buckingham, evidently believed that there was foul play. He writes : 'I have no good opinion of his death, yet I was the last man that did him homage in the extremity of his sickness.' Arthur Wilson, the contemporary historian of the reign records : 'The King, that was very much impatient in his health, was patient in his sickness and death. Whether he had received anything that extorted his agueish fits into a fever, which might the sooner stupify the spirits and hasten his end, cannot be asserted ; but the Countess of Buckingham had been tampering with him in the absence of the doctors and had given him a medicine to drink and laid a plaister on his side of which the King much complained and they did rather exasperate his distemper than allay it and these things were admitted by the insinuating persuasions of the Duke her son, who told the King they were approved medicines and would do him much good. And though the Duke often strove to purge himself for this application, as having received both medicine and plaister from Dr Remington, at Dunmow, in Essex, who had often cured agues and such distempers with the same; yet they were arguments of a complicated kind, not easy to unfold, considering that whatsoever he may have received from the doctor in the country, he might apply to the King what he pleased in the Court.'

What Buckingham's unofficial efforts to 'purge himself' of suspicion were, we have no record; but we have his official answer made to the charges of the Commons in 1626. This defence, which is printed in full in the appendix to this chapter, seems to me to confirm rather than allay suspicion. It explains almost too well those facts of the situation which were incontrovertible. His uncorroborated dove-tailing is a little too perfect. And, it must be reiterated, Charles's dissolution of Parliament to prevent it being tested by evidence is a strong argument against its accuracy.

According to the duke, it was the king who asked for the plaister and the posset-drink, as it had done Buckingham good in a recent attack of ague. Buckingham, though he admitted the efficacy of the remedies, delayed sending for them and only did so after the king had personally ordered the duke's servant, Baker, to go and fetch them from Dunmow. Buckingham asked James not to use them until after they had been tested on one of the Gentlemen of the Bedchamber and two children in the town who had ague and then to use them only on the advice of his doctors. The king promised to do so.

At this point, Buckingham left Theobolds and went up to London, returning to the king's bedside at the precise moment when James was drinking the 'posset-drink' which had, in the meantime, arrived. James asked Buckingham to administer it to him, which he did, after the doctors and various other people in the room had tasted it. Later, when the king grew worse, Buckingham heard the rumour that 'his physic had done the King hurt' and had been given without advice. He told the king of this and James answered : 'They are worse than devils that say it.'

It will be seen by this account that the points which are too well attested by witnesses to be denied are admitted but explained in another sense. The medicine from Dunmow was fetched by Buckingham's servant, Baker – but it was the king, not the duke, who sent him for it. Buckingham administered the fatal draught to James – but the king was already on the point of drinking it when the duke arrived back from London. Buckingham complained to the king of the slanders – but the king's answer was favourable to the duke.

Secondly, Buckingham goes out of his way to assert that other people tasted the drink, including some of the physicians – which cannot be made to tally with the physicians' own evidence before the select committee. Thirdly, no mention at all is made of the administration of the 'plaisters' which, as Buckingham admitted that he had recommended them, were also ultimately his responsibility.

Sir William Sanderson, another contemporary historian who was also the Earl of Holland's secretary, records that 'what Buckingham gave James to drink was a posset-drink of milk and ale, hartshorn and marigold flowers, ingredients harmless and ordinary' – though, as Dr Chevers has pointed out, any drink at that point would much aggravate the illness and nothing could have been less appropriate. (And, on his analogy of the beer and milk drunk by the surgeon in Bengal, it would have been by itself sufficient to cause death.)

There were, of course, more scurrilous tales than these, written by the anti-Royalist pamphleteers. One will suffice – that by Sir Anthony Weldon who, originally Clerk of the Green Cloth at James's court, had been dismissed for satirizing the Scots and who eventually joined the Parliamentarian side in the Civil War. He published in 1650 his *Court and Character of King James I* which contained much unreliable gossip and is rightly regarded by historians, even when they use it, with the maximum of suspicion. He writes: 'He (James) now goes to his last hunting journey (I mean the last of the year, as well as of his life, which he ever ended in Lent) and was seized of an ordinary Tertian Ague, which at that season, according to the proverb, was Physic for a King; but it proved not so to him and, poor King, what was but physic to any other was made mortal to him. Yet not the ague, as himself confessed to a servant of his who cried: "Courage, Sir, this is but a small fit; the next will be none at all"; at which he most earnestly looked and said : "Ah, it is not the ague afflicteth me, but the black plaister and powder given me and laid to my stomach."

'And in truth the plaister so tormented him that he was glad to have it pulled off and with it the skin also. Nor was it fair dealing, if he had fair play (which he himself suspected, often saying to Montgomery whom he trusted above all men in his sickness : "For God's sake, look I have fair play!") to bring in an Emprick to apply any medicines whilst those physicians appointed to attend him were at dinner. Nor could any but Buckingham answer it with less than his life at that present, as he had the next Parliament had it not been dissolved upon the very questioning him for the King's death and all those that prosecuted him utterly disgraced and banished the Court.

'Buckingham coming into the King's chamber even when he was at the point of death and an honest servant of the King's crying : "Ah, my Lord, you have undone us all, his poor servants, although you are so well provided you need not care" : at which Buckingham kicked at him, who caught his foot and made his head come first to the ground, where Buckingham presently rising runs to the dying King's bedside and cried : "Justice, Sir, I am abused by your servant"; at which the poor King mournfully fixed his eyes on him as one who would have said : "Not wrongfully", yet without speech or sense.'

The credibility of Weldon is neither more nor less than that of any other 'gossip' (such as Creevey, for instance, at the Hanoverian court) but the passage about Montgomery – who, as Earl of Pembroke, lived till 1650 and, at least in his earlier days at court as one of James's favourites was well-known to Weldon – has about it the ring of authenticity.

To sum the matter up, it is incontrovertible that the fifty-nine-year-old king was in an enfeebled state of health but that no one expected the tertian ague to be mortal; that certain unknown remedies were applied in defiance of the doctors by Buckingham and his mother; that the king grew worse after each application and that hope for his life was finally abandoned after Buckingham had administered a 'posset-drink'; that two doctors, Eglisham and Craig, publicly accused Buckingham of causing the king's death; that all the doctors, even though under pressure, refused to certify the remedies harmless; that the charge against the duke though in a necessarily modified form, was formally made by the House of Commons and that a proper investigation was officially stopped by the Crown (which Buckingham controlled); that informed contemporary opinion was overwhelmingly in favour of Buckingham's guilt and even those who, like Bishop Goodman, considered the duke personally innocent, were suspicious of foul play on somebody's part. Against this must be set the fact that, after the autopsy, the king's death was 'supposed' to be due to the 'corruption' of his blood which was 'wonderfully tainted with melancholy' – a vague diagnosis which, at this distance of time, is difficult to appraise correctly and which may or may not be compatible with poison.

On all this S. R. Gardiner comments : 'The evidence is worthless in itself and the only ground for supposing it to have any value is cut away when once it is understood that Buckingham had no object in poisoning the King.'

It is therefore necessary to examine the position of Buckingham at the time of James's death.

The Position of Buckingham in 1625

The keystone of James's foreign policy was a Spanish alliance, of which one of the terms was intended to be Spanish aid to restore the Palatinate to his son-in-law, who had been driven out of it. To cement the alliance, Prince Charles was to marry the Infanta Maria, sister of the King of Spain. Gondomar, the powerful Spanish ambassador in London, returned to Spain in 1622 to superintend negotiations in Madrid, with the English ambassador there, the Earl of Bristol.

In 1623 Prince Charles, accompanied by Buckingham, went to Madrid to woo the Infanta in person. Their visit was kept secret as long as possible from the House of Commons in England, who, having inherited all the Elizabethan prejudices, were violently anti-Spanish and did not understand that, in the new century, it was France under Richelieu, not Spain, which was the strongest European power and, as such, the 'natural' enemy of England (whose policy, then as always, was in self-interest to allow no nation to have the hegemony of Europe).

There were seven chief actors in the comedy of 'the Spanish Match'. On the English side, the thirty-year-old Buckingham, the twenty-two-year-old Charles and the forty-three-year-old Bristol, the one competent English statesman of the age. On the Spanish side were the seventeen-year-old King, Philip IV, who cared for nothing but hunting and was entirely dominated by his minister, the thirty-six-year-old Olivares; the Infanta, who was sixteen – and Gondomar, who at fifty-six, was one of the ablest diplomatists in Europe, and whose return to Spain Olivares had insisted on as being the only man capable of coping with Bristol.

Bristol, who believed that the restoration of the Palatinate should be settled diplomatically on its merits and confused neither by concessions to the 'religious' prejudices of Protestant mobs in England nor by secret clauses in a marriage treaty, had been at the outset opposed to the idea of the marriage, but he had loyally endeavoured to carry out his master's instructions. On the one hand, he denied the right of Spain to interfere with the religious policy of England; on the other, he had bargained for the best possible terms from Spain which, he considered, would be safer as an ally than as an enemy of England.

The arrival of Buckingham and Charles undid all his work. They stayed in Madrid exactly twenty-five weeks. During that time, Buckingham contrived to offend everyone, from the populace who said that they would 'rather put the Infanta headlong into a well than into his hands', to Olivares himself, who eventually told him in public that he looked upon his friendship as a thing of no importance. He wrecked all Bristol's diplomacy, destroyed any hope of continuance of good relations between England and Spain and at the same time injured the chances of a satisfactory settlement of the Palatinate question.

The result was due to his unique combination of political incompetence with personal arrogance. In England, though he was the all-powerful favourite and transmitted the king's orders, the details and routine of government had remained in the hands of trained officials. His own contribution had been limited to interference, from personal motives, which lessened the efficiency of the administration or increased the confusion of the king's celebrated 'statecraft'. On his arrival in Madrid, because of his position with James, he took the control of negotiations out of Bristol's hands, and when Bristol was forced to remonstrate with him, treated him 'worse than a dog'. Never before having tried his own unaided hand at diplomacy and having no aptitude for it, Buckingham was consistently out-manoeuvred by Olivares.

As with his lack of political acumen, so with his personal behaviour. In England he was so accustomed to treat king, nobles and commoners alike as if they were his servants that he did not realize how this behaviour would affect those trained in the rigid etiquette of the Spanish Court. It was not so much that he was intentionally rude as that he had no idea of any other code of manners.

The Spaniards, accordingly, were further antagonized by seeing Buckingham lounging in a dressing-gown and without breeches at the prince's table, turning his back on him in public and shouting at him in questionable nicknames. They were disgusted when Buckingham leant rudely forward to stare at the Infanta, and again when he created a scene, followed by a fit of sulking, because Bristol was invited to share a carriage with the king and prince. He offended the clergy by bringing one of the official theological conferences to a sudden and unconventional end by 'expressing his contempt for the Friars by unseemly gesticulations' and then throwing his hat on the ground and jumping on it. The courtiers were insulted by his indiscriminate amours, which were such a source of scandal that he was even suspected of an attempt on Olivares's wife and his illness in the summer attributed to a disease caught from a 'notorious stew' who was sent, heavily veiled, to impersonate her. Bristol was eventually moved to write home to James : 'I must, for the discharge of my conscience and duty, without descending to particulars, let Your Majesty truly know that suspicions and distastes betwixt them all here and my Lord of Buckingham cannot be at greater height.' His judgment was confirmed by the fact that, on the pillar set up in a field by the Escurial to commemorate the visit, the Spaniards omitted the name of Buckingham 'as if he had been none of the company'. But Bristol's honesty in the report meant his ruin.

From the moment he arrived back in England, in the autumn of 1623, Buckingham had only one object—to revenge his wounded vanity by precipitating a war against Spain. In this policy, he had the support of the House of Commons and, indeed, of the country in which, for the first and last time, he became a popular figure – the prince's good angel who had foiled the wicked Spaniards. He had, too, the enthusiastic support of Charles, of whom, in Spain he had made a lasting conquest.

This friendship, indeed, was the most significant fact to emerge from the Spanish journey. No historian has sufficiently recognized (what is abundantly evident from contemporary records as well as Domestic and Foreign – especially Venetian – State Papers) that until 1623 Buckingham and Charles were on exceedingly bad terms. All biographers of Buckingham have put their reconciliation years before it in fact took place and consequently do not allow for the full meaning of Madrid, where, if Charles fell in love with anyone it was not with the Infanta but with Buckingham.

I do not of course mean that Charles had physical relations with him. The favourite's known relation with the prince's father would preclude that, even if there had been no other reason. But Charles became more deeply attached to Buckingham than even James had ever been and from the return from Spain until Buckingham's murder five years later, that passionate affection never wavered. From 1624, Buckingham could control Charles as he could never, even in the first flush of James's infatuation, control James. And from that time, from the point of view of power as well as from the point of view of amorous convenience, Buckingham must have preferred Charles to James as king. What is more, he did not conceal it. To a French visitor, James confided that he did not know what devil had entered into Buckingham since he returned from Spain and the duke himself did not trouble to hide from the king his knowledge that his conduct was causing the comment that 'I am suspected to look more to the rising sun than to my maker'.

It is this which gives a certain poignancy to James's letter to Buckingham in the Christmas of 1624: 'I cannot content myself without sending you this billet, praying God that I may have a joyful and comfortable meeting with you and that we may make at this Christenmas a new marriage, ever to be kept hereafter; For, God so love me, as I desire only to live in this world for your sake, and that I had rather live banished in any part of the earth with you, than live a sorrowful widow-life without you. And so God bless you, my sweet child and wife, and grant that ye may ever be a comfort to your dear dad and husband, James R.'*

*Generations of historians have incorrectly ascribed this letter as written to Charles!

But, throughout 1624, Buckingham, though secure in the support of the prince and the Parliament and the people, knew, that as long as James retained any kind of control of policy, there was the danger that he might learn the truth about Spain and that, in the circumstances, such a revelation might destroy him. Though he seemed all-powerful, he was under no illusions on what, ultimately, his power depended. As he had supplanted Somerset as the Royal minion, so he might be supplanted by some younger and more attractive rival. And if the political and personal motives coincided in James's mind, he was lost.

It so happened that he had a potential rival, a young kinsman of his own, Arthur Brett.

Just before the journey to Spain, at the end of 1622, James and Buckingham had had a violent quarrel over Arthur Brett, who had been made a Gentleman of the Bedchamber and had very obviously attracted the king's notice. It was a matter not only of court gossip but was serious enough to engage the attention of the Venetian ambassador, who reported it to the doge with the comment : 'Some who observed the fate of the earlier favourite, Somerset, think that His Majesty's favour is like the summer sky from which, when quite serene, a thunderbolt sometimes falls unexpectedly'.

Before he left for Spain, Buckingham thought it advisable to take all possible precautions against being supplanted in his absence and Brett was accordingly knighted and sent abroad. Young Monson (who, five years earlier had been thought of as a rival favourite and washed his face hopefully each morning in 'posset-curd') was similarly exiled. In the March of 1624, however, when Brett returned from his Continental travels, he was welcomed by James with such affection that Buckingham dared not let James out of his sight. Unfortunately, that May, various strains had become too much for him. He collapsed and for three weeks was dangerously ill of – as one reported it – 'a fever, the jaundice and I know not what else; so that, beside other physic, he hath been let blood thrice at least; yet the world thinks he is more sick in mind than in body and that he declines apace', and when he was well enough to return to Court – in mid-June – he found Brett in such favour that the Venetian ambassador at least believed that the duke's absence had been due not so much to illness as to James's changed affection.

Certainly Brett's hold had become strong enough for Buckingham to need a month to break it, but by the middle of July he had managed it and Brett was told to keep away from James.

The young man, however, was of an impatient disposition and shortly afterwards, when James was hunting in Waltham Forest, he ignored the ban, rode up to him and laid hands on the bridle of his horse. This was all that Buckingham needed. Brett was sent to the Fleet prison and, though he was released after about six weeks, he was forbidden thereafter to come within ten miles of London or the Court.

But, for the remaining eight months of James's life, Buckingham could not free himself from the fear of the emergence of another rival, or even of Brett's own return.

It is against this background that one must consider the more direct threat to Buckingham's position which would have materialized on the arrival of authentic and incontrovertible news from Spain.

The first danger was the return of Bristol, who arrived in England at the same time as Brett – in the March of 1624. Buckingham's influence was still sufficient to ensure that he was not allowed to see James. His attempt to have the ambassador sent to the Tower was, indeed, unsuccessful, but James, though he promised Bristol he would not condemn him unheard, ordered him for the moment to confine himself to his own manor of Sherborne. When Bristol, though forced to obey, asked that the Commons should make the fullest possible investigation of his conduct, he was told that the end of the session was near and Buckingham tried to bribe him to silence by offering to forget the past. Bristol replied : 'In the matter of my fidelity and loyalty towards His Majesty, the Prince and my country, I hope I shall never see that come into compromise, but shall rather lose my life and fortunes than to admit the least stain to remain on me or mine in that kind.' But he was never allowed to see James again.

Gondomar's confessor, Lafuente, who was also dispatched from Spain to inform James of the truth of things, called for different measures. Buckingham had him waylaid near Amiens and all his papers stolen, so that when he was conducted to James's presence he had to admit that he had lost his credentials. Eventually he managed to get a private audience with the king and told him that it was Buckingham's conduct in Spain, of which he had been kept in ignorance, that had caused the present dangerous situation. James was interested enough to want to know more and two days later, Inojosa, the Viceroy of Navarre, who had been sent to England to support the attempt to save the Spanish alliance, completed the story. If the king refused to go to war with Spain, he said, Buckingham intended to force him to abdicate in favour of Prince Charles.

With Parliament and the country in its present mood, this was quite a feasible plan. James was to be kept amused with hunting and other pastimes at Theobalds until the time was ripe. The king was frightened. In his youth in Scotland men whom he had lovel as much as he loved Buckingham had conspired to hold him in terror of his life. And there was nothing in the present behaviour of the prince and the duke which made the present story intrinsically improbable. James told Inojosa to let him have the charges in writing and left Theobalds immediately for the comparative safety of Windsor Castle. On his way, he called at St James's Palace where Buckingham was with Charles. As they came out to welcome him, he burst into tears and cried: 'Steenie, Steenie, wilt thou kill me?'

Buckingham naturally protested his innocence; the Privy Council, when it was summoned to investigate Inojosa's charges, found they were too vague to be sustained and, the councillors swearing one by one that they had never heard a treasonable word pass Buckingham's lips, they found the duke not guilty. Inojosa was asked to leave the country and forbidden to have another interview with the king.

There is no reason whatever to suppose that his story was untrue; and that the abdication was not seriously planned.

As soon as Inojosa reached Spain, it was determined to send Gondomar himself once more to England. This news was, as even S. R. Gardiner admits, 'very terrible' to Buckingham. With Gondomar's arrival, the duke was likely to be ruined for ever. He could survive the imputations of Inojosa and discredit Lafuente; he could prevent Bristol from ever seeing the king; but Gondomar was invulnerable. Nothing could keep him from James's presence and nothing could bribe him to hold his tongue. Even with Parliament, he could shatter Buckingham's temporary popularity by merely revealing the secret clauses of the Spanish treaty and, being what he was, he was not likely to hesitate, should it become necessary.

At all costs Gondomar must not come; and yet there was no possible way of preventing him. But there was a way of preventing him seeing James. On 11 March, 1625, a courier started for Spain with a safe-conduct for Gondomar, and a personal letter from James. On 12 March, James was well enough to consider moving from Theobalds to Hampton Court. On 23 March, after the treatment of the plasters and the julep, all hope of his life was abandoned and on 27 March he was dead.

Gardiner's suggestion that 'Buckingham had no object in poisoning the King' seems to me, in these circumstances, the exact reverse of the truth and should be dismissed as completely as his other and cognate theory that James's interest in Buckingham was 'paternal' is now repudiated by all historians.

Buckingham's blood-guiltiness stands, in fact, exactly where it did before Gardiner wrote, when the verdict of 'Guilty', which accords with the known facts, was accepted without demur.

Appendix

I. *Article XIII of the charge against Buckingham at his impeachment.*

Whereas special care and order hath been taken by the laws of the realm to restrain and prevent the unskilful administration of physic whereby the health and life of man be much endangered; and whereas most especially the royal persons of Kings of the realm (in whom we, their loyal subjects, humbly challenge a great interest), are and always have been esteemed by us so sacred that nothing ought to be prepared for them or administered unto them in the way of physic or diet in the times of their sickness without the consent and direction of some of their sworn physicians, apothecaries or surgeons; and the boldness of such (how near soever to them in place and favour) who have forgotten their duties so far as to presume to offer anything unto them beyond their experience, hath always been ranked in the high offences and misdemeanours.

And whereas the sworn physicians of our late sovereign Lord King James, of blessed memory, attending on His Majesty in the month of March, in the 22nd year of his most glorious reign, in the times of his sickness, being in ague, did, in due and necessary care of and for the recovery of his health and preservation of his person, upon and after several mature consultations in that behalf had and holden at several times in the same month, resolve and give directions that nothing should be applied or given to His Highness by way of physic or diet during the said sickness but by and upon their general advice and consents and after good deliberations thereof first had more especially by their like care and upon like consultations did justly resolve and publicly give warning to and for all the gentlemen and other servants and officers of his late Majesty's bed-chamber that no meat or drink whatsoever should be given unto him for two or three hours next before the usual time of and for the coming of his fit in the said ague, nor during the continuance thereof, nor afterwards until his cold fit was past: the said Duke of Buckingham, being a sworn servant of his said late Majesty and in His Majesty's said bed-chamber, contrary to his duty and the tender respects which he ought to have had for His Majesty's most sacred person and after the consultations, resolutions, directions and warnings aforesaid, did nevertheless, without any sufficient warrant in that behalf, unduly cause and procure certain plaisters and a certain drink or potion to be provided for the use of his said Majesty, without the direction and privity of his said late Majesty's physicians, not prepared by any of his sworn apothecaries or surgeons but compounded of several ingredients to them unknown; notwithstanding the same plaisters (or some plaister like thereunto) having been administered unto his said Majesty did produce such ill effects as that some of the said sworn physicians did altogether disallow thereof and utterly refuse to meddle any further with his said Majesty until these plaisters were removed as being hurtful and prejudicial to the health of His Majesty; yet, nevertheless, the same plaisters, as also a drink or potion, was provided by the said Duke, by colour of some insufficient and slight pretences, who did upon Monday, the 21st day of March in the 22nd year aforesaid, when His Majesty by the judgment of his said physicians was in the declination of his disease, cause and procure the said plaister to be applied to the breast and wrists of his said late Majesty.

And then also, at and in His Majesty's fit of the said ague, the said Monday and at several times within two hours before the coming of the coming of the said fit and before His Majesty's then cold fit was past, did deliver and cause to be delivered several quantities of the said drink or potion to His Majesty, who thereupon, at the same times within the seasons in that behalf prohibited by His Majesty's physicians, as aforesaid, did by the means and procurement of the said Duke drink and take divers quantities of the said drink or potion. After which said plaisters and drink or potion applied and given unto and taken and received by His Majesty, great distempers and divers ill symptoms appeared upon His Majesty insomuch that the physicians, finding His Majesty the next morning much worse in the estate of his health and holding consultations thereabout, did by joint consent send to the said Duke praying him not to adventure to minister to His Majesty any more physic without their allowance and approbation.

And his said Majesty finding himself much diseased and affected with pain and sickness after his then fit when by the course of his disease he expected intermission and ease, did attribute the cause of his trouble unto the said plaister and drink which the said Duke had so given and caused to be administered unto him.

Which said adventurous act by a person obliged in duty and thankfulness done to the person of so great a King after the ill success of the like formerly administered, contrary to such directions as aforesaid and accompanied with so unhappy event to the great grief and discomfort of all His Majesty's subjects in general, is an offence and misdemeanour of so high a nature as may justly be called, and is by the said Commons deemed to be, an act of transcendant presumption and of dangerous consequence.

II. *The Duke of Buckingham's answer.*

To the Thirteenth Article of the charge, which is set forth in such an expression of words as might argue an extraordinary guiltiness in the Duke who by such infinite bonds of duty and thankfulness was obliged to be tender of the life and health of his most dread and dear sovereign and master, he maketh this clear and true answer:

That he did not apply nor procure the plaister or posset-drink, in the charge termed to be a potion, unto his late Majesty; nor was present when the same was first taken or applied; but the truth is this: that His Majesty, being sick of ague, took notice of the Duke's recovery of an ague not long before and asked him how he had recovered and what he found did him most good. The Duke gave him a particular answer thereto that one who was the Earl of Warwick's physician had ministered a plaister and a posset-drink to him and the chief thing that did him good was a vomit, which he wished the King had taken in the beginning of his sickness. The King was very desirous to have that plaister and posset-drink sent for; but the Duke delayed it; whereupon the King impatiently asked whether it was sent for or not. And, finding by the Duke's speeches he had not sent for it, his late Majesty sent J. Baker, the Duke's servant, and with his own mouth commanded him to go for it; whereupon the Duke besought His Majesty not to make use of it but by the advice of his own physicians, nor until it should be tried by James Palmer, of his bed-chamber, who was then sick of an ague and upon two children in the town; which the King said he would do.

In this resolution, the Duke left His Majesty and went to London and in the meantime the plaister and posset-drink was brought and applied by his late Majesty's own command. At the Duke's return, His Majesty was taking the posset-drink and the King then commanded the Duke to give it him; which he did in the presence of some of the King's physicians, they then no ways seeeming to dislike it, the same drink being first tasted by some of them and divers others in the King's bed-chamber;

and he thinks this was the second time the King took it.

Afterwards, when the King grew somewhat worse than before, the Duke heard a rumour as if his physic had done the King hurt and that the Duke had administered that physic to him without advice. The Duke acquainted the King therewith, to whom the King, with much discontent, answered thus: 'They are worse than devils that say it.' So far from the truth it was; which now notwithstanding, as it seemeth, is taken up by some and with much confidence affirmed.

And here the Duke humbly prayeth all your lordships not only to consider the truth of this answer, but also to commiserate the sad thought which this article had revived in him.

CHAPTER 12

The Assassination of Colonel Rainsborough
29 October 1648

THE NAME OF Colonel Thomas Rainsborough is today little known outside the circle of students of the Great Civil War. Yet in his day, this cold, uncompromising fanatic was at the very centre of events. In the critical eighteen months between the May of 1647 and the November of 1648, there were two names of equal and outstanding importance – Oliver Cromwell and Thomas Rainsborough. When in the autumn of 1647 Rainsborough flung at Cromwell, 'One of us must not live' and threatened to impeach him for betraying the common cause, it was – as the French agent in London duly reported – a matter of speculation at Westminster whether Cromwell would survive. It was, however, Rainsborough who died. And his almost casual assassination a year later has ensured that in popular histories his very name is forgotten while that of his rival has become a household word.

It is probable that the murder of Rainsborough sensationally changed the course of English history. Had he lived he would certainly have been strong enough to carry through Parliament the *Agreement of the People,* which earlier he had failed to do. The *Agreement* was to the seventeenth century all that the *Social Contract* was to the eighteenth and the *Communist Manifesto* to the nineteenth and twentieth. Had the *Agreement* been put into effect, it would have meant that England made in 1649 the constitutional 'levelling' experiment which she has not made fully yet and did not even begin to make till 1884. The implications of this need no stressing.

Rainsborough's murder affected events in another way. As Cromwell's only possible rival, he was the military and political leader of the extreme 'Left' of the revolutionaries as Fairfax was of the extreme 'Right' and as Cromwell was of the 'Centre'. In the autumn of 1647 Cromwell, in conjunction with Fairfax, was working for the restoration of Charles I to the throne, with himself as the power behind it. In the autumn of 1648 he was foremost in demanding the king's execution. Rainsborough's death left him no option but to take, temporarily, Rainsborough's place. Rainsborough had seen from the beginning the logic of the constitutional situation which Cromwell, with his slow-moving, traditional, conservative mind, had refused to admit. As long as Rainsborough lived, Cromwell, even though (helped by Charles's untrustworthiness) he was gradually realizing the strength of his argument, could afford to exercise his influence on the side of moderation and to incline to Fairfax and the 'Right'. Once Rainsborough was dead, Cromwell had no alternative but to carry out the murdered man's policy in so far as it involved the destruction of the monarchy.

In 1648 the pressure of outside events had forced the quarrelling wings of Parliament and army to unite once more. Charles I, though still in captivity, had concluded an agreement with the Scots who were invading from the north; the tide of Royalism was running strongly in England and particularly in London; just off the Isle of Wight the Dutch Brazil fleet was riding at anchor, awaiting a favourable opportunity to attack the island and rescue the king. In these circumstances Fairfax, and Rainsborough became reconciled. And when the Second Civil War broke out, in the May of 1648, Cromwell marched north to deal with the Scots while Fairfax undertook the quelling of revolt in England. The stubborn centre of that revolt was the siege of Colchester at which, though Fairfax was in command, the credit rightly went to Rainsborough, who, in popular opinion, was accounted the victor.

When the siege was over and English Royalists, resistance broken, and when at the same time Cromwell had decisively defeated the Scots invaders at Preston, there were a few centres of Royalist power still to be reduced. One of these was Pontefract Castle. Toward this Rainsborough marched up and Cromwell marched down. On 28 October Cromwell arrived at Boroughbridge, about twenty-seven miles north of Pontefract, and Rainsborough was lying at Doncaster, about fifteen miles south of it. On 29 October Rainsborough was murdered. Why and by whom?

He had, indeed, a sufficiency of enemies on both sides. The

Royalists loathed him for his ruthlessness at the siege of Colchester, culminating in the judicial murder of the leaders of the defence, Lucas and Lisle. The story of Colchester, is, in its heroism and its horror, one of the epics of the century. From 13 June until 28 August, under the leadership of the inseparable friends, Sir Charles Lucas and Sir George Lisle, the beleaguered town held out against hope so that it might prevent Fairfax joining Cromwell in his campaign in the north. When, in mid August, there was nothing left to eat but a few dogs (sold at 6s. a small side) and the citizens were reduced to eating soap and candles, they still would not surrender. When the Royalists sent 500 women dying of starvation across to the Parliamentarian lines in the hope that common humanity would at least secure them nourishment, Rainsborough drove them back by the simple expedient of ordering his men to strip them naked before the grinning army. It was Rainsborough who, on 5 July, destroyed the last hope of the Royalists – a water-mill below the North Bridge. He himself commanded a party which forded the river, set it on fire, and tore up the sluice by which the head of water was formed which turned the mill.

After that exploit – as always with him, a decisive action directed at the critical point – it was merely a matter of waiting on time and hunger. With his regiment, known as the Tower Guards, he kept watch on the north side of the town in his 'Fort Rainsborough'.

When the inevitable surrender came, Rainsborough was appointed as one of the Commissioners and his regiment was the first to enter the town. That evening he presided over the execution of Lucas and Lisle who, in defiance of all the rules of war and of Fairfax's word, were tried by court-martial and sentenced to be shot to death.

Lucas, brought out first said, 'I do plead before you all the laws of this kingdom. I have fought with a commission from those that were my sovereigns. I have often looked death in the face on the field of battle, and now you shall see that I dare to die. Rebels and traitors, do your worst!'

As he fell dead Lisle started forward, caught the body of his friend and kissed the lifeless face. Then he took his own place where Lucas had stood and beckoned to the firing party to come nearer.

'I warrant you, sir, we'll hit you,' called one of the soldiers.

'Friends,' said Lisle, smiling, 'I have been nearer when you have missed me.' And so died.

Rainsborough was now assured of a new fame. When, two months later, he met sudden death at Doncaster, the balladmongers saw it as a just vengeance, and in the song *Colonel Rainsborough's Ghost,* he was imagined as saying :

> *Witness the bloody fights in Kent:*
> *The siege of Colchester likewise;*
> *I served well the Parliament,*
> *All deeds of mercy did despise.*
> *For when the town they did surrend*
> *I plotted all against them then;*
> *I quickly brought unto an end*
> *The lives of two brave gentlemen.*
> *Sir Charles Lucas and Sir George Lisle,*
> *Two worthy men whom I did hate,*
> *The glory of the British Isle,*
> *Whom I did make unfortunate.*
> *With resolution stout they died,*
> *And called me traitor to my face.*
> *I did no whit abate my pride,*
> *I saw them fall in little space.*
> *The death of them revenged hath been*
> *On me by those that loved them well.*
> *Sweet Jesus Christ, forgive my sin,*
> *For by my means these worthies fell.*

Thus, in considering the assassination of Rainsborough, the theory that it was a simple act of vengeance cannot be dismissed.

And a month after the execution of Lucas and Lisle, when Rainsborough was with the army at St Albans before he was ordered north to Pontefract, an attempt was made to kill him. When he was riding between St Albans and London, accompanied only by a captain, he was assaulted 'by three of the king's party'. These would-be avengers, seeing the 'gallantry and resolution' of their intended victims, 'put spur to their horses and rode for it, and being extraordinary wellmounted over-rid them'.

But if Rainsborough was hated by the Royalists for his military ruthlessness, he was almost equally loathed by the 'Grandees' – the right wing of the Parliament and army – for his political activities; for now that the Second Civil War had been brought to a successful finish, the deadly animosities which had been temporarily forgotten in face of a common danger were once more revealed in all their intensity. And Rainsborough's visits to London were not unconnected with the new attempt to force the *Agreement of the People* through Parliament.

To understand Rainsborough's position here it is necessary to go back to 1647 – that is to say, the year before the outbreak of the Second Civil War and the siege of Colchester. In the November of 1647 took place those great debates of the army in Putney Church which are, as 'the Putney Debates', a landmark in constitutional history. The point at issue was whether a complete break should be made with the traditional constitution and in its place be set up a new form of government consisting of a single chamber, elected biennially by manhood suffrage without any property qualification. The document in which this was embodied was called the *Agreement of the People,* and in Rainsborough's defence of it at Putney against Cromwell we can most clearly see the cast of Rainsborough's mind :

'The poorest He that is in England hath a life to live as the greatest He; and therefore truly, sir, I think it's clear that every man that is to live under a government ought first by his own consent to put himself under that government; and I do think that the poorest man in England is not at all bound in a strict sense to that government that he hath not had a voice to put himself under,' he argued, anticipating later centuries. 'Either it must be the law of God or the law of man that must prohibit the meanest man in the kingdom to have this benefit as well as the greatest. I do not find anything in the law of God that a Lord shall choose twenty burgesses, and a gentleman but two and a poor man none. I find no such thing in the law of nature or in the law of nations. But I do find that all Englishmen must be subject to English laws, and I do verily believe that there is no man but will say that the foundation of all law lies in the people.'

Again and again, Rainsborough returns relentlessly to this point, 'I am a poor man, therefore I must be oppressed. If I have no interest in the kingdom I must suffer by all their laws, be they right or wrong. Nay thus : a gentleman lives in the country and hath three or four lordships, as some men have (God knows how they got them); and when a Parliament is called he must be a Parliament-man; and it may be he sees some poor men – they live near this man – he can crush them – I have known an invasion to make sure he hath turned the poor men out of doors; and I would fain know whether the power of rich men do not this and so keep them under the greatest tyranny that was ever thought of in the world.'

When a speaker on Cromwell's side pointed out that such a franchise might result in the abolition of all property, since 'you have five to one in this kingdom that have no permanent interests. . . . If the master and servant be equal electors, then clearly those that have no interest in the kingdom will make it their interest to choose those that have no interest. Thus it may happen that the majority may by law destroy property,' Rainsborough turned his argument against him with, 'Then, I say, the one part shall make hewers of wood and drawers of water of the other five and so the greatest part of the nation be enslaved. . . . I would fain know what the soldier hath fought for all this while? He hath fought to enslave himself, to give power to men or riches, men of estates, to make him a perpetual slave.'

At Putney, in the Army Council, Rainsborough's party was outnumbered and, to avoid the defeat of the *Agreement of the People,* he proposed that the matter should be transferred to a rendezvous of the whole army, where he might reasonably hope to be in a majority. At the same time he declared that it was the sense of the army that all negotiations with the king should cease. And secretly he became involved in a plan to kidnap the king from Hampton Court, where Charles was living under the protection of Fairfax and Cromwell – a plot which, revealed to Charles, caused the panic flight of the king to the Isle of Wight.

In the ten days between the end of the Putney Debates and the first part of the rendezvous of the army to decide on the *Agreement of the People,* Cromwell denounced Rainsborough's proposal as 'tending very much to anarchy' and Fairfax evolved a plan for frustrating a vote. A rendezvous of the whole army was to be held indeed – but in three different parts in three different places on three different days. And a paper had been prepared for the men repudiating Rainsborough and his party.

To the first rendezvous, near Ware, on 15 November 1647, Rainsborough's own regiment was carefully not summoned. But Rainsborough himself was there, and one or two other regiments in sympathy with him attended in spite of Fairfax's orders and marched, as if to battle, with copies of the *Agreement of the People* and the motto : 'England's Freedom ! Soldiers' Rights !' stuck in their hats. As the mutinous regiments appeared on the field, Rainsborough himself stepped up to Fairfax and presented him with a copy of the *Agreement of the People*; but Fairfax waved him aside and rode over to reprimand one of the unexpected regiments. It proved amenable, but the other was sufficiently stubborn for Cromwell to have to take sterner measures. As they refused to remove the papers from their hats, he charged them with his sword drawn, re-established discipline, and had the ringleaders arrested, tried, and one of them shot on the field. Rainsborough had lost the day.

His own regiment, which was reviewed three days later, near Kingston, gave no trouble. He had learnt, if not submission, at least a show of discretion. On the Saturday before the fiasco at Ware, he had 'laboured to impeach Cromwell of treason'; but, when the abortive rendezvous was over, it was Cromwell who let it be known that 'a speedy course must be taken for the outing of' Rainsborough 'from the House and the Army'.

But, though Rainsborough was summoned before the House to give an account of his actions, nothing violent was done. It was at this point that all Parliamentary parties saw the necessity of sinking their differences in face of the impending Royalist menace at home and abroad.

So, from the January of 1648 to the end of August, Rainsborough was occupied, first as Vice-Admiral of the Fleet, then at the siege of Colchester. And in September he emerged from the Second Civil War more powerful than ever. His fame at Colchester was but little inferior to Cromwell's at Preston. What is more, his early insistence that the king could not be trusted and that all negotiations with him were a mistake had been proved by the mere fact of the war. And when, less than a fortnight after the shooting of Lucas and Lisle, a petition to enforce the *Agreement of the People* was laid before the House, it was obvious that the military campaign against the enemy had been a mere interruption of the political warfare among the victors. The probability during those months was a Third Civil War on the subject of the *Agreement of the People* with Cromwell leading one side and Rainsborough the other.

Thus, the murder of Rainsborough, though it may have been a Royalist act of vengeance for Colchester may equally have been a political assassination by the Right wing of the Parliamentarians. At the very least, one may attribute Fairfax's move in sending Rainsborough from St Albans to Pontefract to political and not to military considerations. Cromwell was perfectly capable of dealing with Pontefract on his way to the south with a triumphant army. The dispatch of Rainsborough thither with two cavalry and two infantry regiments was directed rather to removing the dangerous colonel from proximity to London than to any necessity of siege-craft. The Lord General was repeating the tactics of 'divide and rule' which had proved so satisfactory at the rendezvous.

It is, of course, quite true that no one was taking the siege of Pontefract very seriously. The commander in charge of it was Sir Henry Cholmley, a Yorkshireman who had been appointed by the Northern Committee and whose popularity was exceeded only by the nonchalance with which he was conducting operations. A letter of the time gives an instructive picture of Cholmley's idea of a siege. The Pontefract garrison, according to the writer, 'have, since I came from London, taken at least two hundred head of cattle, above one hundred oxen, from graziers. They sound a parley for a cessation and make a fair of their horses near the Castle, sell them to Sir Henry Cholmley's troopers and in the cessation they drink to one another, "Here is to thee, Brother Roundhead!", and "I thank thee, Brother Cavalier!"'

There was no likelihood that such a garrison would be starved into surrender, since they had enough victuals for a year, cattle were being driven in in droves and the Royalists had sufficient salt to cure them, and – according to another observer – the garrison had managed, by their marauding expeditions, so to terrorize the countryside that they 'levied for many weeks together the value of £3,000 per mensem'.

In sending Rainsborough to supersede Cholmley, Fairfax, either by accident or design, had chosen the one man who was likely to provoke deadly resentment. Cholmley had no intention of relinquishing his command to anyone, least of all to the most mischievous and hated leader of the 'Left'. Nor were the Northern Committee, sitting at York, disposed to brook interference from Westminster. This was a local matter and no arguments on behalf of efficiency were to be allowed to wreak havoc on a centuries old social structure. The land-owning nobility were the leaders, their tenants were the led; the besiegers and the besieged were, after all, merely relatives with temporary political differences.

Cholmley wrote to the Speaker of the House of Commons: 'This day [apparently 17 October] Colonel Rainsborough came hither, his regiment now being at Doncaster. He brought an order from the General to command-in-chief the forces here before Pontefract. Though I am not ambitious for the honour myself, yet being by the Committee of this country chosen commander-in-chief. . . . I could not do that wrong to Sir Edward Rhodes and Colonel Maulverer, the late Governor of Hull (who are both elder colonels than Colonel Rainsborough), till I first hear that it is your pleasure to have it so. . . . When you shall command, we shall be ready to obey, though we may perhaps think it a hard recompense for our services that when we engaged in the Kingdom's and our country's greatest need we should now have one put over us that is but a bare Colonel of Foot in the army and a younger colonel than any of us.* Sir, the Kingdom being now in this posture, there may perhaps be little use for us, yet we are unwilling that another should reap the reward of our labours and, with double the force that we have had, come now and gain the prize for which we ventured our dearest blood.'

At the same time Cholmley wrote to Cromwell, asking him to come and take command. This was followed up by a similar request from the Northern Committee, and it was expected that Cromwell would arrive at Pontefract on 28 October (when, in fact, he was at Boroughbridge) to resolve the difficulty. If Cholmley was to be

---

*Rainsborough was thirty-eight. As he was also vice-admiral, the complaint would seem to have been of age, not of precedence.

superseded, it should be by the lieutenant-general himself, not by a 'bare Colonel of Foot'.

Rainsborough, at the outset, behaved with unexpected tact. He agreed that he and Cholmley should each remain in their separate and equal commands until Parliament had pronounced on the matter. But on the following day, according to a letter from the Committee at York to the Speaker, he 'hath been again with us and acquainted us that upon second thoughts he cannot conform to his last night's resolution nor go any whit lower than, according to his commission, to command-in-chief'.

It is thus obvious that Sir Henry Cholmley was not above suspicion, if not as a principal at least as an accommodating accomplice. One of the newspaper reports, which ascribed the murder to a band of Cavaliers who had managed to leave the besieged castle, did not scruple to say so. 'At the return of the party to Pontefract', it alleged, 'there was a mighty shout in the Castle and presently the Governor sent a sealed letter (which is against the law of arms) to Sir Henry Cholmley saying that 'he had now decided the controversy about the command, for his men had left Rainsborough dead in Doncaster street'; at the reading of which the base, treacherous, prefidious Cholmley very much laughed and rejoiced for a long time together, so that it is more than probable that Sir Henry was an absolute complotter in the murder from which, as they came back the same day about two o'clock in the afternoon, his guard of horse (consisting of between two and three hundred) let them quietly pass by in their sight, as their good friends, without discharging one pistol upon them or so much as molesting them.

It may be added that Sir Henry Cholmley subsequently changed sides and formed one of the deputation which visited Charles II to invite him back to England in 1660.

Rainsborough was killed by a party of horsemen about eight o'clock in the morning of Sunday, 29 October 1648. Having said this, one has said all that can be certainly affirmed. It is quite impossible to make the various versions of the murder tally in important particulars. The contemporary accounts, written and printed, were by enraged Parliamentarians, none of whom seem to have been eye-witnesses of the occurrence. They report, almost unanimously, that the murderers gained access to Rainsborough's bedroom where, in revenge for Lucas and Lisle, 'they in a sordid manner stabbed him, dragged him to the chamber door, cut his throat, turned him downstairs and escaped'. There are, however, two other accounts which, unexpectedly corroborate each other and which give a different picture. The account in *A Letter from Doncaster* and published in *The Moderate* for 31 October – 7 November 1648 says that 'Colonel Rainsborough had waited long at Doncaster in pursuance of orders received from His Excellency the Lord General Fairfax either that Sir Henry Cholmley would have submitted to the order for his commanding the siege of Pontefract or that he should receive commands to march elsewhere. The Colonel for the ease of the town (being much importuned) removed eight of his companies into the country, having left only his own and another in the town. He conceived himself safe enough with a guard constantly of three score foot, in that it was at least pretended that the Castle of Pontefract was besieged by Sir Henry Cholmley and his force and a party could not have come with safety from the Castle (in that it must come and go within sight of the besiegers' guards). However, the soldiers on guard proved basely negligent, if not treacherous.

'On the 29 of October, being Sunday, a party of forty-seven Pomfret horse, about eight o'clock in the morning, came into town by the London Road. At the main guard, being demanded by the sentinel who they were, they made answer that they came to bring a letter from Lieutenant-General Cromwell to Colonel Rainsborough. He believing, they soon secured him.

'The Captain of the Guard, instead of being at his duty, was all night at a whore-house in town* (whose husband was a main actor) and three more were found asleep. They divided their party and twenty-two of them went and beset the Colonel's lodging.

---

*The man, whose name was Smith, published his own explanation a fortnight later in Amsterdam, whither he fled. It was entitled *The Innocent Cleared*. In it he admitted that it was his duty to be on guard but that he 'was very ill, as many of the several guards can testify' and was persuaded to sit by a fire. Consequently he went to an inn called *The Hind* and did not know it was a house of evil fame. He complains that his enemies have caused 'ballads and songs to be made' about him and 'sung up and down the London streets'.

'The sentry there, having their former answer, suffered two of them to enter with their pistols in their hands. The door being left open by a maid that went out a little before, they went directly to his chamber (it being only latched), suddenly seized on him in bed, so as he had no opportunity to draw his sword or use a pistol, both of which were near him.

'They by force led him downstairs swearing "Dam-them they would pistol him if he spoke a word". Coming down into the hall, of a sudden he cast them both off from him, saying, "Now, gentlemen, what is your business?" but they straightway seized on him again, having nothing to rescue himself and there being none in the room but the maidservant of the house.

'Being brought out, they bid him horse, but he answered "he would die in that place rather than go with them" (being confident, it's thought, of rescue by his main guard). They attempted per force to have horsed him, but, he striving, they ran him through the body. He then called to his sentry to stand by him, but the man answered "he had no match". He desired them to give him a sword that he might die like a man, but one ran him through the belly. He boldly with both hands pulled the sword out of his body, bending the point almost back to the hilt, endeavouring to have forced it from him; at which they cried, "Pistol the rogue!", but that failing to go off one threw his pistol violently at him, bruised his forehead very much and made him stagger.

'Being again run through the body he fell, having before flung one of them upon the ground. They rode away from him. He got up and followed them some twelve yards, which they seeing swore "the dog was following them", and returned again upon him. With faintness he was fallen before they came back, yet they ran him some eight times through the body.

'The last words the maid of the house heard him say before he fell was that "he was betrayed, oh! he was betrayed!" in all this time not any appearing in the street either for his rescue or to revenge him, not so much as a musket shot off or an alarm by a drum, though his struggling with them was above quarter of an hour. Being got over the bridge, their last words were "Farewell, Rainsborough! Farewell, Cavaliers!"

'The Captain of the Guard is since fled.'

The other account is a Royalist one from the pen of Thomas

Paulden, the brother of William Paulden, who apparently was the architect of the enterprise. He did not publish it till 1702, fifty-four years after the event. Paulden insists that kidnapping, not murder, was the intention of the Royalists. They meant to carry Rainsborough a prisoner to the castle and hold him there as a hostage in exchange for Sir Marmaduke Langdale, who was then a prisoner in Nottingham Castle and who, they feared, was about to share the fate of Lucas and Lisle.*

According to one of Paulden's accounts, his brother William at midnight on Friday, 27 October, chose twenty-two men he could trust and, easily escaping from Pontefract Castle, rode with them to Mexborough, about four miles from Doncaster. They rested for a time and, crossing the river, halted at a hamlet, whence they sent a spy to Doncaster to ascertain that all was safe. The next morning they arrived in the town about half past seven and met a friend from the town walking with a Bible in his hand – the prearranged signal with the spy to be given if all was well. They passed the main guard by representing themselves as being from Colonel White's regiment (which was stationed at Rotherham), with letters from Cromwell to Rainsborough. They were taken to the colonel's lodging, conducted to him by his lieutenant to his room and, upon entering, gave Rainsborough a packet of blank paper. While he was opening it, they told him he was their prisoner 'but that not a hair of his head should be touched if he would go quietly with them'. They had a spare horse at the door upon which they ordered him to mount. At first he seemed willing to do so, 'but looking about him and seeing none but four of his enemies, and his lieutenant and sentinel whom they had not disarmed, standing by him, he pulled his foot out of the stirrup and cried, "Arms! Arms!"'

'Upon this one of our men letting his pistol and sword fall because he would not kill him, caught hold of him and, they grappling together, both fell down in the street. Then General Rainsborough's lieutenant,† who was on horseback, dismounts and runs him through the body, as he was cocking the pistol. Another of our men ran General Rainsborough into the neck, as he was struggling with him that had caught hold of him; yet the General

---

*Actually he escaped on 28 October, the day before Rainsborough's murder.

†William Rasine, son of George Rasine of Pontefract.

got upon his legs with our man's sword in his hand; but Captain Paulden's lieutenant ran him through the body, upon which he fell down dead.'

Thomas Paulden also wrote another account which, in some respects, is fuller than this. Here he says that the spy returned with the news that 'they were very secure and had not any alarm nor suspicion of an enemy, and acquainted us with other particulars of their guards and quarters. So by break of day the next morning we mounted and by sunrise came to the gates of the town, where there stood a sentinel who demanded whence we came. We told him "from General Cromwell's army, come upon business to Colonel Rainsborough". So he bid us "God speed us well".

'Before we came near the town we had divided our horse into four parties – six to fall upon the backs of the guards at the Bridge to make good our retreat; six to fall upon the main guard; six to ride the streets to prevent the enemies making a head; and four to Rainsborough's lodgings; and all succeeded according to our wishes.

'Both their guards were surprised and their foot all ran out at the back doors in their shirts and not any man offered to make head against us, saving Rainsborough himself, who, when he was brought down into the street and saw himself and his lieutenant and the sentinel at his door prisoners to three men and one that held their horses without any party to second them, begun to escape from them and cry. "Arms! Arms!"

'A cornet which was one of our four running after him and not willing to kill him caught him by the waistcoat; and in the struggle Rainsborough got his sword and Rainsborough's lieutenant his pistol; but Rainsborough was thrown down and one of our troopers run him through the throat with his sword whilst my brother's lieutenant ran Rainsborough's lieutenant through and killed him.

'In the meantime, Rainsborough had got upon his feet, though wounded, with a sword in his hand; and receiving another thrust through the body by my brother's lieutenant, fell down dead. This done, we threw what arms we found upon the guards into the river and marched on the road the nearest way to Pomfret and came at noon-day in the sight of all their horse into the Castle.'

It will be noticed that Paulden, in both his accounts, says that Rainsborough's lieutenant tried to defend him and was killed – which is at odds with all other accounts; and that in his later

version the interesting 'man with the Bible in his hand' has
disappeared.

There is one particularly curious circumstance to be noticed. In
all accounts, the murderers – or kidnappers – gain entry by saying
that they are bearers of letters from Cromwell. This may have
been merely intelligent assessment of the situation and a shrewd
guess as to what excuse was most likely to get entrance for them.
On the other hand, we know from other sources that Rainsborough
actually was expecting a message from Cromwell. He was staying
at the chief inn of Doncaster, on the north side of the market-
place, where, some years earlier, Charles I had lodged on one of
his visits to Scotland. At the time of the murder it belonged to a
Mr Mawood. On the Saturday Mawood asked Rainsborough
whether or not he intended to dine at home on the Sunday and
the colonel answered that 'he expected order and was uncertain'.
It is therefore at least possible that this information had been conveyed to the assassins, for the alacrity with which the guards both
at the gates and at the house admitted them suggests that visitors
were expected.

Nor, I think, can the suggestion that 'Innocent' Smith was
– to put it at its most charitable – the victim of a plot be entirely
dismissed. The statement that the husband of the lady of easy
virtue at the Hind Inn was one of the main actors in the drama
is, indeed, unsupported; but it seems a pointless thing to have
suggested if there were not some basis for the accusation.

Thirdly, what is the meaning of the curious-exclamation reported
of the fleeing murderers, 'Farewell, Rainsborough! Farewell,
Cavaliers!' The first part of it is obvious enough; but what is the
significance of the second? The party was, apparently, composed
of Cavaliers posing as Roundheads. Once free of the necessity of
disguise, they might indeed have shouted 'Farewell, Roundheads!'
If, on the other hand, they were Roundheads of the 'Right' wing,
posing as Cavaliers, the reported cry would have a comprehensible
meaning. (It could also, of course, assuming that they were indeed
Cavaliers, be merely a play on the word 'farewell' – 'Farewell,
Rainsborough! Fare well, Cavaliers!')

One must take into consideration also Rainsborough's dying words, 'I am betrayed! Oh, I am betrayed!' which surely imply more than a reflection on the mistake of his lieutenant in admitting bearers of the dispatches. Taking all these factors into consideration, it seems probable that there was some collusion within Doncaster itself – or, at least, that the assassination was not quite the straightforward matter which it would seem from Paulden's narrative which, published so long after the event, had the advantage of blurred memories and of the possibilities of reference to published accounts.

One may therefore say that Rainsborough was killed by a party of men posing as Roundheads, who gained admission to Doncaster (in the absence of the Captain of the Guard who had been lured away), on the pretext of delivering dispatches from Cromwell which Rainsborough was known to have been expecting. If these men were, in fact, Cavaliers from the besieged castle of Pontefract, both their escape from it and their return to it was due to Roundhead indifference or collusion. Politically, the murder was of distinct benefit to Cromwell, who was, the day before it, within easy reach of Doncaster and who is known, on that day, to have written a letter to the Speaker of the House of Commons on behalf of one of Cholmley's relatives.* There must also be taken into account the fact that no attempt seems to have been made to find and punish the murderers even when Pontefract at last fell; and Rainsborough's party made a bitter complaint to Parliament that 'his brother receives no furtherance but rather all discouragement that may be in searching after and prosecuting the causers of that so bloody and inhumane a butchery'.

The whole attitude of Cromwell in regard to the Pontefract siege is also one of the mysteries of the time. W. C. Abbott, in his monumental *Writings and Speeches of Oliver Cromwell,* comments that Cromwell, who arrived immediately after the murder to take charge of reducing Pontefract, 'settled down to a military operation which for length, leisureliness, and final dramatic incident had no parallel in either of the civil wars. It is indeed at this distance and

---

*The letter begins, 'I do not often trouble you in particular businesses; but I shall be bold now, upon the desire of a worthy gentleman, Lieutenant-Colonel Cholmley, to entreat your favour on his behalf.' One can say no more than that the coincidence is odd.

in the absence of detailed information difficult to understand the reasons for the whole incident of Pontefract and not least the position of Cromwell, despite the long and apologetic letter which he wrote presently to explain why the siege presented such difficulties.' And again, 'It is no unfair question why he stayed on at the siege of Pontefract when such tremendous issues (as the king's execution) were being debated at St Albans and Westminster. His presence at the siege seems to have served no good purpose, for it was not until long after he left that the place surrendered, nor is there any indication in his correspondence that he anticipated its speedy reduction nor, indeed, that the siege was pressed with great severity.'

But it was not only in regard to the siege of Pontefract that Cromwell in the weeks after Rainsborough's murder moved mysteriously. Nothing whatever is known of his movements between 25 November, when he wrote to one of his intimates an enigmatic letter which can be taken as meaning that he intended to press for the king's death, and the evening of 6 December, when he reported to Fairfax in London. On the morning of 6 December, 'Pride's Purge' had prevented all Members of Parliament who would not vote for the king's death from entering the House of Commons. As I wrote of this in *Charles and Cromwell*, 'Of all his dramatic entrances, this was the most perfectly timed. How far was he implicated? Where had he been? What did he know? To these questions which contemporaries asked, posterity has been able to give no answer.'

Though there is no possibility of establishing any proof, it now seems to me that Cromwell's actions in the seven weeks from the murder of Rainsborough to Pride's Purge are in some way inextricably connected in a purposive and not in an accidental manner.

At the time, of course, the usual official solidarity was preserved in public acts and pronouncements. As soon as the news of Rainsborough's death reached Westminster, Parliament sent instructions to Cromwell to make forthwith 'a strict and exact scrutiny of the manner of the horrible murder of Colonel Rainsborough and to certify the same to the House'. And Clarendon, in his account of the matter – the accuracy of which is suspect by his dating the murder at the end of August – says that Cromwell bound Lambert, who succeeded him as besieger of Pontefract, to exempt Rainsborough's murderers from pardon. When Lambert started negotiations for surrender he said 'that he knew "they were gallant men and he desired to preserve as many of them as was in his power to do; but he must require six of them to be given up to him, whose lives he could not save; which he was sorry for, since they were brave men; but his hands were bound". The six excepted were Colonel Morris, Sir John Digby, and four more whose names he found to have been amongst those who were in the party that had destroyed Rainsborough; which was an enterprise no brave enemy would have revenged in that manner; nor did Lambert desire it, but Cromwell had enjoined it him.'

The Pontefract garrison thereupon made two separate sallies, under cover of which four of the men escaped : 'The other two thought it to no purpose to make another attempt, but devised another way to secure themselves, with a less dangerous assistance from their friends, who had lost some of their own lives in the two former sallies to save theirs. The buildings of the castle were very large and spacious and there were great store of waste stones from some walls, which were fallen down. They found a convenient place, which was like to be least visited, where they walled up their two friends in such a manner that they had air to sustain them, and victual enough to feed them for a month, in which time they hoped they might be able to escape.

'And this being done, at the hour appointed they opened their ports, and after Lambert had caused a strict inquisition to be made for those six (none of which he did believe had in truth escaped) and was satisfied that none of them were amongst those who were come out, he received the rest very civilly and observed his promise made to them very punctually and did not seem sorry that the six gallant men (as he called them) were escaped.'

If this account be at all accurate, the interesting point is that Cromwell knew certainly who the six were. According to a manuscript written by the antiquary, Dr Nathaniel Johnston (who was twenty-two at the time of the murder and got his information from the woman later in charge of the house where Rainsborough lodged), the five in addition to Colonel Morris were 'Cornet Blackburn' and Marmaduke Greenfield, who were the two who entered Rainsborough's bedroom. Finding him asleep they woke him and asked if he wished for quarter. He yielded, but afterwards resisted and Greenfield wounded him in the thigh. Then came Alan Austwick, Sir Charles Dallison, and Mr Saltonsal, 'and they slew him with several wounds'.

This account, of course, does not agree with Paulden's; nor does it suggest that Rainsborough was killed in the street, though it is not directly incompatible with that theory.

The more important fact is that they all escaped and were, by the Parliamentary general, referred to – if Clarendon is to be believed – as 'gallant men'. The cry of the extremists was unanswered, 'Can the soldiery of this kingdom be silent and not revenge this barbarous murder of their incomparable commander? The Lord stir up your hearts to be avenged of these bloody enemies!' The enemies, secret or open, were too powerful.

But the public ceremony was satisfactory. Rainsborough's body was brought home to his family house at Wapping, where it was accompanied to the grave by 'fifty odd coaches' and 'near 1,500 horse' and his chaplain preached a sermon, subsequently published as *The Glorious Day of the Saints,* 'I think he was one of whom this sinful nation was not worthy; he was one of whom this declining Parliament was not worthy; he was one of whom these divided, formal, carnal Gospellers was not worthy. He served his generation faithfully. Though he died by the hands of treachery, I am fully satisfied, with many more, that he is now triumphing in glory and it will be but a day before he shall see his enemies stand at the bar.'

CHAPTER 13

The Executioner of King Charles I
30 January 1649

ON Tuesday, 30 January 1649, a bitterly cold day even for winter, with the Thames frozen over and a grey sky threatening snow, King Charles I was executed on a scaffold outside the Banqueting House in Whitehall – 'at his own front door barbarously murdered.' He was kept waiting for death for four hours, from ten o'clock till two. This, however, was not intentional cruelty on the part of his enemies; it was because no executioner could be found. And the secret of the identity of the two who eventually volunteered as headsman and assistant was so well kept that it is a mystery still.

Both men were dressed alike in close-fitting woollen frocks, like those worn by butchers or sailors, with frieze trunk breeches. Their faces were impenetrably masked by large vizards and the disguise was completed by wigs and false beards. The executioner's wig, 'a grey grizzled periwig', hung very low : his assistant had a black wig and beard and affected a large flapped black hat, looped up in front.

Early that morning Colonel Daniel Axtell had sent his brother, Elisha, with a guard of soldiers to Wapping to escort the common hangman, Brandon, with his tackle, to Whitehall; but there seems little doubt that when he got there, Brandon, despite bribes and threats, refused to do the deed. He was put under arrest at Whitehall until the execution was over and immediately afterwards sent home with five pounds in half-crowns as compensation.

A waterman named Abraham Smith narrated that 'as soon as that fatal blow was given' he was walking about Whitehall when a file of musketeers in charge of Brandon asked him where the official bargemen were. As there were none to be seen, they directed Brandon into Smith's boat.

'Going into the boat,' said Smith, 'he gave one of the soldiers a half-crown. Said the soldiers : "Waterman, away with him,

Begone quickly"; but I, fearing the hangman had cut off the King's head, I trembled that he should come into my boat, but dared not examine him on shore for fear of the soldiers; so out I launched and having got a little way in the water, said I : "Who the devil have I got in my boat?"

'Says my fellow, says he : "Why?"

'I directed my speech to him saying : "Are you the hangman that cut off the King's head?"

' "No, as I am a sinner to God," saith he, "not I." He shook every joint of him. I knew not what to do. I rowed away a little further and fell to a new examination of him when I had got him a little further. "Tell me true," said I, "are you the hangman that cut off the King's head? I cannot carry you," said I.

' "No," saith he, "I was fetched with a troop of horse and I was kept a close prisoner at Whitehall, and truly I did not do it. I was kept a close prisoner all the while, but they had my instruments."

'I said I would sink the boat if he did not tell me true; but he denied it with several protestations.'

Less than six months after the execution Brandon died. In 1680, over thirty years later, Dr Thomas Tenison became Rector of St Martin's-in-the-Fields and his chaplain has left on record that, during his incumbency, he was sent for to pray by a dying man in a poor house in Gardner's Lane, Westminster. 'He made haste but found the man just expired. The people of the house told him that the man (whose name they never knew) had been very anxious to see him and to confess to him that he was the executioner of King Charles; that he was a trooper of Oliver's and, every man in the troop having refused to do that office, Oliver made them draw lots and, the lot falling upon him, he did the work in a mask, and that he immediately mixed in the crowd, hiding the mask; that he had never been easy in mind since. He had lived some time in their house, was poor and melancholy and much distressed for want of consolation from Dr Tenison.' If this story be true, it is, of course, conclusive evidence against the possibility of Brandon being the executioner. Yet, since the majority of historians, following S. R. Gardiner, incline to the belief that Brandon was the headsman, one more piece of evidence may be adduced.

In the 19–26 June 1649 issue of *The Kingdom's Weekly Intelli-*

gencer, under the date of Saturday, 23 June occurs the following :

On Wednesday last, the hangman departed this life and on the Sunday before, a young man, a friend of his, coming to visit him asked him whether he was not troubled in conscience for cutting off the King's head. He replied, Yes, by reason that upon the time of his trial and at the denouncing of sentence against him, he had taken a vow and protestation wishing God to perish his body and soul if ever he appeared on the scaffold to do the act, or lift up his hand against him; further acknowledging that he was no sooner entered upon the scaffold but immediately he fell a-trembling and hath ever since continued in the same.

He likewise confessed that he had £30 for his pains all paid him in half-crowns within an hour after the blow was given, which money he gave his wife at six o'clock that night and told her that it was the dearest money ever he earned in his life. He was very much disturbed in his sickness and lay raging and swearing and still pointing at one thing or another, which he conceived was visible before him.

A little before the death of the aforesaid Richard Brandon he, being in some discourse with a neighbour touching the executing of the King, said that even at the very point of time when he was to give the blow a great pain and ache took him about the neck and hath since continued; and that he never slept quietly in his mind, saying that he was afraid to walk along the streets or go to his bed and sleep without a candle burning.

The other fellow that was upon the scaffold, that went in the name of his man, was one Ralph Jones a ragman, who liveth in Rosemary Lane. And he who now takes his place as executioner is one William Loe, a dust carrier and cleaner of dunghills.

This account was taken word for word from a pamphlet entitled *The Confession of Richard Brandon,* a pseudo-Royalist satire, which was put about by the Cromwellian government so that, by fixing the crime on a dead man, they could divert suspicion from the real executioners. Such a purpose was admitted. The publication was 'to the end that the world may be convinced of those calumnious speeches and erroneous suggestions which are daily

spit from the mouth of Envy against divers persons of great worth
and eminency by casting an odium upon them for the executing
of the King; it being now made manifest that the aforesaid
executioner was the only man that gave that fatal blow and the
man that waited upon him was a rag-man living in Rosemary
Lane.'

What, therefore, might have been taken – indeed, has been
taken – as evidence that Brandon was the executioner turns out to
be, when all the circumstances are considered, even stronger evidence that he was not. The newspaper item and the pamphlet from
which it was copied prove only, if they can be held to prove anything, that the authorities were exceedingly anxious to conceal the
real identities of the men on the scaffold.

Finally, there is the significant fact that when, in 1660, William
Hulet was on trial on the charge of being the executioner, though
his defence was that the dead Brandon was the real culprit, he
dared not call as a witness the hangman's widow, Mary Brandon,
although he had originally announced his intention of doing so.

Dismissing Brandon, despite S. R. Gardiner and Sir Sidney Lee
(who in the article in the *Dictionary of National Biography* describes Brandon quite simply as 'the executioner of Charles I'), we
must next examine the credentials of this William Hulet who was
tried on the charge and found guilty – though not, as far as any
record exists, executed – at the Restoration.

Hulet's own story was that he was a sergeant in Colonel
Hewson's troop which was on duty in Whitehall on the day of
execution; that he, with six or eight other sergeants from various
regiments had in the morning been called together, sworn to
secrecy and asked to volunteer as executioner; that he had refused
and, because of it, had been kept a close prisoner in Whitehall till
ten o'clock at night.

The name of Hulet as a suspect was first mentioned during the
trial of Colonel Daniel Axtell who must have known the identity
of the executioners. During the Commonweath, Axtell had been
promoted, sent to Ireland and eventually appointed Governor of
Kilkenny. When, after the Restoration, he was indicted, one of the
witnesses was Lieutenant-Colonel John Nelson, second-in-command
of another regiment in Ireland.

'My Lords and gentlemen of the jury,' said Nelson, 'upon a

discourse with the prisoner at the bar in Dublin five or six years since' (that is, in 1654 or 1655), 'upon the platform of that Castle, I desired to know of him who it was executed the King, thinking he might inform me. He was pleased to tell me this.

'Saith he : "The persons who were employed in that service, you know as well as I do."

' "Not I", said I. "I saw them in vizards but not their visage, as I know of."

' "Yes." saith he, "you do know them. It is true myself and others were employed in that affair in the ordering of the execution; but there were several persons came and offered themselves out of a kind of zeal to do the thing, but we did not think it proper to employ persons we did not know; but we made choice of a couple of stout persons."

' "Pray let me hear their names", said I.

'Said he : "It was Hulet and Walker." '

Axtell interrupted the witness : 'You named one man : I did not hear the other.'

'I named Hulet and Walker', said Nelson, loudly.

'Was anybody by?' asked Axtell.

'No, sir', Nelson admitted.

'Did I name anybody to you?'

'You named those two persons.'

'Certainly I must have invented them, then,' retorted Axtell, 'for I had no more knowledge of them than anybody here.'

'You told me', said Nelson, 'that you were one of those who had the managing of the affair.'

The last remark is important in assessing Axtell's denial; for the reason the executioners were mentioned at all in his trial was merely to establish that, since he knew who they were, he must *ipso facto* have been one of the colonels in charge of the final arrangements. As this fact was unchallenged, the matter of the executioners, as such, was irrelevant and Axtell's point in denying knowledge of the men's names was merely to avoid convicting himself out of his own mouth. So well was this understood that, when Hulet himself was brought to trial later the same day, Axtell, in spite of being asked, did not give evidence.

At Hulet's trial, Nelson repeated his evidence, with the additional information that Hulet was the assistant and Walker the headsman. He also asked that Colonel Pretty, then in Ireland, should be sent for to corroborate the evidence, for, though he refused to swear positively, his recollection was that Pretty also had named Hulet.

The first witness against Hulet was Richard Gittens, who claimed to have been a fellow sergeant with him in the same company for about thirteen years. Gittens said: 'A day or two before the King came to the scaffold, Colonel Hewson did give notice to the lieutenant that we should come to him, about thirty-eight of us, and he put us all to our oaths that we should say nothing of what they did. He swore us to the Book. After he had sworn us, he asked us if we would undertake to do such an act. If we would, we should have a hundred pounds down and preferment in the Army. We refused, every person. We thought Hulet did refuse. After all refused, it seems he did undertake to do the deed.

'When the King was brought on the scaffold, we were in Scotland Yard and they were upon the guard in the Banqueting Chamber. When they were there I laid down my arms and got into the Company. Captain Webb kept the guard with his halberd in his hand by the scaffold and I did bustle to come near to them. Then I returned back. Hulet, (as far as I can guess), when the King came on the scaffold for his execution and said: "Executioner, is the block fast?" fell upon his knees to ask him forgiveness. By his speech, I thought it was he.

'Captain Atkins said: "Who would not undertake to do this act?"

'I told him I would not do it for all the city of London.

' "No, nor I either, for all the world", saith Atkins. "You shall see Hulet quickly come to preferment." And immediately after he was made Captain-Lieutenant.'

'Was Hulet with his regiment that day?' asked the counsel.

'We could not see him with the regiment all that day', replied Gittens. 'He was never absent at any time before.'

'Did you know his voice?'

'Yes, sir.'

'Did you mark the proportion of his body, or his habit – what disguise he was in?'

'He had a pair of frieze trunk breeches', said Gittens, 'and a vizard, with a grey beard; and after that time Colonel Hewson called him "Father Greybeard" and most of the army besides. He cannot deny it.'

Hulet, however, denied everything. He denied that he and Gittens were sergeants in the same company; he denied that he was ever called 'Greybeard' and he denied that Gittens had been in a position to hear any voice on the scaffold. The questioning was swift.

'Where were you at the time when the act was done?' asked Hulet.

'Where was I?' said Gittens. 'By Captain Webb.'

'Where was he?'

'At the door of the Banqueting House.'

'Was you on the scaffold or no, sir?'

'I was on the scaffold end.'

'My Lord', said Hulet to the judge, 'I desire you to consider what this person says. He was on guard in Scotland Yard and at the scaffold with Captain Webb!'

The topographical divergence, however impressive as a debating point, is by no means conclusive. What Gittens had said, it will be remembered, was that he was in Scotland Yard, went to the scaffold at the time of the execution and returned. At that time Scotland Yard was one of the three courts of Whitehall Palace and contained the Guardroom; and the end of the the scaffold was at a little building annexed to the Banqueting House on the north side. Anyone today, merely by walking from Old Scotland Yard to the entrance of the United Services Museum, can make the experiment of timing how long it would have taken Gittens (who, as he was in Scotland Yard, was presumably in reserve, not on duty) to get from the one place to the other. Five minutes leaves a comfortable margin for going there and back at a walking pace.

As for Hulet's denial that he and Gittens were in the same regiment, it may be true that, *on that day,* they were separated; but Hulet made no attempt to answer the charge that they had been fellow-sergeants for thirteen years (which could have been checked), in which case Gittens's identification of a well-known voice in the profound silence which fell on the crowd when the king came on the scaffold would have been easy enough.

Later evidence against Hulet from Captain Toogood was more damning. 'I was in 1650, about September, in Dublin Castle about some business with Colonel Hewson', he said. 'Captain Hulet came into the room and talked with Colonel Hewson a little while. I observed them very familiar and I asked Hewson what he was. He told me he was his Captain-Lieutenant of horse. I desired to know where he had got him. He said he had made him so from a sergeant and a very mettled fellow he was. It was he that did the King's business for him upon the scaffold.

'In 1653,' continued Captain Toogood, 'there was a disbanding of the army in Ireland. This gentleman was then continued Captain-Lieutenant in Pretty's regiment. I discoursed with Pretty concerning him and one part of it, I remember, was about the King's death; and he did tell me that he was assured by Colonel Hewson that Hulet either cut off the King's head or held it up . . .

'About twelve months after, I came to live near the prisoner in Ireland. Once I remember at one Mr Smith's, at the White Horse in Carlow I met him there and I asked him whether he was the man who cut off the King's head or no.

'Saith he : "Why do you ask me this question?"

'I told him I had heard so by Hewson and Pretty. Upon that he said : "Well, what I did I will not be ashamed of. If it were to do again, I would do it."

'Once since that time, about half a year afterwards, I was in the same place and there talking with him about the King's death. He was telling me it was true he was one of the two persons who were disguised upon the scaffold. I desired to know what if the King had refused to submit to the block.

'Saith he : "There were staples about the scaffold and I had that about me that would have compelled me" – or words to that effect. . . . I have observed in Ireland that it hath been generally reported that he was either the man that cut off the King's head, or that held it up; as I have said before. And I have heard them sometimes call him "Grandsire Greybeard".'

There was further evidence on both sides, but none of it satisfactory. The story told by a soldier that, in a tavern over several pints of wine, Hulet though not admitting that he did it, yet justified the execution was cancelled out by a 'stranger'*

*So entered in the report of the trial; there is no clue to his identity.

Hulet called to testify on his behalf who did not take the oath and merely reported : 'I was with my master in the company of Brandon the hangman and my master asked Brandon whether he cut off the King's head or no. He confessed in my presence that he was the man that did cut off the King's head.' The evidence of a spectator in the crowd that the executioner was of the same build as Hulet was hardly more valid than the uncorroborated affirmation of another that he once heard Brandon confess to the act. But the fatal weakness of Hulet's case was that he dared not call Mary Brandon, because she had already given evidence on oath before the Lord Mayor which ran counter to that of the witnesses for the defence.

In the evidence of a soldier named Stammers and Hulet's questioning of him, the possibilities are nicely balanced.

Stammers identified Hulet as Captain-Lieutenant of Colonel Hewson's troop in which Stammers served in Ireland. . . . 'When I had entered myself into that troop,' said the witness, 'I was a while in Dublin and I was commanded by the prisoner at the bar, I and the rest, to march to a place named Lutterel's-town, about five miles beyond Dublin. The prisoner at the bar came thither to us two days after. Then, being in his chamber, he sent for me. I went up and sat down. He examined where I had served. I told him I did formerly belong to the Lord of Inchiquin. He asked if I was ever in the King's army.* With that he walks about the room two or three turns. Saith he : "I was the man that beheaded King Charles and for doing it I had a hundred pounds," saying, "I was a sergeant at that time." '

'I desire to ask him a question', said Hulet, 'I confess – what is your name?'

'Stammers', said the counsel. 'His name is Stammers.'

---

*Murrough O'Brien, first Earl of Inchiquin, President of Munster, was a Royalist who temporarily submitted to Parliament because they had command of the seas and therefore controlled the supplies Inchiquin needed for the people of Munster. As soon as he had got the supplies, he gradually made himself master of the south of Ireland; fortified the southern ports against Parliament and openly declared for Charles I once more in 1648. After the king's execution, he fought against Cromwell as long as he could and in 1650 crossed to France. Hulet's question to Stammers is thus quite a natural one, and may, indeed, be taken as confirming the authenticity of the conversation.

'Such a one was under my command', said Hulet. Then, turning to the witness, he said : 'I think I have not seen you these eight years. I desire to know when these words were spoken and the place.'

'In Lutterel's-town in your own chamber, nine or ten years ago.'

'It is about eight years since I left that command', said Hulet. 'Who was by at the time?'

'Nobody.'

''Tis strange. How long had you been in the troop before?'

'I was in Dublin about a fortnight', said Stammers. 'Then you sent for me and I came to Lutterel's-town. The first time that I came to the troop was at Dublin and then you came to me with two orders from Hewson; and then you did pretend you were the brother of one, Mr Chambers; and then we went and quartered in Lutterel's-town.'

'My Lord,' protested Hulet to the judge, 'his examination in Ireland and this doth not agree. You did deny this before Baldwin, a trooper. I desire his examination may be read.'

That examination was therefore read, and, according to the note in the report of the trial, 'agreed with the testimony now given'.

'I desire that he may mention what man that was that I sent for him', said Hulet.

'I cannot tell what man', said Stammers.

'My Lord, I desire that servant may be either named or produced.'

'I cannot remember the man', said Stammers. 'It was seven years ago.'

Hulet's version of the matter was that, at a tavern in Gorran, between Cullen and Munster, he and others were drinking, when the discussion turned on the execution of the king.

'Saith Stammers : "I did hear that you were one of the persons for that purpose."

'Said I : "They that say so do me wrong."

'Saith he : "It is no matter if you were so, for it was a just act."

'Said I : "Whether it was or no, I have nothing to do to justify it."

'He said : "As I hope to be saved, I would have done it." ' '

Between accusation and counter-accusation, the reader may judge, but it seems to me that, taking into consideration not only this but the rest of the evidence, the balance tips against Hulet. And the jury who listened to it all, 'after a more than ordinary time of consultation' decided in that sense. He was pronounced 'Guilty'. On the other hand, as no record of his execution exists, it may have been felt that the identification was not altogether conclusive.

About ten weeks after the trial, two petitions from him and a letter to the Speaker were reported to the House of Commons. Nothing further is known. Hulet slips unnoticed out of history. But he could have been the man who died twenty or so years later, asking for the Rector of St Martin's in-the-Fields to come and ease his conscience.

If Hulet was the headsman, who was the assistant? It will be remembered that Lieutenant-Colonel John Nelson, who first mentioned Hulet's name in the trials, said that Colonel Daniel Axtell named the second man as Walker. Henry Walker was the most famous and popular journalist of the time. Originally an apprentice to an ironmonger in the City, he went to Cambridge in 1639; was ordained, and was almost immediately suspended for his fanatical views. On the eve of the Civil War, he was imprisoned for writing scurrilous but lively libels under the names of Members of Parliament. He then tried to sell himself to the Court by publishing an apostrophe to the king.

> *. . . Charles, all Europe's splendour,*
> *Thine enemies' terror and true faith's defender*

in which he prayed :

> *That God which graced thee with a Royal Crown,*
> *Crown thee with grace, thy honours with renown!*

Finding no answering enthusiasm from the palace, he joined in the Parliamentary army, and, a deadly enemy of the king, became the intimate friend of Cromwell, Hugh Peters and William Hewson. When the war was over, he set up in journalism and edited *Perfect Occurrences,* which became the official newspaper of the Army and the mouthpiece of Cromwell.

A week after the king's execution, Walker was concerned to deny in his paper the rumour that the executioner was a certain Colonel Fox and later he dealt with another *canard* on the subject : 'Some have lately laid an imputation on Captain Edward Frodsham that he was the King's headsman. But the contrary is attested by those in whose company he was. And, indeed, the report is ridiculous.' It is significant, also, that *Perfect Occurrences* made no reference to Brandon's death or suggested that he had been the executioner.

Henry Walker by his position and his contacts with the managers of the execution, also certainly knew who the mysterious men were, though there is no reason to suppose that either he himself or his brother William* was one of them. The name of Walker appears only in Lieutenant-Colonel Nelson's evidence and was neither repeated nor in any way followed up. It is possible that an incident in his career as a professional journalist explains the mention of him.

In the first few months after the execution of the king, Parliament's official astrologer, William Lilly, and Cromwell's secretary, Robert Spavin, collaborated in the lucrative side-line of supplying forged passports to Royalists, some of which they managed to sell for as much as £50 apiece. The passports were all under Cromwell's hand and seal, obligingly supplied by Spavin, and they were distributed by Lilly whose eminence in fortune-telling had given him an immense clientele. When the matter eventually came to Comwell's knowledge, he sent a full account of it to Henry Walker with the curt note : 'Mr Walker. Print this verbatim in your *Occurrences* for satisfying people how they and the Army have been abused.' Walker duly printed it (in June, 1649) and this exposure may account for the rumour that he was the executioner. Between 1649 and 1660 there was ample time for a slander-campaign; and neither Spavin nor Lilly was scrupulous in denigration.

Lilly, however, left on record in print a curious story implicating

*William Walker was secretary to Major-General Lambert, a mathematician, the recipient, in 1681, of the honorary freedom of the Cutlers Company of Hallamshire (which suggests that the apprenticeship of Henry to an ironmonger was of the nature of a son going into the family business and would explain his subsequent appearance at Cambridge), was left undisturbed at the Restoration and was honourably buried in the parish church of Sheffield.

another man, equally unlikely the 'Cornet Joyce' who is known in popular history for his forcible abduction of Charles I from the Parliamentarians at Holmby House.

'The next Sunday but one after Charles I was beheaded,' wrote Lilly, 'Robert Spavin, secretary to Lieutenant-General Cromwell, invited himself to dine with me and brought several others along with him. Their discourse all the dinner time was only who it was that beheaded the King. One said it was the common hangman; another, Hugh Peters; others also were nominated but none concluded.

'Robert Spavin, so soon as dinner was done, took me by the hand and led me to the south window. Saith he : "These are all mistaken. They have not named the man who did the act. It was Lieutenant-Colonel Joyce. I was in the room when he fitted himself up for the work; stood behind him when he did it; when done, went in again with him. There is no man knows this but my master Cromwell, Commissary Ireton and myself." '

Quite apart from the intrinsic improbability of Joyce being the executioner or of Spavin standing behind him on the scaffold, no one is likely to credit any story told by William Lilly which has no independent confirmation. In this case, the business relationship of Spavin and Lilly makes it doubly untrustworthy; and the fact that Joyce was shortly afterwards cashiered and imprisoned for his opposition to Cromwell supplies a motive for Spavin's attempt to slander him.

In considering the identity of the assistant, we have some small clues which are absent in the case of the executioner. One is the man's behaviour; another is his dress. When he held up the head of the king and everyone was waiting for the conventional shout : 'Behold the head of a traitor', he said nothing at all. If any were disposed to think that this strange silence betokened sympathy with the victim, they were rapidly disabused by another solecism. He threw the head down on the scaffold with such force that the still-warm cheek was bruised. And in his dress he had, as we have noticed, a certain panache – a black hat 'cocked up,' not the unobtrusive cap of the executioner.

From such slender evidence it would, indeed, be impossible to draw any valid conclusions were it not that they all fit one who has persistently then and since been suspected – Cromwell's trusted

Army Chaplain, Hugh Peters. He was the one man whose voice everyone would know – which would account for his silence. He was particularly venomous in his sadistic hatred of the king and had, on the morning of the execution, suggested – and superintended – addition to the scaffold of four staples to which hooks and pulleys were attached to drag the king like a beast to slaughter should the executioners think it necessary. And his florid exhibitionism which made him a power in the pulpit, was such that, in the days when Charles was a prisoner, he would ride in a coach before him with his own attendant escort.

The character of Peters in relation to the king may be epitomized in the incident of the sermon he tried to preach to him on the eve of his death. The text he had chosen was 'All the Kings of the nations, even all of them, lie in glory, every one in his own house. But thou art cast out of thy grave like an abominable branch, and as the raiment of those that are slain, thrust through with the sword, that go down to the stones of the pit as a carcass trodden under foot.' 'This I did intend to insist and preach upon before the poor wretch', said Peters, 'and the poor wretch would not hear me.'

Burnet's description of Peters as 'a sort of enthusiastic buffoon (though a very vicious man) that had been of great use to Cromwell and had been outrageous in pressing the King's death with the cruelty and rudeness of an inquisitor', expresses the general judgment of the times, and is borne out by what is known of him. It was indeed his ordinary reputation that made him, at the time, an obvious suspect.

From the trials of the regicides, two points about Peters emerge. He was seen both before and after the execution. Richard Nunnelly, the door-keeper of the Committee for the Army, who went in with Cromwell to Whitehall after the morning session of the Commissioners at Westminster, saw and spoke to Peters in the Banqueting House as he was making the final arrangements for the scaffold. When the execution was over, he saw him again. 'I saw the vizards going into a chamber there,' Nunnelly said; 'about an hour afterwards there comes Hugh Peters in his black cloak and broad hat out of that chamber, (as I take it) with the hangman.'

There is nothing suspicious about these movements of Peters. On the contrary, they were, it might be argued, the natural things for him to do. It might be expected that he would examine the staples which, at his suggestion, had been driven into the scaffold; and it was equally probable that he, in common with others of the Army, would be in conversation with the headsman and with Brandon, after the need was done. Nor was there any reason why he should not acknowledge them. His actions on the day of execution itself would, in view of his known attitude to the king and his proved part in bringing him to trial and death, have no effect on the inevitable sentence to be passed on him. He was not on trial, as Hulet had been, for being an actual participant in the execution.

It is when we find him desperately trying to establish an alibi and denying that he was at Whitehall at all on the day of the execution that our suspicions are aroused. To prove that he was not there was obviously important to him; but, in trying to prove it and failing, he went far to confirm the suspicion that he was not only there, but there in an important capacity.

The witness on whom he relied was his servant, Cornelius Glover, who, alone of all the witnesses, did not take the oath. Glover was twenty-one at the time of the execution and just 'up from the country.' As his personality emerges clearly from the report, it is worth giving the evidence in full.

The Lord Chief Baron started the questioning : 'Where do you dwell?'

'In Paul's Churchyard,' said Glover.

'What is your quality of life?'

Peters answered for him : 'A servant of the King's.'

'I am not asking you, Mr Peters', said the judge.

'I belong to the Post House', said Glover.

'Pray hear him speak', Peters urged.

'What would you have him asked?'

'When I was out of my bedchamber that day the King suffered.'

'What do you say to that?' said Lord Chief Baron.

'I was come to Mr Peters a little before that time to live with him as his servant', said Glover. 'It fell out on that day he was ill in his chamber. The soldiers in St James's House were all gone away. I had a desire to go to see the meeting where they were at Whitehall. Saith he : "Thou seemest to have a great desire to go and look about thee. It is very sad, but if you will go, you may." I did go over the Park.'

'What time?' asked the counsel.

'About noon.'

'What hour?'

'I do not know. I did not stay there. The soldiers and the people filled the place and I went back again to the chamber. I came back again within the matter of an hour's time.'

'Was the King dead before you came back?'

'They said he was not. When I went home he asked me what was doing. I told him there was a great crowd I could not come near. I stayed there an hour and then I went out again and still there was a crowd and I came back again and Mr Peters was in his chamber then.'

'Was he in bed or up?'

'I do not remember.'

'How old were you then?'

'I am not above thirty-two or thirty-three.'

'Was Mr Peters sick?'

'Yes, he was melancholy sick as he used to be.'

That ended the cross-examination. Everything depended on the truth of Glover's assertion that he returned to Peters (who had apartments in St James's Palace) and then went out again. The king was executed at two o'clock. The headsman and his assistant were not found finally till about one o'clock. Peters was seen by Nunnelly leaving Whitehall 'about an hour' after the death of the king. Thus allowing a quarter of an hour to walk across the park from the garden of St James's to the Banqueting House, Peters could have left his apartments at quarter to one and been back at quarter past three. This is to take the reckoning at its longest, for the time between the finding of the executions and the execution could have been less than an hour.

This time is fixed by the fact that, once the two men had been procured, the warrant empowering them to act was signed by Colonel Hacker, after some discussion in Ireton's room in Whitehall, and then 'immediately' after the king was led to the scaffold. It could, therefore, have been as late as half-past one. And, at the other end of the period, if Peters did in fact come out of the room with Brandon and if the waterman's independent evidence of Brandon's coming to his boat 'as soon as the fatal blow was struck' be correct, Nunnelly's 'about an hour' would be nearer half an hour, at the outside. Thus the crucial time for Peters's alibi is from 1.15 to 2.30. And it is precisely this time which is covered by his servant's aimless return. According to his own account, Glover got back about one o'clock and stayed with Peters till two o'clock. The story seems a little too good to be true.

After the counsel had finished with Glover, the Lord Chief Baron asked him : 'Did you desire to go out or did he send you?' which seems a reasonably clear indication that the mind of the Bench was working on these lines.

'I did desire to go', said Glover, 'being newly come to London.'

'This gentleman', said the judge to the jury, 'though not upon oath is examined and it is only to one particular, nothing at all to the main proofs.'

It was at that point that Peters revealed his motive. 'I bring him only', he said, 'to vindicate myself from the aspersion of being on the scaffold.'

'They did not lay the weight of their evidence on that', the Lord Chief Baron reminded him. And, indeed, except in Peters's own mind, it had nothing to do with the charges against him in which it was not even mentioned. What he was accused of was 'compassing and imagining the death of the King' and, in particular, as the Solicitor-General put it, that 'there are five places where he did consult about the King's death – at Windsor, at Ware, in Coleman Street, in the Painted Chamber and in Bradshaw's house and four witnesses to prove this; there are two witnesses to his comparison of the King to Barabbas . . . proof that he called the day of His Majesty's trial a glorious day, resembling the judging of the world by the saints. He prays for this (the King's death) in the Painted Chamber, preaches for it at Whitehall, St James's Chapel, St Sepulchre's. What man could more contrive the death of the King than this miserable priest hath done?'

But what he was anxious to defend himself against was 'the aspersion of being on the scaffold'. And, in trying to extricate himself by Glover from the charge which was never formally made in Court, he was (or so it seems to me) finally confirmed for posterity the suspicion that he was Hulet's assistant, who dared not let his voice be heard and who threw down the severed head of the king with wanton violence.

CHAPTER 14

The Campden Wonder
16 August 1660

IT MAY SEEM a far cry from the high politics of James I's court in 1616 to the disappearance of an old steward from the Gloucestershire village of Chipping Campden in 1660; nor is there necessarily any connection between the Overbury murder and the 'Campden Wonder'. Yet the two cases are linked by at least one man – the disappearing steward – and one family, the Overburys. The steward, William Harrison, had been the servant of Sir Baptist Hicks, who had lent his London house on Campden Hill (named after his Gloucestershire property) to the Somersets for their honeymoon; and as at that time Harrison was thirty-two he would certainly have known them well. And the local magistrate in Gloucestershire who authorized the arrest, in 1660, of the supposed murderers of William Harrison was Sir Thomas Overbury, the nephew and heir of the Sir Thomas Overbury poisoned in the Tower.

These connecting strands *may* be of no relevance to the solution of the baffling Campden Wonder, but it is essential that they be known to the investigator. In my fictional reconstruction, *The Silver Bowl*, I made them the essence of the answer, and though that answer is imaginary there is nothing in it that is impossible. Whatever the true solution, the problem is not truly stated without making allowance for the background. The Campden Wonder is anything but a little village tragedy.

Campden House was a monument to the self-glorification of Baptist Hicks, a mercer and money-lender born in the reign of Edward VI who died, at the age of seventy-eight, in the reign of Charles I. His life spanned a social and economic revolution and his career illustrated how money could be made in it. He started quietly enough in the reign of Elizabeth in a house in Old Jewry and a shop at the sign of the White Bear in Cheapside. He built up a good business with the City Fathers, and when his elder brother, Michael, became secretary to the Cecils – first to the elder, then to the younger – he found he had the entrée to Court circles. As long as Elizabeth was queen, he used it discreetly and confined himself to dealing with courtiers, to whom both the Hickses lent money (Fulke Greville and Francis Bacon were two who are known to have got into their clutches) : but when James and his horde of penniless Scots came over the Border, Baptist Hicks saw his chance. He started by giving the king the best silks he had, lending him £16,000 and accepting a knighthood. Then he proceeded in a similar way with the Court – the secrets of which, financial and otherwise, he knew from his brother (who died in 1612, the same year as Robert Cecil), so that he was able to lend at exorbitant prices and put the screw on at the right moment.

His weath was fabulous. In Kensington he built a great house on Campden Hill; in Clerkenwell a Session House, which he called Hicks Hall, and near it, for the people, an inn which he named *The Baptist's Head*. He showed his power over official circles by defying the law that no knight could keep a shop, by continuing at the White Bear after his knighthood and forcing a legal decision in his favour. He became a Member of Parliament and bought a peerage, calling himself Viscount Campden after the Gloucester-shire estate which he was said to have 'won' from its owner.

There, at Chipping Campden, he spent £30,000 (in the currency of the time) on a great Italianate house – a three-storeyed mansion with a glass dome, in which a light always showed at night for travellers lost on the wolds; two banqueting houses, connected by an underground passage running beneath the Terrace Walk; the various outbuildings, lodges, stables, laundry, and at the gates almhouses for his pensioners.

Sixteen years after his death – during the Civil War in 1645 – the house was destroyed. It was garrisoned for the king under the command of Sir Henry Bard, a friend of the Campden family. So rapacious were his soldiers that the inhabitants of the hamlets round about complained that 'they had not even a shift of Sunday cloathes left'; and complaints were made which eventually reached the king. As, in 1645, the king was marching north, he ordered Bard to join him. Bard had his revenge for the complaint. As Clarendon put it, 'His Majesty marched to Evesham and in his way

The Campden Wonder 213

drew out his garrison from Campden House; which had brought no other benefit to the public than the enriching the licentious governor thereof; who exercised an illimited tyranny over the whole country and took his leave of it in wantonly burning the noble structure he had too long inhabited.'

After Baptist Hicks's death, the property had passed to his daughter Juliana, who went to live with her son, the third Viscount Campden, in Rutlandshire. On the eve of the Restoration, in 1660, she was still there; but the old steward, William Harrison, with his family, stayed on in the ruins of Campden House living in what had once been the stables, administering the estate, and collecting the rents, which he duly forwarded to Lady Juliana.

William Harrison's wife, with whom he was on bad terms, was a Gloucestershire woman of Cromwellian sympathies – she is described as 'a snotty, covetous Presbyterian' – whom he suspected of being in touch with the Roundheads, for which reason he had on several occasions 'hidden all his papers from her sight and mind'. Their elder son, Edward, aged about forty, was said to covet his father's position; and the younger son, William, was married to a wife whose name, Hephizbah, suggests that she shared her mother-in-law's religious outlook. The old man does not seem to have had a happy family life, and his main trust was apparently in his devoted servant, John Perry.

The Perrys lived in a cottage near the great gates of Campden House. There were two brothers, Richard and John; their mother, Joan – who was suspected of being a witch – and Richard's wife and two small children. They lived rent free and their wants were supplied by Harrison from the Campden estate (the father had been a drunken ne'er-do-well who had gone off with the Royalist forces and had been killed at Naseby), and in 1660 Richard was thirty and John twenty-four.

On 16 August 1660 – ten weeks after the Restoration of King Charles II – when all the villagers of Chipping Campden were out in the fields harvesting, William Harrison walked over the fields to Charringworth, two miles away, rent collecting. As he had not returned by nightfall, Mrs Harrison sent John Perry to meet him on the way home. Neither Harrison nor Perry came back during the night, and at dawn Edward Harrison set off for Charringworth in search of them. He met Perry returning alone, with no news of the old man's whereabouts, and together the two went to Ebrington, a hamlet half way between Campden and Charringworth, to continue the search.

Later in the morning a poor woman who was gleaning in the fields picked up by some gorse bushes, within about half a mile of Campden House, a hat, a comb, and a neck-band belonging to William Harrison. The hat and the comb were hacked and cut, and there was blood on the neck-band.

The village decided that William Harrison had been murdered and left the harvesting to hunt for the corpse. They did not find it and gradually suspicion fastened on John Perry. Sir Thomas Overbury, the local Justice of the Peace, rode over from Bourton-on-the-Hill to examine him.

Perry's story of his nocturnal search was that about half past eight, when he had been sent by Mrs Harrison to meet his master, he had gone down the fields 'about a land's length' when he met Will Reed, a labourer, on his way home, whom he asked whether he had seen Harrison. He then invited him to accompany him in the search, as he disliked going alone over the fields in the dark. Reed suggested that he should borrow Edward Harrison's horse and ride to Charringworth by road. Perry, however, decided against this and asked another passer-by, Pearce, whom he met by the courtyard gate, to be his companion. They set off together, but after they had gone 'about a bowshot' over the fields, Pearce said he must return home. Perry went back with him to the lodge gates and, when he had left, lay down in the hen-roost by the churchyard gate until midnight. It was then, because of the full moon, as light as day and he set off at last on his errand. However, a great mist came up and, unable to find his way even by moonlight, he spent the rest of the night under a hedge. At dawn he continued his journey, knocked up one Plaisterer at Charringworth from whom Harrison had collected twenty-three pounds in rents the previous afternoon, and went on to another tenant named Curtis, whose daughter informed him that Harrison had called there also though, as her father was out, he had received no money. With this as the sum of his information, John Perry returned to Campden House, meeting Edward Harrison on the way.

However odd the story might sound, Reed and Pearce and Plaisterer and Curtis confirmed on oath that, as far as they were concerned, Perry was telling the truth. But the fact remained that for the vital hours between half past nine at night (when Pearce had left him) till four in the morning (when he had called on Plaisterer) there was nothing but his unsupported word that he had spent the night first in the hen-roost and then under a hedge.

The magistrate, as might have been expected, considered that he had no alternative but to order Perry's detention for a day or two in the hope that more evidence would come to light; but the following week when Overbury came over again to Chipping Campden nothing had been discovered and Perry repeated point for point his original story.

Then, for some reason, he began to talk in such a way as to draw even more suspicion on himself. First he said that a travelling tinker had murdered Harrison; then that a gentleman's servant in the neighbourhood had robbed and killed him and that the body would be found hidden in a bean-rick in Sheep Street. The villagers hunted in all the bean-ricks in the neighbourhood, with no result.

On 24 August, at Overbury's third visit, Perry said he was at last willing to tell the truth. His deposition on this occasion was that his mother and his brother Richard had murdered Harrison on his return from Charringworth. They had, he said, often asked him to tell them when his master went to collect rents. On this occasion he had done so, with the result that, when Harrison arrived back at Campden House that evening and let himself into the grounds through a side gate opening into one of the fields known as the Conygree, Richard followed him. John Perry himself was not with his brother, but a few moments later he joined him and found Harrison on the ground, Richard Perry kneeling on him and old Joan Perry standing by. He heard Harrison say. 'You rogues, are you going to kill me?' and implored Richard not to do so. Richard said, 'Hold your tongue, you are a fool', strangled Harrison, searched his pockets for the money (which he threw into his mother's lap) and eventually, aided by his mother, dragged and carried the body which they threw into the great sink by Wallington's Mill, just behind the garden of the house. John Perry himself, so he said, had nothing to do with this disposal of the corpse, but stayed in the courtyard by the gate to keep watch. It was then that he saw John Pearce.

After the telling of this story, Joan and Richard Perry were arrested and brought before Overbury the following day. In spite of the fact that Wallington's Sink as well as the Campden fish-pools and all the ruined parts of the house had been thoroughly searched and had yielded no sign of Harrison's body, and in spite of Joan and Richard's denials and their further assertions that John was mad, the Perrys were committed for trial at the next assizes at Gloucester.

As the three were being brought back from Overbury's house at Bourton to prison at Campden on 25 August, Richard dropped 'a ball of inkle' from his pocket. One of the guards picked it up and, asking Richard what it was, was told it 'was only his wife's hair-lace' even though it had a slip-knot at one end. The guard took it to John, who was walking far ahead and had not seen the episode. John said immediately, 'To my sorrow I know it, for that is the string my brother strangled my master with.'

At the Assizes in September, the judge, Sir Christopher Turnor, refused to try the case on the grounds that, as no body could be produced, there was no real evidence that murder had been committed. The Perrys, however, were not released, and in the spring Assizes of the following year, Sir Robert Hyde, who was less scrupulous, decided to hear the case.

At the trial in September, two earlier and unexplained circumstances had been taken into consideration. In February – that is to say, in the uneasy time when General Monck was marching to London and when no one knew whether the Cromwellian Protectorate would be continued under a new military dictatorship or whether Charles II would come home from his exile – there had been a robbery in Campden. It had happened on a particular market day which had coincided with the visit of a famous preacher. At noon, when the villagers were either in church or at the market, a ladder had been set up to the second-storey window of William Harrison's house, an iron bar wrenched away with a ploughshare (which had been left in the room), and £140 stolen. The thieves were never discovered, in spite of an intensive search in which the whole town co-operated.

What many considered a sequel to this daylight robbery occurred three months later on the eve of May Day. The inmates of the almshouses and the casual passers-by in Church Street heard from behind the high garden wall of Campden House agonized screams for help from John Perry. Three men ran as fast as possible to the courtyard gate of the house to be met by Perry himself in a state of obvious terror, a sheep-pick in his hand and his coat slashed about the pocket. He explained that he had been set upon by two men in white with drawn swords who would have killed him had he not defended himself with his sheep-pick – which certainly bore the marks of recent notches, as did also a large key in his pocket.

Perry's conduct in what was assumed to be the invention of mysterious attackers was generally taken to confirm the suspicion that, in some way, he and his family had been responsible for the robbery; and at the September Assizes the Perrys had been induced to plead 'Guilty' to the robbery on the grounds that they would be immediately pardoned for it because of the Act of Pardon and oblivion passed by Charles II on his Restoration in May. They did so plead and they were so pardoned; but their action told against them in that it reinforced the general case against them as undesirable and criminal characters.

Now, in the spring Assizes of 1661, they withdrew their confession of guilt for the robbery and reiterated their plea of 'Not Guilty' to the murder of William Harrison; John Perry retracted all his stories about his mother and his brother, saying that 'he was then mad and knew not what he said'. In spite of the fact that the body of Harrison was still missing, and in spite of the Perrys' insistence on their innocence, they were all found guilty and hanged.

Joan, because of her supposed witchcraft which would have put a spell on her sons, was hanged first. Richard, 'dogged and surly', suffered next, imploring John, by a dying declaration, to clear their characters. John refused to do so, but before he himself was turned off, he said to the assembled crowds, 'I know nothing of my master's death, nor what has become of him; but you may hereafter possibly hear.'

They did. Fifteen months later, at the beginning of August 1662, William Harrison arrived alive and well in Chipping Campden.

Harrison's story, as he wrote it on his return for the magistrate, Sir Thomas Overbury, ran : 'As I was coming home that Thursday evening, there met me a horseman and said, "Art thou there?" and I, fearing he would have ridden over me, struck his horse over the nose, whereupon he struck at me with his sword several blows and ran it into my side while I, with my little cane, made what defence I could. At last another came behind me, ran me in the thigh, laid hold on the collar of my doublet and drew me into a hedge near the place. Then came in another. They did not take my money, but mounted me behind one of them, drew my arms about his middle and fastened my wrists together with something that had a spring lock to it – as I conceived by hearing a snap as they put it on. Then they threw a great cloak over me and carried me away.

'In the night they alighted at a hayrick, which stood near unto a stone-pit by a wall side, where they took away my money. About two hours before day (as I heard one of them tell another he thought it then to be) they tumbled me into the stone-pit. They stayed (as I thought) about an hour at the hayrick, when they took horse again. One of them bade me come out of the pit. I answered that they had my money already and asked what they would do with me, whereupon he struck me again, drew me out and put a great quantity of money into my pockets and mounted me again after the same manner.'

Before continuing with Harrison's narrative, which adds to and complicates the mystery, it may be as well to establish one point which, it seems to me, contains the clue to everything. The vital time, between dusk and dawn, is covered by two accounts, Harrison's and Perry's, either of which may be and both of which probably are untrue. (The murder story for which the Perrys were hanged is an obvious lie, for Perry knew that Harrison was not dead.) Perry's story of sleeping in the hen-roost for three hours and Harrison's story of being set upon at that same time by mysterious armed men are both, it seems to me, covers for what was actually happening – some arrangement which involved them both, a confidential servant and his master. For some reason it was necessary that Harrison should 'disappear' and that his disappearance should be kept a mystery as long as possible. This would account for Perry's odd behaviour in telling various stories and his eventual implication of his family in a murder charge which he knew could not be proved and for which, in consequence – provided the law were properly administered – no one could be punished, since there was no body to find. What could not be foreseen was the maladministration of the law by the second judge, Sir Robert Hyde.

As one contemporary writer put it, 'Many question the truth of the account Mr Harrison gives of himself . . . but there is no question of Perry's telling a formal false story to hang himself, his mother, and his brother; and since this, of which we are certain, is no less incredible than that of which we doubt, it may induce us to suspend hard thoughts of Mr Harrison.' (Much more, in my opinion, does it force us to suspend hard thoughts of John Perry, a paragon of loyalty, keeping his master's secret even at the gibbet – a person unrecognizable in the warped hate-ridden peasant whom John Masefield has portrayed in *The Campden Wonder* or the 'conspicuously crazy' megalomanic Andrew Lang holds up to ridicule in *The Campden Mystery*.)

William Harrison's account continues : 'On Friday about sunsetting, they brought me to a lone house on a heath where they took me down almost dead, being sorely bruised with the carriage of the money. When the woman of the house saw that I could neither stand nor speak, she asked whether or no they had brought a dead man. They answered, "No, but a friend that was hurt and they were carrying him to a surgeon." She answered that if they did not make haste their friend would be dead before they could bring him one one. They laid me on cushions and suffered none to come into the room but a little girl. There we stayed all night, they giving me some broth and strong waters.

'In the morning very early they mounted me as before, and on

Saturday night they brought me to a place where there were two
or three houses, in one of which I lay all night on cushions by their
bedside. On Sunday morning they carried me from thence, and
about three or four o'clock they brought me to a place by the
seaside called Deal, where they laid me down on the ground. And,
one of them staying by me, the other two walked a little off to
meet a man with whom they talked. In their discourse, I heard
them mention seven pounds; after which they went away together
and half an hour after returned.

'The man (whose name, as I after heard, was Wrenshaw) said
he feared I would die before he could get me on board; then
immediately they put me into a boat and carried me to ship-board
where my wounds were dressed. I remained in the ship (as near as I
could reckon) about six weeks.'

All writers on the mystery seem to assume that the 'seven
pounds' is the price the kidnappers were paid for delivering
Harrison to the ship's master for sale as a slave in 'Turkey'. This
is so obviously nonsense – for who would shanghai a man of
seventy-two in so feeble a condition that he had to be nursed? –
that it, in itself, strengthens the theory that the whole of the 'kidnapping' story is Harrison's cover for his secret journey and that
the 'seven pounds' is passage money. The 'wounds', as well as the
alleged attack, merely make his account of his disappearance fit in
with the hat, comb, and band found among the furze bushes which
Perry 'planted' to divert attention from the truth.

The point of importance here is that, by the Monday, Harrison
is safely out of England and that, a day or two later in Chipping
Campden, Perry says he will 'tell the truth' to the magistrate and
accuses his mother and brother of murder.

From the moment of embarkation, Harrison's story becomes, in
the opinion of most writers, so strange as to be obviously false.
His ship, he said, was chased by Turkish pirates; he and other
passengers were captured, taken to Smyrna, and sold in the
slave market. Harrison himself became the slave of an eighty-year-
old Turkish doctor, who employed him to keep his 'still-room' for
him. He was given the nickname 'Boll' because of a little silver
bowl he was given to carry. Eventually, when his master died,
Harrison managed to sell the bowl and with the proceeds get his
passage home – and so back to Chipping Campden, where the

whole matter became a nine days' wonder, and Antony à Wood noted in his diary, 'Wednesday, 6 August 1662 : Mr Harrison, supposed to be murdered two years ago, came out of Turkey to his home in the country.'

If either part of the narrative is true, it is the latter which is the more credible. The seas were infested with pirates, and the numbers of Christian slaves in Turkey and North Africa at this period ran into tens of thousands. A mere twenty-three years before the Campden Wonder, Captain William Rainsborough, Thomas Rainsborough's father, had become a national hero for blockading the port of Sallee and obtaining the release of 339 captives, men, women, and children. This checked for a moment the state of affairs in the thirties of the seventeenth century when the western coasts of England were powerless against Barbary raids. Hiding in the port of Cardiff, the Turkish pirates periodically swept St George's Channel. English fishermen dared not put to sea, even near the coast, for fear of them. They had landed within twelve miles of Bristol, burnt Ilfracombe, captured Lundy Island. They had carried off men, women, and children from Somerset and, at sea, taken and enslaved over 2,000 sailors. In its day, Rainsborough's victory in 1637 was officially reckoned the greatest sea exploit since the last fight of the *Revenge* and worthy to be remembered with it. But the perspective in this matter has been altogether lost through the centuries, and Harrison's narrative, which would seem almost commonplace to men of his own day, earned the ridicule of such Victorians as Andrew Lang as 'conspicuously and childishly false'.

Had Harrison, setting off secretly for some foreign place which we do not know, been captured and sold into slavery as he said he was, it would explain why John Perry retracted his story. The time allowed for the return had long expired; there was neither sign nor news of Harrison and Perry had every right to conclude that he was dead and take what steps he could to save himself.

There is a last factor to be taken into account before a solution can be attempted – the reactions of Harrison's family. Immediately after Harrison's disappearance, his son Edward asked Lady Juliana to appoint him steward in his father's place. This she did, with the result that he became extremely unpopular in the neighbourhood by reason of his harshness and his exactions, and the return of

William Harrison was popularly welcomed as much for the deposition of Edward from his office as for anything else. Edward was also the leader in the feeling and actions against the Perrys. It is probable that he, through Lady Juliana, was instrumental in securing the illegal second trial, and it is certain that he arranged that John Perry's body should be hung on Broadway Hill in chains 'where he might daily see him'.

As for his mother – the 'snotty, covetous Presbyterian woman' – she committed suicide six months after her husband's return. 'Harrison's wife', noted Antony à Wood, 'has hung herself in her own house. Why, the reader is to judge'.

The outline of the case is now clear enough. William Harrison had for some reason or other, to undertake a long journey of which his wife, his son, and the neighbourhood in general must be kept in ignorance. He took into his confidence his trusted servant, John Perry. On the night of 16 August 1660, he set out, either alone or accompanied by persons unknown, leaving Perry to arrange a false trail of murder and to take upon himself and his family an accusation of murder. There would be no danger of death for the Perrys, since there could be no trial without the production of a corpse; and, in any case, Harrison would be speedily back. But on the one hand Harrison's ship was captured and he himself taken prisoner and on the other the Perrys were brought before a corrupt judge who distorted the law.

The question to be solved was the nature of the secret undertaking. When I wrote *The Silver Bowl* it seemed to me that no imperative could be strong enough for such loyalty as Perry's, and for such an expedition by so old a man as Harrison, but a religious one; and in that book I postulated that they were all involved in the witch-cult – which in itself was no more improbable than the capture of Harrison by Turkish pirates. That solution, imaginary as it is, still appears to me to cover *all* the facts and to distort none – and it is reinforced by one obvious clue which, strangely enough, I missed at the time – the inexplicable incident of John Perry's reply when shown the knotted string that Richard had dropped. Those who understand the cult will see clearly enough the significance of this.

But since I wrote I have been given another and a simpler answer which involves no metaphysical aids and which leaves the interrelationships of the characters, as they emerge from the story, undistorted by psychological improbabilities.

According to my informant there is among the Campden papers a letter sent by hand from Algiers from the third Viscount Campden to his mother, Lady Juliana, asking for money from the estate; as well as a receipt and an accompanying letter for money received 'by hand of Harrison, oure good servant, who retourneth forthwithe, and as I will later'. This suggests that young Campden was, like so many Royalists, in exile during the Commonwealth and was spending the time in travel; and it may be noted here that Overbury, the magistrate, had also spent the greater part of his life in distant lands, going as far as India, and had but recently returned to England. His knighthood, at the time he took John Perry's deposition, was only seven weeks old. It is also relevant that Harrison, as Baptist Hicks's confidential servant, could have been an experienced traveller in his younger days, serving his master's vast trading interests with the Levant. Thus Harrison's expedition becomes almost as commonplace a journey as it might be today.

But why the secrecy? The suggestion is that Mrs Harrison (and presumably her son, Edward) with their Cromwellian sympathies would have betrayed the Campdens had she known. This argument seems to me to have no force for the August of 1660, with the Restoration accomplished and the Cromwellian leaders on trial for their lives; but it may well be that the eighteen years of necessary secrecy – from 1642 to 1660 – may have hardened it, for William Harrison, into an irrefragable habit. And, of course, there may still have been local secrets which were involved.

The Campden papers suggest this. My informant, the Hon. Mrs E. M. Bellingham, tells me that William Harrison had, with the aid of the three Perrys, managed to salvage from Campden House most of its portable property and to convey it somewhere unknown through the underground tunnels which are known to have been in existence then.

The work was stated to have been done at night and to draw off the would-be 'nosey parkers' of the period (and there is no doubt that Harrison's wife was one of them), Joan Perry acted as a witch, prowling about the churchyard at the fall of night and only on nights when the rumbling of barrows and hand-carts in the underground tunnels might be heard. My great aunt showed me some beautiful tapestries which had been so carted to a distant house and shed, later built over to hide a trap-door leading to steps and near the Perrys' old home; and in her house at Sudeley I saw the actual handcart made by the Perry brothers which was used. I believe it is still in existence. . . .

'As a girl I often stayed with Miss Mary Anderson at Broad-way and cycled over to the site of old Campden House. The old steward then there showed me where the original tunnels formerly ran underground and, I think it was in 1904, several men went down to investigate. One of the supposed tunnels was a very deep ditch on which the whole family of Perrys had been engaged and it ran between Campden House and a disused mill on the road to Broad Campden. Later, I helped to trace the supposed "ditch" into the underground cellars of an old chapel and it would have been quite an easy thing for any person to have pushed a good sized handcart along it. . . .

'I have great reason to believe that the ditch was actually dug so that the Campden family might have a means of flight at any time; and I do know that in 1897 someone opened the sluice gates of the disused mill and the ditch was flooded; so that if the Cromwellians had discovered the flight of any Royalists, their pursuit could have been cut off very easily. . . .

'For the payment the three Perrys are known to have had a cottage rent-free for all time from the estate. The words I myself saw were "in perpetuity".'

This explanation, in itself, clears up a great deal of the mystery; although it suggests even more behind it than the circumstances of Civil War. In the first place, it was Baptist Hicks himself who had built the underground passage beneath the terrace connecting the two banqueting houses; and some of the other tunnels may have been his work. Could they have acted as secret cellars to store his own treasures? This seems to me more probable than that the treasures should have been carried off from the house itself before – or during – Sir Henry Bard's occupation from 1643 to 1645. They could hardly have been left there after the conflagration in '45;

and this date would have the additional disadvantage of making Richard Perry fourteen and John Perry eight at the time and, in consequence, unable to manipulate the handcart with much effect.

On the other hand, if the treasures were already there, the one person who would know about them would obviously be William Harrison; and it might well be that, after the burning of the house, it was his work to superintend the removal of them to some place of safety — or even to arrange for the sale of them for the impoverished family.

The idea of Joan Perry pretending to be a witch and prowling about the churchyard is not altogether convincing to anyone who knows the climate of the seventeenth century or what witchcraft is. That explanation seems to me to be a later gloss made to fit in with the known fact that she was locally believed to be a member of the cult and that this belief played its part in the execution. No one would have minded an old woman prowling about the churchyard after dark, for the simple reason that no one else was likely to be in the vicinity of it; and no witch would be likely to select the churchyard as the scene of her 'prowls'.

And I am left at the end still uncertain whether the mere family loyalty of William Harrison and the domestic loyalty of John Perry would have stood the enormous strains imposed in this case. Indeed the new evidence, in one way, inclines me even more strongly to suspect that the 'secret' involved was much more than the Campden treasures or young Campden's need of ready money; and now that there is an underground chapel connected by passages with the Conygree (which I had mentally postulated for the last meeting of the coven but did not dare to outrage probability by inventing) I leave with even greater reluctance my original solution. Perhaps one may compromise and call the Campden Wonder, on whichever level you care to find the clue, the Tragedy of the Loyal Servants.

CHAPTER 15

The Mystery of James de la Cloche
11 April 1668 to 13 August 1669

ON 11TH APRIL, 1668, when, in England, Charles II had been on the throne for eight years, a young man who claimed to be his eldest son was admitted as a Jesuit novice at St Andrea al Quirinale in Rome. His entire worldly goods consisted of two shirts, two pairs of stockings, two pairs of shoes, a black stuff doublet, a silk dress, a clerical cloak, three pairs of sleeves, three collars, a leather chest-protector, a sword-belt, and a hairbrush. He gave his name as 'James de la Cloche du Bourg' of the island of Jersey 'under the King of England' and his age as twenty-four – though it seems by other evidence to have been twenty-two.

The General of the Jesuits, Gian Paolo Oliva, a man outstanding both for his intellectual powers and his diplomatic ability as well as his piety, was convinced of the authenticity of de la Cloche's credentials. These consisted of three letters. The first was two and a half years old, bearing the signature of Charles II, 'given at Whitehall, 27th September, 1665, written and signed with our own hand and sealed with our accustomed seal'. The king wrote, 'We acknowledge as our natural son, James Stuart, who in obedience to our command has lived in France and other lands up to the year 1665. . . . We have again commanded him to live under another name, that of de la Cloche du Bourg of Jersey, and for important reasons which affect the peace of the realm we forbid him to speak of his relationship to us until after our death, when he may present this our declaration to Parliament.'

The second letter, dated eighteen months later, ran, 'James Stuart, now known by the name of de la Cloche, whom we have already acknowledged as our natural son, has pointed out that, if he should survive us, he would have nothing to live on. We therefore assign him, out of our estate, if our successor and Parliament agree, £500 a year which, however, he shall not enjoy unless he lives in England and follows the religion of his father and the Anglican liturgy.'

The third letter made it quite clear that he had forfeited this £500 a year by leaving England and becoming a Catholic. It was in Latin and written by Christina of Sweden, who, in the July of 1667, was living in Hamburg. When, twelve years earlier, Christina had become a Catholic and forfeited her Protestant throne, she had, on her first visit to Rome, been confirmed by the Pope himself, and on that occasion Oliva had preached the sermon. Also, on the way to Rome, Charles II, himself in exile under the Protectorate, had made a special journey to meet her. There was, therefore, nothing strange in her writing, 'James Stuart, born in the Isle of Jersey, who now passes under the name of de la Cloche du Bourg, is a natural son of Charles II, King of England, as His Majesty has privately acknowledged to us. Having quitted the sect of Calvin in which he was brought up, he joined the Holy Roman Church at Hamburg on 29th July, 1667.'

On the strength of these three letters – which are still extant in the Jesuit archives in Rome – Oliva accepted de la Cloche for the novitiate of the Society of Jesus.

Four months later, in the August of 1667, two long letters arrived from Charles II, one for Oliva, one for de la Cloche. To the General of the Jesuits, the King of England explained that he had long prayed God to give him a safe and secret chance of conversion to Catholicism, but that he could not use the priests at present in the country without exciting suspicion. It seemed, therefore, almost providential that his son – a 'child of his earliest youth' by 'a young lady of a family the most distinguished in our kingdom' – had decided to become a priest. James could be sent secretly to England to act as his father's confessor and to administer the Sacraments to him. He will ask the Pope to expedite James's reception of priest's orders; but, if that is not easy, the young man could be ordained in Paris, through the good offices of Louis XIV; or even in London. Charles has spoken to the two queens about the matter (his wife, Catherine of Braganza and his mother, Henrietta Maria) and they have agreed with him and are most anxious to welcome James.

To James himself, whom he addressed as 'Our most honoured son, the Prince Stuart, dwelling with the R.P. Jesuits under the name of Signor de la Cloche', Charles wrote that he hoped that it might be possible to recognise him and give him precedence of his younger and less nobly born brother, the Duke of Monmouth. If toleration were gained, and both Charles and his brother, the Duke of York, died without male issue, de la Cloche might even succeed to the throne. If, however, he still wished to be a priest, Charles would not oppose it. The king assured his son of his affection, not only as his first-born but because of the virtues of his character and the solidity of his studies and acquirements. The two queens were anxious to see him. He was to be careful of his health, which was delicate, and he was not to voyage in an unhealthy season.

Should these letters have aroused Oliva's suspicions? On the face of them, they fitted perfectly into the known political situation. About ten days after de la Cloche had arrived in Rome, Ruvigny, the French ambassador in England, reported a conversation he had had with Charles II. The king had said to him that he was most anxious for a very close alliance with France; but that he would need help, as most of those round him were quite another mind. How, the ambassador asked, did Charles intend to achieve his goal? The king would not explain but kept saying, 'Leave it to me. I will tell you about it at the first opportunity!'

An essential part of the plan for the alliance was that Charles should turn, openly or secretly, Catholic, and this step was beset with many dangers. Had it become known, he would certainly have been sent 'on his travels' again; and he could not be certain that anything he said or did was kept a secret. He had had experience of that in 1662 when he had made what he had believed the most perfectly guarded inquiries to the Pope about becoming a Catholic, only to find that his action was known in the country, and that to safeguard himself he had had to sanction new anti-Catholic legislation.

Charles's desire that de la Cloche should become the priestly intermediary would not, therefore, have struck Oliva as anything strange. But one discrepancy the General might have been expected to see. The king asserted that his mother, Henrietta Maria, was anxiously awaiting her grandson in London and that he had con-

sulted her about the plan. But Henrietta had left England for ever
and taken up residence at the court of France in 1665 – three years
before the letter was written. There was also a discrepancy in the
first of de la Cloche's testimonials which was dated from Whitehall
in the September of 1665 – when the Court was far removed from
London because of the Great Plague. Though Oliva could hardly
have been expected to know this, the mistake, considered in conjunction with that of the 'two queens', suggests to a posterity which
has more leisure to examine the documents and more information
to check them by that, assuming that the letters were forged, the
writer of them had not been in England since, at latest, the early
part of 1665.

Three weeks after the first letter Charles wrote again to Oliva.
In this letter, dated 29th August, he says that he has heard that
Christina of Sweden is on her way to Rome and that in no circumstances must de la Cloche be allowed to meet her, since she might
divulge the secret of his identity. De la Cloche must come to
England at once. If there is any suspicion that Charles is a Catholic,
there will be riots and he may even lose his life.

Another – undated – letter asks that the young man may, contrary to the rule for Jesuit novices, travel alone without a *socius*,
since this may arouse suspicion. He is to come by sea, direct from
Genoa, where he is to leave his religious habit to be resumed on his
return. He is to use the name of Henri de Rohan, as if he were a
member of that Calvinistic house, who were friendly with the king;
and he can pose as the son of a rich preacher, deceased, on his way
to visit his mother. He is not to land in London but at some other
port and thence to make his way to the capital.

In this, as in other letters, Charles asks Oliva to supply de la
Cloche with the necessary money, promising not only to repay it
but to make in addition generous donations to the Society of Jesus.

These letters confirm our suspicions that the letters are not
genuine, but they again suggest that whoever composed them was
in touch with political developments. Christina of Sweden did not
in fact leave Hamburg for Rome until the following October. It can
indeed be argued that it was inevitable that she should leave since
she had provoked a riot by her tactlessness, in that violently Protestant city, in welcoming the election of the new Pope by hanging on
the façade of her house six hundred lamps to form the words :

Clemens IX. Pont. Max. vivat. But that episode had occurred in
May, and in August Christina, in spite of her announcements that
she intended to visit Rome, was still in Hamburg. The writer of the
letters seems to have been aware that some definite decision about
her departure was arrived at between 3rd August and 29th August.

Taken together the later letters create an ideal situation for a
confidence trickster. As de la Cloche is to travel alone, no one can
guarantee that he in fact goes to England. As, whatever happens,
he is not to see Christina, the genuineness of her letter authenticat-
ing him cannot be checked. As he, and no one else, is to deliver all
messages and letters to Charles II, Oliva has no chance of communicating with the king independently. And de la Cloche is to
have all the money he needs supplied on the spot by Oliva.

Oliva himself apparently accompanied the young man to Leghorn, the port 150 miles north-west of Rome. On the back of one
of the letters from Charles, he wrote to the king a note, dated
14th October, saying that 'the French gentleman' would tell him
that his wishes had been carried out and would give him all the
necessary messages. This note is undoubtedly genuine and would
seem to establish that Oliva saw de la Cloche aboard ship, so that,
even if he left it at the first port of call, he must at least have set
off for England.

He arrived back again in December, bringing another letter from
Charles dated 18th November, 1668, in which the king says that his
most dear and honoured son is returning as his secret ambassador
and is to go back to London bearing the answers to certain questions which cannot be committed to paper.

And at this point James de la Cloche disappears completely from
history. There is no mention of him anywhere, either in the records
of the Society of Jesus or in the history of England. Those who
believe that he was what he said he was and that the letters are
genuine suggest that once he arrived back in England he changed
his name again and that he was in fact the 'foreign priest' who was
at Court when Charles, on his death-bed, at last became a Catholic.
Or, as Acton suggests, once his return mission to London (with the
answers to the questions too dangerous to commit to paper) was
over, he may have finished under another name his Jesuit training
at a college in France or Flanders. In any case there would be no
need for Charles to write to Oliva about it. De la Cloche may also,

others think, be the priest secretly brought from abroad to Charles during the 'Popish Plot' reign of terror.

These are conjectures merely, lacking any evidence; and, indeed, there is no reason even to suppose that de la Cloche was in England in the November of 1668.

We do know, however, that a short time after de la Cloche left Rome for the last time in the December of 1668 there appeared in Naples a young man calling himself James Stuart, claiming to be the eldest son of Charles II, born in Jersey, using as one of his names 'Roano' (which suggests de Rohan) and carrying papers from Christina of Sweden and Oliva, General of the Jesuits. He fell in love with Teresa, the daughter of a poor inkeeper, Francesco Corona, and married her. Not wishing his future father-in-law to appear as poor as he was, James himself supplied Teresa's dowry. Corona 'could not deny himself the pleasure of exhibiting this money before his friends and he indiscreetly boasted before his neighbours concerning his rich son-in-law'.

The matter reached the ears of the Viceroy of Naples and James found himself arrested on the charge of coining. There were found in his possession many jewels, 200 *doppie* (about £160) – Oliva had given de la Cloche 800 *doppie* – and papers in which he was addressed as 'Highness'. Because he claimed to be the son of Charles II, he was confined honourably in the castle of St Elmo and removed later to Gaeta where he was allowed fifty *scudi* a month for his support, while the Viceroy wrote to Charles II to inquire what should be done with him.

On 16th June, 1669, Kent, the English agent at Rome, wrote, 'The gentleman who would have been His Majesty's bastard at Naples, upon the receipt of His Majesty's letters to that Vice-King was immediately taken out of the Castle of Gaeta, brought to Naples and cast into the Grand Prison called the Vicaria; where, being thrust among the most vile and infamous rascals, the Vice-King intended to have caused him to be whipt about the City; but means was made by his wife's kindred (who was likewise taken with this pretended Prince) to the Vice-Queen, who, in compassion to

her and her kindred, prevailed with Don Pedro to deliver him from
that shame; and so ends the story of this fourb who speaks no
language but French.'

In all the story of James, one thing at least is luminously clear –
that Charles's disclaimer of paternity in this instance is worthless as
evidence. In the circumstances, there was nothing else he could say.
And it is also of interest that, though the vicereine saved James the
whipping, the viceroy himself took the step of immediately releasing
him. It has been thought that Charles may have accompanied his
official denial with a plea for mercy. Unfortunately there is no
portrait of James in existence, for a knowledge of his appearance
would make the mystery easier to solve. If he greatly resembled
Charles II (which in any case, even if he were an impostor, is
probable), the conduct both of Oliva in Rome and of the viceroy in
Naples would be explicable.

Having been released, James disappeared from Naples for a time
and the next news is dated ten weeks later when, on 31st August,
Kent reported, 'That certain fellow, or what he was, who pretended
to be His Majesty's natural son at Naples is dead and, having made
his will, they write me from thence, we shall with the next post
know the truth of his quality.'

The will, however, merely confused the issue. James claimed
Lady Mary Stuart, of the Lennox Stuarts, as his mother; by way
of security for his princely legacies, he 'assigns and gives his lands
called the Marquisate of Juvignis, worth 300,000 *scudi*'; he
appointed Charles II as his executor and begged the king to give
his unborn child 'the ordinary principality either of Wales or Monmouth or other province customary to be given to the natural sons
of the Crown'.

Even assuming that 'Juvignis' should be transliterated 'Aubigny',
there is no trace of any Lady Mary who would fit the case – though,
in spite of the torrents of scorn which have been poured on the will
(which Acton considered 'fatal to the case for the Prince'), it should
be noticed that the Lennox Stuarts were also Seigneurs of Aubigny
and that the sixth Duke (who was seven years older than de la
Cloche) had spent most of his life in France; and that genealogists
are not infallible.

On 7th September Kent wrote his last newsletter on the subject :
'That certain person at Naples who in his lifetime would needs be

His Majesty's natural son is dead in the same confidence and princely humour; for having left his lady, Teresa Corona, an ordinary person, seven months gone with child, he made his testament and hath left His Most Christian Majesty (whom he called "Cousin") executor of it.

'He had been absent from Naples some time, pretending to have made a journey into France to visit his mother, Dona Maria Stuarta of His Majesty's Royal Family, which nearness and greatness of blood was the cause, says he, that His Majesty would never acknowledge him for his son. His mother, Dona Maria Stuarta, was, it seems, dead before he came into France. In his will he desires the present King of England, Carlo 2nd, to allow his Prince *Hans in Kelder* eighty thousand ducats, which is his mother's estate. He likewise leaves to his child and its mother, Teresa, 291,000 ducats which he calls legacies.

'He was buried in the Church of St Francisco di Paolo out of the Porta Capuna (for he died in this religion). He left £400 for a lapide to have his name and quality engraven upon it, for he called himself Don Jacopo Stuarto. And this is the end of that Princely Cheat or whatever he was.'

'Whatever he was.' The latest edition of the *Dictionary of National Biography* is content to accept his credentials and describes him as 'the natural son of Charles II, born in Jersey when his father was just seventeen', thus ignoring the devastating criticism to which his claims have been submitted by various historians. De la Cloche, as his father's secret Jesuit confessor, fits too well into the Protestant myth to be lightly surrendered. On the other hand, Andrew Lang, certain of his impostorship, grants that 'he stands for ever on an eminence' as the greatest confidence trickster of history, one who had indeed 'gauged the depths of human credulity'.

There are two separate problems to be discussed before attempting a solution. First, were the Jesuit novice and the Naples 'prince' the same man? Secondly, if they were, who was he? And, if they were not, what happened to the Jesuit novice?

To dispose of the last question first. If the Naples man were a thief or an accomplice who had stolen or been given the Jesuit novice's papers and acquired or been briefed in his life story, he would either have continued his life as a religious or adopted some secular calling and disguise. There is no reason to identify him with any priests at the Court of Charles II nor is Father Florent Dumas's essay on *The Saintly Son of Charles II* – though valuable for its reprint of the letters – based on solid evidence for the later years. One point, however, Father Dumas brings out – that on his second journey to England in the December of 1668 (when he disappeared) James was to be accompanied by another Jesuit as a companion, whom he had, on his first journey, left and was to rejoin in France.

This companion – or, rather, a companion – also makes an appearance in another account of de la Cloche which we know only at second hand – a letter of 1674 by Vincenzio Armanni, who was interested in the conversion of England and knew the country. This in quoted by Brady in his *Anglo-Roman Papers* (1890), but the original seems unprocurable. Armanni himself owed his information to one of the two confessors of the Naples man. According to Brady's summary of Armanni's account of the confessor's information, James, accompanied by a French Knight of the Order of St John of Jerusalem, came to Naples for his health in the December of 1668. The Frenchman then went by way of Malta to England, having recommended as a confessor to James the parish priest who was Armanni's informant.

One school of thought believes that it was at this point that the 'switch' took place and that it was not the French knight but de la Cloche who returned to England, leaving the Frenchman to impersonate him in Naples. They think that James, once in England, was, after some service to Charles, allowed to retire to the country, where he married and had a family. I myself know one who claims to be directly descended from him and I have seen, not indeed conclusive but certainly circumstantial, evidence that this is so.

There is also another story, current in Jersey, that the eldest daughter of the de Carteret who was responsible for the defence of the island against the probable and subsequent invasion by Cromwell of 1651 was the mother of James de la Cloche. Local rumour has it that he grew up a great impostor and defrauded the Pope of Rome of a large sum of money. The story goes that his behaviour and his strong facial resemblance to his father caused his 'brothers' to have him imprisoned in Reims and to have his head fastened in an iron mask – the circumstance from which Alexandre Dumas took the plot for his famous novel. It is impossible to corroborate the story, but the village where he stayed is still called 'Bel Royal' and the house 'Maison Charles'; his chair and his boots still exist in the local museum; and, according to Jersey historians, Charles stood godfather to de Carteret's child – the only hint they give.

The Armanni version, however, says that, after the Naples man was released from prison and left the city 'it may be supposed he went to England. After a few months he returned to Naples with an assignment of 50,000 *scudi* and died of fever.'

The theory that the Naples man was an impostor has, however, so many difficulties that it is almost impossible to adopt it. If one accepts Armanni at all, one must accept him whole – and this is fatal to the thesis. One example must suffice. According to Armanni's informant, James, while in prison, 'wrote to the General of the Jesuits, beseeching him to interpose his good offices with the Viceroy and to obtain permission for him to go to England *via* Leghorn and Marseilles'. The one person who would know de la Cloche's handwriting would be Oliva; and, since he would be also acquainted with the curious marriage of the erstwhile novice, it is unlikely that he would be taken in by an impostor's imitation of it. This time, at least, he would err on the side of suspicion.

Everything, indeed, points to the identity of James de la Cloche and James Stuart – whether he was a prince or merely a prince of confidence tricksters. As Andrew Lang puts it, 'On the theory that the man at Naples was an impostor, it is odd that he should only have spoken French, that he was charged with no swindles, that he made a very poor marriage in place of aiming at a rich union; that he had, somehow, learned de la Cloche's secret; and that, possessing a fatal secret, invaluable to a swindler and blackmailer, he was merely disgraced and set free'. In fact, the paradox of the situation is that, while the career of de la Cloche in Rome excites every suspicion, his career in Naples allays them. With Oliva, every move he makes proclaims him confidence trickster; in Naples, every move proclaims him – at least in his own belief – the son of Charles II.

To say that he was what he claimed to be is not, of course, to assert the authenticity of the letters of Charles II or to imply that his relations with Oliva were anything but a swindle. Nor – more importantly – is it to suggest that he was born in Jersey, as every writer on the subject seems to do. The only evidence we have that Jersey was the place of his birth is in Kent's newsletter from Naples on 30th March, 1669, in which he states that the unknown Englishman 'seems' to have 'vaunted to be the King of England's son born at Jersey'. Charles's original testimonials merely state that he is to describe himself as 'of Jersey'. One may admit the probability that the king met his mother in Jersey, but can go no further.

A possible reconstruction of events is that he was a son of Charles II, born on his travels, and that, after the Restoration, prompted by his mother, he wrote to the English Court, where he was unofficially recognised by his father. Seeing, however, that no official status was intended, he left England to seek his fortune on the Continent.

Not enough attention, I think, has been paid to the case of Monmouth – on this theory, his younger brother – during the early 1660s. Monmouth was also a child of Charles's exile, and his mother died before the Restoration. Four years after her death – in 1662 – the king's mother, Henrietta Maria, brought the boy, then aged thirteen, to England. By the October of that year Pepys was reporting the whispers that he was 'lawful son of the King, the King being married to his mother'. The king heaped honours on his son, created him Duke of Monmouth, and, on the occasion of his marriage (at the age of fourteen) the following April, it was noticed that his coat-of-arms bore no bend sinister. A week later, when Monmouth was dancing at Windsor with the queen, with his hat in his hand, 'the King came and kissed him and made him put on his hat which everyone took notice of'.

This was public knowledge and may well have inspired de la Cloche to seek his fortune at Court a year or two later. Equally, Charles's extravagant affection for Monmouth would have prevented anything approaching an official recognition for an elder son.

It may also be conceded that were de la Cloche an impostor, the Monmouth episode could have given him the pattern of behaviour, even to the interest which Henrietta Maria was said to manifest in him. But in that case, it is odd that he should have chosen 'James' – Monmouth's name – as his name; and, indeed, the identity of name (since Charles may not have known of his existence) tells in de la Cloche's favour.

Once on the Continent, there is nothing improbable in de la Cloche's having drifted to Hamburg, having been converted to Catholicism, and having been used by some clever intriguer in the entourage of Christina of Sweden. With the aid of one authentic specimen of Charles's handwriting and knowledge of the ways of the English Court before 1665, the production of the later letters would present no insuperable difficulties to one in touch with events.

When examining the Naples period, there is one other obvious fact too often overlooked – that James's marriage was a love-match of some intensity. Whoever he was, he threw away everything to marry Teresa and, dying, his one thought was to safeguard her. She, on her part – a poor innkeeper's daughter – forced her way to the vicereine to plead for him. Could it be that, during the time he was supposed to be in England, he was actually in Naples, had first seen her then and, having got more money from Oliva by his return in December, had gone back to Naples to marry her?

If this be dismissed as a romantic conjecture, unworthy of serious historical consideration, I can only plead that, in a flood of conjecture, the one fact that towers like a rock is that James de la Cloche, 'that princely cheat or whatever he was', married for love and died before he was twenty-six.

CHAPTER 16

The Man in the Iron Mask
1669 to 1703

THE first known reference to the mysterious 'man in the mask', who died in the Bastille on Monday, 19th November, 1703 after thirty-four years in prison, is in a letter eight years later from the sister-in-law of Louis XIV of France to the mother of the future George I of England : 'A man has lived for long years in the Bastille, masked, and masked he died. Two musketeers were by his side to kill him if he unmasked. He ate and slept in his mask. There must, no doubt, have been some reason for this, as otherwise he was very well treated, well lodged and given all he wanted. He received Holy Communion in his mask; he was very devout and was perpetually reading. No one has ever been able to find out who he was.'

Another letter followed about a fortnight later with the information : 'I have just heard who the masked man who died in the Bastille was. His mask was not an act of barbarity. He was an English nobleman who had got mixed up in the Duke of Berwick's affair against King William and he was treated thus so that that King would never be able to find out what became of him.'

This, of course, was impossible, since the man had been in prison since 1669, the year before the Duke of Berwick was born. But the letters are interesting, quite apart from their value as references, because they show by the eight-year interval how closely the secret had been kept even in Court circles and (by the reference to Berwick) how, from the first, the mysterious man was supposed to have some connection with England.

In the May of 1717, the youthful Voltaire made his first acquaintance with the Bastille and during his year's imprisonment there, he talked to people who had waited on the 'Mask' before his death thirteen and a half years earlier. Though the prison officials no more knew the secret than did Louis XIV's sister-in-law, they were at least in a position to hear that kind of gossip which is valuable in any enquiry because it is probably founded on some kind of fact. And they knew the prisoner. Voltaire himself later elaborated and changed the story for his own purposes of propaganda against the Court and Dumas, seizing on it, immortalised it in that romance which generations of schoolboys and filmgoers have assimilated to such an extent that, whatever the true solution, it is the Voltaire-Dumas theory which seems certain of popular survival.

According to this, the Mask was either the elder brother of Louis XIV or his twin, who was kept in prison with his features covered (the mask, incidentally, was not of iron but of black velvet—a simple and comfortable affair) lest there should be two apparent Kings of France, leading to disturbances in the State. Today, of course, this is dismissed as the romance that it is. Later discoveries have revealed Voltaire's many inaccuracies as well as his purpose in discrediting the monarchy by a story which played its small part in preparing a climate for the Revolution. But, at the time, it spread like wildfire and in 1801, nearly a century after the Mask's death, it was given its last and most fantastic twist.

The Mask, so the new legend ran, was really Louis XIV himself, kept in captivity, while on the throne was the illegitimate son of his mother, Anne of Austria and Cardinal Mazarin. And, while he was in prison at one of the earlier places of his incarceration on the Iles Sainte-Marguerite, in the bay of Cannes, he married. A son was born to him who was smuggled out of the castle-prison and taken to Corsica. The boy was given the name of 'de buona parte' (of good family) and became the grandfather of Napoleon. Thus, the Emperor Napoleon I was the rightful heir of the Bourbons!

The fantasy may have served Napoleon at the time – he was crowned Emperor three years after it was first put into circulation – and, when he was in such a position that he had all the State papers of France and of most of Europe at his disposal, he had a thorough search made in all the home and foreign correspondence of the period in the hope of discovering who the Mask really was. But in the end he had to own himself baffled and where he, given those resources, was defeated, it is improbable that anyone else can succeed.

Yet from the Louis XIV story one important lesson emerges. The first thing the historical detective (or, for that matter, any detective) has to learn is not to overlook the obvious and, in rightly dismissing the romances as being the wrong solution, one must be careful to notice that they contain the right clue. In all the thousands of learned pages written about the Mask and all the obscure candidates argued about and all the ingenuity expended in tracking down nonentities, this obvious clue is monotonously forgotten – the simple fact that the unknown man had to wear a mask, because, if he did not, he would have been recognised. In other words, he was exactly like somebody that everyone knew. His face was as well known as, for example, King Edward VII's face would have been in England two hundred years later. If the Mask were not Louis XIV or his brother, he must have been at least someone who resembled him. And this axiom which novelists remember while historians forget, makes it possible to discard at the outset most of the clever academic solutions. The wearing of the mask was a precaution, not a punishment; and the man, on every matter unconnected with his identity, was treated with all possible consideration. Though he was deprived of his liberty, there was no question of endangering his life. He had no friends or (apparently) relatives to be interested in his survival, yet no recourse was had to the convenient and conventional solution of 'died in prison' to remove him.

Two centuries' research has established with certainty one of his names – Eustache Dauger, a valet. M. George Mongrédien in his *Le Masque de Fer*, published in 1951, which gives an admirable summary of all the candidates and all the evidence, has confirmed incontrovertibly, in my opinion, that the Mask (who must be the one survivor of five prisoners originally in charge of M. de Saint-Mars at Pignerol in 1681), was Dauger, and not Matthioli. He thus confirms Andrew Lang's identification published in *The Valet's Tragedy* in 1903. And for many years before that, it was recognised that the Mask must have been either Dauger or Matthioli.

Count Matthioli was the secretary of the Duke of Mantua, who, in 1679 was kidnapped by the French and imprisoned in the mountain fortresss of Pignerol, near Turin, then on French soil, for having betrayed secret negotiations between the Duke of Mantua and Louis XIV. There was no secret about him. A book about him was published in 1682 and the matter was a subject of newspaper comment in 1687. As Lang says rightly, 'for years after his arrest, he was the least mysterious of State prisoners' and, in fact, the only reason for his identification with the Mask is that it is impossible to *prove* whether it was he or Dauger who died at the Iles Sainte-Marguerite in 1694. The argument that the Mask was buried under the name of 'Marchiel' is, considering that all State prisoners were buried under false names, hardly evidence, even if 'Marchiel' is a version of 'Matthioli'.

Without going into the complex details of the various arguments, one may say that today, thanks to M. Mongrédien, Dauger's claim is not likely again to be challenged – adding, for myself, that, had the simple point of the necessity of the *mask* been allowed for, the candidature of the well-known Matthioli could never have been seriously advanced.

The 'man in the iron mask' is, therefore, the valet, Eustache Dauger. But who is Eustache Dauger? No one. The name, indeed, is the really impenetrable disguise. One knows of him exactly nothing. 'You raise the mask,' as M. Mongrédien says, 'and behind it you find a prisoner without a record and without a face.' It is, indeed – but the French expresses it better than a translation : 'C'est par trop irritant et decevant !'

The valet, Eustache Dauger

On 19th July, 1669, Louvois wrote to Saint-Mars, in charge of the prison at Pignerol that the king's lieutenant at Dunkirk was bringing him an important prisoner – a valet named Eustache Dauger. Though he might seem of no great importance, as far as worldly position was concerned, he was one whom it was vitally necessary for the king's service to guard with all the precautions that could possibly be devised. 'It is of the first importance that he is not allowed to tell what he knows to any living person, either by writing or by any other means. I am informing you of this in advance so that you can prepare some lodging for him where no one can pass his windows and where there are enough doors to ensure that the sentinels outside the most remote can hear nothing he says. You must yourself take to him, once a day, the day's necessities and you must never listen, under any pretext whatever, to what he may want to reveal to you. You must threaten him with death if he ever opens his mouth to you on any subject but his day-to-day needs.'

Saint-Mars obeyed his instructions, prepared a safe prison and, in the hearing of the Lieutenant de Vauroy, Dauger's escort across France from Dunkirk, told him that he would run him through with his sword if he made any attempt to impart any secret to him. The valet was safely in prison by 24th August, and on 31st April, Saint-Mars reported to Louvois that everyone at Pignerol thought he must be a Marshal of France – an estimate, it seems to me, which must have been based on Dauger's age and bearing, as reported by the guards who came silently in contact with him.

The search for the identity of Dauger leads backwards – and to England. Charles II was immersed in the negotiations with his cousin, Louis XIV, for the secret Treaty of Dover by which the English king, with the aid of French money, hoped to be able to establish England once more as a Catholic monarchy instead of a Protestant plutocracy and extricate himself from being the virtual prisoner of Parliament. Louis, on his part, wanted Charles's support, or at least, his neutrality in his war with the Dutch. In what was one of the greatest diplomatic duels of that century, the question resolved itself into 'how much pressure Charles could put on Louis by a tacit threat to make terms with Parliament, and how far Louis could compel Charles to go in that direction without the situation becoming too dangerous'.

In the tortuous negotiations, one chief ambassador was, it will be remembered, Charles's favourite sister 'Minette', who was also Louis XIV's sister-in-law; but, just as there were, on the surface, the ministers of both countries, acting openly as regards part of the treaty, so there were, well below it, other mysterious go-betweens to whom, even today, with so much documentation at our disposal, we have no clue. And, among them, was an elusive figure to whom Charles referred as 'the Italian' (which may merely mean 'man from Italy') in a letter to Minette written on the evening of 20th January, 1669 : 'I had written thus far when I received yours by the Italian whose name and capacity you do not know, and he delivered your letter to me in a passage where it was so dark as I should not know his face again if I saw him.' It is at least possible that this man, who was apparently unknown even to Minette, is the same mysterious, unidentified person of whom a year earlier – on 27th December, 1667 – Charles had mentioned : 'You know how much secrecy is necessary for the carrying out of the business and I assure you that nobody does or shall know anything of it but myself and *that one person more*, till it be fit to be public.'

One of the more bizarre figures of the time who was used as an envoy by Charles and Minette was l'Abbé Pregnani. He was among other things an astrologer to whom the Court naturally applied for racing-tips. In one of his letters, Charles tells his sister : 'I came from Newmarket the day before yesterday, where we had as fine weather as we could wish, which added much to the horse-races. L'Abbé Pregnani was there most of the time and I believe will give you some account of it, but not that he lost his money upon confidence that the stars could tell which horse would win, for he had the bad luck to foretell three times wrong and Monmouth had such faith in him that he lost his money.' Pregnani, a man of extremely dissolute habits, who found the stars also foretold that he would one day be Pope, died in Rome at the end of 1678. It seems unlikely that he was trusted with any profound secrets. But might he not have been a 'cover' for the mysterious man whom Minette did not know and whom Charles, in the darkness of the passage, did not see?

Because the theory that Pregnani and Dauger were one and the same was, in 1912, shattered (by the discovery that Pregnani was safe in Rome from 1674, till his death, when Dauger was certainly in prison), it has been unwarrantably assumed that there was no connection between the two. But this seems to me to be a complete *non sequitur*. Why should Dauger – assuming he is the mysterious stranger – not have been posing as Pregnani's valet? Such a hypothesis, not in itself unreasonable since it would be bordering on the eccentric if the abbé had no servant, preserves intact the discovery which is the most brilliant single contribution to solving the mystery. For it has been discovered that Charles himself issued a passport to Pregnani on 15th July, 1669; the abbé left England on the 16th, arrived at Calais on the 17th and on the 19th Louvois wrote to Saint-Mars the letter I have quoted telling him of Dauger's arrest in the neighbourhood of Dunkirk and his dispatch to Pignerol. The coincidence is, to say the least, curious, nor does it seem to me that its relevance is really affected by the discovery that Pregnani and Dauger are not, as was at first believed, one and the same.

But even if it be admitted that the Mask, 'Eustache Dauger', was involved in the very dangerous secret negotiations between Louis XIV and Charles II, it still does not explain why he had to wear a mask or give any clue as to who he really was; and the next stage of the enquiry must concern itself with his possible identity.

The Crisis of 1637

Some years ago, Lord Quickswood suggested to me a theory of the identity of the Mask which immediately made sense. Having heard it, I could not forget it and when, in 1955, I was preparing a broadcast on the Man in the Iron Mask, I wrote to him to ask if I might make it public. He was kind enough to give his permission, with this *caveat* – that there was no 'solid historic basis' to his 'ingenuities'. 'I regard them myself', he said, 'as no more than a very good guess. I must admit that, when you come to hard evidence, there is nothing in favour of the theory that cannot very easily be overthrown : but I do think that it is a better case than any other case that has been put forward. No other theory answers many of the questions that may be put.'

In the broadcast, I mentioned Lord Quickswood's theory but did not adopt it as my own. Yet, subsequently, the more I tested it, the more likely it seemed. To say that it is a guess without any solid historic (in the sense of 'provable') basis is merely to say that it is like every other theory of the Mask's identity which has been or ever will be advanced. And, as on the one hand, it makes more sense than any alternative solution and, on the other – as I hope to show – there is no known evidence with which it is incompatible, I have now come to accept that inspired guess of Lord Quickswood as the solution I am myself prepared to defend. In a sentence, it is that the Mask was Louis XIV's father.

The events leading up to what the *Cambridge Modern History* describes as 'the unexpected, almost miraculous birth' of Louis XIV in 1638 were these. In 1637, the King and Queen of France, Louis XIII and Anne of Austria, had been married for twenty-two years and had lived apart for the last fourteen of them. There were no children. Without being on scandalously bad terms, they were known to have no great regard for each other and there were rumours that the king was impotent.* The real ruler of France at the time was, it will be remembered, the great Cardinal Richelieu.

The king, the queen and the cardinal seldom agreed on any topic; but it so happened that, in 1637, they all intensely wanted the same thing – an heir to the throne of France. In the absence of a dauphin, the next king would be Louis XIII's younger brother, that lamentable young man, Gaston, Duke of Orleans. For different reasons, king, queen and cardinal all loathed him and were all to the last degree apprehensive of his succession to the throne. Louis XIII was, though not old, weak and ill and not expected to live long. All his principles of government were certain to be abolished and all his work undone should Gaston succeed him. Gaston would probably execute Richelieu and certainly remove Anne from any influence.

In the circumstances, the cardinal exerted himself to reconcile the king and queen, who met at one of his country houses. It was shortly announced that the reconciliation had succeeded and that the queen was pregnant. Gaston and his party were extremely sceptical and announced in advance that, if she was, the cardinal must be the father. This, for many reasons, was extremely unlikely, though Richelieu thought the succession sufficiently important to make it prudent for him to show no special interest in the birth of the child and to be away in the country, far from Court, when it was born.

---

*It may be of some interest that the last attempt at a solution of the Mask in France, in 1934, M. Pierre Vernardeau's *Le Médicin de la Peyne* rests on the assumption that Anne of Austria's doctor, when performing the autopsy on Louis XIII, discovered an 'ectopie des testicules', which established scientifically the impotence of the king and, consequently, the illegitimacy of Louis XIV; and that the Mask was a man who knew the secret. The theory seems, according to M. Mongrédien, to have been demolished by M. Geoffroy Tenant de la Tour's nineteen-page pamphlet in reply, issued the same year, which, I fear, I have not read but which, from M. Mongrédien's description of it, appears conclusive in establishing that the particular doctor, Pardoux Gondinet, whom M. Vernardeau mentions, did not enter Anne's service until the year after Louis XIII's death and consequently could not have performed the autopsy. I am not certain, without seeing more of the evidence, that this really disposes of the cardinal point at issue – that the king was impotent – and it in no way affects Lord Quickswood's theory, which does not postulate impotence. He himself, in fact, does not believe it, but holds that Anne's second son, 'Monsieur', was Louis's child.

Anne's confinement was painful and difficult and it was noticed by those in attendance that Louis (who sat in a room next door to her bedroom) showed the utmost anxiety for the life of the child, but was quite uninterested in what happened to the mother. The child was a most magnificent specimen, very strong and as unlike Louis XIII as it was possible to be. He who as Louis XIV 'was to make a mark on history of almost unequalled physical and mental vigour', was indubitably a very odd son for Louis XIII to have had – as Gaston and his supporters quite brutally noticed at the time.

'I am afraid that I cannot claim any direct historical evidence which would point further than these undoubted circumstances suggest,' Lord Quickswood wrote to me, 'but I cannot help asking what so able a man as Richelieu would have done when it was necessary for the King to have a son. Richelieu was unscrupulous, though not to the point of depravity; but he would certainly have felt justified in substituting someone as a father for the Queen's son, if this was the only way out of his difficulties. It is likely that in Paris at that time there were illegitimate descendants of Henry IV* and an able and unscrupulous man like Richelieu, with boundless power at his command, might easily find a young man of seventeen or eighteen who was willing to play the splendid, if ignominious, part which was required. He would pick his man; he would persuade the Queen that union with this man was the only way out of their difficulties; and if the young man was good-looking and attractive, it was even possible that she would welcome him as a mate on those grounds. The circumstances that the reconciliation of the King and Queen took place at a country house of the Cardinal's would make it quite possible for the young man to be smuggled into the house and out again without the knowledge of anyone except the three great conspirators concerned. When success came and it was clear that the Queen was going to have a child, the young man would be loaded with money and persuaded to leave France for Canada. He would there reside until all three of the conspirators were dead. The Queen was the last to die, and

---

*'Likely' seems to me a considerable understatement. Henri Quatre's illegitimate sons would of course, be Louis XIII's half-brothers, though the obliging youth would probably be a grandson.

probably from motives of chivalry the young man would say
nothing as long as she lived, but when she was dead it would be
natural for him to want more money than he had received and he
would come to Europe fishing for gold. The ministers in charge of
France at the time would quickly see the danger of such a claim as
he might make, the more so because he had a marked facial resemblance to the King, Louis XIV.'

Lord Quickswood also cites the later investigation into the Mask's
identity by Louis XV who announced that the man was imprisoned
because he had a remarkable resemblance to the Royal family and
had used it in a mischievous and seditious manner; and the well-
known episode (which, in spite of the fact that Voltaire uses it,
seems to be true) that during his imprisonment in the Iles Saint-
Marguerite fortress, the Mask once wrote something with a steel
fork on a silver plate and threw it out of the window so that it fell
on the beach. A fisherman picked it up and brought it to the castle,
whereupon Saint-Mars asked if the fisherman could read. When the
fisherman answered 'No', Saint-Mars said : 'It is lucky for you that
you cannot, for it would have been necessary to put you to death if
you could.'

I have the greater confidence in Lord Quickswood's theory
because it is he, as himself a statesman and, even more, as a
member of the great 'ruling house' of Cecil, who enunciates it. One
may have various views on the character of the Elizabethan
founders of the Cecilian dynasty (for that term is not too strong),
but there can be no difference of opinion on the fact that it has for
nearly four centuries, been one of the finest families of statesmen
in Europe, continuously concerned in the art of government. And
any statesman, particularly a Cecil, is not likely to view history with
the same eyes as a professional recluse counter-checking manuscripts
or an earnest history teacher trying to instruct his charges in the
principles of good citizenship. Neither of these would probably
assume that it was a natural thing for Richelieu to act in the way
that Lord Quickswood (and, it may be added, the ordinary common
sense of any man of the world) assumes that he acted. But that only
adds another count to one's indictment of the academics who fail
to understand that 'history' and 'life' are synonymous terms. In the
nature of things there can be no 'documentary evidence' that Louis
XIV's 'almost miraculous birth' was compassed in that way; but

that a Cecil assumes that that is how Richelieu would have arranged it, is, for me, as good as any such evidence and better than most.

The one weakness of this solution, which its author admits, is that the Mask, if he were Louis XIV's father, would have lived till the age of eighty-three. 'It is not impossible that he may have done so,' writes Lord Quickswood, 'but it is certainly an element of improbability that must be weighed against the theory, with which otherwise everything corresponds.' Thus the next part of the enquiry must concern the Mask's age.

How old was the prisoner?

The one documentary reference to this is in the parish register of the church where he was buried on 20th November, 1703, under the name of 'M. de Marchiel'. Here it is given as 'about forty-five'. Even if one did not know, from other cases, that State prisoners were given false names and ages, this is patently nonsensical, as it would make him about eleven at the time of his arrest at Dunkirk. There is, therefore, no direct evidence of his age; but if he were the father of Louis XIV he would have been about forty-nine at the time of his arrest – which would not be incompatible with the rumour at Pignerol that he was a Marshal of France.

The Mask was in four prisons – at Pignerol from 1669 till 1681; at Exiles from 1681 to 1687; at Sainte-Marguerite from 1687 till 1698 and in the Bastille from 1698 till his death in 1703. At Exiles, if he were Louis's father, he would have been in his sixties. The nephew of the lieutenant of that prison later wrote : 'My uncle, told me how, in order to see the Mask, he had once taken the place of a sentinel and watched outside his prison. He saw him at night through the window, a tall well-made man and still vigorous in spite of his grey hair.'

This incident probably occurred at the beginning of 1687. Saint-Mars had been promoted from Exiles to Sainte-Marguerite and had asked permission to go and see his new domain. He explained that he had to leave the Mask behind but 'has forbidden the Lieutenant even to speak to that prisoner'. At Sainte-Marguerite, Saint-Mars had a new prison built specially for the Mask with large, sunny rooms at the cost of 5,000 livres (which may, surely, be interpreted as a concession both to his rank and his increasing age). When, finally, Saint-Mars went to take up his command there in the May of 1687, the Mask accompanied him in a sedan-chair. The obvious means of transit was a litter, but a litter might have broken down and the prisoner have then been seen. As it was, after twelve days travel in a closed chair, the Mask was nearly dead (which, though such an experience might have been too much for many people, suggests an old rather than a young man).

There is another, and to my mind, more conclusive argument about the Mask's age. In the controversy, to which I have referred, between those who claim Dauger as the Mask and those who support the claims of Matthioli, there is one passage which turns on the interpretation of the word 'ancient'. From the time of Dauger's arrest till his death, as we have seen Saint-Mars was uninterruptedly in charge of him. As the governor was sent from Pignerol to Exiles and from Exiles to Sainte-Marguerite and from Sainte-Marguerite to the Bastille, so Dauger went with him. But Matthioli did not go to Exiles, but remained at Pignerol until 1694, when he was moved to Sainte-Marguerite and thus, after a seven-year separation, came once more under Saint-Mars's surveillance.

On 17th November, a Government official wrote to Saint-Mars : 'All you have to do is watch over the security of all your prisoners, without ever explaining to anyone what it is that your old prisoner has done (sans vous expliquer à qui que ce soit de ce qu'a fait votre ancien prisonnier).' Saint-Mars on his part regularly mentioned in his letters 'mon ancien prisonnier'. The Matthiolists argue that this means 'my erstwhile prisoner : he who was left at Pignerol and is now restored to me.' The Daugerites insist that it must mean 'my prisoner of long-standing'. As between them, in this particular argument, there is no doubt that the latter are right – especially as, apart from anything else, Matthioli was not imprisoned at all till ten years after Dauger. The 'ancien prisonnier' must be Dauger. But why need 'ancien' mean 'of long-standing' or 'senior'? Why cannot it merely mean 'old'? And in the context, were it not for the strange and untenable theory that Matthioli might have been the Mask, why should anyone have supposed it meant anything else?

The first time the adjective appears in the correspondence between Saint-Mars and government officials is in 1693 – that is to say, when the father of Louis XIV would have been about seventy-three – and it continues till the end. It even appears in the journal of du Junca, the Lieutenant of the Bastille (to whom 'ancien' could not possibly have either meaning applied in the Dauger-Matthioli controversy), when he notes where 'l'ancien prisonnier' is lodged. Must it not mean merely that the Mask was an old man – a probability reinforced by the fact that he spent his time quietly reading or at his devotions and that, one morning after Mass, he felt a little unwell and died quietly the same evening, after making his confession, without having had any disease? So a man of eighty-three might die.

Thus it seems to me that the age of Louis XIV's father, far from impugning Lord Quickswood's theory, actually suports it; and that if one merely looks at the known evidence (without wresting 'ancien', for controversial reasons, to mean something that it obviously does not mean), an old man is, in fact, postulated after 1693. Indeed, as far as I can see, the only reason that the Mask was ever thought of as being young is that he was described as a 'valet' which, by a conventional association of ideas, suggests youth. Had he been described as a 'butler', it would, with equal illogicality, have been assumed that he was old.

It is, therefore, possible to say of Lord Quickswood's 'inspired guess' that it explains every aspect of the mystery – the masking, the precautions against the telling of the secret, the considerate and respectful treatment of the prisoner. It tallies with the suggestion which, however romantically embroidered, has from the first been integral to the story – that there was some connection between the prisoner and the king. It provides as the reason why the prisoner was not simply killed, or at least allowed to die in prison (which, considering the obvious danger of his secret, is a minor mystery in itself) that Louis XIV could not, whatever the danger, commit parricide. Only one question remains to be answered to complete the solution; and that does not really concern Lord Quickswood's theory, which is already satisfied, but my own view, which postulates the visit to England as part of the story. Louis XIV's father could have certainly been 'Eustache Dauger, a valet'; but could he have been the mysterious messenger to Charles II?

Was 'The Mask' in England

There is no need to insist that any reconstruction of the Mask's life between 1637 and 1669 must be purely imaginary. Lord Quickswood's suggestion that he would be banished to the French possession of Canada is likely enough, but, even if he delayed his return till the death of Anne of Austria, it is improbable that he would risk living in France, once he had made – if he did make – his attempt at blackmail. He would be much safer in, for example, Italy.

The more one considers his position, the more impossible, from a practical point of view, becomes the theory that he dared to visit France at all. His only asset was himself. His story alone, divorced from any proof, could be dismissed as a *canard*, which nobody would take seriously. And what proof could he supply except his own person – which would have resulted in instant arrest?

But there was one market in which he could sell his information at a high price. To Charles II of England, in his diplomatic duel with Louis XIV, the secret would have been invaluable. The 'Mask', were he a grandson of Henri IV, would have been cousin to Charles, who was also a grandson of Henri IV; and he could, without too much difficulty, have established the authenticity of his story. The underworld ramifications of the secret treaty of Dover affected, at that moment, most of Europe. In Italy they had already produced the curious affair of James de la Cloche and there is nothing inherently improbable in the suggestion that 'Dauger' (whatever name he may have been going under) might have met Pregnani in Rome and thus gained entry into the secret labyrinth.

Such a theory also fits the odd fact that Minette did not know who he was when he went, in the ordinary course of the secret negotiations, to her brother. Minette, as the wife of Louis XIV's younger brother Philip who resembled Louis XIII as much as Louis XIV differed from him,* was the last person to be entrusted with that secret.

---

*It is this fact which makes Lord Quickswood reject the theory of Louis XIII's impotence, though to my mind it is not conclusive against it. There is no suggestion that the fathers of Anne of Austria's children were not Bourbons.

There is no need to pursue further what are only possibilities. The one point I wish to make is that the Mask's relation to the English diplomatic situation can be explained as well on Lord Quickswood's theory as on any other and better than on most, the conventional 'James de la Cloche' hypothesis included.

In conclusion, to quote from Lord Quickswood's letter : 'All the circumstances recorded in history about the Man in the Iron Mask do exactly correspond to what would have happened if he had been secretly father of the King. No doubt the thesis rests only on theoretical grounds, but those who reject it may be asked what other explanation can be given which is as plausible as this one. Why was he kept in prison instead of being executed for treason? Why, above all, was he not allowed to show his face? Why was the secret of his birth such as could be written on a silver plate and yet be of such a character as would make it unsafe for the Goverment to leave alive the fisherman who had picked up the plate, if he had read it? That Louis XV found out nothing extraordinary is quite intelligible. Very few people would know the truth – perhaps none surviving at the time of his enquiry; and in any case, the truth (if it be what I suppose) would be the last thing that would be told to the reigning monarch of France. Nowhere, we may be sure, would it have been recorded : nowhere would it have been allowed to displace the plausible account that the prisoner was a mere adventurer, trading on an accidental resemblance to the royal family. But I must not overstate my case. The theory that the Man in the Iron Mask was really the father of Louis XIV is just an historical guess, of which it would be foolish to contend that there was any evidence greater than to justify its claim to be a better guess than any other.'

I hope I may claim to have shown in addition that what Lord Quickswood sees as the one weakness of the theory – the man's age ——is really its strength; for the existing documents of the case support the contention that the Mask, who was quite certainly 'Eustache Dauger', was almost certainly an old man. Nor does the theory involve the abandonment of the discovery that Pregnani, with a secret passport from Charles, arrived at Calais the day before 'Dauger' was arrested, about fifteen miles to the east of Calais, and almost in sight of the technical safety of the French border, to be sent, in the strictest custody to Pignerol, over 500 miles to the south. Indeed, if 'Dauger' was posing as Pregnani's 'valet', it increases the value of that discovery by explaining why, as Pregnani was officially on the way to Paris, the 'valet' went in the opposite direction on landing in France.

The case rests.

CHAPTER 17

The Murder of Sir Edmund Berry Godfrey
12 to 17 October 1678

SIR EDMUND BERRY GODFREY, a bachelor of fifty-seven, Justice
of the Peace for Westminster, had the reputation of being
the best J.P. in England. He lived in Hartshorne Lane,
near Charing Cross, and was in business as a coal merchant. He
was a vestryman of the Church of St Martin's-in-the-Fields, and
Sundays and weekdays was a familiar figure in the neighbourhood,
with his tall, thin body, stooping a little; his beak of a nose; his
melancholy expression and his careful dress, always black but with
a gold hatband and cane. A melancholy man, a brave man – his
knighthood had been bestowed on him for his conduct in the
Great Plague of 1665 – and, in the October of 1678, an extremely
frightened man, he disappeared completely for five days during
which all London was searching for him before his dead body was
found in a ditch of Primrose Hill.

On the wet afternoon of Thursday, 17 October, between three
and four o'clock, two men who had been drinking in the White
House tavern in the fields north of Marylebone found the body
in a dry ditch, with a sword driven through it. There were in fact
two sword wounds, as well as a broken neck and very severe
bruises on the chest, as if it had been 'beaten with some obtuse
weapon, either with the foot or hands or something'. That phrase
was used in the surgeon's evidence, who pointed out in addition
that the sword wounds had been made *after* death; that the neck
was not merely broken but that 'there was more done to his neck
than an ordinary suffocation'; and that an examination of his
stomach showed that he had been without food for two days before
his death. Another point that was noticed was that his shoes were
quite clean, so that in that muddy, dirty weather he had obviously
been carried to the place where he was found. And there were
some wax stains, as if from a candle, on his clothes.

As there are at least a dozen different theories about this murder, which precipitated a reign of terror in England, it may be as well to dispose of some of them immediately.

First, Godfrey did not commit suicide. Quite recently an attempt was made to resurrect this theory. It is enough answer to point out the impossibility of Godfrey's having run his sword twice through his body; then broken his neck with violence and, after death, transported himself, without dirtying his shoes, to a ditch in the middle of a muddy countryside.

Secondly, it is established that the body was not put there after death by his brothers who, finding he had committed suicide in his own house, ran their swords through the corpse and arranged it to look like murder. Their alleged motive was that, had suicide been established, his estate would have gone to the Crown.

Thirdly, Godfrey undoubtedly was not murdered by the three men who were later hanged for murdering him. As this is now admitted by every writer on the subject, of whatever school of thought, it is unnecessary to deal at all with the later faking and torture and perjured evidence, except to notice in passing one of the curiosities of history. A silversmith named Prance was tortured till he named three tradesmen – all, like himself, quite innocent – who were known to serve Somerset House, the residence of the queen, where the real instigators of the murder wished to locate the murder. The accused men's names were Green, Berry, and Hill. In those days Primrose Hill was known by its older name of Greenbury Hill. This has been noticed as the strangest known coincidence; but it seems to me much more than that – a kind of macabre joke perpetrated by Prance as an implicit appeal to posterity. If he had to name someone for the Greenbury Hill murder, why not Green, Berry, and Hill?

The background of the murder is the political situation of 1678. Charles II had managed for eighteen years to survive the difficulties and dangers of his reign without 'going on his travels again'. He was actually winning his diplomatic struggle against his cousin, Louis XIV, while at home he was contriving – to use a somewhat later phrase – to 'dish the Whigs.'. The Grandees, the enormously wealthy landowners who disappproved of royal power because it shackled their own, had the 'Country party' as their political organization and the 'Green Ribbon Boys' as their 'ginger group'. They were fanatically anti-Catholic and anti-French. They were also secretly in French pay; since both they and Louis XIV wanted at the moment the same thing – disturbances in England. From Louis's point of view, such disturbances would distract Charles's attention from foreign politics and lessen his influence in the European scene; from their own point of view, the benefits of a potentially rebellious kingdom were obvious; while none of them despised an extra £500 a year (paid through the French ambassador) for doing what they would in any case have done.

The total situation is of such complexity that it would need a volume to do justice to it, but to illustrate concretely what might be termed the Case of the Curious Allies one example will suffice. Charles wished to withdraw the English forces from the continental war, partly on grounds of expense, partly because he inclined to a peace policy which was England's need at the moment, partly because the war could benefit Louis only and not himself. Louis, as obviously, was loth to dispense with any allies in his war against the Dutch and found English troops eminently 'expendable'. The Grandees, on their part, had no desire that the king should in any way economize, since were he solvent he would escape from his financial dependence on them, acting through Parliament. Their even greater fear was that the country as a whole might unite behind a patriot king. As their leaders, Shaftesbury, Russell, and Holles, put it to their paymaster, the French ambassador, the danger was of 'the whole nation being in one way of thinking'. They therefore declared that Charles's withdrawal of his troops from France was part of a design to enslave England, and that by means of a standing army the alternative of Popery or massacre would be presented to the country.

Politically, this was a comprehensible enough tactic, which had been already employed with considerable success in the lifetime of many of its practitioners; but from the point of view of the country as a whole, unaware of these necessary niceties of high politics, there might have been a certain surprise manifested should it be discovered that the party which was indefatigable in shouting 'No Popery!' and 'Down with France!' was in fact being subsidized by France in the interests of a Catholic triumph in Europe.

A rough modern parallel would be if the 1922 Committee of the Conservative party were in fact in the pay of Soviet Russia, accepting Communist gold to prosecute an anti-Communist policy. Such a fantasy was, in 1678, hard fact. Obviously anyone acquainted with the secret would be in danger of his life. And it was that secret, there can be no doubt, which Sir Edmund Berry Godfrey knew from his intimate friend Edmund Coleman, who was the paymaster of the £500 a year (in the currency of the time) on behalf of the French ambassador to the Country party members of the House of Commons.

The leader of the Country party was an unpleasant little dwarf, the Earl of Shaftesbury, who might almost have been the reincarnation, physically, spiritually, and politically, of Robert Cecil. Even Macaulay, whose *History* is a propaganda defence of the Country party and its allies, refers to Shaftesbury's 'deliberate selfishness. He had served and betrayed a succession of governments, but he had timed his treacheries so well that, through all revolutions, his fortunes had constantly been rising.' He lives for ever as Dryden's Achitophel :

> *For close designs and crooked counsels fit;*
> *Sagacious, bold and turbulent of wit;*
> *Restless, unfixed in principles and place,*
> *In power unpleased, impatient of disgrace.*
> *A fiery soul which, working out its way,*
> *Fretted the pigmy-body to decay*
> *And o'er-informed the tenement of clay.*
> *A daring pilot in extremity;*
> *Pleased with the danger when the waves went high,*
> *He sought the storms; but, for a calm unfit,*
> *Would steer too nigh the sands to boast his wit . . .*
> *In friendship false, implacable in hate;*
> *Resolved to ruin or to rule the State.*

He was determined to raise the 'No Popery' wind to a hurricane which might rock the throne, especially since the heir to the throne was Charles's Catholic brother, James, Duke of York. As an alternative candidate, the Country party was backing Charles's bastard, the Duke of Monmouth, an ambitious weakling with some charm but no principles, who was quite prepared to pose as 'the Protestant Champion'.

There was also among Shaftesbury's tools the invaluable Titus Oates, the son of an Anabaptist preacher who had pretended to have aspirations to the Jesuit novitiate and had been given the hospitality of the college at St Omer. He was the chosen instrument for starting the storm, by alleging that he had discovered a Popish Plot, in which the Pope, Louis XIV, the General of the Jesuits, the Archbishop of Dublin, and others had arranged to kill the king, set up the Duke of York in his place, destroy English trade, set fire to London, and massacre all Protestants in their beds.

Charles, when he first heard Oates tell his story, actually laughed in his face. The Commander-in-Chief of the Papist army was, according to Oates, an elderly peer whom Charles knew to be bedridden with gout. Oates described as tall and dark a short red-headed man with whom Charles was well acquainted. The lies, quite apart from the inherent idiocy of the story, were patent. The king, realizing that Oates was a mischievous fraud, and the Secretary of State, thinking it ominous that 'vast concerns are like to depend upon the evidence of one young man who hath twice changed his religion', refused to take him seriously and the plot looked like being stifled at birth.

But though neither king nor council paid the least attention to Oates's revelations, the country believed them to an extent which suggests mass hypnotism. The agents of Shaftesbury, in particular the well-organized 'Green Ribbon Club', which met at the King's Head in the Strand, were indefatigable in manufacturing and disseminating scares. Shaftesbury's wife went about with a pistol in her muff for protection, thereby setting a new fashion. There was daily expected the appearance of a troop of monks from Jerusalem to sing a *Te Deum* for the plot's success; men would have torn to pieces – so an observer remarked – a Papist dog or cat.

Yet, because of the attitude of king, court, and council, the plot still hung fire and Oates, finding that the highest tribunal in the land would pay no attention to him, decided to start the matter in the lowest. He determined to make his depositions in an ordinary magistrate's court and, on 6 September 1678, went for

that purpose to Sir Edmund Berry Godfrey, before whom as a
magistrate he swore the truth of a written statement about the
horrible, vile, and treasonable Popish Plot.

Godfrey immediately told his friend Edmund Coleman about
it* and Coleman, through his contacts with the Duke of York
(he was the duchess's secretary), was able to assure Oates that the
king knew everything about the accusations and was not interested.
Consequently Godfrey did nothing.

But, three weeks later, on 28 September, Oates visited Godfrey
again with more 'revelations', took his oath that they were true,
and went on to Whitehall with another copy to present it to the
king, who detected him in an obvious perjury.

This time Godfrey was exceedingly worried. He knew that Oates
was a conscienceless perjurer; he realized that Coleman was now in
grave personal danger; he knew that the king and the court did not
wish, in view of the propaganda-drunk mobs, that the matter
should be proceeded with. Yet he had no option but to proceed.
He was somewhat in the situation of a modern police officer to
whom a malicious mischief-maker, who has friends among the
great, has laid sworn evidence that there is going to be a crop of
murders in a particular street. Whatever he may privately wish or
think, he is bound to act.

Godfrey's worries increased the next day when he heard the news
of Coleman's arrest. He said to a friend that he 'had taken the
depositions very unwillingly and would fain have had it done by
others'. 'I think I shall have little thanks for my pains,' he said.
'Upon my conscience I believe I shall be the first martyr.' But he
gave no indication as to what party was going to martyr him.
Nor, when he explained that 'he was master of a dangerous secret
which would be fatal to him' did he give any hint of what the
secret was. From the vantage point of posterity, we can see well
enough that the secret was his knowledge from Coleman that

*I am discarding the fable that Godfrey was ignorant of what this first
deposition contained. North is quite clear that he knew; and Coleman's
knowledge three weeks before the deposition of 28 September is confirmed by an independent source – the House of Commons debate about
the events of 28 September, when Sir R. Thomas, following Capel, rose
to say, 'I met Mr Coleman. I told him he was up to the shoulders in
it. Coleman said he discovered it three weeks ago' – that is to say, on the
7th, when Godfrey revealed to him Oates's charges sworn on the 6th.

Shaftesbury and the Country party were in the pay of France* He had every reason to be frightened, though he said to an old friend, 'I do not fear them if they come fairly and I shall not part with my life tamely.' But who were 'they'?

It may be as well to exonerate here another category of suspects – the Catholics. Inevitably, in the atmosphere of the time, whatever or whoever had caused Godfrey's death, the Catholics would have been accused of it. As one writer, quite unbiased by theological preferences, has put it, 'If in full sight of fifty witnesses, Godfrey had slipped on a cobblestone in the street and broken his neck, it would have been believed that the cobblestone was the contrivance of the subtle Jesuits.' And, in the state of popular madness, the Catholics were painfully aware of this. Of all men whom, for their own safety, they would want at that moment to keep alive, the first was the important magistrate who had taken the depositions of Titus Oates.

In the second place, it is unlikely that they would have murdered out of all London the one magistrate who was friendly towards them. They had in fact no conceivable motive for murdering Godfrey, nor nowadays does any historian suppose that they did. All the contemporary evidence against the actual Catholics who were hanged for it was later proved to have been perjured; and any modern defence of Catholic guilt in 'popular' histories is bound up with the acceptance of Oates, that unparalleled liar and scoundrel, as a pillar of rectitude, and the Popish Plot, the most fantastic fake in English history, as genuine.

Again, one example must suffice. The motive alleged for Catholic guilt was the stealing of the depositions of Oates, which were said to have disappeared. Once those had been destroyed and Godfrey killed, no evidence of the plot would remain. Actually, Godfrey sent the depositions to the Lord Chief Justice who had returned them to him the day before his disappearance and, far

---

*The conventional theory that the 'secret' was that Oates was a perjurer has been disposed of by Andrew Lang in *The Mystery of Sir Edmund Berry Godfrey*, where he submits the evidence adduced by Pollock in *The Popish Plot* to a devastating analysis. In any case, Oates's perjury was common knowledge to anyone, from the king downward, who had had anything to do with him, so that it could hardly have been classed as a 'secret'.

from having 'disappeared', they were found in his house after his death and handed over by his brother to the authorities.

If no Catholic was the murderer, neither – for a variety of reasons of which his cowardice and his alibi are sufficient to mention – was the man who seems the obvious suspect, Titus Oates. Nor, personally, was the Earl of Shaftesbury. The motive does not lie in the political situation alone.

On Friday, 11 October, Godfrey received a letter which greatly disturbed him. If we knew the writer, the whole mystery would be dispelled; but unfortunately we have no means of knowing, though it is possible to make a fairly shrewd guess. After reading the letter, Godfrey went to a meeting of the vestry of St Martin's-in-the-Fields where he insisted on settling a few small debts. After the meeting he refused an invitation to dine on the following day on the grounds that he did not know whether or not he would be free to fulfil the engagement and added, 'You ask for news? Why, I'll tell 'ee. In a short time you will hear of the death of someone.'

When at last he got home, he sat up late burning papers. Next morning he rose earlier than usual. He dressed carefully in his best coat – then changed it for an older one. Between nine and ten he left his house at Charing Cross and was seen and heard near St Giles-in-the-Fields, asking the way to Primose Hill. He went, presumably, to Primrose Hill. Someone certainly claimed to have seen his unmistakable figure not far from Paddington Woods.

He returned from the country walk safely, and between twelve and one was met in the Strand by one of his fellow-vestrymen, who invited him to dinner. Godfrey said he was in a hurry and could not stop.

That is the last time that anyone, except his murderers, saw him alive. For five days, from the afternoon of that Saturday, 12 October, till the afternoon of Thursday, 17 October, London was agog with the mystery. Speculation and rumour were rife; every kind of tale was current, but two points were monotonously emphasized. Because he was the magistrate who had taken the first depositions about the Popish Plot, he was obviously the first victim of that plot. And the last words he had been known to utter was to ask the way to Primrose Hill – for his later conversation with the vestryman in the Strand had not yet become public property. The murderers were unaware of it. Consequently the body, when it did turn up, was found on Primrose Hill. That could have been predicted.

There is one piece of missing evidence on which I have never seen any comment, but which would be conclusive. What coat was he wearing when the body was found? Because early in the morning he changed from his best coat into an inferior one, it has always been assumed that he was still wearing it when he was killed. It seems to me more probable that he put on his best coat because he was going out to dinner with a person of importance (from whom he had received the letter) and changed it only because he was *first* going a country walk. But could he not have changed it again after he returned from Primrose Hill?

And there is another piece of evidence which, though plain enough, is often overlooked. On the Thursday afternoon, an hour or two *before* the body was found 'planted' on Primrose Hill, two bishops, who were enthusiastic supporters of the Country party and very friendly with Shaftesbury, heard and repeated that Sir Edmund Berry Godfrey's corpse had been found, with a sword sticking through it, in Leicester Fields – the fields west of Leicester Square.

Here, at last, is a pointer to the real murderer.

Near Leicester Fields was the town house of Philip Herbert, Earl of Pembroke, one of the noblemen of the Country party. He has been described, on the whole kindly, as 'a madman when he was sober and a homicidal maniac when he was not'. And he was usually not. He indulged in drinking bouts which lasted for days and died of them at the age of thirty. He resembles no character so much as Mr Hyde of Jekyll and Hyde. In 1678 he was in his middle twenties. In the January of that year he was in the Tower for blasphemy and was released on 2 February. On 3 February he killed one of his young drinking companions by kicking him to death on the chest. It was by no means his first kill (he certainly committed six murders and the number has been put as high as sixteen) but he had so far evaded the law. This time, however, a Middlesex jury of gentlemen made an indictment of murder against the earl. And at the head of that jury – and so acting, in a sense, as prosecutor – was Sir Edmund Berry Godfrey. It was as brave a thing as 'the best J.P. in England' ever did.

When Pembroke stood his trial on 4 April before the House of Lords he at once pleaded benefit of clergy. In the reign of Henry VII a distinction had been drawn between those actually in Holy Orders and those who, though secular, were 'clerks' in the sense that they were able to read. This latter class was allowed to plead benefit of clergy once only and, on receiving it, were branded on the left thumb so that, should they return to the courts, they would be recognized. At the time of the Reformation, under Edward VI, the branding was abolished and benefit of clergy was extended to the whole House of Lords, any member of which was to be discharged for the first offence (except murder) whether he could read or not. As Pembroke's offence was technically – and, indeed, may have been actually – manslaughter, he was, making use of this device, able to be freed at once, though he was warned by the Lord Chief Justice, 'Your Lordship must give me leave to tell you that no man can have the benefit of that statute but once; and I would have Your Lordship take notice of it as a caution to you for the future.'

Godfrey had no illusions as to what Pembroke's freedom would mean to him; and almost immediately after his release he went abroad 'for his health's sake'. He had, in fact, hardly returned from the Continent when he took Oates's depositions in early September. All through the weeks that followed the sinister figure of Pembroke must, in his mind, have loomed as large as the unpleasant personality of Oates. And, in the end, the two fears met.

It needs so comparatively little imagination to enter into Godfrey's mind at this juncture that one becomes somewhat impatient of orthodox historians who stress Godfrey's 'melancholy temperament' as a reason for morbid fear leading to suicide. In his position the most eupeptic of mortals might have felt dismayed; and what is most apparent is not his melancholia but his realism and his courage. His remark that his fellow-vestrymen would 'soon hear of the death of someone', his other saying that he was not afraid 'if they come fairly', his burning of his papers and his setting of his affairs in order, all point to the fact that he was expecting to die. Taken in conjunction with the mysterious letter and his morning visit to Primrose Hill, they suggest to me that one of Pembroke's friends had challenged him to a duel on Primrose Hill – though this hypothesis has the drawback that it postulates in him a conventional 'honour' taken to to the point of insane risk.

Another suggestion about the contents of the letter, which has been made to me by the historian, Father Basil FitzGibbon, S.J., of all men most deeply versed in the intricacies of the plot, is that it came from one in a position of authority – possibly the Lord Chief Justice – and contained an invitation to dinner, at which the difficulties of the situation that had arisen over the Oates depositions were to be privately discussed. It is easy to see how such a letter could prove an irresistible bait. . . . Godfrey may be an honest man, but popular fury is rising and is on Oates's side. The king's attitude makes the exercise of diplomacy imperative; but how little he can influence events is seen by the arrests already being made, particularly that of Coleman. It would be unfortunate if Godfrey would be accused of 'stifling' the plot. Loyal Londoners would resent it greatly. Perhaps a little friendly advice from the highest judicial quarters . . . ? Such a letter would be quite as disturbing as was the one which Godfrey received – but he would not dare to refuse the invitation.

In choosing between these two possibilities, the evidence of Godfrey's 'best coat' would be a decisive pointer. If he were fighting a duel, the change to second best would be natural. If he were dining with the nobility, it would be equally natural with this uppermost in his mind to put his best one on and then change it for his morning walk, only to resume it after his return to town.

In any case, both suggestions are mere hypotheses, either of which would fit the situation as far as it is known, but neither of which can ever be proved. What seems certain that during that afternoon Godfrey became, by one means or other, the prisoner of Pembroke.

But is there any necessary connection between Pembroke and Shaftesbury? Though Pembroke was a supporter of the Country party, there is no reason to suppose that he took any interest whatever in the political and religious struggle. His interests were more primitive. Nor is it likely that Shaftesbury would wish to be politically identified with Pembroke.

As it happens, there is on this point an important piece of documentary evidence. Two years after the murder – in 1680 – Pembroke murdered another man, by the name of Smeeth, in his usual fashion : the kicking to death on the chest which had become so notorious that 'a Pembroke blow' was a current phrase. There was the usual petition of mercy for him; but on this occasion the king took the unique course of insisting that the petitioners should sign their names and the document be entered in the patent roll. There it remains – practically a roll-call of the Country party, from Shaftesbury and Monmouth downwards. There can be no doubt that the party found Pembroke useful to them and, it may be safely suggested, never more useful than in the murder of Sir Edmund Berry Godfrey, whose chest bore signs that it had been 'beaten with some obtuse weapon, either with the foot or hands or something' – the Pembroke blow. Indeed, that dangerous and undestroyed list of the petitioners for mercy for him in 1680 may have been blackmail on his part for his knowledge of the real circumstances of the more important murder of 1678.

This relationship between Shaftesbury and Pembroke is the clue which makes the story comprehensible. Every investigator of the crime has realized at once that the beneficiaries of the murder were the Country party and that from the moment the body was found the 'Popish Plot' was safe. Godfrey's funeral was the signal for the tumbrils. His dead body was carried into the city attended by vast crowds; it was publicly exposed in the streets, the further to inflame fear and anger; in the funeral procession, seventy-two Protestant clergymen marched before it and over a thousand 'persons of distinction' followed it; and, at the funeral sermon, the preacher was guarded by two able-bodied men in the pulpit lest the Papists should there and then attempt another murder. The king was powerless to protect the innocent Catholics, for had he exercised his prerogative of pardon, revolution would undoubtedly have followed. He procrastinated as long as he could in signing the death-warrants, 'Let the blood lie on them that condemn them, for God knows I sign with tears in my eyes.' He was helpless in the Country party's power. For the moment Shaftesbury had triumphed.

But, however clearly the motive for and the achievement by the assassination may be seen, the insuperable difficulty has been that all the evidence (including psychological evidence for what it is worth) is against the possibility of the personal implication of Shaftesbury or Oates. And if, on the other hand, the death of Godfrey was mere private vengeance, it becomes, unconnected with politics, a coincidence too curious for credence. Yet, once Pembroke is seen as the connecting link the solution is not too difficult.

As soon as Godfrey has accepted the invitation, whatever it may have been, he is lost. Were it a duel, Pembroke can easily have him kidnapped, especially in a lonely country place. Were it an invitation to one of the Grandees (of whom the Lord Chief Justice was one), it needs no more than a whisper to Pembroke where his enemy, Godfrey, may be found. In either case, the unhappy magistrate can be transported to Pembroke's house and there done to death at leisure.

For the missing five days while all London is looking for him, he is in Pembroke's house, no more than five minutes' walk from his own. Here he is tortured, kept without food, and finally killed in the Pembrokian manner. (The wax stains on his clothes are an additional clue, since wax candles were too expensive for any but the very wealthy to use.*) When at last he is dead, the corpse can be disposed of by Pembroke's servants who need not even know who it is they are carrying to dump on Primrose Hill. They must have been accustomed to covering, without curiosity, evidence of their master's unfortunate lapses.

At some point a more convenient place was probably considered to be just outside in Leicester Fields, where suicides and duellists were occasionally found. But it was rather too near home to be safe; though a discussion of it would account for the earlier rumour heard and passed on by the two bishops. And, of course, the death would have had to be made to look like murder or suicide. With two sword wounds and a dislocated neck, no one would pay too much attention to those bruises on the chest.

*Again I am not considering the Protestant theory that the wax came from altar candles.

CHAPTER 18

The Innocence of Sir John Fenwick
1688 to 1697

Dear Life, I always told you from the beginning what would be the end of it. That you will find true. Get leave, if possible to come to me, but I doubt it must be from the King. He will answer now 'that I am in the hands of Parliament'; so he will refuse to meddle; and when they have condemned me by their Act, I expect all barbarity to be used to me. This may be the last, for aught I know, you may have from me. My circumstances alter so often. God bless you and preserve you and reward you here and hereafter for your love and kindness to me and remember your poor unfortunate husband who loved you to his last.

So runs one of Sir John Fenwick's letters to his wife, written from Newgate while the Commons were debating the Bill of Attainder condemning him to death for High Treason in 1696. It had been impossible for the Crown to find more than one witness against him and as this precluded trying him by the ordinary processes of law, King William III ordered him to be disposed of by Act of Attainder. The Bill, which the Tories fought tenaciously in both Houses as compromising the elementary principles of justice, passed the Commons by 189 to 156 and the Lords by only 66 to 60.

Of the various charges against Fenwick, the only one relevant to an enquiry about his innocence is that which charged him with conspiring to assassinate William III. That Sir John remained an open and avowed Jacobite, refusing to break his oath to the exiled James II when William usurped the English throne, no one, least of all himself, denied. He was thus technically guilty of 'adhering to the King's enemies', which was High Treason if William were considered the rightful king. Fenwick, with thousands of others, did not so consider him, and, on the scaffold itself, proclaimed : 'I pray God to bless my true and lawful sovereign, King James, the Queen and the Prince of Wales and restore him and his posterity to the Throne again, for the peace and prosperity of this nation; which is impossible to prosper till the government is settled on a right foot.'

The situation, in fact, was an undecided and revolutionary one, in which 'treason' was a word of no meaning, except in the sense of Harington's couplet :

> *Treason doth never prosper: what's the reason?*
> *For if it prosper none dare call it treason.*

Since Fenwick's side did not prosper, his unswerving loyalty to his king could be termed 'treason', and, in so far as he was guilty in that sense, the accusation was a tribute to his honour. Dying, he could say with truth : 'My religion taught me my loyalty, which I bless God is untainted; and I have ever endeavoured in the station wherein I have been placed, to the utmost of my power to support the crown of England in the true and lineal course of descent, without interruption.'

Assassination, however, was a different matter. That he was in any way implicated in the so-called 'Assassination Plot' he vehemently denied; and no one with any knowledge of his character is likely to doubt his word.

Several years ago, Mr J. A. K. Ferns, who had heard some of my broadcasts on historical mysteries, was kind enough to write to me to tell me that, at the end of 1951, he presented to the British Museum a collection of Fenwick papers including a collection of forty letters written by Fenwick, when he was a close prisoner in Newgate, to his wife, Lady Mary, and smuggled out by his lawyer, Christopher Dighton. 'I do not know how the papers came into the possession of our family,' Mr Ferns wrote, 'but I think a thorough investigation may prove Sir John not guilty.'

These letters, from one of which my opening quotation is taken, do indeed afford final psychological proof of Fenwick's innocence, were any needed. They complete the known picture of him as a man to whom the idea of a cowardly assassination would have been utterly impossible. They also reveal his realism and his understanding of the forces against him. For example, to his wife's hope that the Lords might throw out the Bill even if the Commons passed it, he writes : 'My dear life and soul, I beg you not to grieve for me. It is impossible to save my life or honour either, now; for they will say I am a liar and with that infamy I shall die. . . . I have no hopes of the Lords, for if they will not pass it, they will bring the mob to cry for "Justice!" and the Commons will give no money till I am executed. It is for that that I prepare. All my trouble is that they will be so barbarous as never to let you see me more and that is insupportable to me.'

This new Fenwick correspondence is, I believe, being published in full and must eventually be considered by historians in relation to the other known documents of the time. But the Fenwick that emerges from it is the same loyal, intrepid, intelligent man of the Border whom we know from history – a man whose panache would have made him at home in the company of the Three Musketeers, to which rare company he, in temperament, properly belongs.

Sir John Fenwick

Sir John Fenwick was born, as far as can be ascertained, in 1645, the year of Naseby. He was a Northumberian of some substance, married to Lady Mary Howard, sister of the Earl of Carlisle. He went soldiering when quite young, was a colonel of the Foot at thirty and major-general at forty-three. He was M.P. for Northumberland from 1677 at intervals till 1685. Fanatically devoted to the Stuarts, he opposed the Exclusion Bill designed to debar James II from the Throne and, when James eventually became king, Fenwick took an active part against Monmouth who, as a tool of William of Orange and the Whigs, made armed rebellion against James. When William himself, with the Dutch Armada, came against England in 1688 and successfully overthrew his royal uncle-father-in-law, Fenwick supported James till the last and, in the days of William and Mary's rule, so openly proclaimed his continuing loyalty to the exiled king that William gave order to close Hyde Park against him and his friends whose swaggering behaviour had caused one of the paths there to be known as 'Jacobite Walk'. On one occasion, when William and Mary were passing, Fenwick so far allowed his principles to overcome his manners as to omit to raise his hat – a discourtesy which William never forgave.

During the impressionable years from five to fourteen, Fenwick had grown up under the usurpation of Oliver Cromwell. No loyalist then doubted that the king would come into his own again; nor, when similar forces to those which had killed Charles I drove his son, James II, into exile, did the loyalists doubt that the usurpation of William, too, would end with the king's return.

Because we know the outcome – that Charles II was restored but James II was not – it is never easy for us to enter into the situation as it was before the outcome was known. In this, as in so many other cases, the apparently futile game called 'the Ifs of History' is an essential element in understanding history. One of the main deformations in all thought about the past is the assumption that what did happen had to happen and that the attitude of men involved in an unresolved matter conforms with the judgment and perceptions of those wise after the event.

Even the casual reader today would never describe a man who in 1656 remained faithful to the exiled Charles II throughout the military usurpation of Oliver Cromwell a 'traitor', whereas he is only too prone to apply the term to one who, forty years later, remained faithful to the exiled James II throughout the military usurpation of William of Orange. And the reason, possibly subconscious, is that the one usurpation was successful and the other was not. In so far as the differentiation is conscious, it is due to the Whig propaganda version of events which, equating success with legality, represents William's accession by right of conquest as more 'constitutional' than Oliver's.

Moreover, in 1696, as Mary was dead even William's pretended claim to the throne as her husband was no longer admissible.* And William himself was prepared to recognise as his successor James II's son, the Prince of Wales who was in France with his father, provided that James would allow the boy to be educated as a Protestant. Though his proviso made certain – as presumably it was intended to – that James would refuse to consider the

---

*Mary II's claim was not valid in her father's lifetime, whereas Mary I was indubitably queen in her own right. Those who contend that after Mary II's death, William III was the rightful King of England, are logically forced to admit, *a fortiori*, that Philip I was the rightful King of England after Mary I's death. They are so far from doing this that very few but historians realize that the correct and official description of Mary I's reign after her marriage in 1554, is that of 'Philip and Mary', whereas everyone knows the later 'William and Mary'.

proposition, it at least revealed William's own attitude to a fluid situation.

The state of the country, at that time, bore witness to the Dutchman's rule. William had always hated the English but, in his megalomaniac warfare against France on his own behalf as Stadholder of Holland, he had seen their usefulness as a source of men and money; during his eight years on the English throne he had poured them out unstintingly. By 1696, beside the loss of lives, William was six million pounds in debt, the currency had depreciated to an extent unknown before or since, and the price of corn (which might be considered the equivalent of our modern cost-of-living index) had doubled. The resultant misery and unrest among the ordinary people made the climate of opinion propitious for a Stuart restoration. Even among the real rulers of the country – the multi-millionaire cabal which had financed William in his original attack on James – there was a reaction in James's favour. The very men who, when James was on the throne, had intrigued with William to unseat him – Shrewsbury, Churchill, Godolphin, Russell and the rest – were now intriguing with James to unseat William.

Taking all these circumstances into consideration, Sir John Fenwick's implication in the scheme for a Stuart restoration in 1696 was certainly not regarded by himself and cannot reasonably be regarded by anyone else as 'treason'. On the contrary Fenwick did only what was demanded of him by his original oath of allegiance to King James II, which he had kept when so many others had broken it.

So the Duke of Berwick, when he came secretly to England to organize the Stuart counter-attack, could note that 'there were two thousand horses ready to take the field to join the King [James II] on his arrival. Sir John Fenwick, a Major-General, was to take command of them.'

The Duke of Berwick's Mission

James FitzJames, Duke of Berwick, was twenty-six. He was the eldest son of James II by Arabella Churchill. He was already a hardened and acclaimed soldier when, at the age of seventeen, he had come to England and remained as his father's loved and trusted companion through the revolution of 1688. He went into exile with the king – the father, in fact, escaped to France disguised as the son's servant – and fought for him throughout the Irish campaigns from 1689 till 1691, when James recalled him to France. He then joined with the French armies in the Low Countries in the war against William and earned and incurred William's lasting hatred by one episode.

At the battle of Neerwinden, Berwick, in charge of the two centre brigades, had carried the village and driven the enemy beyond it, when he found his retreat cut off. To regain his own lines, he took out his white cockade in order to pass as an officer of the enemy. Unfortunately his aide-de-camp was recognized by one of Berwick's Churchill uncles, who was fighting for William. He – as Berwick tells it – 'suspected immediately that I might be there and, advancing to me, made me his prisoner. After mutual salutations he told me he must conduct me to the Prince of Orange. We galloped a considerable time without meeting with him; at last we found him at a great distance from the place of action, in a bottom, where neither friends nor enemies were to be seen.' William did not like that and the meeting of the brothers-in-law was not, at least on Berwick's side, cordial. 'The Prince made me a very polite compliment, to which I only replied by a low bow : after looking steadfastly at me for an instant, he put on his hat and I mine; then he ordered me to be carried to Lewe.'

William, contrary to the rules of war, continued to hold Berwick. 'The Prince of Orange certainly had a design of sending me prisoner to England where I should have been closely confined in the Tower of London, though that would have been contrary to all the rules of war; for, though he pretended that I was his subject and consequently a rebel, yet he had no right to treat me as such, since I was not taken prisoner in a territory that belonged to him. We were in the country of the King of Spain and I had the honour to serve as Lieutenant-General in the army of the Most Christian King [Louis XIV] : so that the Prince of Orange could be considered in no other light on that ground than as an auxiliary.'

Eventually Berwick was released in an exchange of prisoners and for more than a year continued to fight with the French against William. Then, at the beginning of 1696, his father decided to send him secretly to England to report on the situation there. Hardly had he landed, than William issued a proclamation offering the reward of £1,000 for his arrest.

Berwick's own account of what he did was : 'King James had privately concerted measures for an insurrection in England, whither he had sent a number of officers; his friends there had found means to raise two thousand horse there well appointed, and even regimented, ready to take the field on the first notice [under Sir John Fenwick]. Several persons of the highest distinction had also engaged in the business; but all were unanimously agreed not to throw off the mask before a body of troops was actually landed in the island. The Most Christian King readily consented to supply them; but he insisted that previous to the embarkation, the English should take up arms, not choosing to risk his own troops without being sure of finding a party there to receive them.'

Berwick had therefore the difficult task of convincing the loyalists in England to start the insurrection without James and his troops to lead them – a proceeding which they naturally refused. And, indeed, Berwick saw their point : 'I had several conversations with some of the principal noblemen; but it was in vain that I made the strongest representations I could think of, and urged the necessity of not letting slip so fine an opportunity. They continued firm in their resolution not to rise until the King of England had landed with an army. To say the truth, their reasons were good; for it is certain that, as soon as the Prince of Orange had discovered their revolt or had information of the design (which could not remain long concealed considering the preparations that would be necessary for transporting the troops), he would immediately have ordered out a fleet and blocked up the sea-ports of France; by which means the insurgents would have found themselves obliged to risk a battle with their raw, undisciplined troops against a good army of tried and experienced soldiers, and they must inevitably have been destroyed.'

The risk of recognition that Berwick ran in England (where, only eight years earlier, he had been a prominent figure at Court) was too great for him to prolong his stay for more than a few days. He was, in fact, on one occasion recognized in spite of his disguise, but the man put him immediately at his ease by whispering 'God speed you in all your enterprises' – a sentiment which was probably representative of the country as a whole. On the other hand, Berwick's own ingenuousness in the matter of secrecy was partly to blame for his danger. Dressed in a French uniform suit and a blue cloak, he bought a pair of silk stockings in a hosier's in the New Exchange and paid for them from a purse full of louis d'ors. The shop-woman, naturally suspicious, informed the authorities.

Like the other followers of James, Berwick made use of the isolated house in Romney Marsh belonging to a farmer named Hunt, who made his real living by smuggling. Hunt was, as the event proved and as might have been predicted, anything but reliable; but Berwick was able to make his way from there, guarded by a loyal captain and his troop, to the lugger waiting off the Sussex coast to take him back to France.

Berwick escaped just before the betrayal of the so-called 'Assassination Plot' (which was, in fact, a kidnapping plot) led to the arrest of many of King James's partisans, including, eventually, Sir John Fenwick, who knew nothing about it.

The 'Assassination Plot'

It is unnecessary to assure anyone with the slightest knowledge of the character of King James II that the idea of assassinating William was to the last degree abhorrent to him. When some scoundrel suggested it, he had him immediately arrested; and when he found that he had been represented, however guardedly, as possibly approving of it, he instantly dismissed the man who had so misrepresented him.

Kidnapping, on the other hand, had a different complexion; and I see no reason to suppose that James would not have rather enjoyed turning the tables on William by successfully carrying out the manœuvre which William had tried to practise on him in 1688 and which had failed only because of James's violent attack of nose-bleeding.* 'Kidnapping the King' might, in fact, almost be described as a favourite Stuart pastime, which had been practised with success on both James I when he was King of Scotland and Charles I when he was a prisoner of Parliament.

On the other hand, nothing could better suit William than an

*See *James by the Grace of God*, p. 179.

apparent (but unsuccessful) attempt at assassination, which would restore his popularity and utterly discredit James; and it was this that one of his *agents provocateurs,* an unpleasant desperado named Porter, who posed as a Catholic and a Jacobite, eventually engineered.

There was a third type of man, the conscienceless hanger-on at James's court or the young enthusiast, who was quite prepared for murder in a profitable or a godly cause; and men of this kind, discrediting the king they served, were also implicated in the politics of the day – as, throughout history, they as well as the honest men and the *agents provocateurs* have appeared in similar revolutionary situations.

It was one such, by the name of Crosby, a secretary under Lord Middleton, who in the spring of 1695 had come over to England with the news that King James had issued a commission for levying war and seizing William – which meant, in effect, procuring his assassination. He seemed surprised that the English Jacobites had not received the commission and insisted that he had seen James sign it before he left France.

The mythical commission, of course, never arrived and the idea of murdering William so shocked the English Jacobite gentlemen, including Sir John Fenwick, that no steps were taken in the matter. Indeed Fenwick's attitude was such that he could claim that it was he who 'partly by dissuasions and partly by delays' was the main preventer of the design. He suggested to his friends that one of them should go direct to James to ascertain the truth. Before he went, he told some of the more important Jacobites in England of his intention and they encouraged him, saying 'it would be a great service to inform King James what an infamy Crosby had thrown upon him and that he ought to be severely punished to prevent any such thing for the future.' The delegate 'affirmed to King James before Crosby what he had said. King James reproved Crosby and told him that he would no more be employed in his service.'

The delegate may have been Fenwick himself; but in any case Sir John had made his attitude to an attempt on William's life so unequivocally clear that when, a year later, a new 'Assassination Plot' was hatched, those involved in it were careful to exclude him from their counsels.

This plot of 1696, which has still many unsolved features, took place at the same time as the discussions about the intended Stuart insurrection with which Berwick and Fenwick were concerned. On the part of the genuine conspirators, who considered it (I think, rightly) as a kidnapping plot which had the approval of James II, it was a piece of monumental ineptitude, which played directly into the hands of Porter, William's *agent provocateur*. By its coincidence with the insurrection (and this was probably intended by William) it made a legitimate *coup* by loyalist gentlemen appear to be a foreign invasion relying on murder; for the general public, even if William's intensive propaganda had allowed them to, were not likely to discriminate between the two plans, utterly different though they were.

Impressed by the way in which Crosby had misrepresented him in 1695, James in 1696 chose the sixty-year-old Sir George Barclay, a Scot who had fought under Dundee at Killiecrankie and a man of unimpeachable honour, to carry his commission to his followers in England, giving them the authority to 'take arms and make war on the Prince of Orange' at the appropriate moment. They were also empowered 'to do such acts of hostility against the Prince of Orange . . . as may conduce most to our service.' This was taken to mean that William might, if possible, be kidnapped.

The men Barclay gathered round him, through his contact with two of James's agents in London, Charnock and Parkyns, included Ambrose Rookwood, John Bernardi, Sir John Freind – respectively Brigadier, Major and Colonel – and others of proved physical valour to the number of forty, whom he called his Janissaries. Unfortunately for everyone, Barclay, though cautious enough to refuse to employ one of William's spies, Fisher, eventually fell in with Porter who had recently added to his *bona fides* from the Jacobite point-of-view by spending some weeks in prison for riotously loyal conduct on the Prince of Wales's birthday.

Though Barclay at first distrusted Porter as one given too much to drinking, he eventually not only gave him his confidence but adopted the plan which Porter obligingly outlined. On 15 February, William had arranged to go hunting in Richmond Park. He was in the habit of going by road from Kensington to Turnham Green and there crossing the river in a boat. From the place where he was accustomed to land on his return a lane led to Turnham Green 'something narrow, with hedges and ditches on each hand, so that a coach and six horses cannot easily turn, at least on a sudden'. The forty 'janissaries' were to be in readiness in the various ale-houses and taverns scattered about the Green so that, on a signal, they could assemble when William's coach arrived, at which point it should be a comparatively simple matter to overpower the guards and kidnap the prince.

Thus far the plan had been worked out when Berwick arrived in England and was told of it. 'Sir George Barclay, lieutenant of my troop of Life Guards', he wrote, 'meeting one day at a tavern a Mr Porter, the latter said that to facilitate the intended insurrec-tion he had thought of a scheme which would make the matter almost sure. He explained to him all the movements of the Prince of Orange and said that with fifty men he would undertake to beat off the guards and seize upon his person. Barclay communicated this to me; and thought I did not look upon the affair to be as certain as they concluded it was, I thought myself in honour bound not to dissuade him from it; but one of the conspirators, terrified at the danger or in hopes of a reward, betrayed it, so that the design was frustrated, just at the instant it was to be carried into execution.'

Which was, after all, what might have been expected.

William duly went in state to the House of Lords, sent for the Commons and from the throne informed them that, but for the intervention of Heaven, he would at that moment have been a corpse and the kingdom invaded by a French army. Some of the traitors were in custody and warrants were out for others. The Houses instantly voted a joint address in which they thankfully acknowledged the Divine Goodness which had preserved him to his people. They suspended Habeas Corpus, exhorted him to arrest anyone he regarded as dangerous and thoughtfully provided that they themselves should not be dissolved by his death. Meanwhile the common people reacting as might be expected to the words 'foreign invasion' and 'assassination' forgot their grievances and indulged in the usual concomitants of Protestant indignation in the way of pillage and panic which recalled the good old days of Titus Oates.

Many of the leading Jacobites were arrested, though Barclay as well as Berwick got safely to France. They were put on trial as quickly as possible so that they might be tried under the existing law of High Treason which denied the prisoner the right of knowing the crime he was accused of until he heard the indictment in court. This state of affairs had already been abolished in principle by an Act which was to come into force on 25 March 1696. Consequently as many as possible of the conspirators were put on trial and condemned before that date; though even those who were covered by the new procedure gained little benefit from an action whose conclusion was foregone. Porter, together with two informers, gave the convenient, necessary evidence which convicted them all. Charnock, King, and Keyes were the first to die, to be followed by Sir John Freind and Sir William Parkyns who were tried and condemned on 23 March and 24 March respectively.

As the two knights, unlike most of the others (but like Sir John Fenwick) were devout Anglicans, they were attended on the scaffold by three Church of England clergymen, who in common with many more, including Archbishop Sancroft and Bishop Ken, had refused to break their oath of allegiance to James by swearing one to William. Their action moved Bishop Burnet, William's creature, to intense wrath. He recorded : 'All three of them [the nonjuring clergy] at the place of execution joined to give them public absolution, with an imposition of hands in the view of all the people : a strain of impudence that was as new as it was wicked. . . . Two of them were taken up and censured for it in the King's Bench, the third made his escape.'

After 25 March, Rookwood, Cranburne, Lowick, Cook and Knightley were tried and condemned, Porter still obliging.

But Sir John Fenwick so far remained at liberty.

Fenwick's Arrest

In William's original proclamation, offering rewards for the capture of the 'wicked and traitorous persons' who had 'entered into a horrid and detestable conspiracy to assassinate and murder His Majesty's Sacred Person', the name of Fenwick was absent. Berwick and Barclay and Parkyns and Rookwood and twenty-six others were mentioned, but not Fenwick who, as we have seen, though consulting Berwick on the insurrection, was ignorant of the kidnapping.

Yet in the indictment subsequently framed against him, the main charge was of 'compassing and imagining the death and destruction of His Majesty', by which the 'Assassination Plot' was meant. And even the secondary insurrection charge was so worded that it emphasized, irrelevantly, the murder attempt – 'adhering to his [William's] enemies, by consulting and agreeing with several persons (whereof some have been already attainted and others not yet brought to trial for their said treason) at several meetings to send Robert Charnock (since attainted and executed for High Treason for conspiring to assassinate His Majesty's Sacred Person, whom God long preserve) to the late King James in France.'

In the opening speech against Fenwick in the House of Commons, Sergeant Gould deliberately linked and confused the two. Having spoken of the insurrection, he said : 'That fell to Sir John Fenwick's part. As to the assassinating part, you have had several examples already. This we have evidence to prove; and if we prove this matter as we have opened it, then I think there is no person whatsoever but will agree that this is high treason in the highest degree.'

The actual evidence given against Fenwick asserted his presence in 1695 at a meeting of various of James's sympathizers in England at which they decided to send Charnock to France to consult the king about details of the insurrection and report to him that the 2,000 horse were in readiness whenever he should need them. At this meeting were the inevitable Porter and an ex-actor who had once been kept by the Duchess of Cleveland named Cardell Goodman, popularly known as Scum Goodman. It was on the words of these two alone that the charge against Fenwick rested; and even these referred only to the 'insurrection' meeting. Not even Porter had the effrontery to suggest that he had any knowledge of the Turnham Green affair.

During the high treason trials of February, March and April, 1696, Fenwick was safely in hiding. Though he had not been named in any proclamation, he knew that ultimately he would be sought for and he decided (or, possibly, had been ordered by Berwick and Barclay before they left) to go to France until the hue-and-cry was over. But, before he went, he determined to make a last gesture to help those of his imprisoned colleagues who were still alive, in particular the Earl of Ailesbury. The witness who was sending one after another loyalist to death was Porter, whom Fenwick imagined to be a terrified renegade Jacobite and whom therefore he supposed that a passage to France, a pardon from King James and a substantial bribe could silence.

That May, from his hiding place, he got in touch with two Irishmen he could trust implicitly, Clancy and Donelagh, and gave them their instructions. The result may be told in Porter's own words to the House of Commons : 'I had a meeting with one Clancy, first in Mitre Court and afterwards at the King's Head Tavern by the Playhouse. At those meetings he proposed to give me 300 guineas to bear my charges to France and send me a bill for 300 more; and likewise that I should be allowed £300 a year. He said he had been with Sir John Fenwick, who desired him to make this proposal to me. I met him about seven or eight times. The day before I was to go I met with my Lady Fenwick. She said, what Clancy had proposed should certainly be made good. I received 300 guineas of Clancy and he brought me a letter which, he said, was written by Sir John Fenwick to King James on my behalf. I had it and read it before it was sealed up and he delivered it to the gentleman that was to go with me, one Captain Donelagh. The contents, as much as I remember, was, He desired His Majesty, by reason that my going away was to save my Lord Aylesbury and my Lord Montgomery etc. to pardon what I have done.'

At this point, after the three hundred guineas had been counted on the tavern table and Porter had pocketed them, the *agent provocateur* gave a signal, at which several messengers from the office of the Secretary of State rushed into the room, and arrested Clancy, who was eventually tried, convicted and pilloried. Porter had once again served his Dutch master well.

At the next sessions of the City of London, on 28 May, Fenwick was indicted of High Treason, with Porter and Goodman supplying the evidence. And, at this point, since no further service could be rendered by him in England, Fenwick made his final preparations for crossing to France. He left his hiding place and went to the usual rendezvous at Romney Marsh where, though Hunt's establishment had been broken up, he was confident of finding shelter till the boat arrived. But just before he turned off the high road, he had the misfortune to run into an official who was on his way to London with two smugglers he had caught and who at once recognized him.

'It is Sir John Fenwick', said the guard to his prisoners. 'Stand by me, my good fellows, and I warrant you you will have your pardons and a bag of guineas besides.'

Fenwick dashed through them, pistol in hand and, because he was better mounted, threw off their pursuit. But the hue and cry was up. The bells of all the little Marsh churches rang out the alarm, every hut was searched and at last Fenwick was run to earth in the cottage where he was to await the ship to safety. Just as he was arrested, indeed, she approached the shore, showing English colours, waited a little while and then, disappointed of her passenger, stood out to sea.

Sir John managed so far to elude the vigilance of his captors as to be able to scrawl a note to his wife : 'What I feared is at last happened; had I gone alone I had done it; but the other was betrayed from London.* It is God's will, so we must submit. I know nothing can save my life but my Lord Carlisle's going over to him [William] backed by the rest of the family of the Howards to beg it and offering that I will be abroad all his time, where I cannot hurt him; and that I will never draw sword against him. I must leave it to you what else to say. . . . The great care must be the jury, if two or three could be got that would starve the rest. Money, I know, would do it; but, alas! that is not to be had, nor shall I get enough for counsel. I beg of you not to think of being shut up with me; I know it will kill you, and besides I have no such friends as you to take care of my business; though it would be the comfort of my life, the little time it lasts, to have you with me; and I have this only comfort now left, that my death will make you easy. My dearest life, grieve not for me, but resign me to God's will. You will hear, as soon as they bring me to Town, where they put me and then I would have a servant or somebody with me. I am interrupted, so can say no more now. . . . '

When Fenwick arrived in London to be arraigned before the Lords Justices, he learnt that the letter had been intercepted and taken to Whitehall.

*This suggests – though the dates are rather confusing – that Fenwick was crossing at the same time as Donelagh and Porter should have done.

Turning the Tables

Everything seemed lost. But it was not in Fenwick's nature to accept defeat, and his next move – though he knew it must mean inevitably his death – was a desperate throw to retrieve the general situation. He approached Devonshire, the Lord Steward, and informed him that he threw himself entirely on William's mercy and would disclose everything he knew about the Jacobite plots to unseat William. He would even give a list of plotters.

William, at the moment, was in Holland, but Devonshire thought Fenwick's offer sufficiently important to delay the trial until William's pleasure was known. William, in reply, authorized him to take Fenwick's confession in writing and send it to him as quickly as possible.

So Fenwick, using the knowledge that Berwick had given him, made a list of those who had been intriguing with James for William's downfall – Churchill, Shrewsbury, Godolphin, Russell and their peers; in fact, almost the entire Government. He also suggested that 'the Assassination Plot' was planned by the Government. The resultant alarm and despondency, were it not for its tragic outcome, provides one of the most hilarious moments in seventeenth-century history. For everyone conversant with the real state of affairs knew the accusation was true. Even William knew it, for as Monmouth said of him : 'He pretends not to believe these charges and yet he knows' (and here Monmouth confirmed his assertion with a tremendous oath) 'he knows that every word of the charges is true.' Yet he dared not officially believe or admit it. He wrote back furiously : 'I am astonished at the fellow's effrontery. You know me too well to think that such stories as his can make any impression on me. Observe this honest man's sincerity. He has nothing to say except against my friends. Not a word about the plans of his brother Jacobites.' The impression, nonetheless, was considerable, though the political and personal repercussions belong rather to the history of William III's reign than to a consideration of Fenwick's case. It is enough to say that Shrewsbury was not seen again at Court, that Godolphin was dropped from the Ministry and that Churchill was temporarily disgraced.

William returned from Holland to find that the news of Fenwick's confession had got abroad in the country. Knowing the damage likely to be done by a full and open enquiry, he ordered that Fenwick was to be tried by the ordinary courts and the matter not debated by Parliament. The accused statesmen, however, especially Russell, wished the matter to be brought up in the Commons and their honour publicly vindicated in solemn debate. And they suggested that, as a prelude, William should himself see Fenwick. Accordingly at the beginning of November, Fenwick was taken from prison, where he had been for five months, and interviewed by William in the presence of some ministers and the Crown lawyers.

'Your papers, Sir John,' said William, 'are altogether unsatisfactory. Instead of giving me an account of the plots formed by you and your accomplices, plots of which all the details must be exactly known to you, you tell me stories without authority, without date, without place, about noblemen and gentlemen with whom you do not pretend to have had any intercourse. In short your confession appears to be a contrivance intended to screen those who are really engaged in designs against me and to make me suspect and discard those in whom I have good reason to place confidence. If you look for any favour from me, give me, this moment and on this spot, a full account of what you know from your own knowledge.'

Fenwick said that this request took him by surprise and asked for time.

'No, sir', said William. 'For what purpose can you want time? You may indeed want time if you intend to draw up another paper like this. But what I require is a plain narrative of what you yourself have done and seen; and this you can give, if you will, without pen and ink.'

At this, Fenwick refused to say another word.

'Be it so', said William. 'I will neither hear you nor hear from you any more.'

Fenwick was thereupon taken back to Newgate to await his trial for High Treason. But next day it was discovered that a trial was impossible. Of the two necessary witnesses against him, 'Scum' Goodman had disappeared. Lady Fenwick had discovered a tougher man than Clancy named O'Brien, who, accompanied by one of the picked Jacobites, had met Goodman at the Dog in

Drury Lane and offered him the alternative of going to France and enjoying an annuity or having his throat cut then and there on the spot. Goodman chose France and O'Brien did not leave him till he was safely at St Germains.

The Bill of Attainder

The immediate reaction to Goodman's disappearance was the usual 'anti-Popish' outcry. A human head was found severed from its body and so mutilated that it was unrecognizable. Obviously Goodman had been foully murdered by Papists. A little enquiry, however, in Goodman's usual haunts revealed the undoubted fact that he had chosen to go away and a Royal proclamation promptly appeared offering a reward of £1,000 to anyone who should stop him. But by this time Goodman was beyond William's reach.

Macaulay's pen, indignant for William, has recorded the ensuing dismay : 'This event exasperated the Whigs beyond measure. No jury could now find Fenwick guilty of high treason. Was he then to escape? Was a long series of offences against the State to go unpunished merely because to those offences had now been added the offence of bribing a witness to suppress his evidence and to desert his bail? Was there no extraordinary method by which justice might strike a criminal who, solely because he was worse than other criminals, was beyond the reach of the ordinary law? Such a method there was. . . . To that method the party that was now supreme in the State determined to have recourse.'

On 5 November – an appropriate date – the Commons ordered Fenwick to be brought to the Bar of the House and, uncertain what other tricks the extraordinary man had up his sleeve, added a special caution that he should have no opportunity of making or receiving any communication, oral or written, on his way from Newgate to Westminster. When he arrived, strongly guarded, he was three times exhorted to confess his crimes. Three times he refused, giving his reasons cogently enough : 'I was in hopes that His Majesty would have informed the House himself. He hath all that I know. My circumstances are hard. I am in danger every day to be tried and I desire to be secured that what I say shall not rise up in judgment against me. It is hard to make me accuse myself under these circumstances and very hard to put it on me now.' He remained painfully unimpressed by the Speaker's assurance : 'You have no reason at all to apprehend that you shall suffer anything if you make a full and free discovery here. No man that ever did so, and dealt candidly with this House, ever did.'

Fenwick's courteous but adamant refusals to implicate anyone at last exasperated the House and the Speaker rapped out : 'Sir, you know what the House doth expect. You must either give them satisfaction in it or withdraw.'

He withdrew and a motion was immediately carried to proceed against him by Bill of Attainder – that is to say, merely to declare that he was guilty without the necessity of proving it and to pass this decision by a majority, like an ordinary Government Bill.

For three weeks, the outnumbered Tories fought tenaciously to prevent the Bill's passage. However they may have disagreed with or even disliked Fenwick, they saw the action as a sacrifice of every principle of justice. Sir Godfrey Copley put it succinctly : 'I dread the consequence of this for our nation in general and for our posterity. It is not Sir John Fenwick's life I argue for. I do not think it worth a debate in this House* nor the consideration of so great an assembly; but I do say, if this method of proceeding be warranted by an English parliament, there is an end to the defence of any man living, be he never so innocent.' Young Foley, the Speaker's son, contemptuously disposed of those who had argued precedents from the Earl of Strafford's case and the Duke of Monmouth's and others within living memory : 'There hath been no precedent that comes up to this – that we should pass a bill to attaint Sir John Fenwick because he will not give evidence or because there is no evidence against him. If Sir John Fenwick is to be hanged because there is but one witness against him, any man in the world may; and then I think every man's life depends on whether this House likes him or not.'

One of the most balanced speeches was made by Sir Francis Winnington, who twenty years before had been Attorney-General

---

*When Lord Cutts subsequently reproached him for this remark, saying : 'I think the life of a gentleman may be thought worth ours', Copley hastened to explain that he meant 'that, Sir John Fenwick considered in his single capacity, I did not think it was worth the while of this House to act in their legislative capacity on him.'

to King James II when he was Duke of York. It was nearly eleven at night when he rose to speak and the debate had been proceeding since eleven in the morning, so the old lawyer, who was now M.P. for Tewkesbury, made his points as tersely as possible. From the 230 columns which the report of the debate occupies in *State Trials,* it is worth quoting him, substantially in full.

'I shall trouble you but a little while, it being late,' he said, 'but gentlemen, seeing it is an extraordinary case, I shall give my reasons why this Bill ought not to be committed; for every Member here is now a judge and he must take the blood of this gentleman upon him, either to condemn or acquit him, though I must confess I have been amazed to hear the doctrine preached that every man, as he is satisfied in his private conscience, ought to judge this man guilty!

'I desire to know by what authority we sit here? We sit here and have a legislative authority and it is by the King's command we come together. But at this time we are trying a man for his life; and therefore I humbly conceive that we ought to proceed according to what is alleged and proved – "secundum allegata et probata" – and if any man in his private opinion says he is guilty he is not acting by the commission by which he sits here. For to tell you of the "Lancashire Plot" or that a man shall not be dealt with this way thereafter seems to be an argument to inflame but having no bearing on the question.

'I agree with all the precedents, good and bad, that have been cited and do not question that in extra-ordinary cases it is in the legislative power of Parliament to look after the safety of the Kingdom; but I shall submit why this does not fall in that category.

'You have one witness, but I do not apprehend you have one good witness, for you must consider what Porter says upon his word; and I appeal to you, if you take what he says upon his word, did you ever know of a Bill of Attainder brought against any man on a bare affimation? No! In that case, you should have turned it into an Impeachment, if the thing looked probable, and then you would have witnesses upon oath. . . . The ancient method of Bills of Attainder used to be first by the impeachment of the person and then to turn it into a Bill of Attainder.

'Next, look what is insisted on by the King's Counsel and recited in the Bill – that there was a bill of indictment found by the oath of two witnesses, Goodman and Porter. Under favour, I think they are not to be accounted witnesses in the point, because it is natural justice in all courts of the world that, if a man be accused as a malefactor, he had the liberty to cross-examine the person who accuses him. Now we all know very well that Bills of Indictment, when they are found by the Grand Jury, never allow the prisoner to put cross-questions, because a Bill of Indictment is only an accusation. And, if an accusation alone is sufficient, who can be innocent? In this case, the oath of Porter that was given to the Grand Jury is not an oath on which you can put any value.

'Next, Sir, consider the paper of Goodman, which you would read, and consider the validity of that. Goodman being now absent, the prisoner has no opportunity for cross-examination. I beseech the House to consider the ill consequences of this. Any Minister of State may come and get an examination before a Justice of the Peace or Secretary of State, and the witness is conveyed away and a Bill of Attainder is clapped on the man's back and the statement shall be read as evidence against him. He is but half a witness – and a witness to the accusation, not a witness in a trial.

'Now I come to Sir John Fenwick's particular case. Sir John Fenwick is indicted, issue is joined and he has notice of his trial. One of the witnesses goes away. No man can tell why he went. (I may believe why, in my private opinion, but that is not my judicial knowledge.) Has it ever been known that when any man has been indicted and issue joined, a Bill of Attainder has been brought against him because his trial was deferred? Here are plots against the Government, and it may be forty are arrested for them. In the case of twenty, there may be two witnesses, but the others may have the good luck to have only a single witness against them. Will you have Bills of Attainder against all the rest?

'If this had been an extraordinary case, wherein the Government had been particularly concerned, it might have weighed with you. But no man can show me any precedent for a Bill of Attainder except where men of great power were concerned to subvert the government. But what is Sir John Fenwick's case? He is in custody and the plot has been detected. If he had run away, you might still suppose he was plotting against the Government because he was fled from justice.

'Gentlemen say the Government *is* concerned. So it is in every felony and particular treason; but must there therefore be a Bill of Attainder to punish it? When there is a Bill of Attainder, it must be because of an immediate danger that threatens the government established that such a man is attainted. But I do not see that any of these circumstances apply to Sir John Fenwick.

'All men agree that this is an extraordinary way of proceeding. Then the question is : Is Sir John Fenwick's case extraordinary or is he anything more than a common malefactor who is in a wicked conspiracy? For myself, I cannot agree that this case of Sir John Fenwick's is so extraordinary that, unless he is hanged, the Government will fall.

'And, under favour, once a precedent is established, who knows what Time may produce from it? It may be that after the death of His Majesty who came to restore our liberties, we may have wicked Members and Members chosen as in Henry VI's time.* Sir John Fenwick's may be the condition of every subject in England.

'We must govern the power of Parliament by reason and common justice; and, as there is no urgent necessity to use this extraordinary remedy, I am against this Bill because it may be dangerous to posterity.'

When he sat down, Sir Thomas Littleton, one of the most active of the Whigs who was shortly to become Speaker of the House of Commons, sprang to his feet to make an objection. It was he who, urging the Commons not to 'consider little niceties' had tried to inflame them against Fenwick by talking of 'plot upon plot' and adding that he had heard so much gossip about the 'Lancashire Plot' that if anyone voted against the Bill, their constituents would be sufficiently incensed that their candidature would probably not be renewed at the next election. Littleton now said that Winnington had accused him of irrelevance in mentioning the 'Lancashire Plot' and that, if it came to a matter of irrelevance, 'I have heard him several times bring his wife and children into his speeches to no purpose at all.'

---

*That is to say, by the victorious side in a Civil War. Winnington's parallel is here exact, since a restoration of James II could have resulted in similar acts of Attainder, on the precedent of Fenwick's, being legally used against all the Members of Parliament who were now voting for it!

'I have a wife and children and that gentleman none', Winnington replied. 'Therefore I think I may make use of that expression.'

The next speech was by Sir Thomas Seymour, who, having reminded the House : 'You may judge the prisoner, but others will judge you', pointed out that, 'upon the whole there has been so much said by the counsel for the prisoner and so little said by the counsel against him that there is not evidence enough for you to proceed.'

The outspoken 'Jack' Howe (so known to distinguish him from his contemporary the Dissenting divine, John Howe) who had once been in William's household and, appalled by what he had seen and heard there, had severed his connection with both Court and Government, put the matter realistically : 'I believe, if Sir John Fenwick had been told when he was Major-General of King James's army that I should come here to sit upon his life, he would have laughed at it and thought it impossible. But the contrary has happened. And I have seen parties hang one another with such violence, I pray God we may keep from it. I do not know; we are all concerned in some measure. It has been the unhappiness of this nation that, at one time or another, everyone has been concerned in such a way as they could have a proceeding of this sort brought against them.'

But even the reminder of what they all knew – that this was an act of vengeance in a revolutionary situation – had no effect. Indeed, Howe's speech, by its very honesty, may have had the effect of hardening the Government in their determination to carry out William's orders.*

In his prison, Fenwick had no illusions. His wife had tried to comfort him by suggesting that the Commons would make another attempt to come to an understanding. But he knew that he would be pardoned only if he would betray his friends and wrote back : 'You speak as if you thought they would offer something to me. If they do, they shall never have another answer from me but what they have had.' After the Second Reading of the Bill in the Commons, he wrote : 'I am satisfied that nothing can save my life. There can be but one Reading more and then it goes up to the

*Macaulay's sneer at Howe is most revealing: 'He was what is vulgarly called a disinterested man; that is to say, he valued money less than the pleasure of venting his spleen.'

Lords. I believe now you have as little hopes as I have to succeed in that House better than I have done in the other. Tell me the truth, as you are my friend as well as my wife, and flatter me not. You give credit, I fear, to people who would see me dead and give you hopes till that hour come.'

On the day the Lords finally passed the Attainder, by a mere majority of six (which, if the bishops had behaved legally and refrained from voting 'in the case of blood', would have been only two.*) The Lords adjourned for a fortnight for the Christmas recess – an interval which was used by Fenwick's friends to plan his escape and by his enemies to put a strong military guard round Newgate.

In prison, Fenwick's one desire was to see his wife again. Throughout all his letters, this persists in a heart-breaking refrain : 'My dear life and soul, all my grief is I fear I shall never see you more, for if you hope for leave from the Lords I doubt you will be deceived, for though they should grant liberty for counsel and solicitor, yet they will stay you must have leave from the King, the other being allowed in a judicial way, but yours as a favour; and what you may expect of that, you may judge. This is the only fear I have. Fear of death, I bless God I have none; but if I should not see you again, it would break my heart before I die. And I believe, too, they will be so cruel as not to allow me a desire [for you] to come to me, for this tyrant would destroy my soul as well as my body. If I am once in his power, I expect no other.'

He wrote an apologia (which seems to be lost) to which he refers in another letter : 'I am writing a paper which I would leave with you which I would have you publish as much as you can safely when I am dead, but know not how to get it to you.'

The strain on Lady Fenwick, making her ill, was an additional anxiety. One letter, on the torn outside sheet of which is written in her hand : 'When the bill was passed', shows his gallant attempt to cheer her : 'My dear life, I had yours dated last night and this by

*And as Churchill and Prince George of Denmark (Anne's husband who was entirely under his influence) as well as Sunderland and others who had been intriguing with James and had been listed by Fenwick also voted with the majority, the result was even closer than it seemed. Godolphin, to his lasting credit, voted against the Bill and Shrewsbury, of course, was absent.

Dighton. He is in haste so I have only time to tell you I am glad to hear you are better. God be thanked for it. I am very well, too, as one in my condition can be. I long to know the particulars you mention. God in heaven bless my dear, dear life and send us a happy meeting.' But both knew that the consolation of meeting would be denied, and Fenwick dropped the pretence, setting himself to answer what may have been (we have not her letters) a threat of suicide after his death : 'My dear life, if you have that love for me you express, which I believe, in God I beg of you as I beg of Him that you will not grieve for me. Resign me to the will of God, offend Him not by your immoderate grief to destroy yourself. Indeed I am cheerful and all the sorrow I feel is the want of you : but how to have the comfort to see you I know not.'

On 11 January 1697, William gave his assent – which had never been in doubt – to the Bill. To Lady Fenwick's petition which she presented to him, throwing herself at his feet, he answered that he must consult his ministers. Her petition to the House of Lords that they would intercede with William to commute her husband's sentence to banishment took the Government by surprise and it was thrown out, after considerable difficulty in whipping up a majority, by only two votes. Alarmed by this, the Government saw that the Commons was properly prepared lest she should decide to appeal to them and when she did, on the last day of Fenwick's life, they refused her by a majority of forty-five.

Fenwick was executed on 28 January 1697, having been shriven by Thomas White, the nonjuring Bishop of Peterborough deprived of his See for refusing to acknowledge William's right to the throne. It was noted that Fenwick died with a composure and bravery which surprised even those who knew him.

Epilogue

It is, I hope, unnecessary to insist further on Fenwick's innocence on the one charge which is relevant to his condemnation – his participation in the 'Assassination Plot'. There is not a shred of evidence that he was even aware of it, though it is of course possible that Berwick may have mentioned it to him when they were discussing the general situation.

The story of this judicial murder has an epilogue which is one of the most edifying examples of unexpected justice in English history. Five years after Fenwick's execution, William was riding at Hampton Court, when his horse stumbled on a mole-hill. William broke his collar-bone and shortly afterwards died. Everyone knows of the famous Jacobite toast to the mole – 'the little gentleman in black velvet'. But not everyone knows, I think, that the horse was Sir John Fenwick's favourite horse, Sorrel, which William had taken for his own after its master's execution.

CHAPTER 19

The Appin Murder
14 May 1752

ALL WRITERS ABOUT the shooting of the 'Red Fox' suffer from one disadvantage. They seek to solve a mystery of which the true solution is known to certain people. The eldest males in the direct line of the Appin Stewarts know who fired the shots that killed Campbell of Glenure as he rode from Fort William to superintend evictions in Appin. Many others in the district share the secret which may not be told. Robert Louis Stevenson, when writing *Kidnapped,* asked indeed in vain. Andrew Lang was given a name which he did not disclose – though it is easily identifiable to those who read his *The Case of Allan Breck* – but which is not, as he supposed it was, that of the marksman. Sir William Mac-Arthur, whose essay *The Appin Murder,* published in 1952, is the last word on the subject, writes : 'I was initiated into the 'secret', the name of the person being told me in a whisper, with cautious over-the-shoulder glances to make sure that no eavesdropper was by. I have faithfully kept their confidence ever since, a quixotic loyalty, for accusations against the person concerned have been made in print, unjustly as I believe. There are brother 'secrets' too, involving other persons, and they cancel one another out. In fact I do not believe that there is any real 'secret' at all. . . . To my mind, everything points to it as an act of private vengeance at the hands of some desperate men crazed by a sense of tyranny and injustice and caring nothing for any consequences so long as their oppressor could be struck down.'

Yet, though the 'secret' as it is in tradition may be misleading, there is no doubt that the truth is known at least to the Chief of Appin; and probably to others.

The background of the story is the aftermath of the '45; of a Scotland held down by garrisons of English soldiers, the clans suppressed and the kilt forbidden, and the lands of loyal Highlanders confiscated and given to Hanoverian partisans; of a venal government in Edinburgh which was merely the instrument of the Pelham administration in London – the most unblushingly corrupt government that even the eighteenth century produced; of three clans, the Appin Stewarts and the Camerons, who had been together in the front line of Bonnie Prince Charlie's Army at Culloden; and the Campbells, who had supported the English; and of a Campbell mysteriously shot in Appin Stewart territory, for which an undoubtedly innocent Stewart was hanged, after a trial in the Campbell country before a jury packed with eleven Campbells and the clan chief of the Campbells presiding.

Charles Stewart of Ardsheal, who led the Appin Stewarts at Culloden (where they lost a third of their fighting force), himself escaped to France. His estate was confiscated and the Hanoverian Government appointed the owner of the neighbouring estate, Colin Campbell of Glenure – the Red Fox – to administer it and collect the rents. He, with some cunning, appointed as his assistant, James Stewart 'of the Glen' – 'Seumas a Ghlinne' – a large farmer in Glenduror, who was the half-brother of the exiled Ardsheal. James of the Glen, who described Ardsheal as 'a very affectionate and loving brother', had been 'out' with him in the '45 but had been pardoned. He returned to his farm in the lovely glen from which he took his nickname and here, kindly, industrious, and beloved by his people, he became what might be called the 'peacetime leader' of a broken cause.

He was also foster-father to one of his younger kinsmen, Allan Breck Stewart, whose father on his death-bed had entrusted the boy to James. In 1752 Allan was about thirty, twenty years younger than James. He had, for excitement, originally enlisted in the English Army, but had deserted as soon as there was the chance of a Jacobite rising. Joining the Young Pretender, he had fought at Culloden with the rest of the Appin Stewarts and had escaped with Ardsheal to France, where he joined one of the Scottish regiments in the French Army. From time to time he came back to the Highlands in search of recruits for King Louis and he was thus 'wanted' by the English Government on three counts – he was a deserter, a Jacobite, and a recruiter for France – any one of which would have hanged him.

Allan was nearly six feet, but somewhat round-shouldered and a trifle knock-kneed; with great dark eyes looking out of a face pitted with smallpox (for which reason he was nicknamed 'breck', meaning 'spotted') and with long, bushy black hair 'put up in a little bag'. He was a conspicuous figure in his French uniform – a yellow-buttoned long blue coat lined with red, a scarlet vest, black breeches, tartan stockings, and a feathered hat – and for obvious reasons, on his visits to his home, he preferred to change it for some of his foster-father's clothes. His character was not, on the whole, considered good. Even some of his own clan thought him 'an idle, fair-spoken clever rascal', a wastrel and a sponger who had only once in his life been known to do a day's work.

Allan's visits to the Appin Stewart country were not concerned solely with recruiting. The loyal tenants on the confiscated estate of the chief were voluntarily paying double rent – an official rent which went by the hands of Campbell of Glenure to the Hano-verians and an unofficial one which they paid to James of the Glen, and which went at intervals by the hands of Allan Breck to support Ardsheal in France. The arrangement was working as amicably as, in the circumstances, it could, in spite of the fact that, on Whit Sunday, 1751, James of the Glen, on the orders of Campbell of Glenure, vacated his own land in Glenduror, which was given to a Campbell. Then the Government decided to take a further step. By the following Whit Sunday, 17 May 1752, all the loyal Stewart tenants were to be evicted from their farms. Glenure, therefore, served notices on them in the April, appointing 15 May – the Friday – as the last day of their tenancy.

Such treatment seemed to James of the Glen a disgrace and he immediately took up the cause of the tenants. He went up to Edin-burgh to put their case before the barons of the Exchequer, but found that the court was not in session and that, consequently, no ruling could be given. He did, however, manage to have an interview with one of them, Baron Kennedy, whom – as he wrote to his lawyer – he found 'very kind and seemed to sympathize much with the tenants' case, gave it as his private opinion that they should sit their possessions for this year and that all justice would be done them; and thought they should take a protest against the factor's (Campbell of Glenure) proceedings in a body. . . . The same advice I had from all I consulted, who were not a few; and all were of the same mind that the tenants had a good chance once their case came before the Barons.'

The difficulty was, of course, that the barons would not be in session before 3 June and the tenants would be evicted by 15 May. James's next move, therefore, was by some means to gain a respite. He managed to get a Bill of Suspension from Lord Dun on 18 April, but this was overruled by Lord Haining, a creature of the Government, who, according to an impartial diarist, 'with a slight knowledge of the law had been made a judge by the interest of potent friends'. James, however, was advised that the tenants might still be saved if, at the eviction on 15 May, they made a formal protest in the presence of a lawyer and two responsible witnesses; and that even if that protest should fail, the worst that could happen would be an enforced fine which the Exchequer Court would remit when it heard the case in June. Whether or not this was sound in law is doubtful, but there is no doubt that James believed it was. He had secured the two witnesses and was trying to get the services of a lawyer, since his own was absent from the district. On the day before the eviction, 14 May, he was talking, in a potato field on his new farm in Acharn, to the messenger he had sent to try to procure the services of this lawyer, when they heard a horse galloping at break-neck speed.

'Whoever the rider is', said James to his companion, 'he is not riding his own horse.'

As the rider passed them, he shouted to them that Campbell of Glenure, the 'Red Fox', had just been shot dead in a wood four miles away.

'Well,' said James quietly, 'whoever did the deed, I am the man they will hang for it.'

And six months later, after a trial which is a classic among deliberate and purposed miscarriages of justice, they did.

During James of the Glen's fight for the tenants in Edinburgh, Campbell of Glenure had also been present in the capital, working against him. James, supposing his work was done when he had been granted the Bill of Suspension, had returned home to Appin and was there when he heard that Lord Haining, the Government's creature, had reversed the decision. But Glenure had stayed on – and, apparently, was instrumental in bringing the necessary pressure to bear on Haining. Immediately it was given he left Edinburgh and rode hard for home, which he reached on Saturday, 9 May. On the Monday he set out for the English garrison town of Fort William, to make arrangements for the evictions in Appin on the Friday. He began his return journey on Thursday, 14th May, with the sheriff-officer who was to superintend the proceedings, his nephew, Mungo Campbell, a young Edinburgh lawyer, and his servant, Mackenzie.

The ride down the long road from Fort William to the Balla-chulish Ferry (which took the traveller across Loch Leven into the Appin Stewart country) was through Cameron territory. The Camerons were as loyal as the Appin Stewarts, had fought with them at Culloden and, like them, had had their estates confiscated and given to Campbell of Glenure to administer for the Crown. But there was a difference in their attitude to the 'Red Fox', for he was, on his mother's side, himself a Cameron. If to the Stewarts Glenure was a clan enemy to be killed if necessary in fair fight, to the Camerons he was a traitor who could not claim the conventions of honourable warfare. And that day, on the last part of his journey before he reached the ferry, Camerons lurked on the wooded hillside, each with a gun and within hearing distance of each other, waiting to shoot.

Glenure had, however, been forewarned of this and ordered Mackenzie to ride so close to his elbow all the way, shielding his body on the left – the hill side – that he was an impossible target; for no Cameron would shoot an innocent man. And when at last he was clear of that long, deadly ambush and in the Appin Stewart country on the other side of the ferry, he exclaimed, with understandable relief, 'I am safe now that I am out of my mother's country.' In less than an hour he was shot dead, as with his three companions he was going through the Wood of Letter-more ('the great, overhanging coppice'), about three-quarters of a mile beyond the ferry.

Mungo Campbell, in a letter written nine days after the murder, describes the manner of it : 'Upon entering the middle of a thick wood, poor Glenure was shot, and had power to say no more than, 'Oh, I'm dead : Mungo, take care of yourself; the villain's going to shoot you.' On which I immediately dismounted and being a few paces before him returned to where he was, and started up the brae where I imagined that the shot came from, and saw a villain with a firelock in his hand, who on seeing me, though unarmed, made off without firing. Glenure still kept his horse; and I removed him off, unable to utter a word, but opened his breast to show me the wound. We had two servants along with us, but not a nail of arms among the whole. Immediately I dispatched one of them to bring us some people; and he, being near an hour away, night coming on, and on reflection having had reason to suspect his attachment, I with great difficulty prevailed on the other to see and find some people, lest we should lie in the wood all night, and that one person would be as good a defence as two against armed villains. Judge them on my situation, in the middle of Appin, surrounded by my enemies, and the doleful spectacle of my dead uncle before me, expecting every moment to be attacked and entirely defenceless. In this situation, however, I continued about an hour and a half, when the Appin people flocked about me in shoals (none of whom but pleased at everything had I shared my uncle's fate). I got a boat and conveyed the corpse to a house in Appin where Glenure and I intended to lodge in that night. . . .'

Besides Mungo Campbell, one other person saw the murderer. A woman, More MacIntyre, the wife of Donald MacDonald of Balloch, in her examination immediately after the murder declared that 'upon that foot road in the Wood [she] met a man running very hard, of whom she asked if he saw Glenure, who told her that he was a little before her on the road'. He was someone this Appin woman had never seen before and the mystery of his identity is still unsolved. But it is interesting to notice that she was not called on at the trial, so that her evidence was suppressed.

The only admitted identification was thus Mungo Campbell's, and the young lawyer was careful to change his description to fit the man whom the authorities wished to incriminate – Allan Breck who, they insisted, was acting in collusion with his foster-father, James of the Glen.

As James was hanged as having 'art and part' with Allan Breck (who was, at the time of the trial, safe in France) it is important to stress that no one today doubts James's complete innocence or quarrels with the inscription on his monument that he was condemned 'for a crime of which he was not guilty', or disputes his words after sentence of death was passed on him, 'My Lords, I tamely submit to my hard sentence. I forgive the jury and the witnesses who have sworn several things falsely against me, and I declare, before the great God and this auditory, that I had no previous knowledge of the murder of Colin Campbell of Glenure and am innocent of it as a child unborn. I am not afraid to die, but what grieves me is my character, that after ages should think me capable of such a horrid and barbarous murder.'

And in his speech on the scaffold he gave simply what is, in fact, the final reason which disposes of the charge against him – and, indeed, against Allan. It was psychologically impossible. The Stewarts did not act that way. They did not shoot men from ambush.

'To do my friends justice,' he said, 'as far as I know I do declare that none of my friends, to my knowledge, ever did plot or concert that murder; and I am persuaded they never employed any person to accomplish that cowardly action; and I firmly believe there is none of my friends who might have a quarrel with that gentleman but had the honour and resolution to offer him a fairer chance for his life than to shoot him privately from a bush.'

Allan Breck's movements and the clothes in which he was dressed on the day of the murder were known beyond any doubt. The previous evening he stayed at Ballachulish House, a few moments' walk from the ferry and about half a mile from the place where Glenure was shot. He spent the morning helping with work on the farm and after dinner – about midday – he decided to fish. He borrowed a fishing-rod which had no hook. He fixed a hook of his own and went to a burn on the hillside from which he could see the surrounding country and watch for Glenure's arrival down the road the other side of the ferry. Later in the afternoon he went down to the ferry and asked the ferryman if the party had yet crossed. He was told that they had not – which he must have known. He then returned up the hillside, disappeared apparently into the wood, and was not seen again. He had no gun.

His conduct, indeed, appears to have been deliberately designed to draw attention to himself. He even got so far out of character as to do some work in the morning; he went to a conspicuous place to fish, so that he was in sight of everyone : he came down to ask an unnecessary question about a man about to be murdered. The obvious explanation seems to be that he was endeavouring to establish that, whatever might happen to Glenure, should he come through the Cameron country alive, he was not to blame for it. For he must have known that he would be immediately suspected. He had never made any secret that he hated Glenure. He had said publicly 'twenty times over he would be "fitsides" with Glenure wherever he met him and wanted nothing more than to meet him at a convenient place'. Though this implied fair fight, not murder, there had been one occasion at an inn (when he was very drunk indeed, for he had been drinking all through the night and his indiscretion was in the morning) when he had given a poor man 'twenty pence to buy 2 Pecks of Meal' and, when the man thanked him profusely, had said, 'If you bring me the Red Fox's skin I will give you more.'

As for the clothes that Allan was wearing on the day of the murder, they had been borrowed from James of the Glen (whose clothes he was in the habit of borrowing during his stays in Scotland as being less conspicuous than his French uniform). They consisted of a short black coat with silver buttons, with the breast and sides lined with scarlet; and a pair of plaid trousers of a kind of blue tartan striped with white. This dress was itself noticeable and supports the theory that he was drawing attention to himself. It became even more widely known, for it was eventually produced at the trial.

Mungo Campbell's first description of the murderer he saw 'running up the brae' was given in his 'precognition' as 'a man with a gun in his hand, clothed in a short dun-coloured coat and breeches of the same'. This he altered at the trial to 'a man with a short dark-coloured coat with a gun in his hand'. The difference is vital. Though the 'dun-coloured coat' changed to 'dark-coloured coat' might pass muster, in no circumstances whatever could 'dun-coloured *breeches*' fit blue and white tartain *trousers*. To make assurance doubly sure, Mungo Campbell was not shown the famous suit at the trial. As a lawyer he had to be careful about the limits of perjury.

Thus we can say with some certainty that Allan Breck was not the murderer; and the question narrows down to the identity of the *other man*. That there was another man is unquestionable on quite other grounds, even apart from More MacIntyre's meeting with him; and it is noteworthy that, from the correspondence between Glenure's brothers and relations, they did not suspect Allan Breck of the deed, but assumed that his disappearance and flight to France after the murder was a move to divert attention from the real assassin. They even wished to advertise a pardon for him, if he would come in and give evidence.

Who, then, was the other man? It may be as well first to state the name of the man which was given as the 'secret' to Andrew Lang – and may, for all I know, be still a tradition in the Highlands. It is Donald Stewart.

Donald Stewart was about thirty. He was certainly about at the time of the murder and in contact with Allan Breck; he lived in the district; he was one of those who was called to the scene of the murder and he helped to carry the corpse of Glenure to Kentallen. But there is really no case against him at all, except that on the day of the hanging of James of the Glen, he wanted to go to the scaffold and give himself up for the crime. His kinsmen told him that, whatever he did or said, he would not be able to save James of the Glen, but would probably only share his fate. Nevertheless he struggled so violently that they eventually tied him up with ropes and locked him in a room (which is still existing and is said to be haunted) until the execution was over.

Donald Stewart's own account of himself, as he told it at the trial, was that, after helping to carry the corpse of Glenure to the boat, he went out at nightfall up the brae where he met Allan Breck and accused him of committing the murder. Allan denied it, but said that 'he believed he would be suspected of the murder, and upon that account, and as he was a deserter formerly from the army, it was necessary for him to leave the kingdom'. He said he was very short of money and asked Donald Stewart to see James of the Glen, who would, he hoped, send the money to the place where he intended to stay until he made his escape.

Next morning, about ten o'clock, Donald Stewart went to James of the Glen's house and in conversation with him 'regretted that such an accident as Glenure's murder should happen in the [Stewart] country'. James replied that he had been told that 'one, Sergeant Mor, *alias* John Cameron, had been threatening in France to harm Glenure'.

Having given this evidence, Donald Stewart, in answer to interrogation, deposed 'that, to his knowledge, Sergeant Mor had not been in Appin these ten years'. As for the money which Allan Breck asked James of the Glen to send, James asked why Allan did not come for it himself if he wanted it. Donald Stewart explained Allan's reasons, whereon James answered that 'he hoped in God Allan Breck was not guilty of the murder' but said no more about the money.

The mention of the Sergeant Mor introduces a character even more of a legend than Allan Breck. After the '45, in which he fought with the Jacobites, he organized a band of outlaws and became the Robin Hood of the Western Highlands. He plundered his enemies in much the same manner as Robin Hood; he had the same quixotry; he robbed but he did not kill and once, when a man was accidentally killed in a scrimmage, he abandoned his booty. Like Allan Breck, the Sergeant Mor was in the French Army; like Allan Breck, he hated Glenure and had threatened to kill him. As a Cameron, his attitude to 'the Red Fox' was even more deadly than Allan Breck's; and, had Glenure been killed in the Cameron country, the Sergeant would have been the inevitable suspect.

He has been exonerated by historians only because he was not present at the time. But what is the alibi worth? It rests solely on the deposition of Donald Stewart. There is no other evidence, as far as I have been able to discover, that on the fatal fourteenth of May the Sergeant Mor could not have been in the wood of Lettermore. And if he were indeed the assassin the case becomes clear. The death would have been the vengeance of the Camerons on a traitor. The action of Allan Breck in calling attention to himself would be comprehensible as cover to a friend and fellow-outlaw. And the curious behaviour of Donald Stewart on the day of the execution would have been because he wished to retract the alibi which he had given the murderer. The identity of the Sergeant would have been unknown to More MacIntyre, as she said it was; and his carefully indistinguishable clothes would fit Mungo Campbell's original description of them. What is more, Murdo Cameron, who organized the long ambush through the Cameron country, said that if the Red Fox escaped them there, he would not come alive through the wood of Lettermore – which strongly suggests that at least one Cameron had stationed himself in the Appin Stewart country. And the keeping of the 'secret' by the Stewarts would have been not to shield the memory of one of their own clan but out of a kind of royal courtesy to the Camerons.

As the editor of the *Trial of James Stewart* has put it, 'Two men had openly declared their intention to be "fitsides" with the deceased. One was Sergeant Mor, the famous Cameron outlaw, and the other was Allan Breck Stewart. If the murder had been committed on Cameron soil, the Sergeant would have been the suspect; but Glenure died on Appin ground and suspicion fell on Allan Breck.' It is an acceptance of this simple alternative which has, I think, for so long obscured the obvious theory, which fits the facts, that the Cameron was operating in Appin.

And, as a last cogency, an outlaw, especially one of the calibre of the Sergeant Mor, would not care that the consequence of his action would spoil the peaceful, legal settlement at which James of the Glen was aiming. Both Allan Breck and the Sergeant were believers in 'rough justice' and the tragedy of their action was not so much that it resulted in the death of Glenure as that it brought the innocent James of the Glen to the scaffold.

It is, of course, possible that even without the murder, means would have been found to do away with James of the Glen after his fight for the tenants and the determination he had shown in Edinburgh. From first to last he himself was sure of it. From his remark in the potato field when he heard Glenure was shot – 'Whoever did the deed, I am the man they will hang for it' – to his last moments of life when he said on the scaffold, 'There are many ways taken upon some emergencies for answering a turn, and it appears I must have been made a sacrifice, whoever was guilty', he knew himself doomed.

His last words were, 'My dearest friends and relations, I earnestly recommend and entreat you, for God's sake, that you bear no grudge, hatred, or malice to those people, both evidence and jury, who have been the means of this, my fatal end. Rather pity them and pray for them, as they have my blood to answer for. And though you hear my prosecutors load my character with the greatest calumny, bear it patiently, and satisfy yourselves with your own conviction of my innocence. And may this my hard fate put an end to all discords among you and may you all be united in brotherly love and charity. And may the great God protect you all and guide you in the ways of peace and concord and grant us a joyful meeting at the great Day of Judgment.'

In England, as soon as the result of the trial was announced, the Prime Minister wrote to his brother, 'Our friends in Scotland have done extremely well. The chief villain concerned in the murder of Glenure is convicted and will be hanged in chains upon the spot where the poor man was killed as soon as the law will allow. The Duke of Argyll tried him himself and the jurymen were his countrymen, almost all Campbells.'

CHAPTER 20

The Diamond Necklace

1772 to 1791

Jeanne de la Motte

THE *Public Advertiser* of Friday, 26 August, 1791, recorded:
'The noted Countess de la Motte, of Necklace memory, and who
lately jumped out of a two-pair-of-stairs window to avoid the
bailiffs, died on Tuesday night last, at eleven o'clock, at her lodgings near Astley's Riding School.'

Jeanne de la Motte, a descendant of the Valois, was thirty-four
at the time of her death. As one of the chief actors in the Diamond
Necklace affair – if not, indeed, the chief – she had been sentenced, five years earlier, to whipping, branding and imprisonment. Young Mr Eden, who was in Paris at the time as a special
envoy had described the event in a letter to the twenty-seven-year-
old Prime Minister, William Pitt: 'Madame de la Motte was
called up at five and informed that the Court wished to see her.
She had no suspicion of the judgment, which is not communicated
here to the accused, except in the case of a capital sentence. She
went in an undress, without stays, which proved convenient. Upon
the registrar reading the sentence, her surprise, rage and shrieks
were beyond description. The *bourreau* and his assistants instantly
seized her and carried her into an outer court, where she was
fastened to a cart with a halter round her neck. The *bourreau*
talked to her like a tooth-drawer and assured her most politely
that it would soon be over. The whipping was slight and *pro
forma,* but the branding was done with some severity. It is a good
idea that the V (*voleuse*) on her shoulders stands also for Valois.'

She was then imprisoned in the Salpêtrière.

At the time of her arrest, her husband and accomplice, the self-
styled 'Count' de la Motte, had managed to escape to England,
where on an earlier visit he had exchanged £10,371 6s. worth
of the diamonds from the stolen Necklace for less dangerous jewels
at Robert Gray's, the jeweller in New Bond Street. An attempt
by French agents to kidnap him one evening as he came out of the

Haymarket Theatre, convinced him that London was less safe
than he had hoped and, after visiting Lancaster, Dublin and
Glasgow, he settled in Edinburgh at the house of an old Italian
teacher of languages. The French ambassador in England, through
his agents, offered the old man 10,000 guineas to arrange for him
to be drugged and put aboard a French collier at South Shields.
The ambassador paid in advance 1,000 guineas (less £63 which
was his secretary's 'cut') but the Italian instead of fulfilling his
bargain promptly shared the money with his intended victim and
at the time of his wife's trial and branding in Paris, de la Motte
was living, in comparative safety, at the corner of Charlotte
Street and Rathbone Street in Soho.

During that autumn of 1786, he talked so openly about printing
in England an apologia which would shake the French court that
the Duke of Dorset, who was concerned with French affairs, wrote
to Eden that a memoir was to be published about the Necklace
affair which, as it was certain to contain nothing but falsehoods
and calumny, the French Government should arrange to be
answered immediately on its appearance by some clever journalist
such as the editor of the *Courrier de l'Europe* (who was in French
government pay).

Meanwhile, de la Motte started to implement his threat by writing to the *Morning Chronicle* a long letter in which he declared
that, unless he received justice from the French authorities, he
would consider himself free to publish letters which he fortunately
had in his possession which would reveal the truth of the Necklace
affair. 'For the purchasing of the Necklace I shall account in the
clearest manner by *making mention of its real owner* who made my
wife a present of some of the most brilliant diamonds which I sold
in London as my property. By a concatenation of circumstances
which happened pending the process, my wife and I were abandoned and inhumanly sacrificed . . . I am not to be told that my
memorial, if published, will, by the secret and curious anecdotes it
contains, raise against me a host of powerful foes, who will not fail
to seek for, and meet with, sufficient opportunity to wreak their
vengeance on me. But what of that? My intentions shall have been
fulfilled; and, whatever be my fate, I shall have the comfort of
having left behind me an authentic justification, and of having
unveiled the whole of the intrigue. And who knows I may be

fortunate enough to hear one day or other, for the good of my country, that my memorial has opened the eyes of him who has been kept so long in the dark! [King Louis XVI.] But for that I shall be told the memorial must not reach him and all avenues will be strongly beset. I am aware of it. But, on the other hand, I shall observe that there exists a powerful party, whose interests it is to forward it, who have been long employed in working a mine which only waits a favourable opportunity for explosion. To hasten this, if my memorial has, as it were, the effects of a match, I shall look upon all the misfortunes I have encountered as the path leading directly to that event.'

The 'explosion' was, of course, the French Revolution which started with the fall of the Bastille two and a half years later and there is no doubt that the eventual de la Motte memorial was indeed one of the "matches" which touched it off. Though this could hardly have been foreseen by the French Court, the appearance of the 'Count's' letter (which was again published in the same paper two days later, this time in the original French, and sent in quantities to Paris) taken in conjunction with the Duke of Dorset's warning, which Eden had passed on to the highest quarters, created considerable consternation at Versailles, in particular among the friends of Marie Antoinette.

About four months later in the spring of 1787 (the exact date is in dispute) two of these friends, the Duchesse de Polignac and her sister-in-law, went to England, ostensibly to drink the waters at Bath, actually to come to terms with de la Motte through the agency of Georgina, Duchess of Devonshire. One suspects, from Marie Antoinette's letter to the Duchesse de Polignac enquiring whether she has received any benefit from the Bath waters that 'benefiting by the waters of Bath' was merely a code phrase for 'securing the memorial from de la Motte'; and, in the June of 1787, there appears in a letter to the King of Poland a report of the gossip at Versailles that the Duchess de Polignac has paid Count de la Motte four thousand louis for certain letters said to have been written by the queen.

At the end of July, Jeanne de la Motte, having escaped from the Salpêtrière and for seven weeks eluded capture in France, arrived in London to add fuel to the already considerable flame.

In so far as the case of the Diamond Necklace is still a mystery, the question is : Who helped Jeanne de la Motte to escape and why? This remains the one enigma, for the idea that Marie Antoinette was in any way concerned in it has long been dismissed by all students of the matter. As Andrew Lang put it half a century ago : 'the pyramidal documents of the process, still in existence, demonstrate the guilt of the de la Mottes and their accomplices at every step and prove the stainless character of the Queen.'

Yet, in the last few hours of her life, Marie Antoinette, facing the revolutionary tribunal, had to answer the calumny, when the president asked her : 'Was it not at the Petit Trianon that you first met the woman de da Motte?'

'I never once saw her', answered the queen.

'Was she not your victim in the business of the famous Necklace?'

'She could not have been, as she was quite unknown to me.'

'So you persist in denying that you were acquainted with her?'

'Mine is not system of denial', said the queen. 'What I have said is the truth. That, I will persist in.'

The great Mirabeau himself pronounced : 'The case of the Necklace was the prelude of the Revolution' and Saint-Just hailed it with : 'What a triumph for Liberal ideas! A Cardinal a thief! A Queen implicated! Mud on the crosier and the sceptre!'

And to this result, Jeanne de la Motte's memoirs, which she published once she was safe in England, contributed almost as much as the case itself. They gave the interpretation, the twist, which made it invaluable propaganda to the organizers of the Revolution. How could the French Government, which had been warned by English diplomatists, which had made such elaborate cloak-and-dagger plans to kidnap de la Motte, and the French Court, which had sent emissaries to 'benefit by the waters of Bath', have permitted the escape of the most dangerous criminal in the case, once they had her safely in prison? Who engineered her escape?

But before examining the possibilities, it may be as well to refresh the reader's memory by giving a short resume of the famous 'Case of the Necklace'.

The Necklace

In the year 1772, King Louis XV was hopelessly at the mercy of his mistress, Dubarry. He regretted that he could not present her with a palace composed entirely of gold and precious stones. She announced her willingness to be satisfied instead with a necklace made of the finest diamonds which could be found. The Court jeweller, Böhmer and his partner, therefore scoured Europe for the stones and eventually 629 diamonds, of the finest water, were collected, mounted and strung together in this fabulous necklace. Unfortunately for Böhmer, at this moment the old king died of smallpox and the jewellers were left with it on their hands, with no prospect of a purchaser willing or able to pay the two million livres (which would be equal to about £2,000,000 in today's currency) that Louis had promised. And as Böhmer had got most of the diamonds on credit, to be paid for when he was paid by the king, he faced virtual ruin unless the new king and queen, Louis XVI and the twenty-year-old Marie Antoinette would buy it.

The queen, though impressed by the diamonds, refused it – the thing was in ghastly taste and she had no desire for a necklace 'like a comforter' – and, when her husband offered to buy it for her, she forbade him on the grounds that France had more need of a ship of war than a set of jewels.

Böhmer was beside himself. He had sent his partner to all the other courts of Europe and he had brought the price down but there was still no prospect of a sale. For the next five years, whenever a Royal baby was born, the jeweller went to the palace in the hope that the queen would change her mind and buy it for the christening festivities. In fact, it became a joke in Court circles and whenever anyone met Böhmer on the way to Versailles, they asked : 'Another Royal baby?'

At last, in 1777, Böhmer, who was almost ruined by the interest he had to pay (he had borrowed 800,000 livres from the Treasurer of the Navy), craved an audience, threw himself at the queen's feet, sobbed considerably and threatened, if she did not buy it, to throw himself in the Seine.

'Get up, Böhmer', said the queen. 'I do not like such scenes and honest people do not find it necessary to kneel. You know I have more than once refused the Necklace. Never mention the matter to me again. Try to break it up and sell it – but don't drown yourself over it.'

If Böhmer would have done practically anything to get the

queen to buy the Necklace, the Cardinal de Rohan, Grand Almoner of France, would have done anything merely to prevent her cutting him. Marie Antoinette loathed the tall stout handsome man of fifty or so who had been ambassador to her mother, the empress's Court of Austria. She disliked him on every count, including his notorious lechery, and his selling of ecclesiastical preferments. Two anecdotes give a clue to the man better than any description. On one occasion in Vienna, he and his entourage, dressed in hunting costume, had broken through a procession of the Blessed Sacrament. On another, in France, he went riding in his carriage with his mistress by his side disguised as a young abbé.

His Eminence Louis-René-Edouard de Rohan, Cardinal of the Holy Roman Church, Bishop and Prince of Strasbourg, Prince of Hildesheim, Landgrave of Alsace, Grand Almoner of France, Commander of the Order of the Holy Ghost, Commenator of St Waast d'Arras, Superior General of the Royal Hospital of the Quinze-Vingts, Abbé of the Chaise Dieu, Master of the Sorbonne, Member of the French Academy, etc., etc., etc. had only one ambition left – to get into the good graces of Marie Antoinette at least to the extent that, on the state occasions when she was bound to meet him in his official capacity, she would refrain from cutting him dead.

The third actor in the tragi-comedy was the Jeanne de Saint-Remy, with whom, under her married name of Countess de la Motte, the reader is already acquainted. She was descended from the Saint-Remy who was one of the illegitimate sons of Henri II and she never forgot her Valois blood. She was born at the château of Fontette near Bar-sur-Aube in 1756 to impoverished parents who sent her out to beg crying : 'Pity a poor orphan of the blood of the Valois : alms, in God's name !' The Marquise de Boulainvilliers, investigating her story, found that the claim was true, adopted her and sent her to be educated at a convent. Later she married one of her lovers – La Motte 'calling himself Count and to all appearance a stupid young officer of the *gendarmie*'. The pair lived in the way that might have been expected of them and, in 1781, again 'made prey' of the Marquise who was then at Strasbourg as a guest of Cardinal de Rohan and his friend and, in a sense, master, the strange and sinister Cagliostro, of whom more will be said later.

Jeanne de la Motte had the gift of charming people into believing almost anything she wanted them to believe. Without allowing for this, which is testified on all sides by contemporaries, her incredible story cannot be understood. She is, indeed, *the* 'confidence-woman' of history. And in due course, she made the Cardinal de Rohan believe that she had such influence with the queen (whom she did not know) that she was able to restore him to the Royal favour as well as to dispose at last of the Diamond Necklace.

The de la Mottes engaged the services of an extremely able forger, Villette, who also became Jeanne's lover the more firmly to bind him to their purposes. By the April of 1784, Jeanne was able to show the cardinal letters from the queen, forged by Villette on paper stamped with blue *fleur-de-lys,* which proved to his satisfaction not only that she was deep in Marie Antoinette's confidence but that she had used her influence on his behalf and that the queen was relenting of her hard treatment of him.

In the July of 1784, the de la Motte ménage was completed by a young mistress whom the count had taken, Marie Laguay, whom Jeanne (in virtue of her Valois blood) created Baronne Gay d'Oliva (anagramistically, Valoi). Fortunately for them all the 'Baronne' had a distinct resemblance to the queen.

Before long Jeanne told Gay that the queen wanted her help in a practical joke, for which she was willing to pay £600. 'You are only asked to give, some evening, a note and a rose to a great lord in an alley in the gardens of Versailles. My husband will take you there.' Gay, apparently, asked for more information for what seemed to be an overpaid service, but, as Jeanne de la Motte noted in her memoirs : 'It was not very difficult for me to persuade the girl, for she is very stupid.'

And so it came about that, on 11 August 1784, in the Grove of Venus in the gardens of Versailles, under a clouded, heavy sky without moon or star, the Cardinal de Rohan was forgiven by Marie Antoinette – or so he imagined as he knelt and kissed the skirt of her dress and she dropped a rose and said words which he understood to mean that the past was pardoned.

Gay (who had been dressed by Jeanne de la Motte in a simple white blouse like that worn by Marie Antoinette in the portrait of her by Madame Vigée-Lebrun, which had been exhibited at the

Salon of 1783) gave her own account of the proceedings : 'M. and Madame de la Motte took me into the Park. There a rose was put into my hand by Madame de la Motte, who said to me : "You will give this rose and the letter you have to the person who will present himself and say to him these words : 'You know what this means.'

'She accompanied me to a hedge of yoke-elms, leaving me there while she went to fetch the great nobleman to whom I was to speak. It was a dull night, not a speck of moonlight, nor could I discover anything but those persons and objects which were familiar to me. It would be quite impossible for me to describe the state I was in. I was so agitated, so excited, so disconcerted and so tremulous that I cannot conceive how I was able to accomplish even half of what I had been told to do.

'I offered the rose to the great nobleman and said to him : "You know what this means" or something very similar. I cannot say whether he took it or let it fall. As for the letter, it remained in my pocket. I had entirely forgotten it. As soon as I had spoken, Madame de la Motte came running up to us, saying in a low hurried voice : "Quick! Quick! Come away." '

For obvious reasons, Jeanne de la Motte dared not risk any conversation. A sentence or two from Gay would have convinced the cardinal that she was not the queen. As it was, he was full of gratitude to the clever and charming and influential Jeanne de la Motte who had had him restored to favour and he was not as surprised as he otherwise might have been when, some months later, she brought him the news that the queen wanted him to buy the Diamond Necklace for her. The price by now had come down to 1,600,000 livres and the queen would pay for it in four instalments at intervals of six months – the first 400,000 to fall due in the August of 1785.

The cardinal, easily impressed as he was, insisted on seeing the Necklace to examine it before he bought it. He remarked, truly enough, that it was in excessively bad taste. He also insisted that the queen should send him some kind of written guarantee. With Villette the forger at hand, the guarantee was easily forthcoming, with the further information that, bad taste or not, the queen wanted to wear it at the Candlemas ceremonies on 2 February.

So on 1 Februray 1785, the cardinal got the Necklace from

Böhmer, who was satisfied both with the contract and the information that it was not to be talked about. On the same day, he received a note from the queen, asking him to be at Jeanne de la Motte's house at Versailles with the casket containing the Necklace.

When he arrived, the cardinal was slightly surprised that he was not allowed to take it to the queen himself; but she sent a note saying that the king was with her, that she did not know how long he would stay and that he could safely entrust the casket to the messenger she was sending. He did so and the 'messenger' (who was Villette the forger) delivered the Diamond Necklace to the person who had decided she wanted it. Not that it left the house. But as soon as the cardinal had, Jeanne de la Motte and her husband cut the Necklace up with a heavy and rather blunt knife. Taking the best stones, the 'Count' crossed to England where, as we have seen, he sold or bartered them for other pieces with Gray of New Bond Street and Jeffreys of Piccadilly. With the proceeds, the de la Mottes, with six carriages and a stud of horses, with silver plate and a superb wardrobe and a dazzling display of jewels went back to Bar-sur-Aube, where Jeanne had once cried : 'Pity a poor orphan of the blood of the Valois !'

Five months went by. The cardinal wondered why the queen still did not see him and the jeweller wondered why she never wore the Necklace; but neither of them took any steps until, on 12 July, Böhmer decided to send her a tactful note which might remind her that the first instalment would soon be due. The cardinal dictated the note and when the queen received it she was very puzzled. She read it aloud to her lady-in-waiting : 'Madame, we are extremely happy to think that the last arrangements which have been proposed to us and to which we have submitted with respectful zeal will be received as a new instance of our submission and devotedness to Your Majesty's commands and we feel truly rejoiced to think that the most beautiful set of diamonds in the world will be worn by the best and greatest of Queens. . . . You hear that, Madame Campan?'

'Yes, Your Majesty. What does it mean?'

'I thought as you managed to solve the puzzle in the *Mercure* this morning you might be able to tell me. That madman Böhmer's just sent it to me. You might see him and find out what it means – and tell him I do not require his services any longer.'

And, with that, the queen twisted the note up and burnt it at a taper which stood alight in her library for sealing letters. Had she not done this, but instead sent for Böhmer there and then and asked him what it meant the whole plot would have been exposed and none but the villains would have been hurt. But she can hardly have been blamed for thinking that Böhmer's monomania about the unsaleable Necklace had at last driven him out of his mind.

It was not until exactly a month later, 12 August, that the queen extracted from Böhmer (who in the meantime had been told by Jeanne de la Motte that the queen's guarantee to the cardinal was a forgery)* all the facts as far as the jeweller knew them; and on 15 August – the Feast of the Assumption – just before the cardinal was about to celebrate at High Mass, the king asked him : 'My cousin, what is this tale of a diamond necklace bought by you in the name of the Queen?'

The cardinal was so taken aback that he was unable to speak coherently and was allowed to write the story in as short a space as he could. He managed to compress it into fifteen lines which, when the queen saw them, made her say furiously : 'How could you believe that I, who have not spoken to you for eight years, entrusted you with such a commission?'

The king and queen, most foolishly, refused the cardinal's offer to pay for the Necklace in return for the hushing-up of the scandal. Napoleon's comment later exactly expresses the situation : 'The Queen was innocent, and to make her innocence the more public, she wished the Parlement to be the judge. The result was that she was taken to be guilty.'

At the subsequent trial in the January of 1786, the cardinal was acquitted, though suitable punishments were meted out to such of the others as were within reach – de la Motte himself, it will be remembered, had escaped to England in time – and 'officially' Marie Antoinette's reputation was vindicated. But the populace, inflamed by the revolutionaries, continued to believe that the cardinal was the queen's lover, who had stolen the Necklace to please her and that the wicked aristos had put the blame on good defence-less bourgeois like Jeanne de la Motte and Villette and Gay

*Her motive here seems to have been the calculation that the cardinal, to escape scandal, would pay the money himself.

d'Oliva. Of the three, it was Gay who was the most popular. 'Pretty, a young mother and profoundly dissolute, she was the darling of Liberal and *sensible* hearts.'

The Escape from the Salpêtrière

The escape of Jeanne de la Motte from her imprisonment is best told in her own words, not because her account of it is necessarily more true than any of her other statements but because it is the only one there is; and it is on this statement as a whole, whatever its value, that any solution must be based.

'It was about the latter end of November or the commencement of December, 1786', she wrote, 'that one of the soldiers doing duty as sentinel in the court of the Salpêtrière, to see that the women made no holes in the dormitory to escape by the aqueducts, passed the end of his musket through a broken part of the wall and attempted to touch Angelica, who waited upon me as a servant and who was sentenced to be confined for life in the Salpêtrière.

' "What do you want with me?" asked Angelica.

' "Is not your name Angelica?" he said softly : "Are you not the person who waits upon Madame de la Motte?"

' "Yes", replied she.

' "Very well", said he. "I heard many lords and ladies in the Palais Royal yesterday mention your name as being the person who is so attentive to her. Tell me if you want anything. I always carry about me an inkstand, paper etc., which I will furnish you with, as I know you have not permission to write. Prepare your letters if you wish to write to anybody and I will take charge of them."

'Angelica thanked him for his kindness, but frankly confessed she could neither read nor write.

' "No matter", replied he. "There is your mistress, Madame de la Motte. I would advise you to get her to write for you to the different ladies who come here and beg her to recommend you to their goodness."

'Two days after this, about three in the morning, the same soldier again touched Angelica with his musket and gave her a packet of gilt paper, a large bundle of quills, a bottle of ink and a letter for herself. "Madame de la Motte will read it to you", said he. Next day Angelica brought me the letter, at every line of which I was struck with such astonishment that I could scarcely believe my eyes. This mysterious letter was as follows : "Assure yourself, Mademoiselle Angelica, that I shall be extremely happy if I can be instrumental in procuring your liberty. Command me and believe that I shall seize every opportunity of being useful to you [and, immediately preceding the last line] *Unfortunate,* put this letter before the light – *'Tis understood* – be sure to be discreet."

'After having read to Angelica so much of this letter as concerned her, I made use of some pretext to send her to the dormitory, and the moment I was alone put the letter to the light, when writing began to appear as if by the power of magic. At length all was visible and the following words astonished my eyes :

' "You are earnestly exhorted to keep up your spirits and to take proper nourishment that you may have sufficient strength to support the fatigue of your journey. *People* are now intent on changing your condition. Speak your wishes and mention the day you are willing to depart, that a post-chaise may be prepared which you will find at the corner of the King's garden. Be discreet : 'tis your interest to be so. Confide implicitly in the bearer, without entertaining the smallest suspicion.' "

'Judge of my astonishment on perusing this mysterious paper ! Surely, said I to myself, I am awake and in sober certainty of the truth of what I see. But who can be the persons who have thus interested themselves in my misfortunes? This singular expression, "It is understood" was never used by any person but myself, the Cardinal and the Queen. Perhaps they both, repenting of what they have done, ashamed of having the weakness to suffer me to be sacrificed, at this moment wish to give me liberty.'

To this letter, Jeanne de la Motte says that she wrote an answer, saying that she was anxious to escape from her confinement and begged her unknown correspondent to aid her in the attempt. In due course, she received the following reply : *'People* have reflected; endeavour to procure the model of the key that will open easily that side where you wish to go out. Act for the best and compose yourself !'

'For two months', she continued, 'I laboured at the attempt and at length succeeded in making two designs – one small and the other large – in which I thought I had fortunately delineated the wards of the key, and which, the moment I perceived to be perfect, I enclosed in a letter which I gave to Angelica to convey to the soldiers who, about a fortnight afterwards, brought a key made exactly after the paper model.*

'I had the patience to wait two whole days without sufficient resolution to make the experiment; but on Sunday, between six and seven in the morning, when Angelica and myself were together in the gallery, the opportunity seeming favourable, with a trembling hand and palpitating heart I applied the key to the lock when, gracious Heaven! what was my surprise and joy at the finding the door opened! We both endeavoured as much as possible to conceal our emotions and proceeded to try whether the same key would open the other three doors. In the afternoon of the same day I pulled off my shoes and crept softly along to the second door, which, to my great joy, was also obsequious to my touch. I shut it again, ascended the steps softly by three at a time, all in a tremble for fear of discovery, and found, as I wished, all was fast and everything quiet. I then attempted to open the door on the other side of the gallery near the second dormitory. This I did with wonderful facility, and with as little trouble as I had opened the others.'

Angelica was released on 1 May and it is obvious that, until she was safely out of prison, Jeanne de la Motte was also unable to leave it. She had – according to her own account – the necessary key in February; but she did not actually leave till June. By the hands of Angelica, presumably, or someone whom Angelica had arranged to see her, she sent on 13 May a letter to one of her old lovers, the Baron de Crussol (who had played Basile in the famous production of *The Barber of Seville* when Marie Antoinette had played Rosina). The letter was, in the main, one of her usual appeals for money, but in it she mentioned that the following week the Duchess de Duras, *dame du palais* to the queen was to pay her a visit. 'I shall see her alone; the public must not know it, as it might get talked about on account of my being forbidden to see anyone for fear I should speak.' Of this visit, there does not seem to be any other confirmation and it sounds intrinsically improbable.

*I am inclined to agree with Vizetelly who, in his book on the Diamond Necklace writes: 'We suspect the whole of this key business to be fudge.'

The motive of mentioning it to de Crussol would seem to be to propagate the pretence that the queen and the cardinal were 'relenting' and consequently facilitating her escape.

The narrative continues : 'I reflected within myself that if I should run the hazard of going out in the dress of the Salpêtrière, I should be easily discovered in the event of being met by any of the Sisters. I conceived also that a male habit would be more favourable for my escape and communicated this to my unknown correspondent, to whom I wrote : "I wish to have a large blue coat, a flannel waitcoat, black breeches, a pair of half-boots, a round high-crowned hat to make me appear taller, a switch and a pair of leather gloves."

'All these the guard brought me about ten or twelve days after; he carried the great-coat under his cloak, the waistcoat in his pocket and the switch in the barrel of his musket; and about two nights after he brought the half-boots and a man's shirt. Thus furnished with wings for my flight, I was wholly intent on my game and, what is not a little singular, without the least fear of not being able to effect my escape. . . . I reflected that I was under the immediate protection of the Queen and would not suffer myself to entertain a doubt that it was the Queen and no one else who had taken this interest in my behalf.

'After a time, however, a feeling of apprehension came across my mind and led me to suspect the sincerity of my unknown correspondent. Surely, I thought to self, this cannot be a plot concerted to lull me to security that I may be more easily got rid of. It cannot be so! They really wish to render me service. There can be doubt of it since I have the key and the proper dress; but whither will this post-chaise conduct me? Probably to some convent; and does the Queen suppose that I can be happy there? I will never consent to go to a convent, and only to some place where I can be free – where I am at liberty!

'About this time I was not a little surprised by a visit from M. de Crosne, Lieutenant of Police. About six o'clock one afternoon I was conducted to Sister Martha's apartment, where I saw M. de Crosne, with M. Martin, secretary, and another person who was a stranger. M. de Crosne at first did not know me; he appeared much surprised and affected to find me so reduced, so altered; and his sensibility deeply affected me. . . . I stood for some moments unable to articulate a single syllable. At length, awaking from my reverie, I saluted him, when the amiable man kindly enquired if there was anything I was in want of as, if so, he would give the necessary orders. At these words I quite lost myself and, forgetting every consideration that should have restrained me, I drew near him and repeated : "Want anything? O, sir, it is too much to bear – that I should be thus confined !" M. de Crosne, greatly affected, would not suffer me to recite the melancholy catalogue of my woes. . . . I could not help thinking that M. de Crosne was sent hither expressly to see me, and the more I reflected upon this visit of him, the more suspicious I became. I began to see that they were fearful I should say too much and that it was judged expedient rather to endeavour to soothe than to drive me to extremities; for if I had really any ill-will, any grudge towards the Queen, I thought to myself, neither the Baron de Breteuil nor the Lieutenant of the Police would take the pains to favour me with the slightest attention.'

At last the final plan was made. One day between 8 June and 11 June, at either eleven in the morning or six at night, the guard was to disguise himself as a wagoner and, with a whip in his hand, was to walk round the King's Garden (the Jardin des Plantes). Jeanne de la Motte in her male disguise was to be accompanied by Angelica's successor, Marianne, who knew her way about the prison.

The time eventually chosen was the morning of 11 June. The key opened the four doors, as it had done in rehearsal. Though she had lost sight of Marianne, Jeanne de la Motte records : 'I did not lose my courage but passed on until I found myself in a large hall wherein were a great number of small beds in each of which was a child. After having cast my eyes round me, I enquired of the Sisters the way out. I did not well understand the directions they gave me, but, after traversing many courts, found myself at length in a spacious court among a number of people who had come to gratify their curiosity by a sight of this prison. I followed a part who entered the chapel to view it, taking care to mix myself up with the rest of the company. After addressing a fervent prayer to Heaven to inspire me with courage, I soon had the gratification of finding myself outside those doors which I had always looked on as impassable. Here I saw no one but the Sisters, to whom I gave some money as though I were an ordinary visitor, and at length fortunately reached the high road. Here, after some delay, I discovered my good Marianne waiting for me near the river.'

Eventually she reached Luxembourg where a Mrs MacMahon met her, on 27 July, bringing a note from her husband in London. With Mrs MacMahon, she immediately set off for London, where she was reunited with the 'Count' and with Angelica, who re-entered her service. At the time it was commonly supposed that the authorities not only connived at the escape but abetted it and that, at the moment of departure, the Superior of the Salpêtrière said jokingly : 'Farewell, Madame, take great care you are not remarked' (which meant also re-marked by the branding-iron). This suggestion, however, merely brings the whole escape into line with the de la Motte propaganda-version that the queen and cardinal 'relented'. But as the queen had nothing to relent of and as she was now on even worse terms with the cardinal than she had been before, finding his presumption the last and intolerable insult, it is quite impossible that they could have co-operated in procuring the escape of the one person it was essential to keep in prison.

On the other hand it was quite clear that Jeanne de la Motte had powerful friends who, for revolutionary if not for personal reasons, were prepared to help her; and it seems to me that the obliging guard, as well as Angelica and Marianne and Mrs Mac-Mahon may well have played the parts that the Memoir assigns to them. The story, indeed, suggests members of a secret society, (of which, of course, there were many at the time, all intent on, in their own way, fanning the flame of revolution). And, if we accept Jeanne's account of the letters she received as being substantially accurate and the phrasing such as the cardinal and only the cardinal was accustomed to use, then there is an obvious and even inescapable clue pointing to one person – Cagliostro.

Cagliostro

'That unutterable business of the Diamond Necklace!' writes Carlyle. 'Red-hatted Cardinal Louis de Rohan; Sicilian jailbird Balsamo Cagliostro; milliner Dame de Lamotte "with a face of

some piquancy"; the highest Church Dignitaries waltzing, in Wal-
purgis Dance, with quack-prophets, pick-purses and public women
– a whole Satan's Invisible World Displayed!'

'Jail-bird Balsamo', 'quack-prophet' and, usually 'Charlatan' or
even 'Prince of Charlatans' – these are the epithets conventionally
applied to Cagliostro which, though true, tend to obscure the
real nature of the man. His name was indeed Balsamo; he was
several times in prison and died in one; he indulged, since his
public wanted it and was infinitely credulous, in quack-prophecy
and charlatanry. Yet that façade was of his own choosing. It hid
his true motives and intentions. And it is difficult not to think that
it was deliberately assumed for purposes of safety, as Hamlet
assumed his madness.

Joseph Balsamo was the son of a tradesman in Palermo, where
he was born in 1743. (He derived the name Cagliostro from a
great uncle.) In his early youth he belonged to a religious order – the
Brothers of Charity. He was remarkable for his intelligence and
his brilliance in the study of medicine. He became a practising
alchemist and when he was about thirty came into contact with
the Illuminati who thought, correctly, that he would be an
admirable missionary for their doctrines. He was initiated in a
cave not far from Frankfort, when for the first time he discovered
that the real object of this powerful secret society was to over-turn
the thrones of Europe and that the first blow was to fall in France.
He also found that the society had enormous funds, subscribed by
its members, which were invested in the banks of Amsterdam,
Rotterdam, Basle, Lyons, London, Venice and Genoa. A considerable sum of money was placed at his own disposal (which he
later pretended he had 'made' alchemically) to propagate in France
the disruptive doctrines of the sect. It was on this mission that he
first visited Strasbourg in 1780, when he adopted for his device
L.P.D., meaning *Lilia pedibus destrue* (Trample the lilies under
foot).

He was probably a hypnotist, certainly a physician, who healed
the poor without charge and thereby gained an enormous (and
deserved) popularity among the masses, which further served his
real aims. He was an adept at alchemy, knew something of
natural magic and was an enthusiastic Freemason. One who met
him thus described him : 'Cagliostro was anything but handsome; still

I have never seen a more remarkable physiognomy; above all, he had a penetrating look which seemed almost supernatural. I know not how to describe the impression of his eyes; it was at once fire and ice; attracted and repelled you at the same time; made you afraid and inspired you with an irrepressible curiosity. One might draw two different portraits of him, both resembling him and yet totally dissimilar.'

This remarkable man entirely dominated the Cardinal de Rohan and was intimate with the de la Mottes. He arrived in Paris just at the time the cardinal was making the final arrangements for the purchase of the Necklace.

He was tried, but acquitted, for a share in the affair. He was, however, told to leave France and, in the June of 1786 went to England where he remained for two years. In 1789, after the Revolution had broken out in France, he went to Rome (which was the city next on the list of the Illuminati) where he fell into the hands of the authorities and, after a trial by the Inquisition, was condemned as a leading member of the Illuminati and died in prison in 1795.

During the time that Jeanne de la Motte was escaping from the Salpêtrière, Cagliostro was safely in London and in touch with de la Motte. With his wide 'secret society' contacts in France and with boundless money at his disposal for organization and bribes, it would be stranger if he were not the organizer of the escape (the result of which so notably helped his cause), than if he were. All the people involved – the guard, the women, the 'friends at Court', Mrs MacMahon – fit into that pattern; and by his intimate knowledge of the cardinal and his conduct of the Necklace affair, he would be able to send the right kind of messages to Jeanne de la Motte in prison.

On the other hand, as he and she had publicly quarrelled when at the trial he had brought to earth her fantasies about a *séance* he had once arranged, he would not let her know that he was the mysterious benefactor. She, whose friendship had turned quickly to the hate that is born of wounded pride, called him a 'low empiric' and determined to revenge herself on him. But it is clear that he was not of a nature which would let personalities stand in the way of his grand design; and the purpose of the Illuminati would be best served by having Jeanne de la Motte in England where she could safely write and publish the calumnies which were to be the final fuel to kindle the revolutionary flame.

That the clue to the enigma of the escape is Cagliostro – not the 'charlatan' but the real Cagliostro with his convictions and his underground army – I have personally no doubt; and I hope that one day a Frenchman will reconsider the whole of the Diamond Necklace affair with him in mind. It might well be that the 'Charlatan' would then be found to play anything but the subsidiary and rather comic role now assigned to him. I should not be surprised if he were the ruthless originator of the whole plot.

CHAPTER 21

The Wives of King George IV
15 December 1785 to 19 July 1821

Question and Answer 1956

WHEN I was asked to investigate more dark corners of history, I decided to use the occasion to probe what lay behind the trial of Caroline, Queen of George IV. This attempt of the king to divorce his wife in 1820 brought England to the verge of revolution. It led, among other things, to the formation of the modern police force and to the founding of the magazine, *John Bull*. It contained psychological puzzles, especially as regards the characters of George and Caroline, for George seemed altogether too stupid and vindictive and Caroline too indiscreet and at the same time too innocent. And the great trial, which was European news less than a century and a half ago, had been so completely forgotten that I was able to buy a report of it – 1,100 pages of small print – for a mere four shillings.

Having read the available printed sources, I went to manuscripts. At the Public Record Office, I asked for material on Queen Caroline and was duly brought a folder marked HO 126/3 which contained many letters, documents and official copies of State papers connected with the case. There was, however, one odd thing about the folder. The list of documents which it was said to contain did not tally with the documents which it did in fact contain.

As it was marked 126/3, I thought it might be worth investigating 126/1 and 126/2, but the catalogue on the open shelves bore no reference to the whereabouts of these bundles. More by good luck than good management, I was able to see a catalogue not generally accessible to the public which listed the elusive 1 and 2 thus :

1. Transferred to Buckingham Palace
   for incorporation in the Royal Archives
   at Windsor in July 1935   1 chest
2. As above   1 bundle

The mystery suddenly became modern, though the question why the removal had been made, interesting as it was, took for the moment second place to the historian's natural annoyance that the Public Record Office could be thus raided and a chestful of once-public documents put beyond the researcher's reach. As it seemed to involve a matter of principle which, if continued, could lead to even more falsification – or, at least, falsification at a different level – than is, by definition, inherent in 'history', I wrote a short letter to the Press, stating the facts.

Mr Montgomery Hyde, M.P., the authority on George IV's Foreign Secretary, Castlereagh (who was vitally concerned in the matter of Queen Caroline) saw my letter and was good enough to table a question in the House of Commons. The result, as reported in *Hansard* for 2 February 1956, I quote in full so that the reader may form his own judgment.

Public Record Office
(Removal of Documents)

MR SPEAKER : Mr. David Jones – Question No. 59.

MR HYDE : On a point of order. You have not called Question 58, which is in my name, Mr Speaker.

MR SPEAKER : I understood that the hon. Member's Question was withdrawn.

MR HYDE : It is not.

MR SPEAKER : Mr David Jones.

MR HYDE : Further to that point of order. I asked the Table to withdraw the Question if it were not reached.

MR SPEAKER : The hon. Member ought not to give such hypo-thetical instructions. Mr David Jones.

MR HYDE : Further to that point of order, Mr Speaker, am I not right in saying that it is customary to ask the Table to withdraw a Question if it is not reached?

MR SPEAKER : I understand the custom has grown up for a Member to ask his Question to be withdrawn if it is not reached, but I understood the hon. Gentleman's Question was definitely withdrawn.

MR HYDE : No, Sir, only if it were not reached. I asked that in that event it should be put off until next Thursday.

MR SPEAKER : Mr Hyde.

58. Mr Hyde asked the Secretary to the Treasury why two
bundles of documents relating to Queen Caroline, wife of King
George IV, covering the years 1804 to 1820, have been removed
from the Public Record Office; and where they are now located
and whether they can be seen by students.

MR H. BROOKE : The documents concerned were, on examination
   in 1935, considered to be not public records or State papers but
   part of the Sovereign's private family archives. They were
   accordingly transferred, with the written authority of the then
   Master of the Rolls and the then Secretary of State for the
   Home Department, from the Public Record Office to the Royal
   Archives at Windsor, where they now remain and where, it is
   understood, they are not open to inspection.

MR HYDE : Is my right hon. Friend aware that these papers
   arrived at the Public Record Office over a hundred years ago
   from the old State Paper Office, and that they remained there
   for the best part of a century, where they were seen by the
   public? Will he make it clear now that they were eventually
   transferred to Windsor, not on account of the nature of their
   contents but because of their character?

MR BROOKE : My information is that they were transferred
   because of their private nature.

There is no doubt that the answers are strictly true. But the
question remains as to what is meant by 'private family archives'
in such a matter as the relationship between King George IV and
Queen Caroline which was the pivot of the political and constitutional history of England for twenty years. Enough is known
about the characters of George and Caroline to make any further
revelations on that score irrelevant; and the attempt of George IV
to divorce Queen Caroline can only be called a private family
matter if the same description is allowed to the attempt of Henry
VIII to divorce Queen Catherine.

By this time, the enigma of 1820 was in my mind taking
second place to the enigma of 1935, and eventually, puzzling over
it, the possible solution of the one gave the clue to the probable
solution of the other. I was convinced, by what I had now read,
that Caroline had been 'framed' by George, at least as far as the
adultery charge went; and the manner in which it was done

showed that the King was going to lengths so extraordinary that they must have been dictated by a relentless personal imperative. Was the reason that, as he was married privately to Maria Fitzherbert (who was by the Pope, by the king and by the Royal family, as well as by Mrs Fitzherbert herself, considered his only true wife) he never considered Caroline as his wife at all? Certainly he never forgave her her celebrated remark at the time of the trial that she had only committed adultery once and that was with the husband of Mrs Fitzherbert. And though, at the time of her trial, he was no longer living with her but was the victim of many mistresses, she remained the only woman he loved and he died and was buried with her miniature round his neck. Was it not possible that for this reason he was determined that, cost what it might, no other woman should share his throne?

I had, up to this point, considered the Fitzherbert marriage as one among several factors to be taken into account; but it was the date – 1935 – of the removal of the chest of papers to Windsor that suddenly made me see its unique importance. For we know that, according to J. G. Lockhart's official life of the then Archbishop of Canterbury, Cosmo Gordon Lang, that in 1935 King George V had a 'long and intimate' conversation with the Archbishop about the attachment of the Prince of Wales to Mrs Simpson. It was not many months later that the question of Edward VIII's morganatic marriage was mooted; and it was possible that George IV's marriage to Mrs Fitzherbert had received such emphasis in the Caroline papers that George V, feeling as he did about his son's love for Mrs Simpson, considered that the public interest was best served by their removal to the privacy of the Windsor archives, where references to an unwelcome precedent could, if necessary, be destroyed at leisure.

There had already been, on Mrs Fitzherbert's death, a wholesale destruction by the Crown of papers in her possession, from which only the marriage certificate and one or two other documents necessary to vindicate her character and status had survived in the safety of Coutts' Bank.

There can be, I think, no doubt that Mrs Fitzherbert knew the truth about many relationships at the court of George IV of which today we have no clue left. To Caroline she was always a friend and during the time of the queen's trial, she went to Paris so that there was no chance of her being impounded as a witness. For she was a woman of the most unbending principles and one to whom the committing of perjury was inconceivable.

But there is one curious fact which has survived the general destruction, though not – as far as can be discovered – the documentary proof of it. Her son-in-law, George Dawson-Damer has left on record a remark she made long after the people concerned were dead :

'Princess of Wales (Caroline) married to Prince Louis. Could have bastardized Princess Charlotte. Compounded with the mother – Lord Loughborough by George III's commands. She saw Princess Charlotte who implored her. A peer still alive, who had been a lover of the Princess of Wales, who implored him to destroy the certificate of marriage to Prince Louis.'

Was it possible that Caroline as well as George was married before their stage-marriage to each other?

And, finally, how did all this bear on the true identity of 'William Austin' – the boy whom Caroline adopted and who was officially pronounced to be the son of poor parents, but whom everybody (including George) assumed to be Caroline's own child and whom Caroline swore to James Brougham was the son of the Prince Louis Ferdinand who was killed at Jena in 1806?

William Austin was never separated from Caroline till her death and she made him her heir. He was born during the time that she and George were married and were both living in London and therefore, had the boy been proved to have been her child he would have been 'legally' also George's, under the law that, if the husband was in the kingdom ('within the four seas') he was presumed to be the father of his wife's children, unless it could be proved that access was impossible or that he was impotent. This surely explains what the Duke of Sussex meant when he told his brother George in 1806 that Caroline's conduct must be investigated since facts had come to light which 'might affect the royal succession'.

And, as 'William Austin' did not die till 1849, the question must have been of more than academic interest in the year 1837 which saw both the death of Mrs Fitzherbert and the accession to the throne of George IV's younger niece, Victoria.

The public events, which culminated in the trial and acquittal of

Queen Caroline and her subsequent exclusion from Westminster Abbey on the occasion of George IV's coronation, thus lead back to mysteries which were, then and now, altogether hidden from the public, and the probabilities, as far as they can be unravelled, reveal a tension of personal relationships as fascinating as any in history.

George dared not reveal his marriage to Mrs Fitzherbert (though, at one point he threatened to) for, as she was a Catholic, he would, under the Act of Settlement, have had to abdicate. Caroline for fear of a European scandal dared not admit her marriage (if it existed) to Prince Louis Ferdinand, who visited her in England when, to cover their relationship, she pretended in public to be interested in one of his staff. Neither George nor Caroline, for different reasons, wished the Royal Commission to establish that William Austin was Caroline's child – though George believed it and Caroline behaved as if it were true. George, determined by some means to get rid of Caroline caused her to be cited for an act of adultery with an Italian, of which she was undoubtedly innocent; Caroline, though knowing that her character would be irrevocably damaged during the proceedings, insisted on standing her trial, despite George's offer to her of £50,000 a year to remain out of England. In the same year as Caroline's trial, he increased Mrs Fitzherbert's allowance to £10,000 a year.

In *The Dynasts,* Thomas Hardy has given his Chorus of Ironic Spirits the well-known lines on the doubly-married and monotonously unfaithful king :

A wife of the body, a wife of the mind:
A wife somewhat frowsy, a wife too refined –
Could the twain but grow one and no other dames be,
No husband in Europe more faithful than he!

Though this is misleading in its simplicity, any attempt to unravel the historical complexity must start with the inter-relation of the two marriages.

Maria Fitzherbert

Maria Anne Smythe was born in 1756, the daughter of an old Catholic family who had sacrificed everything for the Stuarts. She was twice widowed before she was twenty-five; her second husband, Thomas Fitzherbert of Swynnerton, by whose name she is known in history, was the twenty-fifth Lord of the Manor of Norbury, in direct male line from the reign of Henry I, which gave the family 'an antiquity which made most of the English nobility seem mushrooms'.

When in 1783 the Prince of Wales, four years her junior, first saw her riding in her carriage in the park, the 'widow Fitzherbert' was accounted one of the beauties of London and George was immediately captivated. Nevertheless, she resisted all his advances until the day when, to quote Lord Stourton's *Narrative,* she met 'a species of attack so unprecedented and alarming as to shake her resolution. . . . Keate the surgeon, Lord Onslow, Lord Southampton and Mr Edward Bouverie arrived at her house in the utmost consternation, informing her that the life of the Prince was in imminent danger – that he had stabbed himself – and that only *her* immediate presence would save him. She resisted, in the most peremptory manner, all their importunities, saying that nothing should induce her to enter Carlton House. She was afterwards brought to share in the alarm but, still fearful of some stratagem derogatory to her reputation, insisted upon some lady of high condition accompanying her as an indispensible condition : the Duchess of Devonshire was selected.

'They four drove from Park Street to Devonshire House and took her along with them. She found the Prince pale and covered with blood. The sight so over-powered her faculties that she was deprived almost of all consciousness. The Prince told her that nothing would induce him to live unless she promised to become his wife and permitted him to put a ring round her finger. I believe a ring from the hand of the Duchess of Devonshire was used upon this occasion and not one of his own.

'Mrs Fitzherbert, being asked by me [Lord Stourton] whether she did not believe that some trick had been practised and that it was not really the blood of His Royal Highness, answered in the negative and said that she had frequently seen the scar . . .

'They returned to Devonshire House. A deposition of what had occurred was drawn up and signed and sealed by each one of the party. . . . On the next day she left the country, sending a letter to Lord Southampton protesting against what had taken place, as not being then a free agent. She retired to Aix-la-Chapelle and afterwards to Holland.'

For over a year she remained abroad, the recipient of constant letters from the prince. 'The speed of the couriers', writes Lord Stourton, 'exciting the suspicion of the French government, three of them were at different times put into prison. Wrought upon and fearful, from the past, of the desperation of the Prince, she consented formally and deliberately to promise she would never marry any other person; and lastly she was induced to return to England and to agree to become his wife on these conditions which satisfied her own conscience, though she could have no legal claim to become the wife of the Prince of Wales.'

The letter of forty-two pages, dated 3 November 1785, by which George finally prevailed on her is the longest love-letter in the language. In it he made it clear that, since the curious scene in Carlton House, he had always considered himself married to her and he even suggested that his father, the king, was not averse to her becoming his wife. The letter ended : 'Come then, oh come, dearest of wives, best and most sacred of women, come and for ever crown with bliss him who will through life endeavour to convince you by his love and attention of his wishes to be the best of husbands and who will ever remain unto the latest moments of his existence, *unalterably thine.*'

The prince had already determined to marry no one else and to let the crown descend through the family of his brother, the Duke of York. 'I will never marry,' he had declared. 'My resolution is taken on that subject. I have settled it with Frederick. No, I will never marry. Frederick will marry and the crown will descend to his children.'

Accordingly, George, Prince of Wales and Mrs Fitzherbert were privately married on 15 December 1785, with her brother, Jack Smythe, and her uncle, Henry Errington, as witnesses. The ceremony was performed by the Vicar of Twickenham, according to the marriage service of the Church of England, which was valid in Catholic eyes, though it was, of course, illegal, because it contravened both the Act of Settlement and the Royal Marriage Act. On the one hand, Mrs. Fitzherbert was a Catholic; on the other, George lacked the necessary consent of his father, the king.

The first years were happy enough. The honeymoon was spent

at Mrs Fitzherbert's villa at Twickenham and when, after Christmas, they returned to Town, though she refused to live at Carlton House, he 'never forgot to go through the form of saying to Mrs Fitzherbert with a most respectful bow : "Madam, may I be allowed the honour of seeing you home in my carriage?" ' She was given the position of honour; all precedence was waived in her favour and the prince would accept no invitations where she was not given first place. Eventually George, to the extreme displeasure of the king, closed Carlton House and went with his wife to live at Brighton where he built his fantastic Pavilion and she, though living in a small house near, reigned as queen of it. 'Her own manners', a diarist noticed, 'ever remained quiet, civil and unperturbed and in the days of her greatest influence she was never accused of using it improperly.' He, on his part, was scrupulous of her honour and dismissed Beau Brummell from his circle of friendship for his bêtise in calling for *'Mistress* Fitzherbert's carriage'.

Unfortunately for them both, the Prince of Wales's mounting debts could be settled only by a grant from Parliament and the now nation-wide rumour of his secret marriage to a Catholic made Pitt, as Chancellor of the Exchequer use his necessity as a lever to prise out the truth. Fox, apparently in good faith, denied the marriage in the House of Commons and, according to Lord Stourton, 'this public degradation of Mrs Fitzherbert so compromised her character and her religion and irritated her feelings that she determined to break off all connection with the prince, and was only induced to receive him again into her confidence by repeated assurances that Mr Fox had never been authorized to make the declaration.' Sheridan's historic and chivalrous speech in her defence 'affirming that ignorance and vulgar folly alone could have persevered in attempting to detract from a character upon which truth could fix no just reproach and which was in reality entitled to the truest and most general respect', retrieved the situation and in the May of 1787 a correspondent recorded that 'the Prince sat at table with Mrs Fitzherbert and all her particular friends near him. His attention to her has been more marked lately than usual.'

The separation of the prince and his wife did not occur till seven years later when, in the June of 1794, he had fallen under the influence of the notorious Lady Jersey. 'From that time', says

Stourton, 'she never saw the Prince and this interruption of their intimacy was followed by his marriage to Queen Caroline [ten months later]; brought about, as Mrs Fitzherbert conceived, under the two-fold influence of the pressure of his debts on the mind of the Prince and a wish on the part of Lady Jersey to enlarge the Royal Establishment, in which she was to have an important situation.'

As the prince's debts by this time had mounted to £350,000 and were in the nature of a European scandal, he was indeed bound to accede to the terms imposed on him for their settlement – marriage to his first cousin, Caroline of Brunswick.

To understand the pattern into which this State marriage falls, it will be most convenient to epitomize the subsequent relations of George and Maria Fitzherbert. She is said to have fainted when the actual news of the wedding was brought to her and, in spite of the fact that George separated from Caroline immediately an heiress, Princess Charlotte, was born in 1796, Maria refused to return to him.

The prince's state of mind, during this second period of separation, was even more excitable, if possible, than during the first. Three days after the birth of Charlotte, when he had given Caroline her *congé,* he made a will in Mrs. Fitzherbert's favour, as passionately written as his unparalleled love-letter ten years earlier. In it he bestowed all his worldly property on 'Maria Fitzherbert, my wife, the wife of my heart and soul' asking that 'my coffin should be taken up and buried next to Hers, wherever she is to be buried and, if she has no objection, that the two inward sides of the two coffins should be taken out and the two coffins then to be soldered together'. Throughout the will, the phrases 'my only true and real Wife', 'the beloved and adored wife of my heart and soul', 'my beloved and adored Maria Fitzherbert, my Wife, my Second Self' witness to his feelings. His mother, the queen, fearing for his health and his reason, wrote to Mrs Fitzherbert, asking for a reconciliation.

By the spring of 1799, George was prepared to make the fact of the Fitzherbert marriage public, no matter what the consequences to everybody involved, and one of the diarists of the time noted : 'Is it that there is a foundation for what is generally whispered, viz., that the Prince of Wales is going to declare his marriage with Mrs Fitzherbert? But what will be proposed for the Princess and her child? Shall we have the old case renewed of Henry VIII and the tables turned on the Protestants?'

In her dilemma, Mrs Fitherbert appealed to Rome. Father Nassau, one of the staff at the Catholic chapel in Warwick Street, went to the Pope to lay the case before him on the understanding that, if the answer allowed it, she would at once return to her conjugal duties but, if not, she would leave England. The answer from the Vatican confirmed Mrs Fitzherbert's status as the prince's true and only wife and on the day she rejoined him on 16 June 1800 she gave her famous 'public breakfast to the whole town of London'. The wedding-breakfast (and the world understood it as such) thus took place nearly fifteen years after the marriage.

'She told me', records Lord Stourton, 'she hardly knew how she could summon resolution to pass that severe ordeal, but she thanked God she had courage to do so. The next eight years were, she said, the happiest of her connection with the Prince. She used to say they were extremely poor, but as merry as crickets and, as proof of their poverty, she told me that once, on their returning to Brighton from London, they mustered their common means and could not raise £5 between them. . . . She added, however, that even this period, the happiest of their lives, was much embittered by the numerous political difficulties which frequently surrounded the Prince, and she particularly alluded to what has been termed "the Delicate Investigation" [about the parentage of William Austin] in which Queen Caroline and His Royal Highness were concerned.'

By 1809, George had succumbed to a new mistress, Lady Hertford, and Mrs Fitzherbert felt bound to refuse to submit to the treatment she now received when, at George's request, she visited him at the Pavilion. 'Whatever may be thought of me by some individuals,' she wrote to him, 'it is well known Your Royal Highness four and twenty years ago placed me in a situation so nearly connected with your own that I have a claim upon you for protection. I feel I owe it to myself not to be insulted under your roof with impunity. The influence you are now under and the conduct of one of your servants, I am sorry to say, has the appearance of your sanction and support, and renders my situation in your house, situated as I am, impossible any longer to submit to.'

Nevertheless she visited him, at his order, on 31 January, 1811, when she pleaded with him to show more kindness to his and Caroline's child, the Princess Charlotte. But in the summer of that year, Lady Hertford persuaded the prince not to invite her to the great party given to celebrate the inauguration of the Regency (George III having at last gone hopelessly insane) as well as to honour the family of Louis XVI of France—the famous dinner when 'the son of the demented entertained the family of the decapitated'.

Mrs Fitzherbert asked for an audience to receive confirmation of the insult from George herself and the following day she wrote him a letter reminding him that he was 'excluding the person who is not unjustly suspected by the world of possessing in silence unassumed and unsustained a rank given her by yourself above that of any other person present'.

From that day, she rarely saw and never spoke to her husband again, though, nineteen years later in his last illness – she was then seventy-four – she could not resist writing him a letter which began: 'After many repeated struggles with myself, from the apprehension of appearing troublesome or intruding upon Your Majesty after so many years of continual silence, my anxiety respecting Your Majesty has got the better of my scruples.'

George seized the letter, read it with joy and put it under his pillow. But it was too late. Death summoned him before he could summon her. He was buried, as he had wished, with her miniature on his heart.

Caroline of Brunswick

On 24 August, 1794, about two months after Mrs Fitzherbert had left her husband for the first time (on Lady Jersey's account), George III wrote to Pitt from Weymouth: 'I have this morning seen the Prince of Wales, who has acquainted me with his having broken off all connection with Mrs Fitzherbert and his desire of entering into a more creditable line of life by marrying; expressing at the same time that his wish is that my niece, the Princess of Brunswick, may be the person.'

This official version is as far from the truth as official versions tend to be. Caroline of Brunswick herself had no illusions about the matter, and summed it up with: 'I was the victim of Mammon. The Prince of Wales's debts must be paid and poor little I's person was the pretence.' And the queen, when the prince discussed the king's insistence on his marriage, told him, with Mrs Fitzherbert in mind, 'It is for you, George, to say whether you can marry the Princess or not.' The combined effect of the king's financial blackmail, Lady Jersey's influence and Mrs Fitzherbert's refusal to return to him made George decide that he could marry the princess and James Harris, Earl of Malmesbury, went to Brunswick to report.

Malmesbury, meeting Caroline who was nearly twenty-seven, was bound to agree that 'old as she was, her education was not yet completed.' His observations on her were those of an acute and trained diplomatist and accurately portray a character which over the years changed little in essentials.

'Princess Caroline very *gauche* at cards – speaks without thinking – gets too easy – calls the ladies (she never saw) "Mon coeur, ma chère, ma petite." I notice this and reprove it strongly. . . . Princess Caroline very "missish" at supper. I much fear these habits are irrecoverably rooted in her – she is naturally curious, and a gossip – she is quick and observing, and she has a silly pride in finding out everything; she thinks herself particularly acute in discovering likings, and this leads her to the most improper remarks and conversation. . . . On summing up Princess Caroline's character today, it came out to my mind to be that she has quick parts without a sound or distinguishing understanding; that she has a ready conception, but no judgment; caught by the first impression, led by the first impulse; turned away by appearances or *enjouement*; loving to talk and prone to confide and make missish friendships that last twenty-four hours. Some natural but no acquired morality and no strong innate notions of its value and necessity; warm feelings and nothing to counterbalance them; great good humour and much good nature; no appearance of caprice; rather quick and *vive* but not a grain of rancour. From her habits, from the life she was allowed and even compelled to live, forced to dissemble; fond of gossiping and this strengthened greatly by the example of her good mother [George III's sister] who is all curiosity and inquisitiveness, and who has no notion of not gratifying this desire at any price. In short, the Princess, in the hands of a steady and sensible man would probably turn out well; but where it is likely that she will find faults perfectly analogous to her own, she will fail.'

As Malmesbury perceived, she was altogether too like her first cousin whom she was about to marry; and the points on which she differed from him were even more likely to precipitate disaster. 'Argument with the Princess about her toilette. She piques herself on dressing quick; I disapprove this. She maintains her point; I, however, desire Madame Busche to explain to her that the Prince is very delicate and that he expects a long and very careful *toilette de propreté*, of which she has no idea. On the contrary, she neglects it sadly and is offensive from this neglect. Madame Busche executes her commission well and the Princess comes out the next day well washed all over.'

The improvement seems to have been only temporary. Three weeks later, Malmesbury regretfully notes : 'I had conversations with the Princess Caroline on the toilette, on cleanliness and on delicacy of speaking. On these points I endeavoured, as far as was possible for a man, to inculcate the necessity of great and nice attention to every part of dress, as well to what was hid as to what was seen. (I knew she wore coarse petticoats, coarse shifts and thread stockings and these never well washed or changed enough.) I observed that a long toilette was necessary and gave her no credit for boasting that hers was a short one.'

Malmesbury accompanied Caroline to England and introduced her to the prince on 5 April, 1795. 'I according to the established etiquette introduced (no one else being in the room) the Princess Caroline to him. She very properly, in consequence of my saying it was the right mode of proceeding, attempted to kneel to him. He raised her gracefully enough and embraced her, said barely one word, turned round, retired to a distant part of the apartment and, calling to me, said : "Harris, I am not well : pray get me a glass of brandy." I said : "Sir, had you not better have a glass of water?" Upon which he, much out of humour, said *with an oath* : "No, I will go directly to the Queen." And away he went.'

Caroline, bewildered by George's strange behaviour asked : 'Mon Dieu ! Is he always like that? I find him very fat and not at all like the picture sent me.'

Three days later, the marriage took place with customary state. It was performed at night and the Archbishop of Canterbury officiated. In the morning, the Prince of Wales had driven down to Mrs Fitzherbert's house at Twickenham. Immediately before the wedding, the Royal family dined at Buckingham House and, as they went to dress for the ceremony the king instructed his second son, the Duke of Clarence (the future William IV) to go with the Prince of Wales and not to leave him because of the state of depression that he was in. Clarence recorded that the prince never uttered a word until they were on their way back to St James's Palace when he suddenly said : 'William, I wish you to go to Mrs Fitzherbert tomorrow and tell her I assure her she is the only woman I have ever loved.'

During the wedding itself the prince, who seemed dazed, rose impatiently from his knees before the ceremony was half over. The archbishop stopped, but the king stepped forward and recalled his son to his situation. At the end of the service he 'shook his son's hand with a force that brought tears to his eyes'. It is improbable, considering what had gone before, that George's 'daze' was due to drink any more than his tears were the result of a septuagenarian handshake. But once the marriage was a fact, he certainly got as drunk as he could and spent most of his wedding night in the grate 'where he fell'' said Caroline 'and where I left him'.

Charlotte, the child of George and Caroline, was born on 7 January 1796; on 10 January, George made the passionate will in favour of Mrs Fitzherbert. He then openly left Caroline and eventually, in response to her complaints and enquiries, wrote to her on 30 April : 'Madam, as Lord Cholmondeley informs me that you wish I would define in writing the terms upon which we are to live, I shall endeavour to explain myself on that head with as much clearness and with as much propriety as the nature of the subject will admit. Our inclinations are not in our power, nor should either of us be held suitable to each other. Tranquil and comfortable society is, however, in our power; let our intercourse, therefore, be restricted to that and I will distinctly subscribe the condition which you required through Lady Cholmondeley that, even in the event of any accident happening to my daughter (which I trust Providence in its mercy will avert) I shall not infringe the terms of the restriction by proposing, at any period, a connection of a more particular nature. I shall now finally close this disagreeable correspondence, trusting that, as we have completely explained ourselves to each other, the rest of our lives will be passed in uninterrupted tranquillity. I am, Madam, with great truth, very sincerely yours, George P.'

Caroline replied in a letter beginning : 'The avowal of your conversation with Lord Cholmondeley neither surprises nor offends me; it merely confirmed *what you have tacitly insinuated for this twelvemonth.*' She retired to a villa at Charlton, which had once been occupied by Mrs Fitzherbert. In 1801, she removed to Montague House, Blackheath and here she continued to receive many visitors, including some from abroad who took advantage of the Peace of Amiens to visit England. At the end of 1802 she adopted, as a newly born baby, William Austin.

That Caroline had what can only be described as a craze for children is undoubted. It was of such dimensions as to be something more positive than what is loosely described as a 'thwarted maternal interest'. In her later years, the parents of any child to whom she took a fancy were destined for promotion. Her interest in 'petite Victorine', the daughter of Bartolomeo Bergami, was to be the cause of her advancement of the father, which provided a lasting scandal and led to her trial. At the end of her life, the attraction of the little son of Parson Wood which she 'could not control' and which, according to Brougham, 'amounted almost to a craze', caused her to dismiss her faithful friends Lord and Lady Hood as Lord of the Bedchamber and Mistress of the Robes 'in order to appoint Wood and his wife who had not the proper rank and indeed in all respects were unfit for the situation'. And in these early days at Blackheath there was a veritable nursery.

In his *Travels in England in the year* 1803, a French visitor, J. H. Compé, encouraged by Caroline, described her life at Blackheath with 'eight or nine poor orphan children to whom she had the condescension to supply the place of mother'. The author draws a picture which bears the stamp of Caroline's approval and was later incorporated into the official defence of her character. 'These poor children were boarded by her with honest people in the neighbourhood; she not only directed everything relative to their education and instruction but sent every day to converse with them and thus contributed to the formation of their infant minds. Never while I live shall I forget the charming, the affecting scene which I had the happiness of witnessing when the Princess was pleased to introduce me to her little foster-children . . .

'The children appeared clothed in the cleanest, but at the same time in the simplest, manner just as the children of country people are in general dressed. They seemed perfectly ignorant of the high rank of their foster-mother, or rather not to comprehend it. The sight of a stranger somewhat abashed them; but their bashfulness soon wore off and they appeared to be perfectly at home. Their dignified benefactress conversed with them in a lively, jocose and truly maternal manner. She called to her first one, then another, and another and, among the rest a little boy, five of five or six years old, who had a sore upon his face. Many a parent of too delicate nerves would not have been able to look at her own child in this state without an unpleasant sensation. Not so the royal mother of these orphans. She called the boy to her, gave him a biscuit, looked at his face to see whether it had got any better and manifested no repugnance when the grateful infant pressed her hand to his bosom.

'What this wise, royal instructress said to me on this occasion is too deeply impressed upon my memory to be erased. "People find fault with me," she said, "for not doing more for these children, even after I have taken them under my care. I ought, in their opinion, to provide them with more elegant and costly clothes, to keep masters of every kind for them that they may make a figure as persons of refined education. However, I laugh at their censure, for I know what I am about. It is not my intention to raise these children into a rank superior to that in which they are placed : in that rank I mean them to remain and to become useful, virtuous and happy members of society. The boys are destined to become expert seamen and the girls skilful, sensible, industrious housewives – nothing more—"

'Such was the wise and philanthropic manner in which this admirable Princess, in the flower of her age, passed one day after another. . . . She devoted one day in the week to her own daughter, the Princess Charlotte, who came to see her and spent the day with her. There was nothing to prevent her from enjoying this gratification oftener, for the child was to be brought to her whenever she pleased. For wise reasons, however, she denied herself and her daughter the more frequent repetition of a pleasure of which both of them every day were ardently desirous. "If," she said, "I were to have the child with me every day, I should be obliged sometimes to speak to her in a tone of displeasure and even of severity. She would then have less affection for me and what I said would make less impression upon her heart." '

What M. Compé omitted to notice was that William Austin, the child of a sail-maker from Deptford, was inseparable from his foster-mother and brought up not at all according to his station. And what posterity has noticed is that, making all allowance for the thirty-five-year-old Caroline's undoubted interest in other people's children, this kind of establishment was the perfect way of concealing any personal experiments in maternity she might be inclined to make.

Meanwhile 'Willikin' became only too well known to many illustrious visitors, including Mr Pitt. 'Oh! how Mr Pitt used to frown', recorded Lady Hester Stanhope, 'when he was brought in after dinner and held up by a footman to take up anything out of the dessert he liked, bawling and kicking down the wine and hung up by his breeches over the table for people to laugh at . . . the Princess used to say to Mr Pitt: "Don't you think he is a nice boy?" To which Pitt would reply: "I don't understand anything about children." Once he cried for a spider on the ceiling and, though they gave him all sorts of playthings to divert his attention, he would have nothing but the spider. Then there was such a calling of footmen and long sticks and such a to-do!'

Caroline's most intimate friends at this period were Sir John and Lady Douglas, her neighbours at Blackheath. At the end of 1804, Lady Douglas was suddenly dismissed from intimacy, found herself the recipient of unpleasant letters and drawings and ultimately retaliated by making the charges against Caroline which led Augustus, Duke of Sussex, in the November of 1805 to wait on his brother, George, Prince of Wales, with news which 'might affect the royal succession'. The so-called 'Delicate Investigation' was thereupon by order of the king undertaken by Lords Erskine, Grenville, Spencer and Ellenborough who in the July of 1806 furnished a report acquitting Caroline of being the mother of William Austin, but adding that 'as on the one hand the facts of pregnancy and delivery are to our minds satisfactorily disproved, so on the other hand we think that . . . circumstances . . . particularly those stated to have passed between Her Royal Highness and Captain Manby must be credited until they shall receive some decisive contradiction, and, if true, are justly entitled to the most serious consideration.'

The former Chancellor Lord Eldon; Spencer Perceval, the former Attorney-General; the Solicitor-General, Sir Vicary Gibbs, and others leapt to Caroline's defence. (Perceval even gave tongue to the sentiment : 'To the Tower or the scaffold in such a Cause' – which makes Caroline's later admission to Brougham that 'she had humbugged Perceval, Eldon and the whole lot' sound rather shabby.) Under their expert legal advice and tuition, she made a masterly defence of herself in letters to the king and was eventually received at Court once more. But, in the years that followed, the matter intruded into politics and finally into the popular consciousness. The Government were asked why Lady Douglas had not been prosecuted for perjury and could be given no answer other than that there were reasons which made it inadvisable. It was to the general relief of everyone concerned that in 1813 Caroline asked and was by Parliament granted permission to reside abroad and in the summer of 1814, accompanied by her attendants and 'young Mr Austin', set out, under the name of the Countess of Wolfenbüttel on her fantastic odyssey.

William Austin

On Christmas Day, 1814, George, in the presence of his sister, Mary, had a serious conversation with his daughter Charlotte about William Austin. He told her : 'As long as I am alive this boy can be no sort of consequence, but if I should die then the boy may be a very serious misfortune to you as well as to the country.' For years both the prince regent and the king had prohibited Charlotte, on her visits to her mother, ever seeing William Austin, because 'from two points of view he was an improper companion' for her.

Charlotte told her father that 'she had never seen him in the drawing-room from the time the order was given that she was not to keep company with him' but that as her mother greatly preferred him to her and always had him with her in whichever of her houses she was, it was impossible altogether to avoid meeting him. She had in fact met him on the staircase, 'a sickly-looking child with fair hair and blue eyes'.

Her father's theories impressed Charlotte. When she discussed the matter with her aunt Mary, she said : 'Now I see clearly that my mother's object is to bring this boy forward.'

'But as long as your father is alive,' said Princess Mary, 'he can be of no consequence.'

To which Charlotte surprisingly answered : 'So my father thinks, but I am not so sure of that.'

'But,' said Princess Mary, 'I believe the Prince can prove that he has not been for *many* years under the same roof with the Princess.'

'The Princess of Wales,' replied Charlotte, 'has been at Carlton House since she had Blackheath and, though I was very young, I am sure I remember seeing Captain Manby and Miss Manby his sister at Carlton House.'

Towards the end of February, George wrote to his daughter, who had now had two months to see the situation in perspective : 'You are now completely sensible and satisfied that she has interests, attachments and views which must render it the object of her most anxious wish and endeavour to prejudice you in the opinion of the whole world and if possible, however unnatural it should seem, to ruin you for the benefit of another. That the time may come when she will thus exert her utmost efforts in favour of the boy . . . there can be no doubt. In such a sad predicament, when I am gone you have no protector but a husband; and that husband cannot be a protector unless he shall have a name, a station and a character in Europe calculated to repel what may be, and what you and I now do clearly see will be, attempted.'

It seems to me, from this, to be quite clear that whatever they might officially pretend and however publicly (and even thankfully) they might accept the finding of the 'Delicate Investigation' that William Austin was the son of Sophia Austin, the entire Royal family was satisfied that Caroline was the mother of the boy and that the father, though possibly Captain Manby, must be presumed to be George because Caroline had been careful, at the critical time, to spend the night under the same roof with him at Carlton House. In other words, Caroline could, if she wanted, establish William Austin as the heir-male to the throne.

Caroline's answer at the time, when someone accused her of being the boy's mother : 'Prove it – and he shall be your King' was not, therefore, as it has usually been interpreted, a laughing assertion of her innocence, a light dismissal of a monstrous *canard* against a faithful wife. It was an equivocal, double-edged remark and the edge turned against the Royal family was the sharp and cutting reminder that if they allowed the 'Delicate Investigation' to establish her maternity, it would also establish William Austin, as George's presumed child, as the future sovereign.

It is also noteworthy that Princess Charlotte's remark about her mother being at Carlton House (which it was altogether against her interest to admit) corroborates the vital evidence, ten years earlier, of Lady Douglas (which the 'Delicate Investigation' dismissed as untrue) that when Caroline had told her of her pregnancy, though she would not reveal who was the father, she did say that she hoped it would be a boy and that 'if it was discovered she would give the Prince of Wales the credit of being the father, for she had slept two nights at Carlton House within the year.'

These facts are an essential clue to the meaning of the 'Delicate Investigation'. All historians and biographers, as far as I know, have made the situation appear simpler than it was. They have assumed that George wished to prove Caroline guilty in order to have an opportunity of divorcing her. But in fact, as is now obvious enough, it was far more important to George than it was to Caroline to establish that she was innocent, even though no one, least of all George himself, believed it.

Lord Glenbervie, Lord North's son-in-law, who was a lawyer, a scholar, a privy councillor, a lord of the treasury – an observer both responsible and knowledgeable – records in his diary how, during a visit to Caroline, ' "Little Willy" as the Princess calls him, concerning whose parents the enquiry was during the *Delicate Investigation*, was in the room after dinner as, it seems, is usual on such occasions, and was playing with an orange which Lady Glenbervie had given him when the Princess, in a sort of reverie, after looking at him steadfastly, said, in her imperfect English, "It is a long time since I brought you to bed, Willy." The boy not hearing distinctly showed that he did not by some gesture or expression, on which she said again, "It is a long time now since I brought you to bed." Still not understanding what was meant, he seemed to have thought she had said it was a long time since he ought to have gone to bed, for he replied that he would go to bed immediately and went out of the room. Lady Glenbervie, prepared as she is for many strange things, was astonished and confounded beyond measure. This is a secret that must be at least a century old before it ought to be whispered, and I give my son that solemn caution if ever this part of this journal shall fall under his eyes.'*

Glenbervie also recorded the relationship of Caroline and Prince Louis Ferdinand : 'Prince Lewis of Prussia, nephew to the old Princess of Orange and to the late King of Prussia, was *l'amant de coeur* of the Princess of Wales and had *les prémices de son coeur* long before she came to England. There is reason to believe he came to England *incognito* after her marriage and when she was living at Charlton and saw her in private and those who have the best means for guessing believe little Edwardina, a protegée of Her Royal Highness, was the result. Willie is thought to be the offspring either of Captain Manby or of Sir Sidney Smith.'†

Caroline's own account of William Austin's parentage was given in the March of 1819 under the seal of secrecy to James Brougham, the brother of her lawyer, Henry Brougham, who was to defend her at her trial. The only person to whom James was allowed to reveal it was to Henry, under the same seal of secrecy.

'She began by saying', recorded James Brougham, 'she had "humbugged Perceval, Eldon and the whole lot" and that William was not the son of Austin; that he was the natural son of Prince Louis Ferdinand and was brought over to England in 1803 by a German woman who died about five years ago; that Louis Ferdinand sent him to her to take care of. On his arrival (she expected him) she got a child from Austin, which accidentally had a mark on its arm the same as William; that this child was taken God knows where, but sent away, and that William was substituted in his place; that she contrived so that the mother did not see it for some time and she never knew or suspected that it had been changed and of course believes to this hour that William is her son.

'In 1805 or 1806 Louis Ferdinand came over to see the Princess. Captain Manby, who had been introduced to her by Lady Town-

---

*This part of the diary was not published till 1928. Considerable portions of it are still unpublished.
†Princess Charlotte, on the other hand, said she thought that Edwardina was Sir Sydney Smith's child and that she was certain that Willie was Captain Manby's. It seems more probable that both children were Prince Louis's, who, it will be remembered, Mrs Fitzherbert had reason to suppose was Caroline's real husband, just as she was George's real wife.

send, was on that station and was entrusted to bring him over. She saw him as often as she could during the week he was here.

'She was always attached to Louis Ferdinand and said she could never love the Prince as her heart was engaged to Louis Ferdinand, but had he treated her well she would have respected him and been a good wife, though there could be no love. Says she made a fool of Manby . . .

'Louis Ferdinand was nephew to Frederick the Great and was killed at Jena. She says he courted death and insinuated that he was in love with her all his life. . .

'After she told me, she said her mind was easier at having told someone of this and frequently afterwards asked me if I thought William looked like a carpenter's son – and whether he did not betray his blood by looking so like a German and things of that sort.'

But it seems that James Brougham was not the only recipient of this confidence. Years after everyone concerned was dead, Henry Brougham placed it on record about 'the sailmaker's child at Deptford, who was called Billy Austin, but for whom another was substituted after a few years, the child of one of her ladies in Germany by Prince Louis of Prussia', that 'she had often mentioned this to Lady Charlotte Lindsay and Mrs Damer, but they supposed it was a jest. However, when Lushington and Wilde went with the funeral to Germany and one of them presented the other to the general who came to receive the body and then said : "And here is Mr Austin, of whom you have often heard," he said, "Yes, I have often heard of Billy Austin, but this is not he; this is the son of my old general, Prince William,* and so like him that I at once knew him before you named him." '

In assessing the truth of Caroline's story that, though Louis Ferdinand was the father, she was not the mother, it must be borne in mind that the one man above all to whom she could not admit her maternity (if it were true) was Henry Brougham. He had to defend her against the charges which were being prepared for her trial and the whole basis of his case was her complete innocence. Psychologically she had to believe that he believed it and it is

---

*Louis Ferdinand had both an uncle and a cousin who might be this 'Prince William' who is unidentifiable.

unlikely that she ever noticed – as the wits did – that in his subsequent declaration that 'the Queen is pure innocence' the last word sounded like 'in a sense'.

Secondly, if Captain Manby was in the secret, it would explain as nothing else can, Caroline's public indiscretions, 'making a fool of him'. To shield Louis Ferdinand, any ruse was permissible; and one must read the following entry in Glenbervie's diaries with this in mind : 'I can never forget my astonishment when on going to dine at Blackheath some time before the "Delicate Investigation" I found Captain Manby there . . . He was certainly not, from his situation, birth or manners, a person one would expect to meet in the society of the Princess of Wales. We were only five : Her Royal Highness, Lady Glenbervie, Miss Vernon, myself and the Captain. She placed him next her at table and directed all her *looks*, words and *attentions* to him at and after dinner, when we went to coffee and then she made him sit very close to her on the same sofa. After a time he withdrew and the moment he shut the door she started up and said in her broken English, "Child cry" and then hurried into the adjoining room which has a communication with her garden and park. She has a private key to this which she sometimes lends. She was absent from us perhaps three-quarters of an hour and to do her justice she returned with an air and look of confusion. In about ten minutes we took our leave, having to return to Town that night. I never saw Manby with her but that time. The child was little Billy.'

It need only be added that by the date this occasion could easily have coincided with Prince Louis Ferdinand's visit to England under Captain Manby's escort and that it is thus not beyond the bounds of possibility that the private invitation to the Glenbervies was part of a deliberate plan on Caroline's part.

Thirdly, Caroline always treated William Austin as if he were her own child. As long as she lived, he was never parted from her. On 5 March, 1818 she wrote to her bankers, Messrs Coutts instructing them to invest £200 a year (the rental of her house at Blackheath) in Government stock on William Austin's behalf. On her death in 1821, she left him all her property and though her estate was insolvent, he received £4,000 from the executors.

He spent most of the rest of his life abroad where (since he had left England with Caroline when he was ten and had only returned

for the unhappy months that saw Caroline's trial, her exclusion
from the Coronation and her death), he was more at home than in
the country of his birth. He was certified insane by Italian doctors
in the autumn of 1841, which by an odd coincidence was the time
that Queen Victoria gave birth to the future Edward VII. He was
kept in an asylum in Milan until 1845 when he was taken to
England and immured in Dr Sutherland's private asylum in
Chelsea till his death four years later.

One may say, therefore, that there is a considerable probability
that William Austin was the son of Caroline at a time when George
could have been presumed the father and that the boy was therefore legally heir to the throne. That, in the chestful of documents
removed from the Public Record Office in 1935, the proof of this
lay is a possibility which is supported by the fact that the remaining
folder HO 126/3 does not contain many of the documents which it
is said to contain.

The documents listed as being there but in fact abstracted from
it included a letter from Caroline to the king, 8 December, 1806 :
the Lord Chancellor to the king, 27 November, 1806 : the king
to the Lord Chancellor, 29 November, 1806 and 11 December,
1806 : the minutes of the Cabinets of 23 December, 1806 and
25 January, 1807 : Lord Chancellor to the king with enclosure
from Lord Ellenborough : a letter from Caroline to the king, 16
February, 1807 : Prince of Wales to the king and opinion of
H.R.H.'s Law Offices annexed 28 February, 1807 : the king to
the Lord Chancellor 3 March, 1807 : the Lord Chancellor to the
king on the same date and again on 11 March : Minute of the
Cabinet of 20 March, 1807, and a separate Minute annexed from
the Chancellor, 25 March – all of which obviously relate to the
'Delicate Investigation'.

The status of William Austin is of mere academic interest today.
Even if he were, and could be proved to have been, the titular
Prince of Wales, it would only mean that he, and not the Duke of
Clarence, should on George IV's death have been King William IV
and that Queen Victoria should not have succeeded to the throne
until 1849, instead of, as she did, in 1837. She was, in any case, the
eventual heiress.

But, when Caroline left England, with William Austin safely in
her possession, in 1814, the matter was anything but academic. And

it is this which explains the subsequent events which were to culminate in Caroline's trial. The Crown had two explosive secrets. One was the fact that the prince regent's true wife was Maria Fitzherbert, which, had it been known, would have meant that George would immediately have had to renounce the Succession under the Act of Settlement. The other was the existence of William Austin who, if Caroline cared to proclaim and prove him her son, could complicate the succession even more hopelessly. George, in fact, could be blackmailed by both his wives. Though there was no danger of it from Maria Fitzherbert, Caroline of Brunswick was incalculable.

Thus, for the remaining seven years of Caroline's life, George's one desire was to discredit and, if possible, divorce her. To attain this end, there was nothing that he would stop at and, when the trial is put in perspective, the reader may be disposed to think that there is very little that he did.

Prelude to the Trial

Caroline, after making various visits, determined to settle in Italy where she eventually bought the Villa d'Este on the shore of Lake Como. As most of her English attendants, outraged by her eccentric conduct at Courts she called at, left her, she collected a household of Italians of whom the most notable was Bartolomeo Bergami, a six-foot military man with 'large mustachios and whiskers, dark complexion and eyes, a bold but agreeable countenance and of robust form', to whose small daughter, Victorine, she had taken a violent fancy. She made him her Chamberlain.

'As to my household,' she said, 'all de fine English folk leave me. I know people are very ill-natured and choose to abuse me. No matter, I do not care – from henceforth I will do just as I please, that I will. Since de English do not give me the great honour of being Princess of Wales, I will be Caroline – a happy, merry soul.' In her merriment, she sang duets with Napoleon's wife, the Empress Marie Louise, at Berne; gave a grand party to Murat in Naples, where she appeared as Glory and 'even more ridiculously dressed than the others, tripped forward, took a feather from the wing of Renown and wrote in large golden letters on a panel she held the names of the different battles in which Murat had distinguished himself'; and organized a *fête champêtre* at the Villa d'Este where she exhibited herself as a Druidical priestess with Willikins as the sacrificial victim. She then decided to spend the next year, 1816, in making an expedition to the East.

Her impending absence suited George. At the end of 1815, the marriage was arranged between the Princess Charlotte and Prince Leopold of Saxe-Coburg-Saalfeld and, with the prospect of the succession now being safeguarded, it had become more imperative than ever to rid himself of the menace of Caroline. In the January of 1816, Castlereagh, the Foreign Secretary, acting on George's instructions wrote a 'Most Private and Secret' letter (which fortunately has survived) to his brother in Italy to instruct him that any evidence which might be to Caroline's discredit was to be scrupulously collected.

'You will keep in mind', the letter ran, 'that there are two objects to be aimed at. The first and best would be unqualified proofs of what no person could morally doubt as would for ever deliver the Prince Regent from the scandal of having a woman so lost to all decency in the relation of his wife – to effect this, or to justify in prudence a proceeding for Divorce, the proofs must be direct and unequivocal and the evidence such with respect to the parties to be examined as would preclude their testimony from being run down and discredited. . . . But there is another most important object short of Divorce viz., to accumulate such a body of evidence as may at any time enable the Prince Regent to justify himself for refusing to receive the Princess in this country or to admit her to the enjoyment of any of those honorary distinctions to which his wife, if received into his Court and family, would be entitled.'

In February, 1816, Prince Leopold arrived in England formally to ask for Charlotte's hand : in the March of 1816, Castlereagh's brother was able to report that, in Italy, everything was in train in Caroline's absence and that he had 'written to the gardener's boy and the cook at the Villa d'Este and they are expected here to finish the Carnival when we shall see if there is anything to be done with them' : on 2 May, 1816, in London, Charlotte and Leopold were married : and at the beginning of September, 1816, Guiseppe Rastelli, who was to give the crucial evidence against

Caroline, successfully applied to her immediately on her return from her journeyings for the post of her Superintendent of Stables at the Villa d'Este.

These dates are necessary for understanding the true course of events, because the official version (which was the only one known at the time and which is still repeated by historians apparently ignorant of Castlereagh's 'Most Private and Secret' letter) was that is was not until over a year later, in 1817, after the death of Princess Charlotte in child-birth, that George started to investigate Caroline's conduct. And as Rastelli left Caroline's service in 1817, months before the setting up of the Milan Commission which considered the evidence collected against her, it is assumed that he was, even if a rascal and perjurer, at least a relatively impartial witness. Once the real sequence of events is seen, it is quite obvious that he was 'planted' at the Villa d'Este by George's agents. And even in assuming that he was engaged by Caroline immediately on her return, I am giving him the benefit of a doubt. He said in his evidence that he entered her service 'at the latter end of August or the beginning of September, 1816' and that she was, at that time, in residence at the Villa d'Este. No reliance can really be placed on his word, but it is worth noticing that, if the August date were the true one, he would have been introduced into her household on the eve of her return.

The public proceedings against Caroline were not long delayed. Princess Charlotte died in the November of 1817, when Caroline was, in the course of further journeyings, visiting Warsaw. Prompted, so it was averred, by the reports to the Admiralty of Captain Pechell, who had been in command of the frigate *Clorinde* which had taken Caroline to the East, and by the gossip of some of Caroline's servants which the Duke of Cumberland had heard in Brussels, enquiries were set on foot. Immediately after Charlotte's death, George instructed his creature, Leach, to ask for a commission to be set up to investigate Caroline's conduct. The ministry agreed and the tribunal assembled in Milan in the September of 1818. From time to time it sent copies of the evidence collected to Leach who passed it on to the Prime Minister. A prominent member of the Commission was Lord Stewart the brother of Castlereagh who had received the secret instructions at the beginning of 1816 and the courier and carrier of Lord Stewart's private messages to

Westphalia and Frankfurt, to Paris and Vienna, scouring Europe for witnesses, was Guiseppe Rastelli.

The Commission returned to England and made its report in the July of 1819. When George's ministers (including Castlereagh) had studied it, they felt bound to advise the prince regent in these terms : 'According to these opinions Your Royal Highness's servants are led to believe that the facts stated in the papers which have been referred to them would furnish sufficient proof of the crime, provided they were established by credible witnesses; but it is at the same time the opinion of Your Royal Highness's confidential servants that, considering the manner in which a great part of this testimony has unavoidably been obtained, and the circumstances that the persons who have afforded it are foreigners, many of whom appear to be in a low station of life, it would not be possible to advise Your Royal Highness to institute any legal proceedings upon such evidence, without further enquiry as to the characters and circumstances of the witnesses by whom it is to be supported.'

As a comment of this important memorandum, one can only endorse Fitzgerald's remark that it is 'as damaging a piece of evidence against the Regent's ministers as could be conceived; for here was the deliberate opinion as to the value of the evidence on which they later brought the Queen to trial.' Fitzgerald thought that it showed 'how flexible were their principles'; a truer estimate which we may make, having at our disposal more facts of the case than he had, is that it showed how imperative it was for George, at whatever risk, to discredit Caroline.

The death of the old, mad king, at the end of January, 1820 – six months after this Cabinet advice – and the accession of the prince regent as George IV made the matter even more urgent. Caroline, though by now aware of the extent of the plot against her, determined to come to England and assert her rights as queen. Neither the obstacles that were put in her way – such as a refusal of a *visa* – nor the offer of £50,000 a year if she would remain on the Continent, had any effect. In February, George threatened to dismiss his Ministers and retire to Hanover unless the Government instituted proceedings against the queen. Again they replied that they were in duty bound to advise him that 'the body of testimony consists almost exclusively of the evidence of foreigners, most of them not above the rank of menial servants, or that of waiters and attendants in hotels, wholly unacquainted with the English language and some of the former class standing in the questionable situation of having been dismissed or removed from Her Royal Highness's service.'

On the other hand, they agreed that Caroline's name was to be omitted from the Prayer Book.

Caroline, when she heard of it, immediately wrote to know why and, intimating that she intended to be crowned queen, started her return journey to England. At the beginning of June she landed at Dover where she was unexpectedly (owing to a failure of Government staff-work) greeted with a royal salute from the castle. The whole town lined the shore and she was given the first of those hysterical popular ovations which were to become a feature of English life for the next five months and bring the country to the brink of revolution.

On 6 June, London saw her for the first time for seven years. She was dressed for the occasion in a black twilled sarcenet gown, a fur tippet and a ruff, with a hat of black satin and feathers. She was now fifty-two, stout and matronly, and neither her ringlets nor the roses on her cheeks were her own. But her tears of emotion were. She had not dared to hope for such a welcome. The streets were almost impassable. Every window was filled with eager faces and men and women waving white handkerchiefs. Cries of 'Long Live Queen Caroline' mingled with 'God bless her. She has a noble spirit. She must be innocent.' To give point to their sentiments, the crowd smashed Lady Hertford's windows in Manchester Square.

Though Caroline's cavalcade had not intended to take the Pall Mall route to South Audley Street where she was staying temporarily in the house of one of her principal supporters, Alderman Wood, the pressure of people and the cries of 'To Carlton House!' forced it. The sentries presented arms and Caroline waved her handkerchief and called 'God save the King' as she passed.

Meanwhile, earlier that same day, George had declared open war. He had sent this message to the House of Lords, commending his queen to be dealt with by them – the first instance of the kind since the precedent of King Henry VIII:

'The King thinks it necessary, in consequence of the arrival of the Queen, to communicate to the House of Lords certain papers respecting the conduct of Her Majesty since her departure from this kingdom, which he recommends to the immediate and serious attention of this House.

'The King has felt the most anxious desire to avert the necessity of disclosures and discussions which must be as painful to his people as they can be to himself; but the step now taken by the Queen leaves him no alternative.

'The King has the fullest confidence that, in consequence of this communication, the House of Lords will adopt that course of proceeding which the justice of the case and the honour and dignity of His Majesty's crown may require.'

The papers were deposited on the table of the House in two large green brief bags. From this moment 'green bag' meaning 'tainted evidence' became one of the catchwords of the nation.

Princess Lieven wrote to Metternich. 'We live in continual tumult and anxiety. The Queen will age us all. Troops have been brought up round London and, at night, cavalry pickets occupy the principal quarters of the town.' Later, she added, 'The Queen is greeted with respect and enthusiasm not only by the mob – make no mistake about that – but by the solid middle-classes who have won England her reputation for virtue and morality. The streets are full of well-dressed men and respectable women, all waving their hats and their handkerchiefs. In a few days there will be a serious crisis in the country. The Queen's trial begins next week.'

The Trial and Death of the Queen

The method of proceeding against Caroline eventually chosen was by a 'Bill to deprive Her Majesty Caroline Amelia Elizabeth of the Title, Prerogatives, Privileges and Pretensions of Queen Consort of this realm and to dissolve the marriage between His Majesty and the said Queen'. The Bill stated that 'whereas in the year 1814 Her Majesty, being in Milan in Italy, engaged in her service in a menial situation one Bartolomeo Bergami, a foreigner of low station; and whereas, after the said Bartholomeo Bergami had so entered the service of Her Royal Highness, a most unbecoming intimacy commenced between them and Her Royal Highness not only advanced the said Bartolomeo Bergami to a high situation in Her Royal Highness's household but bestowed on him other great and extraordinary marks of favour and distinction, obtained for him orders of knighthood and titles of honour and conferred upon him a pretended order of knighthood which Her Royal Highness had taken upon herself to institute without any just or lawful authority; and whereas her said Royal Highness, while the said Bartolomeo Bergami was in her said service, unmindful of her exalted rank and station and of her duty to Your Majesty and wholly regardless of her own honour and character, conducted herself towards the said Bartolomeo Bergami, both in public and private, in the various places and countries which Her Royal Highness visited, with indecent and offensive familiarity and freedom, and carried on a licentious, disgraceful and adulterous intercourse with the said Bartolomeo Bergami, which continued for a long period of time during Her Royal Highness's residence abroad, by which conduct of her said Royal Highness great scandal and dishonour have been brought upon Your Majesty's family and this Kingdom :

'Therefore, to manifest our deep sense of such scandalous, disgraceful and vicious conduct on the part of her said Majesty, by which she has violated the duty she owed to Your Majesty and has rendered herself unworthy of the exalted rank and station of Queen Consort of this realm, and to evince our just regard for the dignity of the crown and the honour of this nation, we, Your Majesty's most dutiful and loyal subjects, the Lords Spiritual and Temporal and Commons in Parliament assembled, do hereby entreat Your Majesty that it may be enacted :

'And be it enacted by the King's most excellent Majesty, by and with the advice and consent of the Lords Spiritual and Temporal and Commons in this present Parliament assembled, and by the authority of the same, that her said Majesty Caroline Amelia Elizabeth, from and after the passing of this Act, shall be and is hereby deprived of the title of Queen, and of all prerogatives, rights, privileges and exemptions appertaining to her as Queen Consort of this realm; and that her said Majesty shall, from and after the passing of this Act, for ever be disabled and rendered incapable of using, exercising and enjoying the same or any of them; and moreover that the marriage between His Majesty and the said Caroline Amelia Elizabeth be, and the same is hereby from henceforth, for ever wholly dissolved, annulled and made void to all intents, constructions and purposes whatsoever.'

The day appointed for the opening of the debate on the Bill

(the proceeding popularly known in history by its less exact if truer description, 'the trial of Queen Caroline') was 19 August, 1820. For the previous three days London had been in a ferment. Westminster was a network of barricades with bodies of those soldiers who could still be trusted not to mutiny at every corner. As the queen, on the way to the House, passed Carlton House, the crowds watched with feverish anxiety to see whether the guards would present arms. When they did so, men surged forward to shake hands with them and women to kiss them. Cries were heard thunderously : 'The Queen or Death' and 'We'll give our blood for you.' On walls were chalked 'The Queen for ever : the King in the river.' Beams a foot square which had been thrown across the streets were broken as if they had been reeds by the mere pressure of the multitude. The crowd outside Westminster was estimated at between twenty and thirty thousand. The king did not dare show himself. Castlereagh, though willing to, was officially prevented lest he should be lynched and had a bed installed in the Foreign Office in the room in which he gave audience to foreign ambassadors.

The House of Lords was crowded. There was a fine of 500 guineas a day for non-attendance unless age, infirmity, absence abroad or the Roman Catholic faith provided a valid excuse.

Caroline, cheered to the echo outside, took her place in silence inside on the crimson and gilt chair facing the Throne which had been provided for her. She wore a black figured gauze dress, trimmed with much lace, a high ruff, white sleeves and a white veil. Though she had by nature light hair, blue eyes, a fair complexion and a good-humoured expression, she had by artifice spoilt her appearance with much rouge, a black wig and a profusion of false curls, which 'gave her features an air of boldness and defiance'. It was Caroline's misfortune that she always managed to dress, act and speak in a part which was not herself and to do all of them badly. She was a figure of simplicity and tragedy. She appeared a rather shady figure of fun.

The witnesses, a motley crew from the Italian underworld whose depositions the Green Bag contained, were living in a state of seige in the houses of the officers of the House of Lords. Walls had been hastily built to prevent them being seen as they took exercise and they were guarded by a gun-boat patrolling the Thames and a regiment of soldiers on the land side. Nevertheless, as Lord Albemarle put it, 'about the building in which they were immured from August until September, the London mob hovered like a cat round the cage of a canary'.

Caroline's reaction to the first witness, Theodore Majocchi who had been her postilion, was unfortunate. When he came forward Caroline 'stood up close to him and threw her veil completely back, held her body very backward and placed both her arms at her sides. In this position she stared furiously at him. For some seconds there was dead silence. Then she screamed out "Theodore!" in a most frantic manner and rushed violently out of the House.'

People were divided in opinion as to what this exhibition meant. Some, forgetting that the queen knew he would be there, considered it a proof of her guilt. Others, more reasonably, construed it as an indignant protest at 'seeing her servant dressed up and turned into a gentleman' as well as at his ingratitude. The Prime Minister immediately sent a messenger to inform the king, who considered the 'O, Theodore!' a fact of greatest importance.

But whatever advantage George might have hoped to gain from it was speedily dispelled by Majocchi's cross-examination by Brougham in the course of which he provided London with a new catchword: 'Non mi ricordo' – 'I don't remember'.

A mere sample must serve as illustration of what was a long process:

ATTORNEY-GENERAL: At what time did you meet with Bergami at Naples?

MAJOCCHI: About Christmas 1814.

ATTORNEY-GENERAL: In what situation was he at the time?

MAJOCCHI: He was a courier – and, it was reported, equerry.

ATTORNEY-GENERAL: Did you afterward enter the service of the princess?

MAJOCCHI: I did.

ATTORNEY-GENERAL: How long after you had met with Bergami?

MAJOCCHI: About a fortnight.

ATTORNEY-GENERAL: What was then the situation of Bergami?

MAJOCCHI: He was a lackey and wore a livery.

ATTORNEY-GENERAL: Can you recollect any accident happening to Bergami?

MAJOCCHI : Yes.

ATTORNEY-GENERAL : What was it and where did it happen?

MAJOCCHI : A kick from a horse. When they went to the lake Aniano.

ATTORNEY-GENERAL : In consequence of it, was he put to bed?

MAJOCCHI : Yes.

ATTORNEY-GENERAL : Did you see the princess in his room during his sickness?

MAJOCCHI : Yes.

ATTORNEY-GENERAL : Did you carry broth to him?

MAJOCCHI : Yes, often.

ATTORNEY-GENERAL : Did you see the princess on that occasion?

MAJOCCHI : Non mi ricordo – I don't remember.

ATTORNEY-GENERAL : Were any instructions given to you as to where to sleep after this accident?

MAJOCCHI : Yes, I slept on a sofa in the cabinet.

ATTORNEY-GENERAL : Did you see anyone pass during those nights through the corridor?

MAJOCCHI : Yes, I did. Her Royal Highness.

ATTORNEY-GENERAL : In what manner?

MAJOCCHI : Very softly; she came to my bedside, looked and passed on.

ATTORNEY-GENERAL : How long did she remain in Bergami's room?

MAJOCCHI : About ten or fifteen minutes.

When the Attorney-General sat down, Brougham rose to cross examine.

BROUGHAM : Was it not a very severe accident Bergami met with?

MAJOCCHI : Yes.

BROUGHAM : He was much hurt?

MAJOCCHI : Yes, he could not ride.

BROUGHAM : Were you not taken into the service of the princess to attend Bergami in his illness?

MAJOCCHI : Yes.

BROUGHAM : You have said he could not ride. Could he walk?

MAJOCCHI : I don't know.

BROUGHAM : Did he go out walking?

MAJOCCHI : I don't know whether he could walk.

BROUGHAM : Did you ever see him walking?

MAJOCCHI :   I – I – don't remember. Non mi ricordo.

BROUGHAM :   Was he attended by any medical man?

MAJOCCHI :   Non mi ricordo.

BROUGHAM :   Did you see Her Royal Highness go into the room of Hieronymus when *he* met with an accident?

MAJOCCHI :   Non mi ricordo.

BROUGHAM :   Have you not seen her go to Sir William Gell's room when he, too, was confined by illness?

MAJOCCHI :   Non mi ricordo.

BROUGHAM :   Was it not her constant practice to go into the apartment of any of her suite who happened to be ill to see after their health and their treatment?

MAJOCCHI :   Non mi ricordo.

BROUGHAM :   You were never ill yourself at Naples?

MAJOCCHI :   Non mi ricordo.

BROUGHAM :   Did the princess make any difference between the highest and the lowest of her servants during any illness of any of them?

ATTORNEY-GENERAL :   I object to this mode of pursuing the cross-examination. It is assuming that some of them were ill, of which there is no proof.

BROUGHAM :   Then I will put the question another way, for I mean to assume nothing. Were all the servants in Her Majesty's suite always in perfect health, except Bergami during his illness from the kick of a horse?

MAJOCCHI :   Non mi ricordo.

And so the farce continued, justifying completely Brougham's final and devastating comment : 'I have heard it asserted that the great prevailing feature of Majocchi's evidence, his lack of memory, signified but little because memories differ. They do. So does honesty. It will be my duty to point out parts of Majocchi's evidence in which I defy the wit of man to conceive any stronger or more palpable instances of false swearing than can be traced in the words "Non mi ricordo". I shall put it to Your Lordships that while Majocchi's testimony has abounded in guilty forgetfulness, no single example supporting the idea of an innocent forgetfulness has occurred.'

Another important witness was Louisa Demont, a one-time chamber-maid of Caroline's. 'She is the smartest dressed of *femmes de chambre*, but neither the youngest nor the prettiest', an observer noted. 'In complexion she is a brunette; her cheeks sunk and shrivelled and her eye more remarkable for an expression of cunning than of intellect. She advanced to the bar with a degree of confidence which even the penetrating glance of Mr Brougham, who eyed her most perseveringly "from top to toe", did not at all affect.'

Brougham left the cross-examination to the junior counsel, John Williams, and a portion of it throws a light on the government methods. The Mr Powell referred to was a member of the Milan Commission.

WILLIAMS: You entered the service of the princess in the year 1814?

DEMONT: Yes.

WILLIAMS: And remained in it until the year 1817?

DEMONT: Yes.

WILLIAMS: Did you quit the princess's service of your own accord or were you discharged?

DEMONT: I was discharged.

WILLIAMS: Were you not discharged for saying something which you afterwards admitted to be false?

DEMONT: Yes.

WILLIAMS: You were applied to by some person or other soon after you were discharged from the princess's service?

DEMONT: Yes, nearly one year after I had left her service.

WILLIAMS: To know what you had to say with respect to the princess? Is that not so?

DEMONT: Yes.

WILLIAMS: Where were you examined?

DEMONT: At Milan.

WILLIAMS: How many examined you?

DEMONT: Four.

WILLIAMS: Was Mr Powell one?

DEMONT: Yes.

WILLIAMS: You have been thirteen months in England?

DEMONT: Yes.

WILLIAMS: Were you ever in England before?

DEMONT: No.

WILLIAMS : Have you finally agreed what you are to have for your evidence?

DEMONT : They have promised me nothing for my evidence.

WILLIAMS : No benefit or profit of any kind?

DEMONT : I expect no profit for coming here.

WILLIAMS : You do not believe, upon your oath, that you are to receive any money or benefit of any kind for coming to England?

DEMONT : I expect no advantage from coming here, only that they pay my expenses back to Switzerland.

WILLIAMS : Did Mr Powell examine you at any time in England?

DEMONT : No.

WILLIAMS : Has he not seen you frequently since your arrival in England?

DEMONT : He has not seen me often.

WILLIAMS : Has he seen you a dozen times since your arrival in England?

DEMONT : Yes, more.

WILLIAMS : Twenty, perhaps?

DEMONT : I do not know how often.

WILLIAMS : It was not upon the subject of this evidence you have given that he visited you?

DEMONT : No.

WILLIAMS : Did he never speak to you on the subject of this evidence?

DEMONT : No.

WILLIAMS : What? During those twenty visits, more or less, you had no talk whatever with him on the subject of your evidence?

DEMONT : I canont say he said nothing about it, because I do not remember.

WILLIAMS : Have you ever said that the princess was surrounded by spies in Italy?

DEMONT : I do not remember.

WILLIAMS : Or represented it in any manner?

DEMONT : I do not remember.

WILLIAMS : Will you swear you have not?

DEMONT : I will not swear, but I do not remember.

WILLIAMS (showing a letter to Demont casually and then folding it so that only the signature is seen and holding it near her) : Is that your writing?

DEMONT : It is not exactly like my writing.

WILLIAMS : Do you believe it to be your writing or not?

DEMONT : It is not exactly like my writing.

WILLIAMS : Do you believe it to be your writing – yes or no?

DEMONT : I do not think it is exactly my handwriting.

WILLIAMS : Do you believe it to be your handwriting – yes or no?

DEMONT : I cannot decide whether it is my handwriting. It is not quite like it.

WILLIAMS : Do you believe it – yes or no?

DEMONT : I cannot say yes or no, because it is not exactly like my handwriting.

WILLIAMS : Do you believe it to be your writing?

DEMONT : I cannot tell what to answer. I cannot answer to a thing of which I am not sure.

SOLICITOR-GENERAL : The paper is held so that she can only see part of the writing. The question can therefore only refer to the part which she sees.

WILLIAMS : I want her to prove or to disprove her handwriting, with respect to any given part of the paper. (He refolds the letter lengthwise). You can now see the first half of every line clearly, can you not?

DEMONT : Yes.

WILLIAMS : Is that your handwriting?

DEMONT : I cannot tell exactly.

WILLIAMS : Was it not in the month of November, 1817, that you quitted the service of the princess?

DEMONT : Yes.

WILLIAMS : Of course, at that time, you knew all the things about the princess that you have been deposing these last two days before their lordships?

DEMONT : Yes.

WILLIAMS : After you left her service but before you saw Mr Powell at Milan, did you never represent the character of the princess to be of a very high description?

DEMONT : I do not remember.

WILLIAMS : Do you remember having said or written or represented that if the princess could read your heart she would be convinced of the infinite respect, the unlimited attachment and the perfect affection you entertained for her august person?

DEMONT : I recollect I have written several times to my sister, but I do not remember the contents of my letters.

WILLIAMS : Will you swear that you did not write to your sister to that effect after you were discharged?

DEMONT : I have written to my sister.

WILLIAMS (reading) : Have you not written to your sister : 'How often in a numerous circle have I with enthusiasm enumerated her rare talents, her mildness, her patience, her charity; in short all the perfections she possesses in so eminent a degree ! How often have I seen my hearers affected and heard them exclaim that the world is unjust to cause so much unhappiness to one who deserves it so little?'

DEMONT : I do not remember whether I used those expressions.

WILLIAMS : But you admit to the sense?

DEMONT : Yes.

WILLIAMS : Do you not remember writing to this effect or these words : 'You know that when the princess is my subject I am not barren, for my journal is embellished with the effusion of my heart, my greatest desire having always been that the princess should appear to be what she really is and that full justice should be rendered to her.' Do you remember having written to that effect?

DEMONT : I recollect that I wrote very often to my sister and spoke of Her Royal Highness.

WILLIAMS : And to this effect?

DEMONT : I do not remember.

WILLIAMS : Will you swear you did not?

DEMONT : No.

WILLIAMS (taking out another letter and pausing) : Did you not write this to your sister? Listen carefully : 'I had almost forgotten to tell you a thing which will surprise you as much as it has done me. I was taking some refreshment at Aunt Clara's when I was informed that an unknown person wished to deliver me a letter and that he could trust it to no one else. I went downstairs and asked him to come up to my room. Imagine my astonishment when I broke the seal. A proposal was made to me to set off to London under the pretence of being a governess : I was promised high protection and a brilliant fortune in a short time. The letter was without signature; but to assure me of the truth of it, I was informed I might draw on a banker for as much money as I wished.'

SOLICITOR-GENERAL : I have not interposed when the counsel against the Bill asked about particular expressions used by the witness; but now that he is reading a letter, I feel it necessary to submit that the regular course is for him to put it in the hand of the witness and to ask whether it is her handwriting or not.

WILLIAMS : (giving the letter to Demont): Is that your handwriting?

DEMONT : Yes.

WILLIAMS : The whole of the letter to the end?

DEMONT : Yes.

WILLIAMS : You swear that?

DEMONT : Yes.

Mr Creevey, writing his daily account of the trial noted : 'The *chienne* Demont turns out everything one could wish on her cross-examination. A most infernally damaging day for the prosecution.' There were to be three more such days before, on 4 September, Guiseppe Rastelli appeared at the bar of the House to give the evidence which was to be the *coup de grâce*.

Rastelli was obviously nervous. He gave his evidence in so low a voice that Thomas Denmam, Caroline's Solicitor-General, intervened : 'Speak louder, sir : we must hear your voice as well as the interpreter's !'

After establishing Rastelli's identity, the king's Solicitor-General asked : 'Did you ever see Bergami ride out in any carriage with the princess?'

'Several times.'

'Describe how they were seated.'

'She was seated on Bergami's knees.'

'Do you remember Bergami's sometimes wearing a cloak?'

'Yes, a cloak that was a present.'

'How have you seen it placed?'

'I have seen the princess extend it over herself and Bergami also, so as to cover Bergami with it.'

'Was it your duty to accompany the carriage on horseback?'

'It was my duty to ride in front and to come near the carriage when I was called to or sent for.'

'Do you recollect any particular occasion when you went near the carriage?'

'I once went near the carriage to enquire what road I should take.'

'Was the carriage open?'

'It was.'

'When you came near the carriage, what did you observe?'

Rastelli described what he observed and added that he was so ashamed that he turned away.

There was a sensation in the House at this first-hand account which could leave no shadow of doubt that Caroline and Bergami were on intimate terms. One of the peers, thinking that he had misheard, asked that the questions and answers should be read over by the shorthand-writer.

Denman immediately rose to cross-examine. He suggested that Rastelli had been dismissed from Caroline's service for theft and, when the witness denied it, persisted : 'You never said to any-body that you had been dismissed on the charge of stealing corn?

'I have not,' said Rastelli, 'because I never told a lie.'

Denman turned on the interpreter : 'Does he mean to say he never told a lie or that he never told a lie without being well paid for it?'

There were cries of 'Order! Order!' and the king's Solicitor-General appealed to the Lord Chancellor against the question. But, considering the state of indignation in the House, the Lord Chancellor overruled the objection.

'Do you understand English?' Denman asked Rastelli.

'Not at all.'

Then, suddenly, Denman snapped unexpectedly : 'How long have you been in England?'

'Since the day before yesterday.'

A hush fell on the House as Denman proceeded to underline the oddity of the sudden visit by establishing that for the last two years Rastelli had been a most active agent of the Milan Commission, gathering the 'Green Bag' evidence and posting over Europe with it.

'When you left Milan, did you bring your father with you and your wife and your children?'

'I did not.'

'What are you to have for coming?'

'They have promised me nothing.'

'What do you expect to have?'

'Nothing. They have promised me nothing. I have nothing to expect.'

'You mean that you expect nothing?'

'Yes.'

Denman then returned to the episode in the carriage. 'You came back for orders, did you?' he asked.

'I did.'

'When you had not received your orders on setting out, you were in the habit of coming back to the carriage in order to receive them?'

'Not always. They had given me their orders before we set out and on this occasion they thought they would be sufficient.'

'Did they call you to the carriage?'

'No. They did not hear me. I went of my own accord.'

'To whom did you first tell this story?'

'I never told it before except to the Commission.'

'How long was that after you saw it?'

'About eleven months or a year afterwards perhaps.'

'Just tell us in what month it was.'

'I don't know precisely.'

Brougham's comment on this when later he opened the defence was pertinent enough : 'When Rastelli swore to scenes too disgusting to be detailed, he had never opened his mouth on the subject. His lips had been hermetically sealed until he was called on by the Commission at Milan. Through ten long months that witness was silent. Is it credible he could have been so reserved if he had anything to tell? Is there one, even among your Lordships, whose lips are schooled to enact the courtier even when no court is present, who would not have repeated it to someone or other? Yet this low person never mentioned a syllable to any living person? But I shall not admit that he concealed these extraordinary things for days, weeks or even hours. I believe he concealed it from the time of his hearing that others had been liberally paid for slanders and resolved to imitate their example.' For the defence did not know, any more than the people knew, the real circumstances of Rastelli's entering Caroline's service. But the people, at least, estimated his evidence at its true worth.

Two days after Rastelli's evidence, Creevey could write : 'This bill will never pass. My belief is that it will be abandoned on the adjournment. The entire middle orders of people are against it and are daily becoming more critical of the King and the Lords for carrying on this prosecution.' He was wrong about the abandonment, but on the day before the adjournment, he had to report : 'The Queen went down the river yesterday. I saw her pass the House of Commons on the deck of her state barge. . . . Erskine, who was afterwards at Blackfriars Bridge, said he was sure there were 200,000 people collected to see her. . . . There was not a single vessel in the river that did not hoist their colours and man their yards for her, and it is with the greatest difficulty that the watermen on the Thames are kept from destroying the hulk which lies off the House of Commons to protect the witnesses.'

The defence opened on 3 October. 'You can form no conception of the rage of the Lords at Brougham fixing this time', Creevey wrote. 'It interferes with everything – pheasant shooting, Newmarket, etc., etc. . . . He has performed miracles and the reasons he has just been giving me for fixing the time he has done show his understanding (if one doubted it) to be of the very first order.' Handicapped, as he was, by his ignorance of the real circumstances of the Government intrigues, Henry Brougham had indeed made an almost miraculous attack and in the days that followed his opening of the defence, this forty-two-year-old Edinburgh lawyer, son of a Scottish manse, who from the depths of his soul hated and despised the accusers of the queen he had served for eleven years, kept his ear very close to the ground. And on Friday, 13 October, he was able to bring the prosecution crashing to ruin.

In a deceptively quiet and courteous voice, he asked the king's Attorney-General : 'I wish to know of my learned friend whether we can have access to Rastelli. Is he here? Is he in this country?'

The king's Attorney-General stretched across the Bar and answered Brougham in a very low voice that no one could hear.

The Lord Chancellor gave the Crown counsel time to think by leaving the House for a few moments.

On his return, Brougham, in a voice which echoed round the Chamber, said : 'My Lords, I wish Rastelli to be called.'

'If my learned friend wishes to call Rastelli,' said the king's Attorney-General, 'he can certainly call him.'

'I wish to know', roared Broughham, 'if Rastelli is in the country and, if in the country, where he is?'

The House was tense. The Lord Chancellor could delay no longer. 'Mr Attorney,' he said, 'is Rastelli here?'

The King's Attorney-General realized that Brougham had out-manœuvred him. The answer could no longer be evaded. 'No,' he said, 'he has been sent to Milan.'

'Then', said Brougham, his long arms waving in their characteristic angular fashion, 'I wish to know whether I am obliged to go on with this Bill?'

The king's Attorney-General stumbled through explanations . . . Rastelli had been sent to Milan with dispatches . . . there was no idea that he would be wanted again as he had already been cross-examined . . . he had gone to assure the relatives of the witnesses that those witnesses were indeed safe and sound from the indignation of the London mobs . . .

Brougham refused to argue. 'If witnesses are allowed to leave the country during the proceedings,' he said, 'there is an end to the security which Your Lordships think you possess that no perjury shall be permitted with impunity at your Bar. I ask again, am I obliged in these circumstances to go on with the case?'

Lord Holland sprang to his feet and moved that counsel withdrew from the House. When they had done so, he addressed his fellow peers : 'I rise to state on behalf of Your Lordships and the cause of justice that the fact that has just come out is absolutely monstrous.'

He was interrupted by a cry of approval which even the cold language of the official report describes in parenthesis : 'Loud cries of "Hear ! Hear !" from both sides of the House re-echoed for many moments.'

'Gracious God,' Holland continued when the noise died away, 'can Your Lordships suppose that after such a proceeding as this we are safe from the suspicion that must be cast upon us?' (Loud cheers.) 'Here is Rastelli, who stated one of the most disgusting things heard in a court of justice – a man on whom suspicion now

rests that he has been engaged in suborning witnesses for the
prosecution, not merely escaping, but being sent away by the
Government. If Your Lordships submit to being dragged through
the mire in this matter, you will taint this branch of the legislature.
Considering these circumstances as forming a *prima facie* case of
the existence of a conspiracy to pervert justice, Your Lordships will
do well to get rid of the disgust and fatigue of this infamous
proceeding.'

The Lords insisted on themselves examining the Government
agent who had engineered Rastelli's return, but when Lord Holland
asked him to produce a letter concerning it, he refused, saying that
he did not consider himself at liberty to produce it, 'being, as I
am, a man confidentially employed.'

This gave Brougham his second great opportunity. He could
now carry the war into the enemy's country. 'With the permission of Your Lordships I wish to ask the witness who is his
employer in this case?'

It was a master-stroke. At last he had forced into the open,
as nearly as he dared within the Constitution, what indeed everyone knew but none could say – that the proceedings were nothing
but George's personal vendetta against Caroline. Feverishly the
Government peers tried to rule his question out of order, but he
persisted and began the speech which, of all speeches George, who
was becoming increasingly touchy on the subject of his obesity
and his curious shape, never forgot or forgave.

'My Lords,' said Brougham, 'I consider it essential that this
question should be put. This is the first witness who can give us
the important information which I now seek. To whom are we
opposed? When we are acquainted with the unknown, the interesting unknown, we may trace its actions and its conduct and bring
from its own mouth – if it have a mouth – who and what he is. I
know nothing of this shapeless being, if shape it can be
called.

His hands outlined the shape, but even the dullest of their Lordships, noticing the suppressed laughter of those who had seen the
point, had begun to realize who the 'shape' was.

'I know nothing about this retiring phantom, this uncertain
shape,' Brougham continued,

'"If shape it might be called that shape had none

Distinguishable in finger, joint or limb"
And such, Your Lordships will admit, "that shadow seemed for
each seemed either" and
> "what seemed his head
The likeness of a kingly crown had on."
Yet under this shape, this "airy nothing" I am to face the
adverse party. I am to be met at every turn in the proceedings by
not being able to put a single question to this visionary personage.
I am to pursue this shape——'

But, of course, it could not be allowed. The Lord Chancellor
called the gale of guffaws to order and told Mr Brougham he
could not continue his quest.

Nevertheless, the case was won. Though the trial dragged on
for three more weeks, the conclusion was foregone. The Bill indeed
passed its Third Reading, but only by a majority of nine and those
nine were the Archbishop of Canterbury and eight obliging bishops.
The Government abandoned the Bill.

As this was announced by the Prime Minister, Lord Liverpool, in
the House, a supporter of the queen met her 'coming out alone
from her waiting-room, preceded by an usher. She had a dazed
look, more tragical than consternation. The usher pushed open the
folding doors of the great staircase and she began to descend. She
was all shuddering and she took hold of the banister, pausing for a
moment. That sudden clutch with which she caught the railing was
as if her hand had been a skinless heart.'

Outside, when the news was known, there was at first 'a kind
of stupor'. Then, according to one who was there, 'everyone
instantly between Charing Cross and Whitehall, turned and came
rushing down, filling Old and New Palace Yards, as if a deluge
were unsluiced. The generous exultation of the people was
beyond all description.'

On that fantastic evening London went mad and Caroline was
cheered and toasted as no hero had ever been. But her great
moment was in the little retiring-room at the House, where she
had spent so much time during the trial quietly playing back-
gammon in preference to hearing herself slandered.

Here she thanked Brougham and Denman and signed a document they had brought her. After she had written 'Caroline', she
returned the pen to Brougham. Then, suddenly, she asked for it

again and added in a firm hand 'Regina' to her signature, saying as she did so : 'Caroline Regina, in spite of them all.'

But George said that he would rather die or lose his crown than submit to any compromise of any sort with her and swore that she should never be crowned.

In due course she was officially notified that 'His Majesty having determined that the Queen shall form no part of the ceremonial of his coronation, it is therefore the Royal pleasure that the Queen shall not attend the said ceremony.' In the circumstances, it became a necessary point of honour for her to be in Westminster Abbey on Coronation Day, 19 July 1821. And now not only the country but the Government were divided. Until five in the evening of 18 July, the Government had not decided whether to obey the king or to resign.

The two people who had no doubts about what to do were George and Caroline. George spent the previous night barricaded in the Speaker's House in Old Palace Yard, a stone's throw from the Abbey; Caroline, hoping to take everyone by surprise, arrived at the Abbey at 5.30 in the morning.

But she found all entrances closed against her. One door was banged in her face. The crowds, which had been dense since midnight, watched the scene and even the occupants of the expensive seats 'applauded her loudly in most places'. Some one pointed out an opening to the platform by which she could gain the covered way leading to Poets' Corner.

At this last door, Lord Hood, who was in attendance on her, demanded admission. The door-keepers requested to see her ticket.

'I present to you your Queen', said Lord Hood. 'Surely it is not necessary for her to have a ticket.'

'My orders are specific and I feel bound to obey them', replied the door-keeper.

Caroline laughed and Lord Hood drew from his pocket a peer's ticket for one person.

'This', said the door-keeper, 'will let one person pass and no more.'

Lord Hood passed the ticket to the queen, but she refused to go in without her attendants, since no provision had been made for accommodating her. She would go only as queen and without a ticket.

'You refuse the queen admission', said Lord Hood.

'We only act in conformity with our orders', answered the unhappy door-keeper.

So Caroline returned to her carriage and drove back to South Audley Street, accompanied by a tremendous concourse of people who broke the windows of all the houses on the route which had 'G.R.' or other decorations in them and, on passing Carlton House, were thunderous with groans and hisses.

Her attendants urged Caroline to rest after the strain and her equerry was able to record during the morning : 'Her Majesty is gone to bed while the better and stronger half is in the act of getting crowned.'

Caroline, however, had no intention of repining. A few nights later Denman found her with a large party, dancing and laughing even though 'her spirits were frightfully overstrained'.

At Drury Lane the following week Kean's performance of *Othello* was turned into a demonstration in her favour. Every passage that could be construed as an allusion to her case was received with plaudits and when Emilia made her outburst about the 'odious, damned lie', a voice from the audience cried out : 'O what Iagos have beset the Queen' and was received with applause from every part of the theatre.

Caroline decided herself to see Kean's *Richard III* on Monday, 30 July and though, during the performance, she felt unwell she stayed till the end. On Tuesday a doctor diagnosed internal inflammation.

A week later she was dead.

One circumstance of her quick illness, from which she predicted she would not recover, was memorable. When Denman suggested sending a messenger to Italy to seal up her papers lest they fell into her enemies' hands, she said : 'What if they do? They can find nothing, because there is nothing and never has been to impeach my character.'

Caroline's funeral provided a last occasion for a triumphant demonstration in her favour. Authority decided that the cortege to Harwich (for she was to be buried in her native Brunswick) must on no account be allowed to pass through the City of London. She had died at her residence, Brandenburgh House, in Hammersmith and it had been ordered that at Kensington the procession should turn off the main road, through Church Street, to Bayswater Road and then north up Edgware Road. Londoners decided otherwise.

An enormous barricade of overturned waggons and other impediments blocked the entrance to Church Street and the procession was halted while messengers were sent to the Prime Minister for instructions. A troop of Life Guards was sent, with orders to divert the procession through the park and gain Edgware Road by way of what is now Marble Arch. But the populace closed the park gates and clung to them so that, without a massacre, they could not be opened. For a second time the authorities had to give in and for the third time the crowd forestalled them and threw up another barrier at the bottom of Park Lane.

This time the procession was made to turn back and the Hyde Park Gate opened, so that the cortege could pass but the people were excluded. The crowd thereupon made for Cumberland Gate (Marble Arch), tore down the railings and used them for weapons, and attacked the soldiers with brickbats and stones. The troops opened fire, killing two and wounding several more and, for the moment, the planned route up Edgware Road, along the New Road (Marylebone Road and Euston Road) was followed. But at Tottenham Court Road there was another impassable barricade and once more the people had their way, driving the procession down Drury Lane and so into the City by Temple Bar. The people having thus gained the victory, the body was taken triumphantly through the City. The Lord Mayor was forced to leave a meeting and come rapidly to Temple Bar to recieve the cortege, which, with him now at its head, passed through streets where all the shops were closed, the windows crowded with citizens for the most part dressed in deep mourning and the streets full of orderly crowds which 'exceeded all calculation.'

So, in triumph, the 'Injured Queen of England' – the words were inscribed on the coffin – left the capital for the last time.

The story of Caroline remains mysterious. The old question: Was she innocent or guilty? is, indeed, no longer to be asked. There can be no serious doubt of her innocence of the charges brought against her at her trial. But her sudden, unexpected and most convenient death provokes inevitable speculation, especially when considered in the context of the political ferment of the time and the undisguised relief with which George regarded it.

But, above all, there is the mystery of George's conduct. The depths to which he stooped in his efforts to get rid of Caroline and to humiliate her are altogether disproportionate to the apparent causes and inappropriate to his basic character. And the solution, I suggest, is to be found in the persons of William Austin and Maria Fitzherbert. Because of the menace of the first, George was forced in 1806 to find Caroline 'innocent' when she was 'guilty' and in 1820 to try to prove her guilty when she was innocent. Because of the status of the second, who was his true and only wife, he could not, without violating the ultimate decencies, allow his State-wife (who was no wife even though she might claim to be the mother of a legal 'Prince of Wales') to be crowned.

It is probable that the now-inaccessible papers removed to Windsor in 1935 contain much enlightenment on both these points. Even without them, we know so much more than the crowds of 1820 knew that it is impossible to withhold admiration that, despite their almost total ignorance, their instincts were so sound.

The circumstances may at least provoke the reader, even though he cannot answer these questions, to ask a larger and more important question : 'What is "History"?'

READ MORE IN PENGUIN

In every corner of the world, on every subject under the sun, Penguin represents quality and variety – the very best in publishing today.

For complete information about books available from Penguin – including Puffins, Penguin Classics and Arkana – and how to order them, write to us at the appropriate address below. Please note that for copyright reasons the selection of books varies from country to country.

In the United Kingdom: Please write to *Dept. EP, Penguin Books Ltd, Bath Road, Harmondsworth, West Drayton, Middlesex UB7 0DA*

In the United States: Please write to *Consumer Sales, Penguin Putnam Inc., P.O. Box 12289 Dept. B, Newark, New Jersey 07101-5289*. VISA and MasterCard holders call 1-800-788-6262 to order Penguin titles

In Canada: Please write to *Penguin Books Canada Ltd, 10 Alcorn Avenue, Suite 300, Toronto, Ontario M4V 3B2*

In Australia: Please write to *Penguin Books Australia Ltd, P.O. Box 257, Ringwood, Victoria 3134*

In New Zealand: Please write to *Penguin Books (NZ) Ltd, Private Bag 102902, North Shore Mail Centre, Auckland 10*

In India: Please write to *Penguin Books India Pvt Ltd, 11 Community Centre, Panchsheel Park, New Delhi 110017*

In the Netherlands: Please write to *Penguin Books Netherlands bv, Postbus 3507, NL-1001 AH Amsterdam*

In Germany: Please write to *Penguin Books Deutschland GmbH, Metzlerstrasse 26, 60594 Frankfurt am Main*

In Spain: Please write to *Penguin Books S. A., Bravo Murillo 19, 1° B, 28015 Madrid*

In Italy: Please write to *Penguin Italia s.r.l., Via Benedetto Croce 2, 20094 Corsico, Milano*

In France: Please write to *Penguin France, Le Carré Wilson, 62 rue Benjamin Baillaud, 31500 Toulouse*

In Japan: Please write to *Penguin Books Japan Ltd, Kaneko Building, 2-3-25 Koraku, Bunkyo-Ku, Tokyo 112*

In South Africa: Please write to *Penguin Books South Africa (Pty) Ltd, Private Bag X14, Parkview, 2122 Johannesburg*

INSPECTION COPY REQUESTS

Lecturers in the United Kingdom and Ireland wishing to apply for inspection copies of Classic Penguin titles for student group adoptions are invited to apply to:

Inspection Copy Department
Penguin Press Marketing
27 Wrights Lane
LONDON
W8 5TZ

Fax: 020 7416 3274

E-mail: academic@penguin.co.uk

Inspection copies may also be requested via our website at:
www.penguinclassics.com

Please include in your request the author, title and the ISBN of the book(s) in which you are interested, the name of the course on which the books will be used and the expected student numbers.

It is essential that you include with your request your title, first name, surname, position, department name, college or university address, telephone and fax numbers and your e-mail address.

Lecturers outside the United Kingdom and Ireland should address their applications to their local Penguin office.

Inspection copies are supplied at the discretion of Penguin Books

READ MORE IN PENGUIN

PENGUIN CLASSIC MILITARY HISTORY

 This series acknowledges the profound and enduring interest in military history, and the causes and consequences of human conflict. Penguin Classic Military History covers warfare from the earliest times to the age of electronics and encompasses subjects as diverse as classic examples of grand strategy and the precision tactics of Britain's crack SAS Regiment. The series will be enjoyed and valued by students of military history and all who hope to learn from the often disturbing lessons of the past.

Published or forthcoming:

Corelli Barnett	**Engage the Enemy More Closely**
	The Great War
David G. Chandler	**The Art of Warfare on Land**
William Craig	**Enemy at the Gates**
Heinz Guderian	**Panzer Leader**
Heinz Höhne	**The Order of the Death's Head**
Anthony Kemp	**The SAS at War**
Martin Middlebrook	**The Kaiser's Battle**
Philip Warner	**Sieges of the Middle Ages**
Cecil Woodham-Smith	**The Reason Why**

READ MORE IN PENGUIN

PENGUIN CLASSIC BIOGRAPHY

 Highly readable and enjoyable biographies and autobiographies from leading biographers and autobiographers. The series provides a vital background to the increasing interest in history, historical subjects and people who mattered. The periods and subjects covered include the Roman Empire, Tudor England, the English Civil Wars, the Victorian Era, and characters as diverse Joan of Arc, Jane Austen, Robert Burns and George Melly. Essential reading for everyone interested in the past.

Published or forthcoming:

Ernle Bradford	**Cleopatra**
David Cecil	**A Portrait of Jane Austen**
Roger Fulford	**Royal Dukes**
Christopher Hibbert	**The Making of Charles Dickens**
Christopher Hill	**God's Englishman: Oliver Cromwell**
Edward Lucie-Smith	**Joan of Arc**
George Melly	**Owning Up: The Trilogy**
Lytton Strachey	**Queen Victoria**
	Elizabeth and Essex
Gaius Suetonius	**Lives of the Twelve Caesars, translated by Robert Graves**

READ MORE IN PENGUIN

PENGUIN CLASSIC HISTORY

 Well written narrative history from leading historians such as Paul Kennedy, Alan Moorehead, J. B. Priestley, A. L. Rowse and G. M. Trevelyan. From the Ancient World to the decline of British naval mastery, from twelfth-century France to the Victorian Underworld, the series captures the great turning points in history and chronicles the lives of ordinary people at different times. Penguin Classic History will be enjoyed and valued by everyone who loves the past.

Published or forthcoming:

Ernle Bradford	**The Mediterranean**
Alan Moorehead	**The Fatal Impact**
Samuel Pepys	**The Illustrated Pepys**
J. H. Plumb	**The First Four Georges**
J. B. Priestley	**The Edwardians**
A. L. Rowse	**The Elizabethan Renaissance**
G. M. Trevelyan	**English Social History**
T. H. White	**The Age of Scandal**
Lawrence Wright	**Clean and Decent**
Hans Zinsser	**Rats, Lice and History**